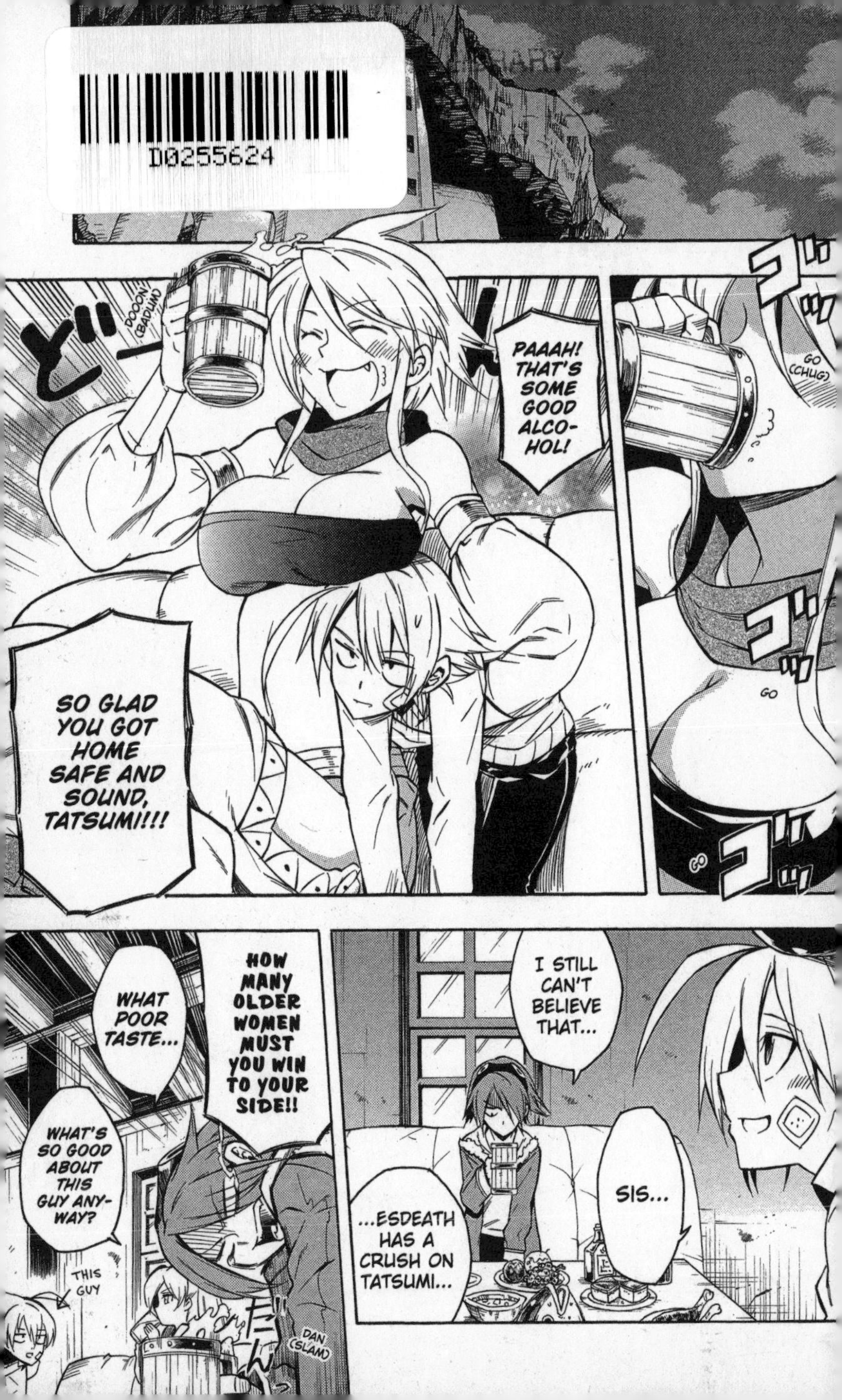
GO
(CHUG)
GO
GO
DOOON
(BADUM)
PAAAH! THAT'S SOME GOOD ALCO-HOL!
SO GLAD YOU GOT HOME SAFE AND SOUND, TATSUMI!!!
I STILL CAN'T BELIEVE THAT...
SIS...
...ESDEATH HAS A CRUSH ON TATSUMI...
HOW MANY OLDER WOMEN MUST YOU WIN TO YOUR SIDE!!
WHAT POOR TASTE...
WHAT'S SO GOOD ABOUT THIS GUY ANY-WAY?
THIS GUY
DAN
(SLAM)

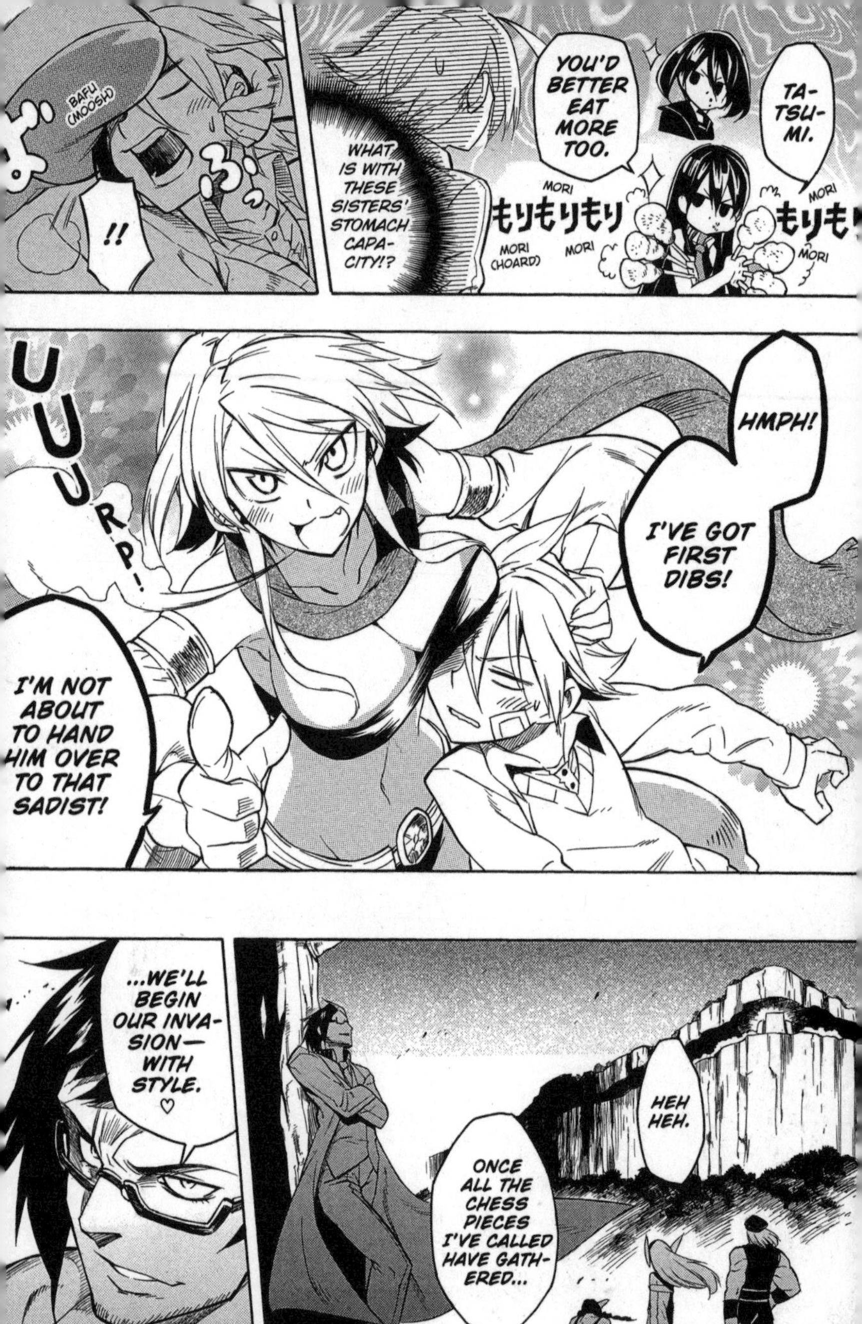
TA-TSU-MI.
YOU'D BETTER EAT MORE TOO.
もりもり
MORI MORI
もりもりもり
MORI MORI (HOARD) MORI
WHAT IS WITH THESE SISTERS' STOMACH CAPACITY!?
BAFU (MOOSH)
!!
HMPH!
I'VE GOT FIRST DIBS!
I'M NOT ABOUT TO HAND HIM OVER TO THAT SADIST!
UUURP!
HEH HEH.
ONCE ALL THE CHESS PIECES I'VE CALLED HAVE GATHERED...
...WE'LL BEGIN OUR INVASION—WITH STYLE. ♡

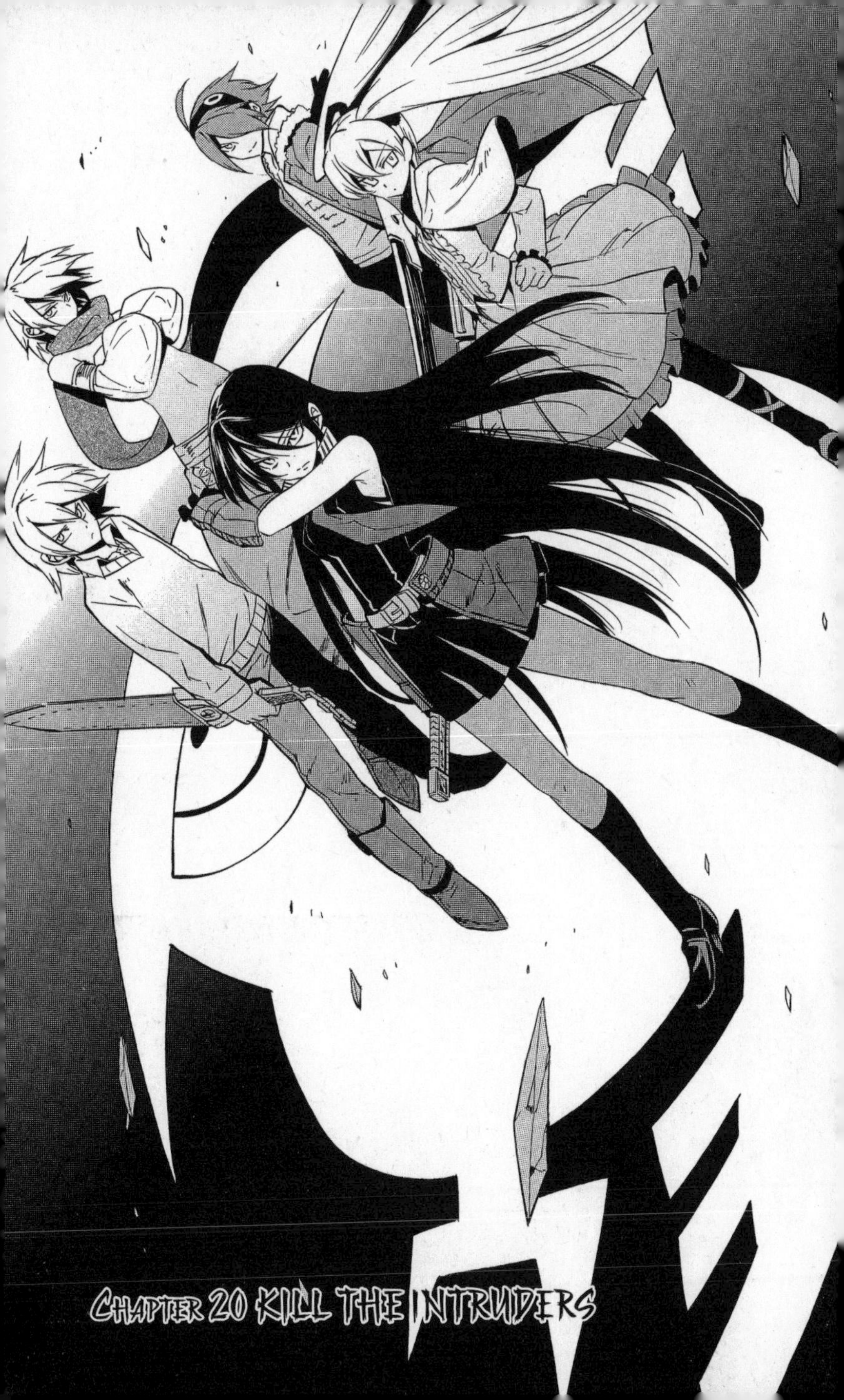
Chapter 20 Kill the Intruders

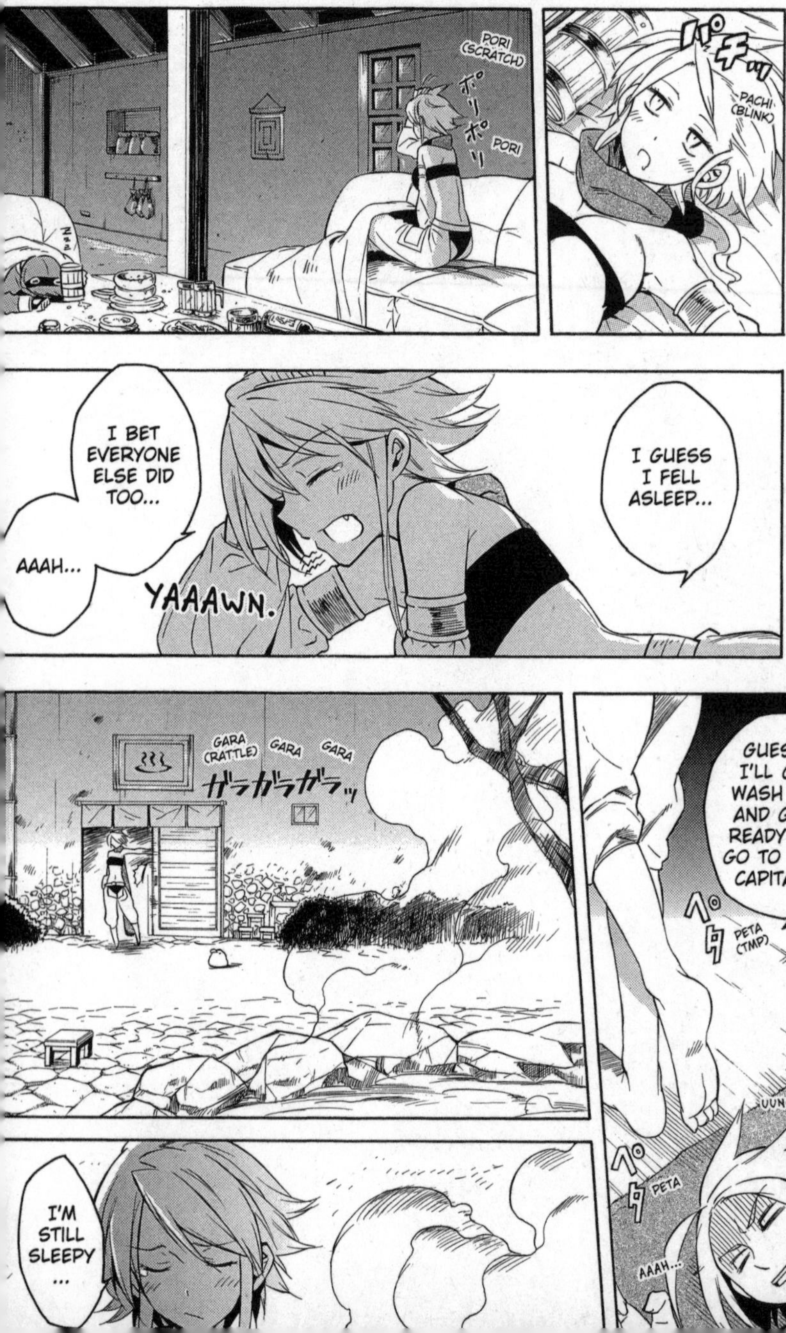
パチッ
PACHI (BLINK)
PORI (SCRATCH)
ポリポリ
PORI
ZZZ
I GUESS I FELL ASLEEP...
I BET EVERYONE ELSE DID TOO...
AAAH...
YAAAWN.
GUESS I'LL GO WASH UP AND GET READY TO GO TO THE CAPITAL.
ペタ
PETA (TMP)
GARA (RATTLE)
GARA
GARA
ガラガラガラッ
UUNGH...
ペタ
PETA
AAAH...
I'M STILL SLEEPY ...

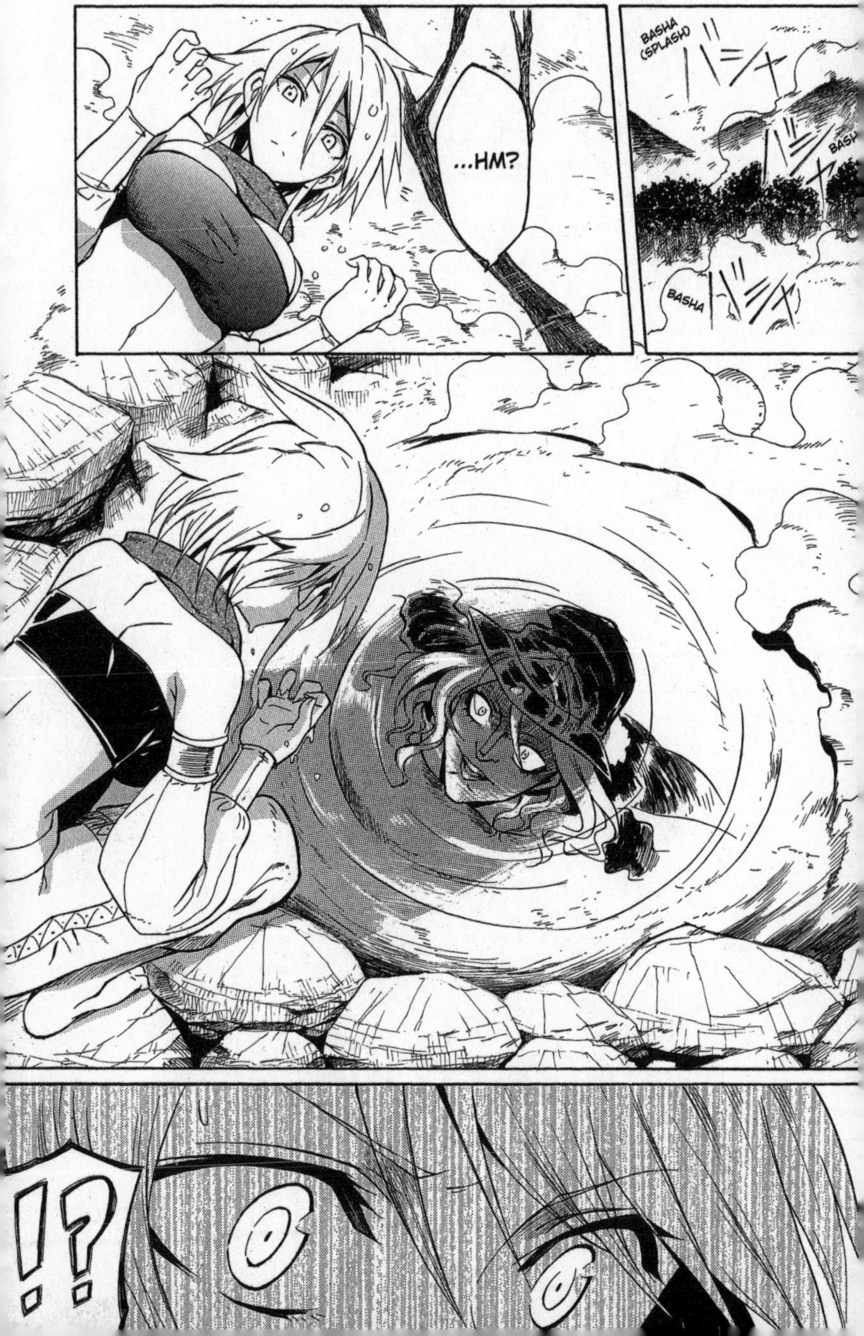

BASHA (SPLASH)
BASH
BASHA
...HM?
!?

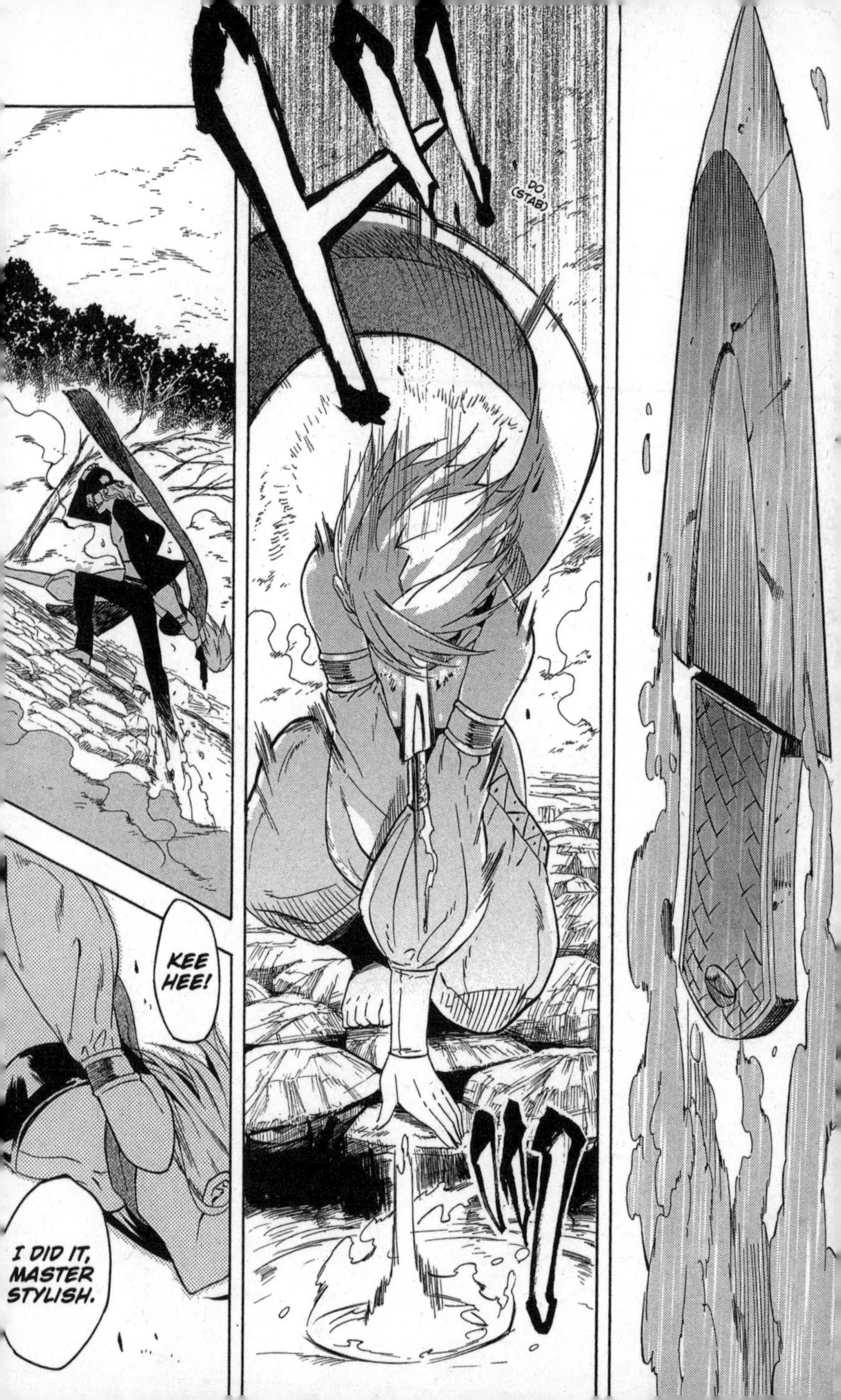
DO (STAB)
KEE HEE!
I DID IT, MASTER STYLISH.

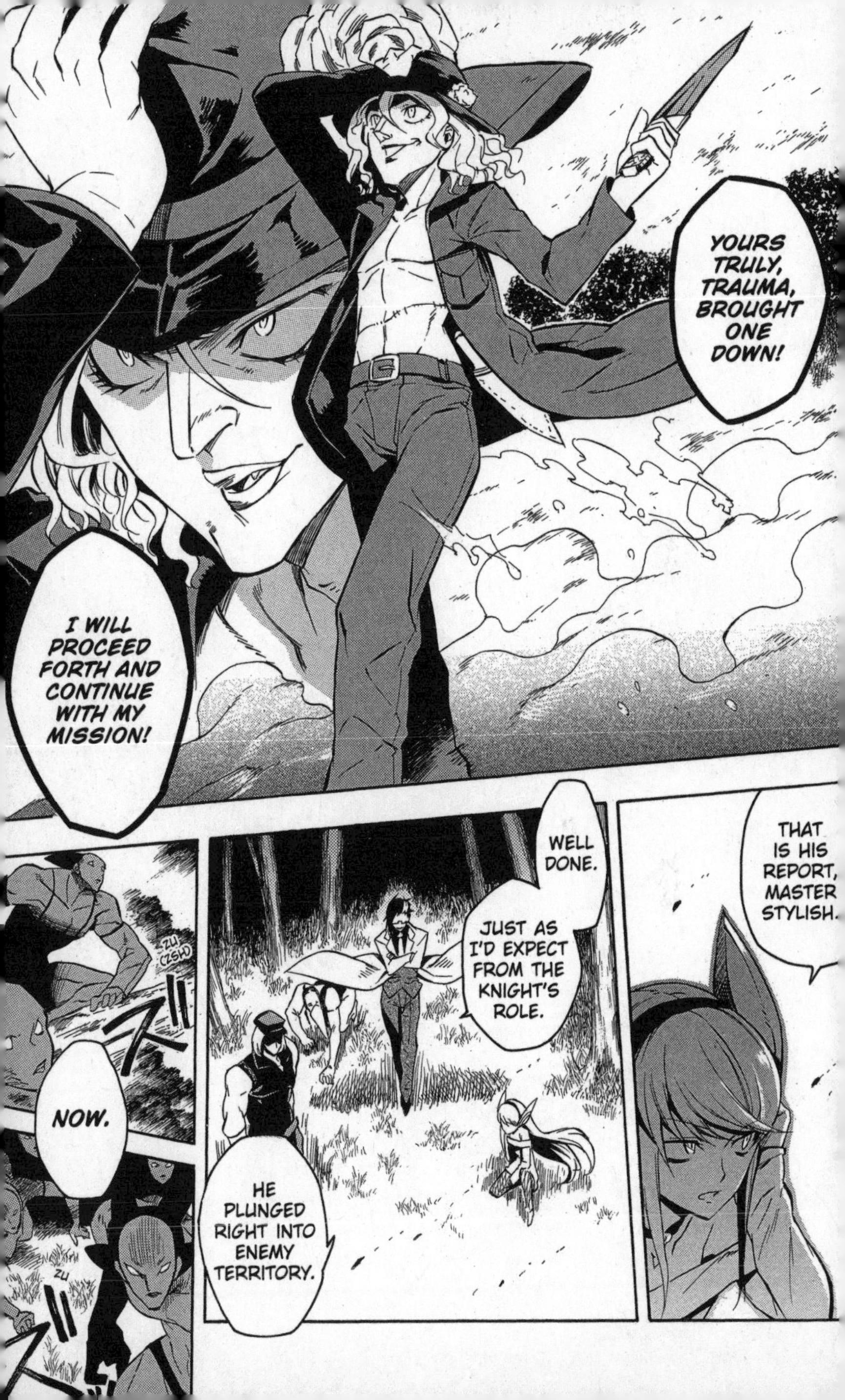
YOURS TRULY, TRAUMA, BROUGHT ONE DOWN!
I WILL PROCEED FORTH AND CONTINUE WITH MY MISSION!
THAT IS HIS REPORT, MASTER STYLISH.
WELL DONE.
JUST AS I'D EXPECT FROM THE KNIGHT'S ROLE.
HE PLUNGED RIGHT INTO ENEMY TERRITORY.
ZU (ZSH)
NOW.
ZU

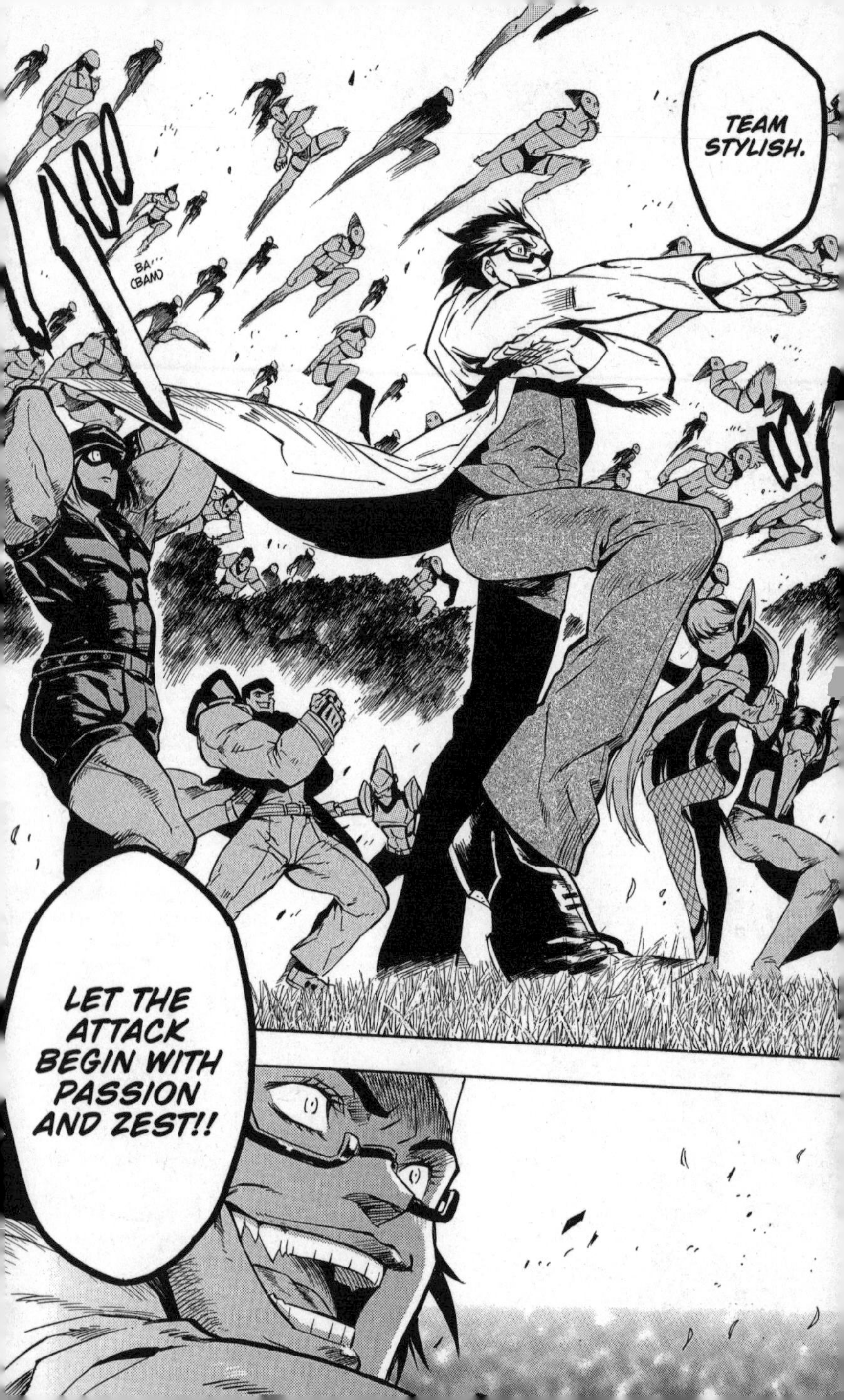
TEAM STYLISH.
BA... (BAM)
LET THE ATTACK BEGIN WITH PASSION AND ZEST!!

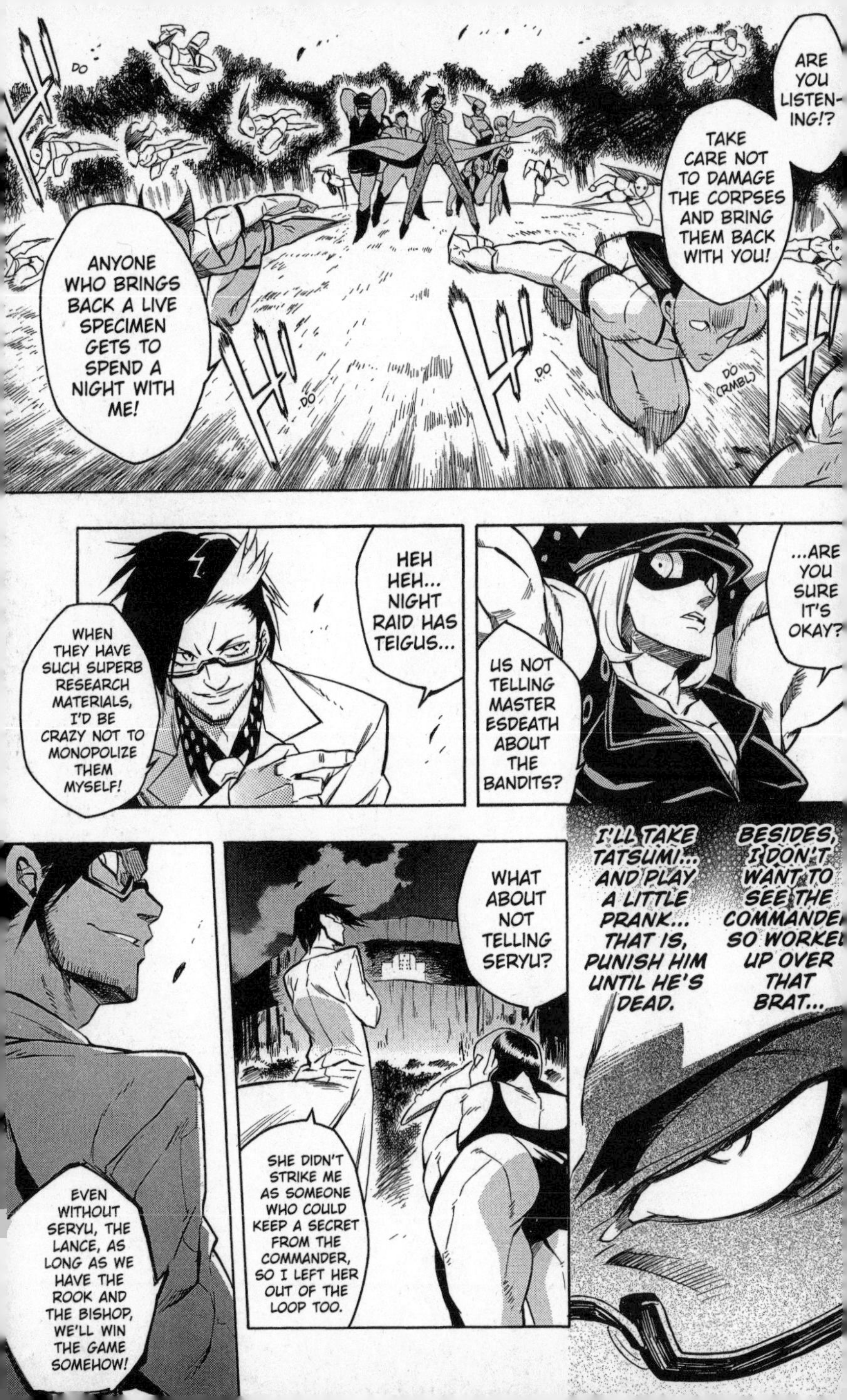
ARE YOU LISTENING!?
TAKE CARE NOT TO DAMAGE THE CORPSES AND BRING THEM BACK WITH YOU!
DO
ANYONE WHO BRINGS BACK A LIVE SPECIMEN GETS TO SPEND A NIGHT WITH ME!
DO (RMBL)
DO
DO
...ARE YOU SURE IT'S OKAY?
US NOT TELLING MASTER ESDEATH ABOUT THE BANDITS?
HEH HEH... NIGHT RAID HAS TEIGUS...
WHEN THEY HAVE SUCH SUPERB RESEARCH MATERIALS, I'D BE CRAZY NOT TO MONOPOLIZE THEM MYSELF!
BESIDES, I DON'T WANT TO SEE THE COMMANDER SO WORKED UP OVER THAT BRAT...
I'LL TAKE TATSUMI... AND PLAY A LITTLE PRANK... THAT IS, PUNISH HIM UNTIL HE'S DEAD.
WHAT ABOUT NOT TELLING SERYU?
SHE DIDN'T STRIKE ME AS SOMEONE WHO COULD KEEP A SECRET FROM THE COMMANDER, SO I LEFT HER OUT OF THE LOOP TOO.
EVEN WITHOUT SERYU, THE LANCE, AS LONG AS WE HAVE THE ROOK AND THE BISHOP, WE'LL WIN THE GAME SOMEHOW!

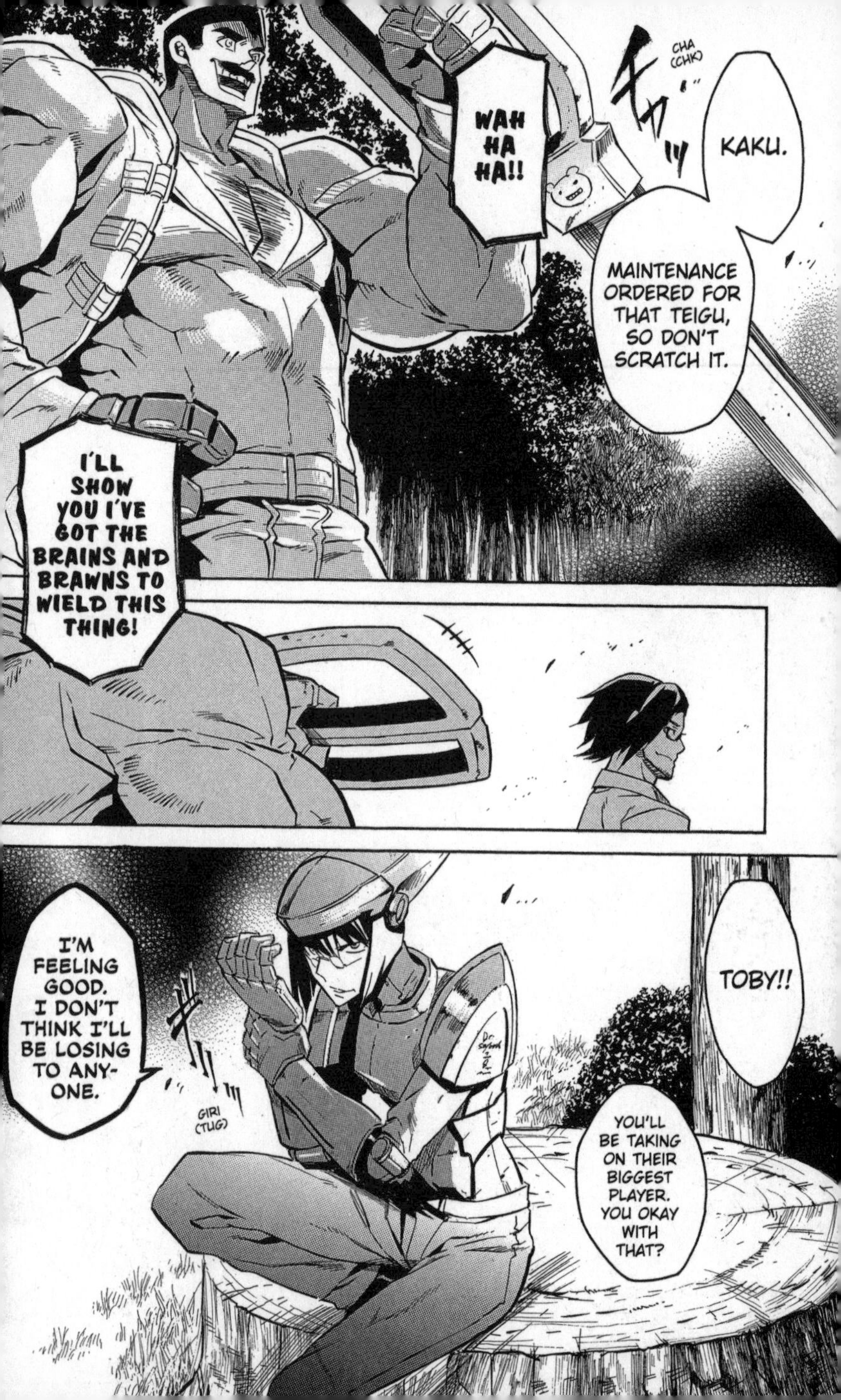
CHA (CHK)
KAKU.
MAINTENANCE ORDERED FOR THAT TEIGU, SO DON'T SCRATCH IT.
WAH HA HA!!
I'LL SHOW YOU I'VE GOT THE BRAINS AND BRAWNS TO WIELD THIS THING!
TOBY!!
YOU'LL BE TAKING ON THEIR BIGGEST PLAYER. YOU OKAY WITH THAT?
I'M FEELING GOOD. I DON'T THINK I'LL BE LOSING TO ANY-ONE.
GIRI (TUG)

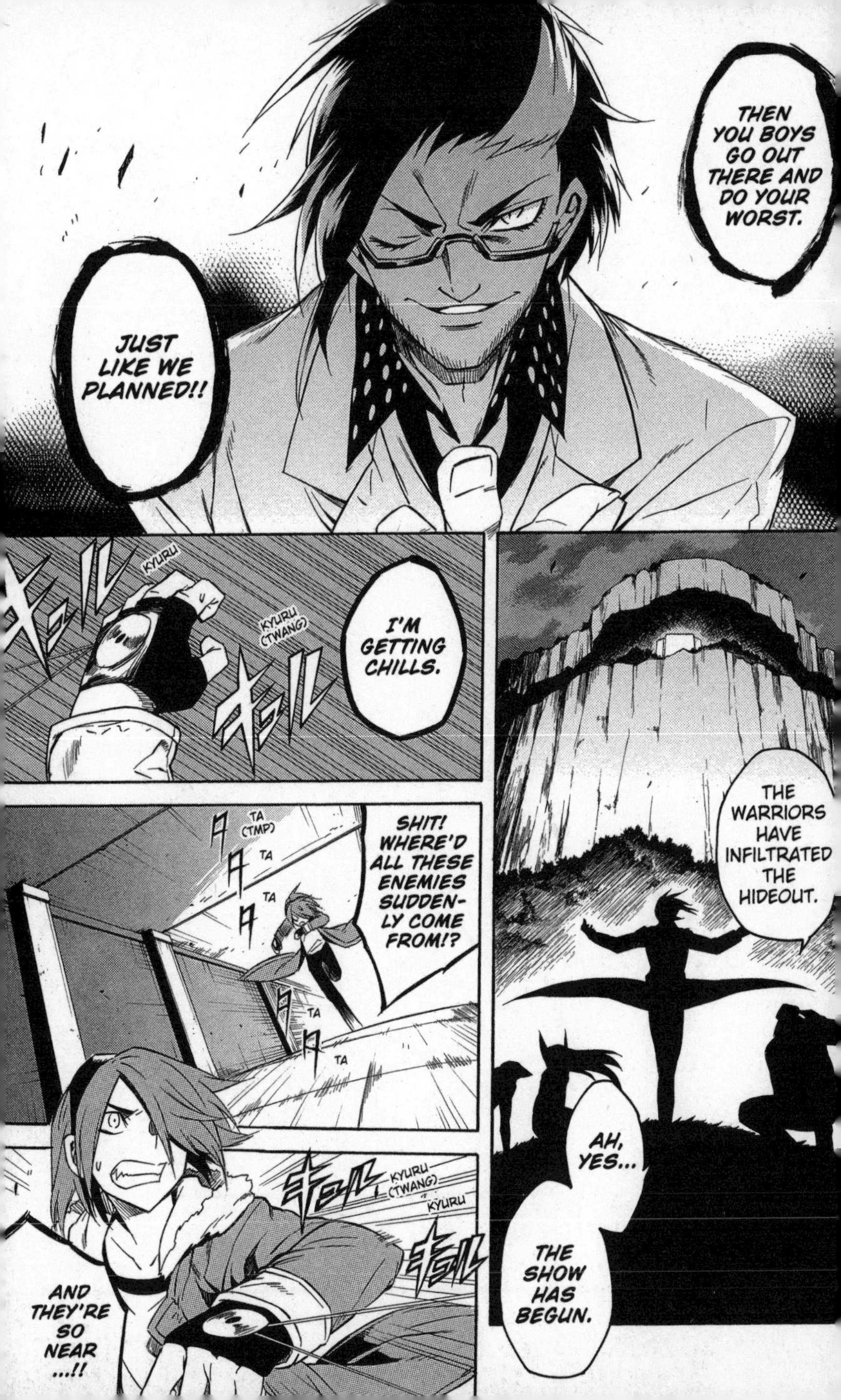

THEN YOU BOYS GO OUT THERE AND DO YOUR WORST.
JUST LIKE WE PLANNED!!
THE WARRIORS HAVE INFILTRATED THE HIDEOUT.
KYURU
KYURU (TWANG)
I'M GETTING CHILLS.
TA (TMP)
TA
TA
TA
TA
SHIT! WHERE'D ALL THESE ENEMIES SUDDEN-LY COME FROM!?
AH, YES...
THE SHOW HAS BEGUN.
KYURU (TWANG)
KYURU
AND THEY'RE SO NEAR ...!!

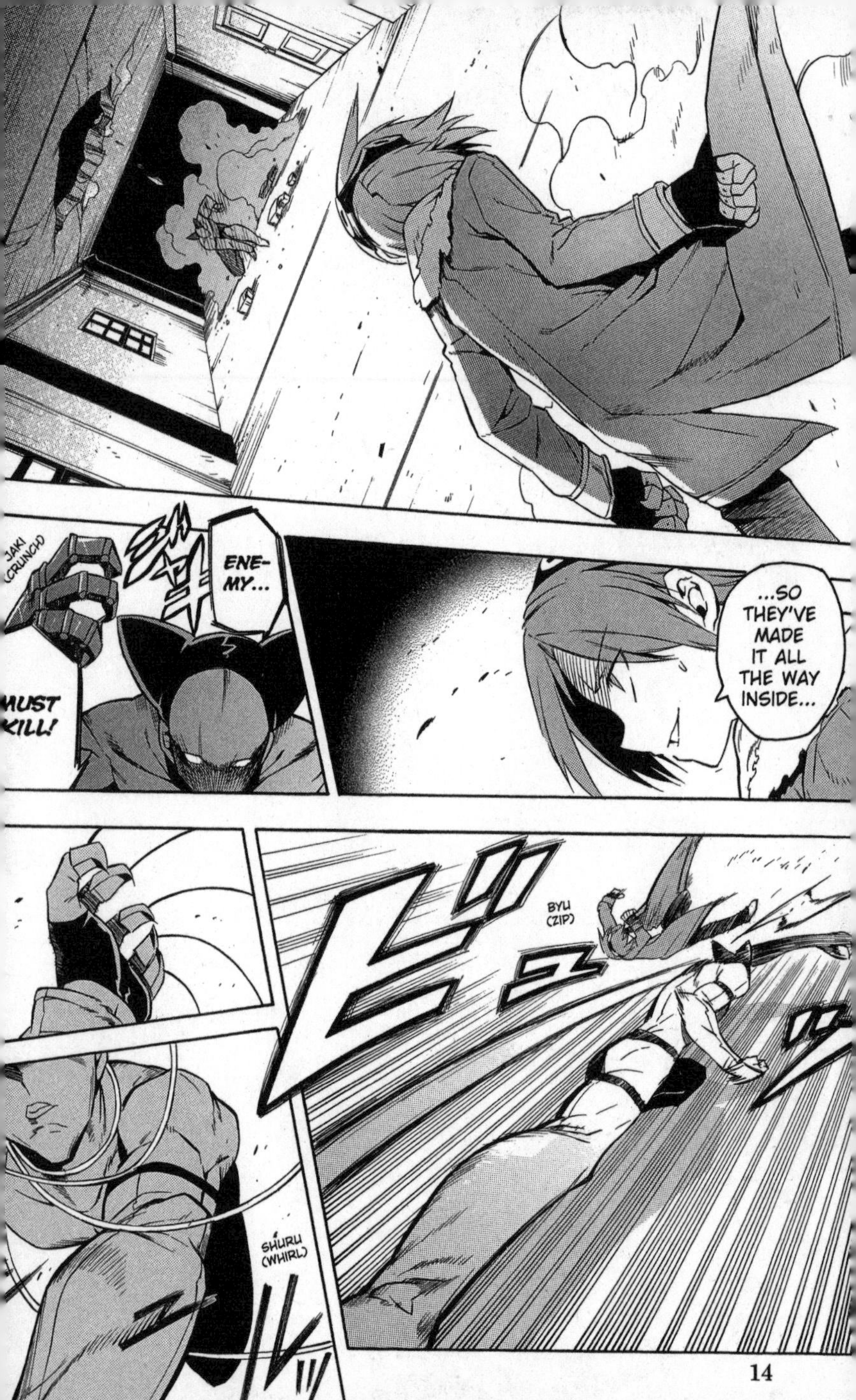
...SO THEY'VE MADE IT ALL THE WAY INSIDE...
ENE-MY...
JAKI (CRUNCH)
MUST KILL!
BYU (ZIP)
SHURU (WHIRL)

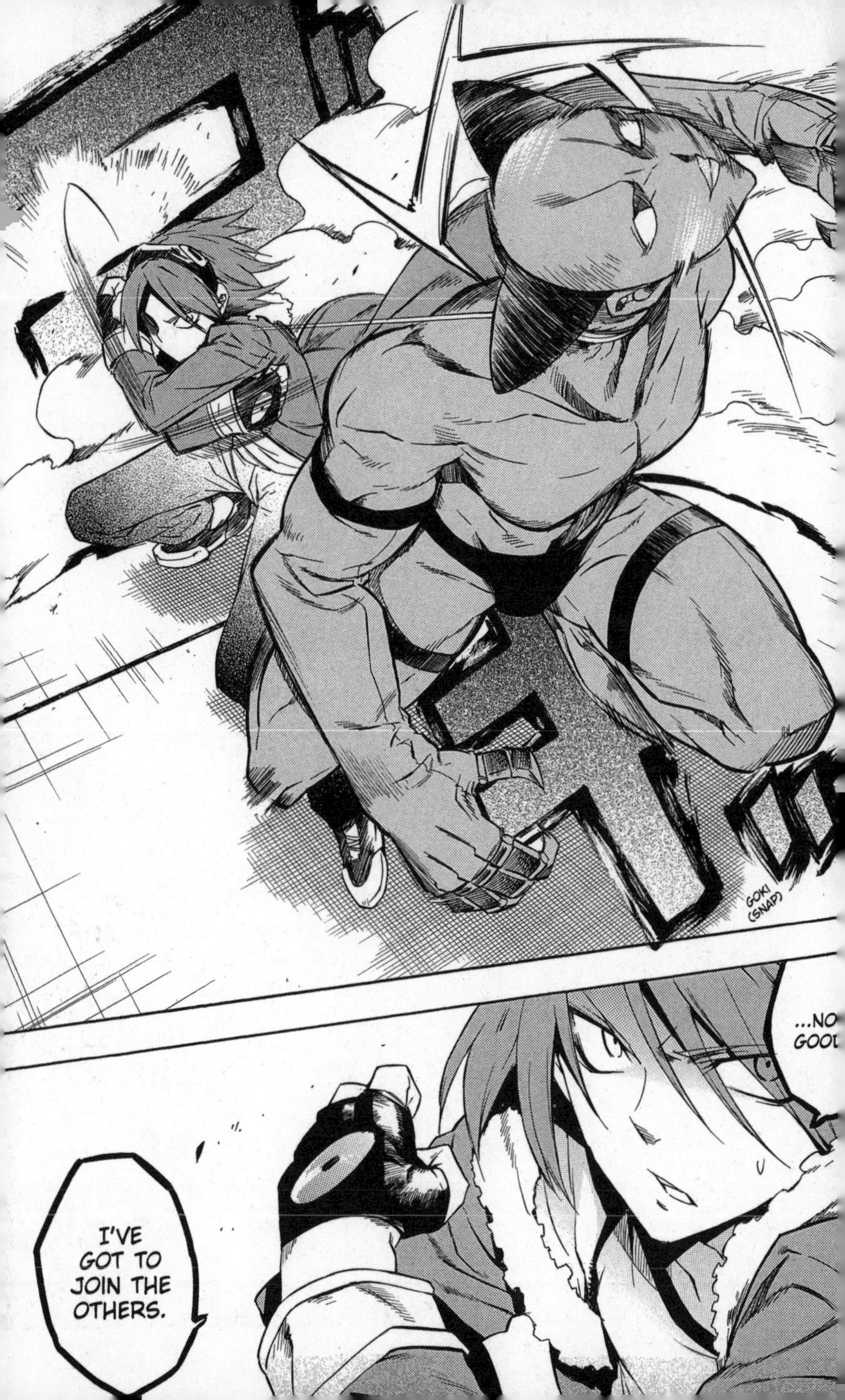
GOKI (SNAP)
...NO GOOD
I'VE GOT TO JOIN THE OTHERS.

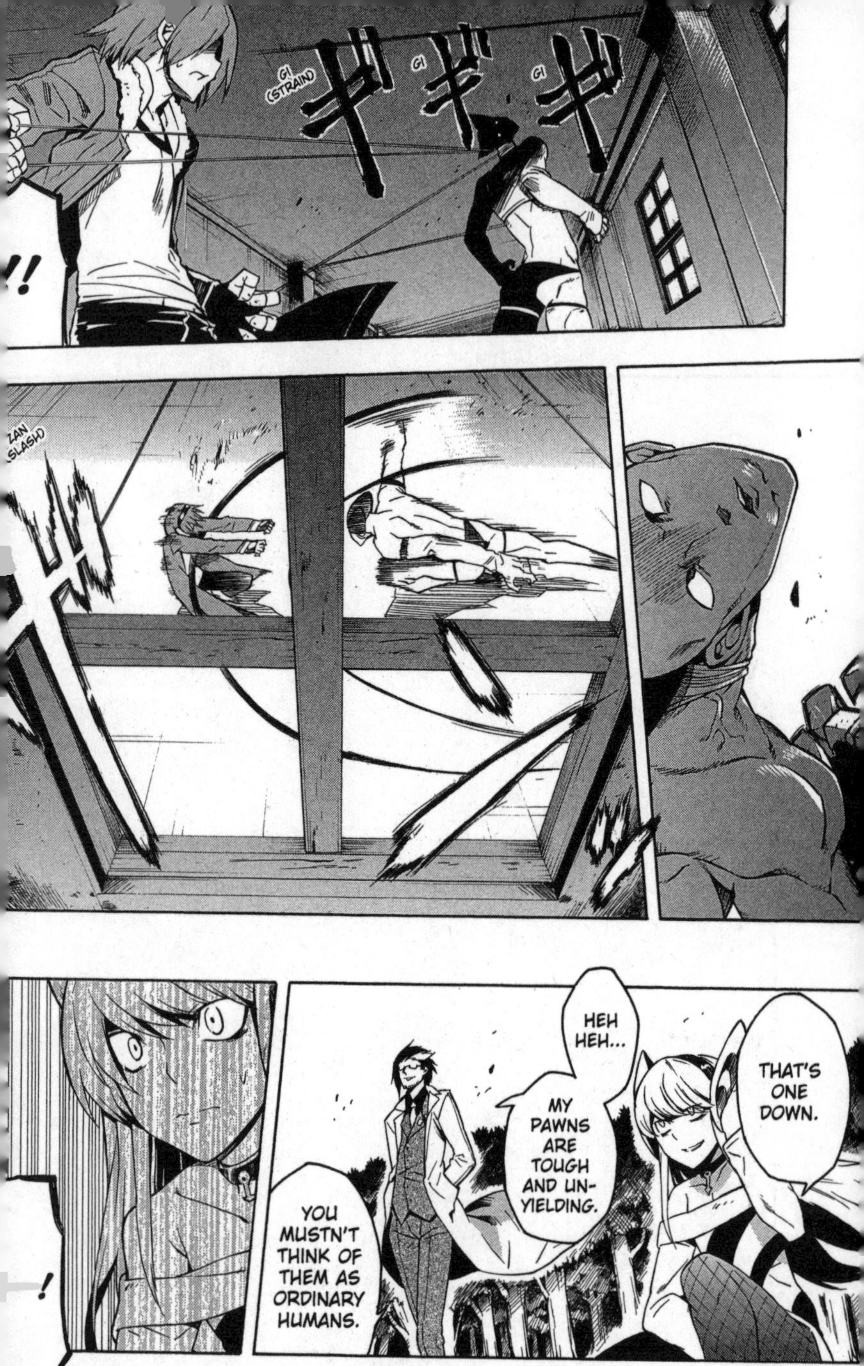
GI (STRAIN)
GI
GI
!!
ZAN (SLASH)
THAT'S ONE DOWN.
HEH HEH...
MY PAWNS ARE TOUGH AND UN-YIELDING.
YOU MUSTN'T THINK OF THEM AS ORDINARY HUMANS.
!

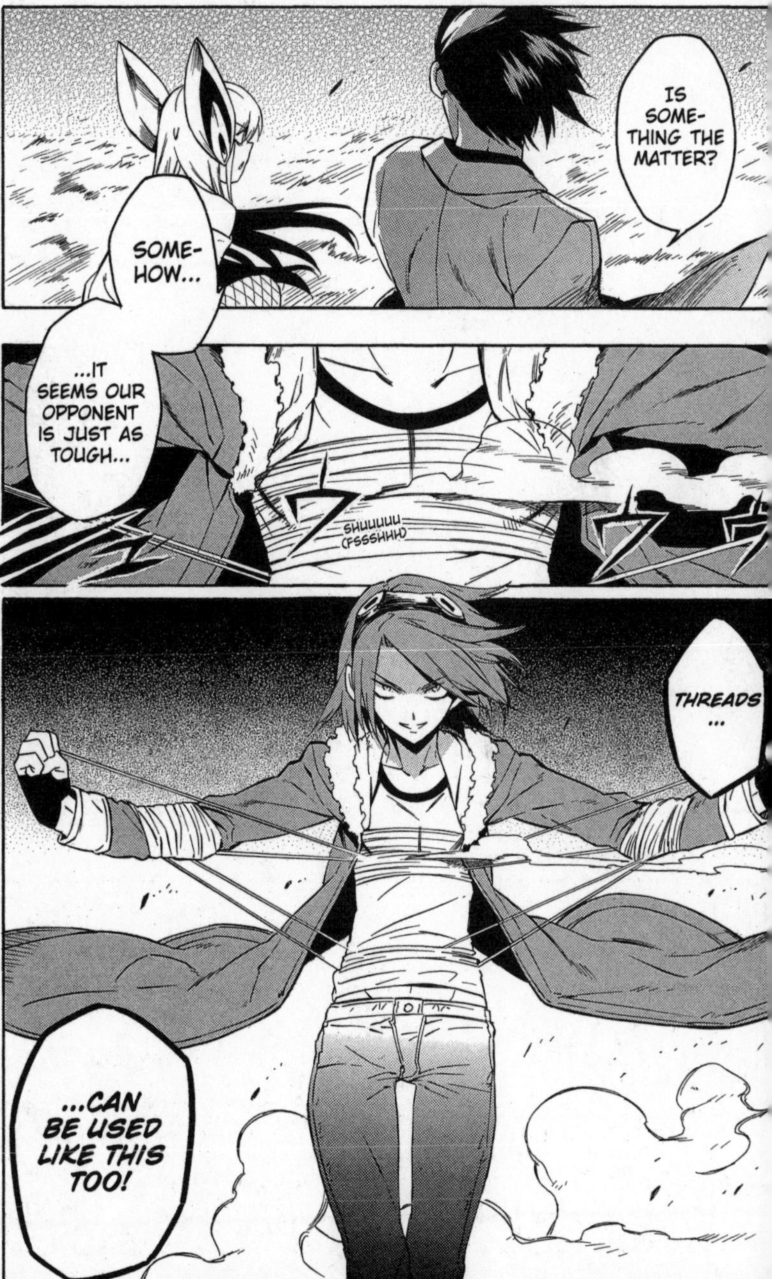

IS SOME-THING THE MATTER?
SOME-HOW...
...IT SEEMS OUR OPPONENT IS JUST AS TOUGH...
SHUUUUU (FSSSHHH)
THREADS...
...CAN BE USED LIKE THIS TOO!

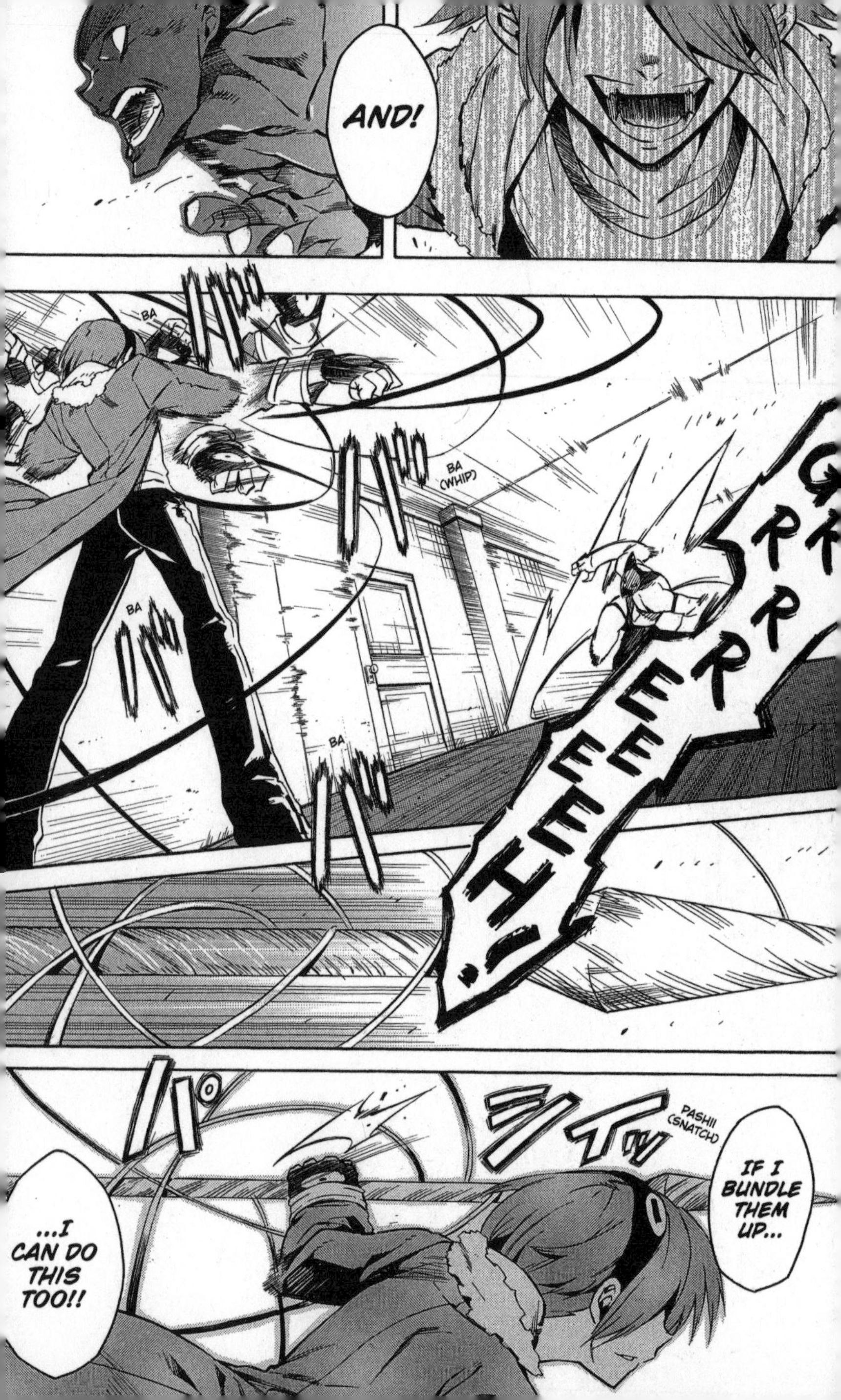
AND!
BA
BA (WHIP)
BA
BA
GRRRRREEEEH!
PASHII (SNATCH)
IF I BUNDLE THEM UP...
...I CAN DO THIS TOO!!

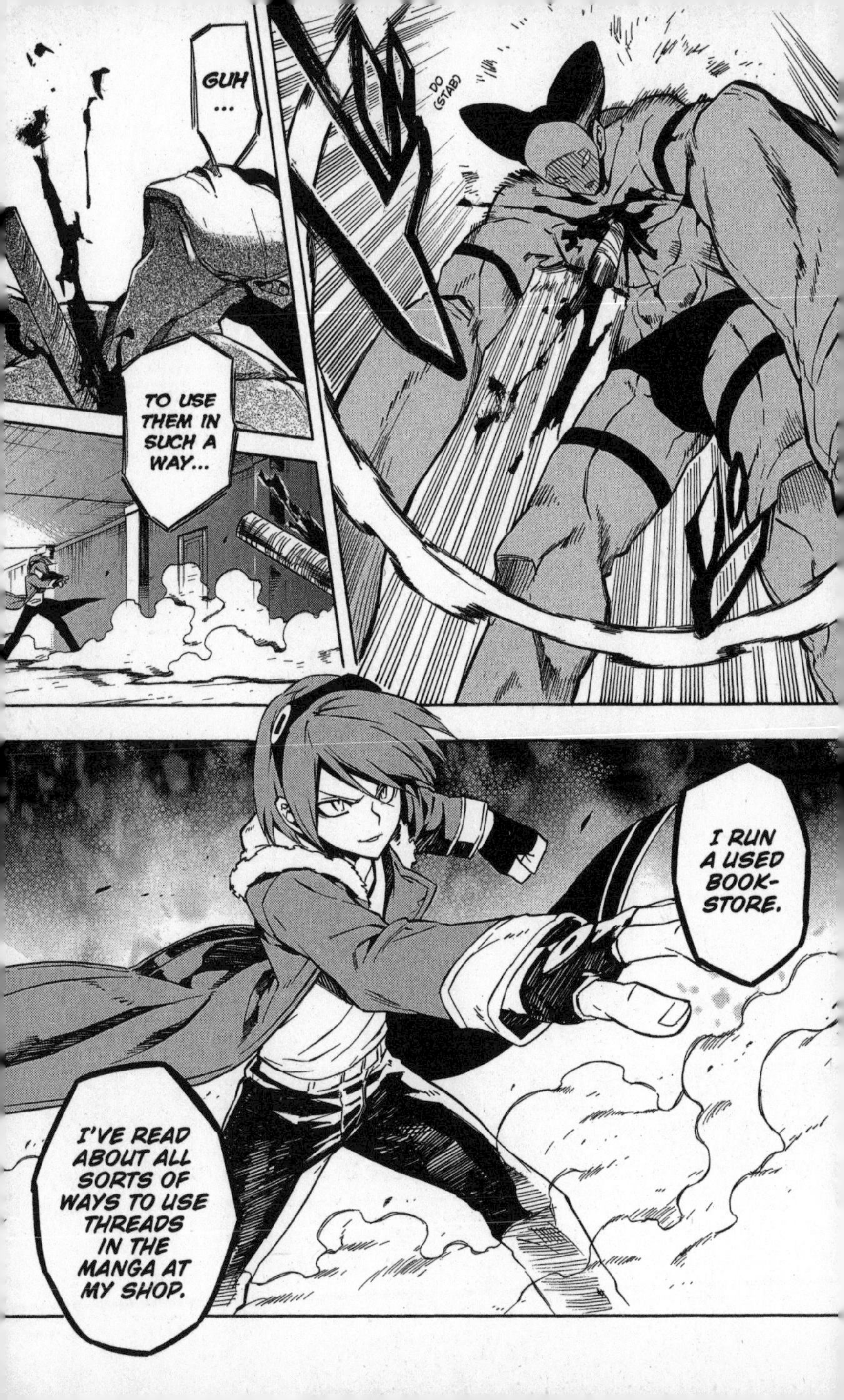
DO (STAB)
GUH ...
TO USE THEM IN SUCH A WAY...
I RUN A USED BOOK-STORE.
I'VE READ ABOUT ALL SORTS OF WAYS TO USE THREADS IN THE MANGA AT MY SHOP.

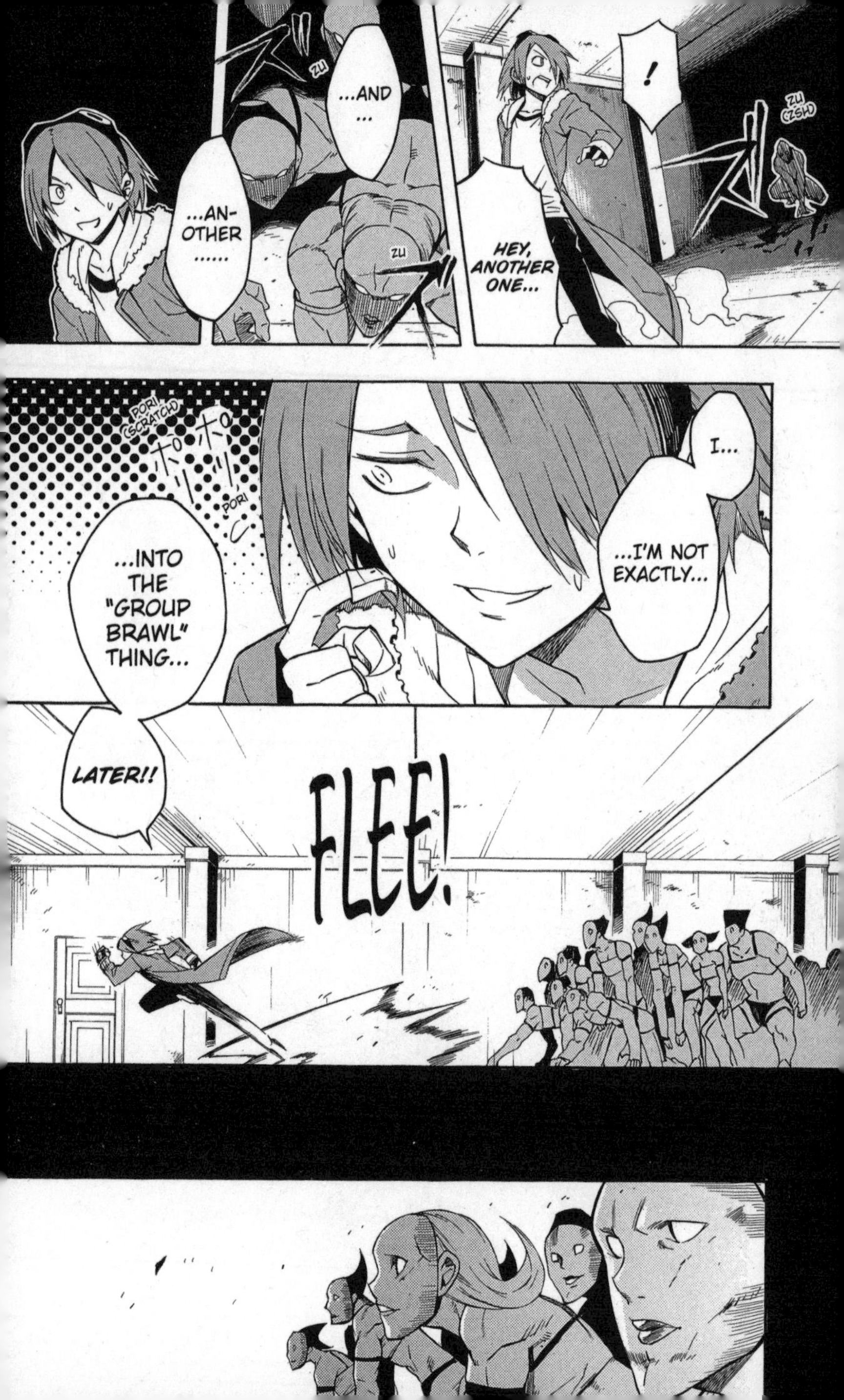
!
ZU (ZSH)
HEY, ANOTHER ONE...
...AND ...
ZU
...AN-OTHER ......
ZU
I...
...I'M NOT EXACTLY...
PORI (SCRATCH)
PORI
...INTO THE "GROUP BRAWL" THING...
LATER!!
FLEE!

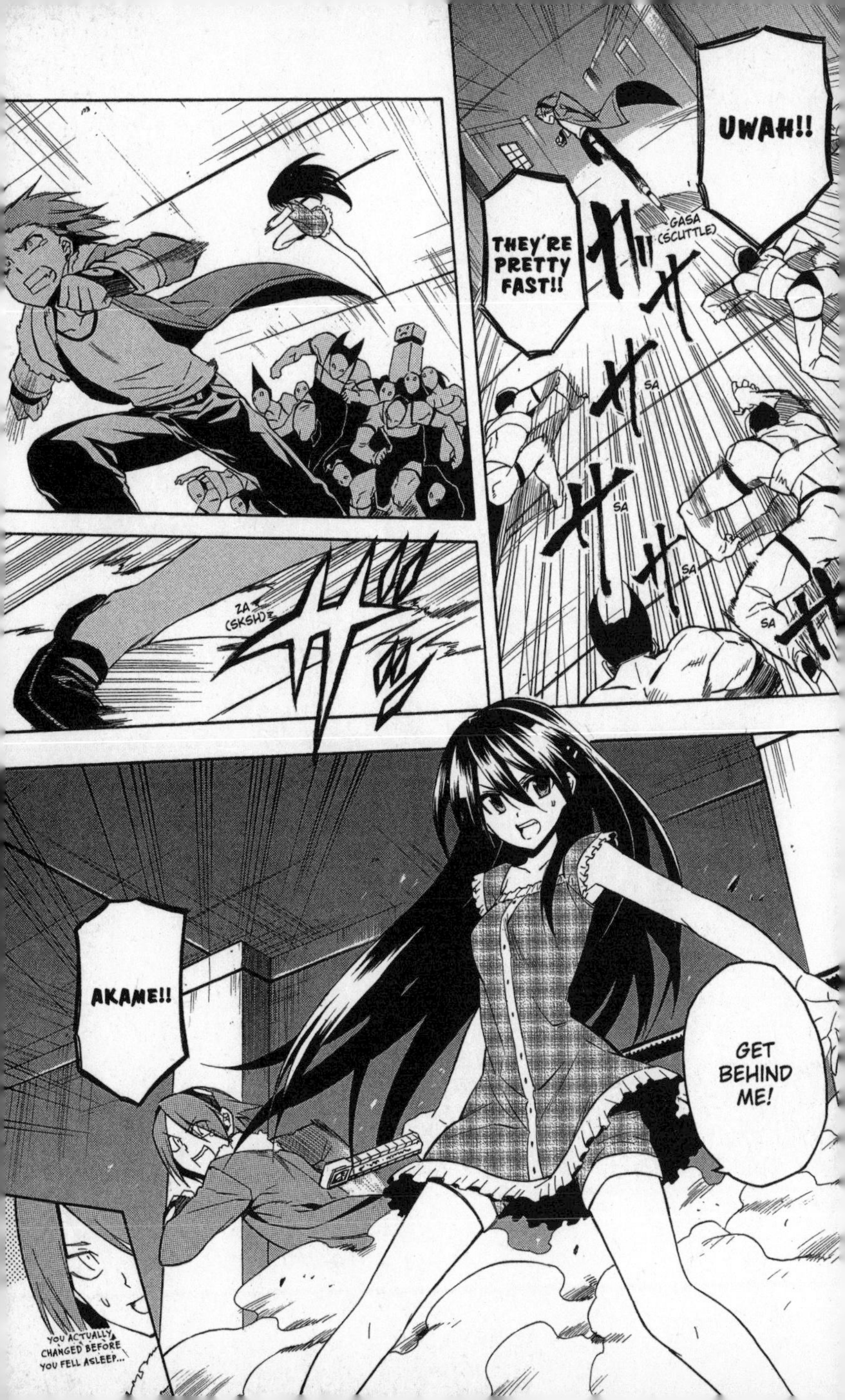
UWAH!!
THEY'RE PRETTY FAST!!
GASA (SCUTTLE)
SA
SA
SA
SA
ZA (SKSH)
GET BEHIND ME!
AKAME!!
YOU ACTUALLY CHANGED BEFORE YOU FELL ASLEEP...

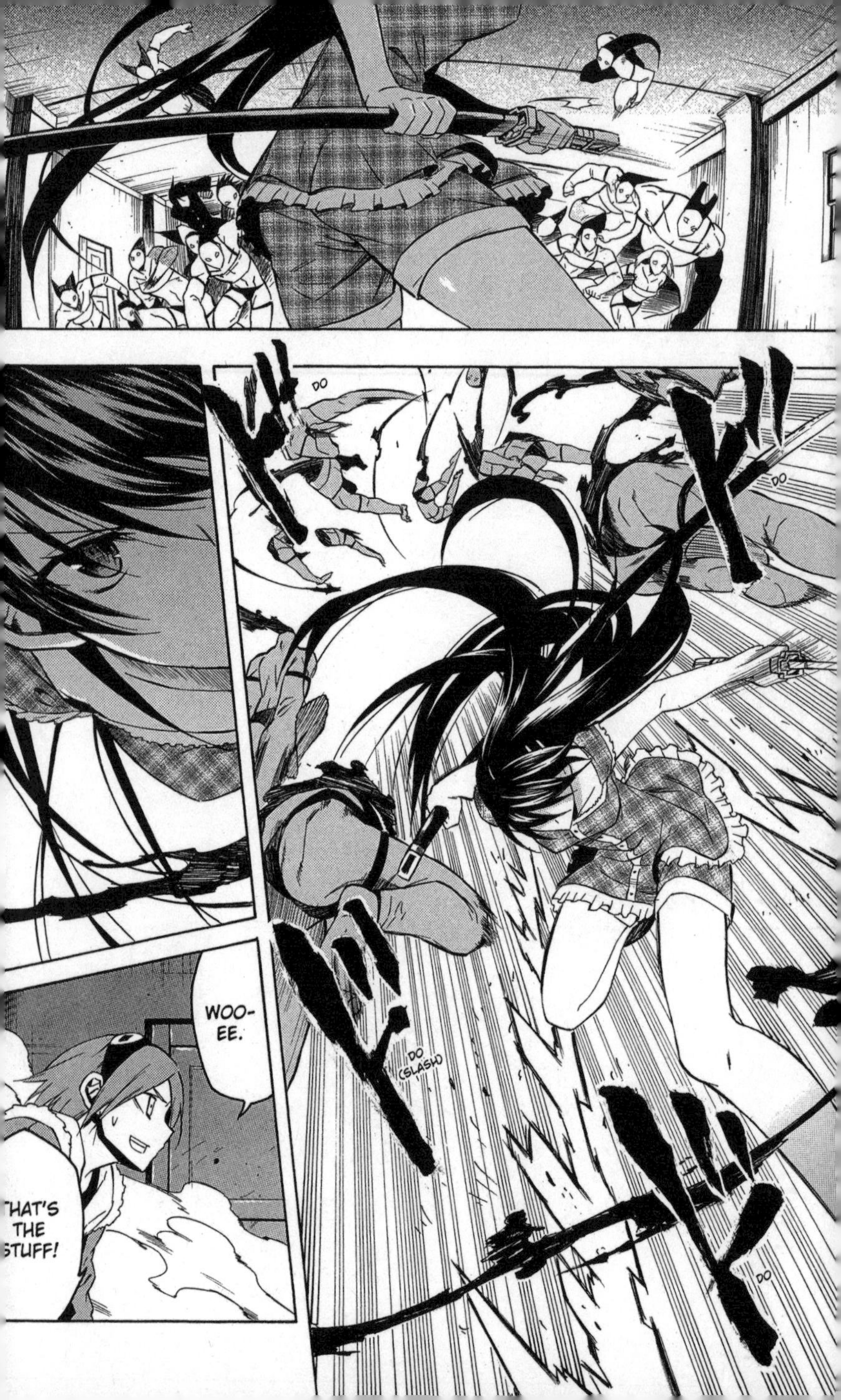

DO
DO
WOO-EE.
DO (SLASH)
THAT'S THE STUFF!
DO

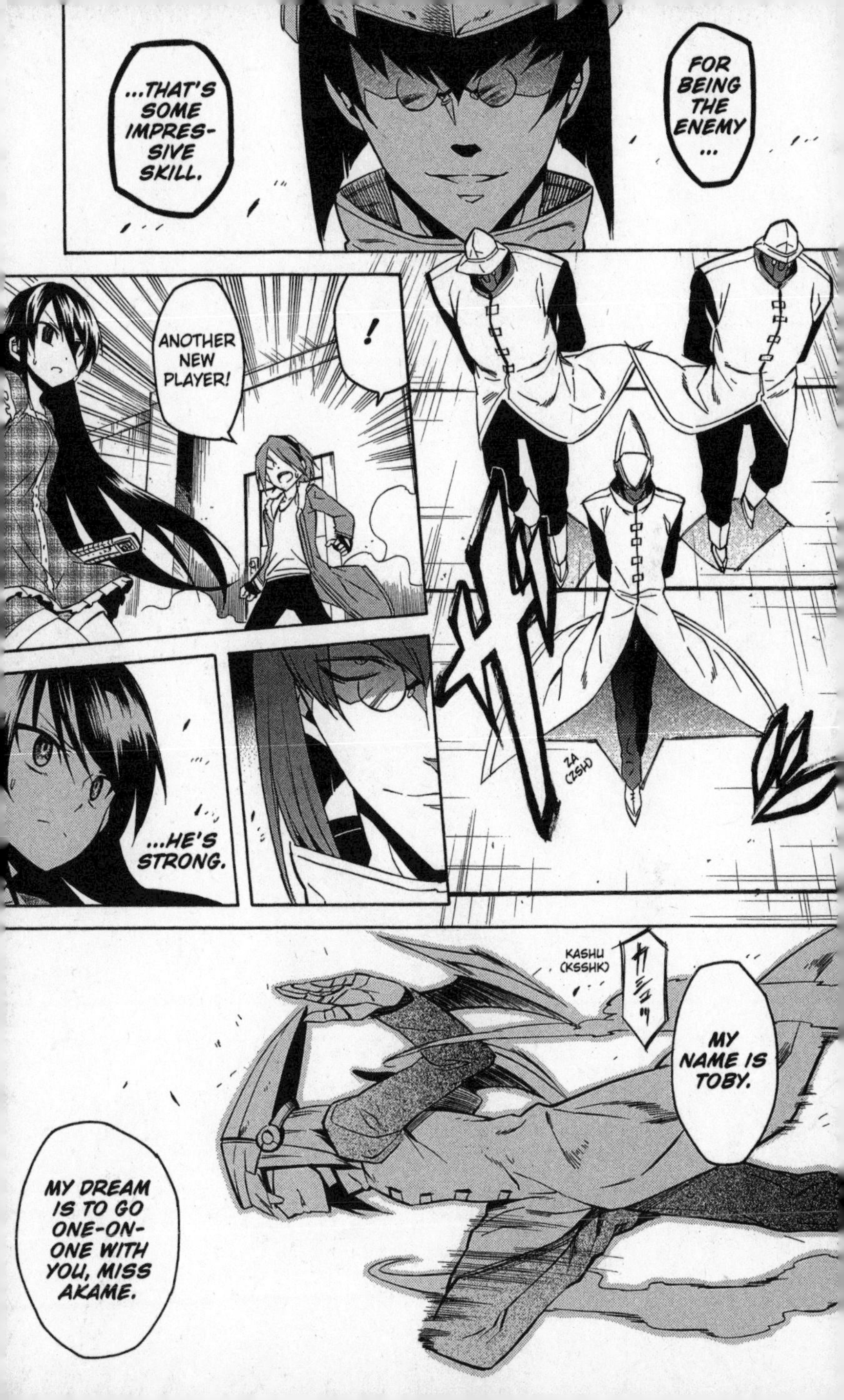
FOR BEING THE ENEMY ...
...THAT'S SOME IMPRES-SIVE SKILL.
ZA (ZSH)
!
ANOTHER NEW PLAYER!
...HE'S STRONG.
KASHU (KSSHK)
MY NAME IS TOBY.
MY DREAM IS TO GO ONE-ON-ONE WITH YOU, MISS AKAME.

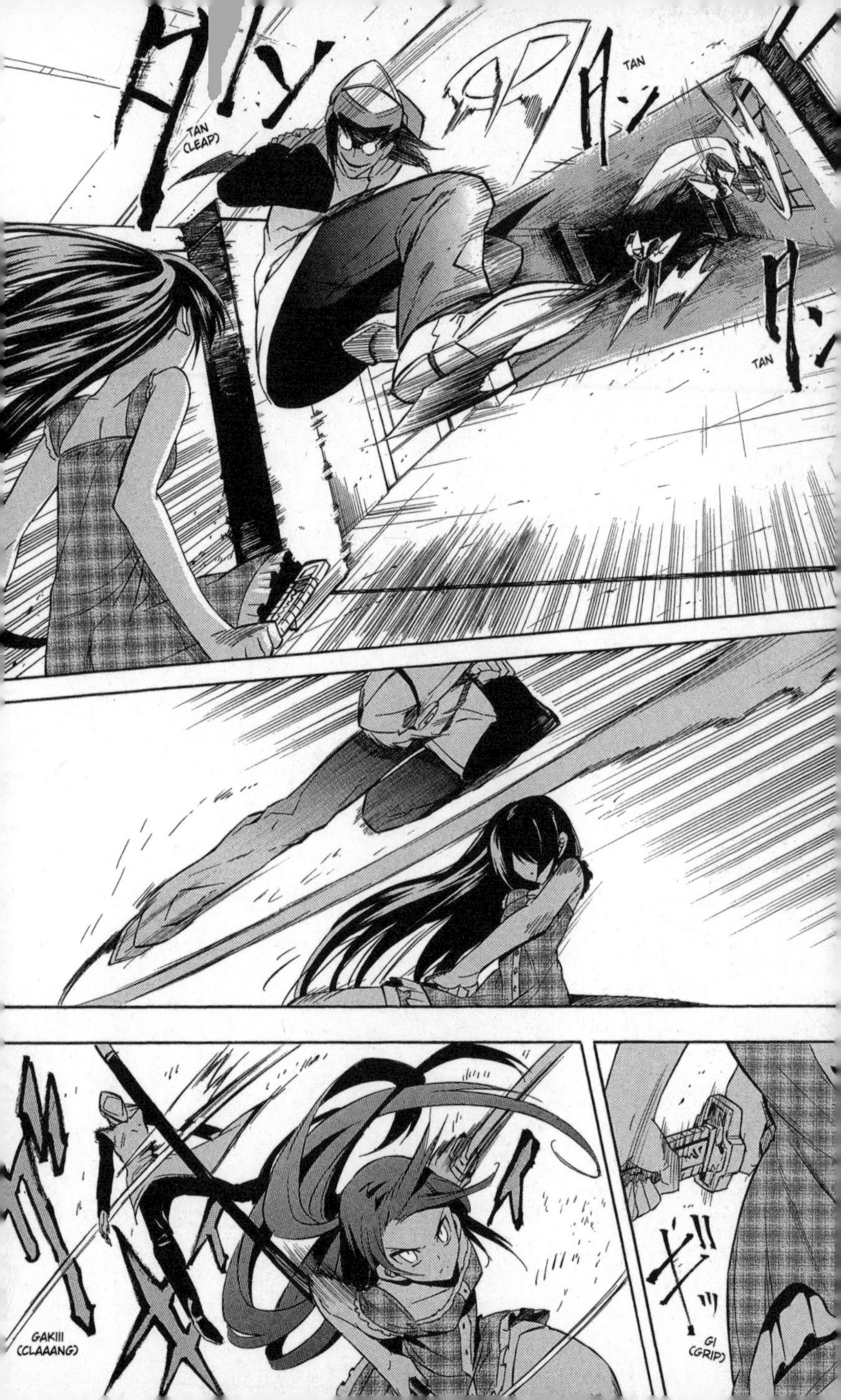
TAN
(LEAP)
TAN
TAN
GI
(GRIP)
GAKIII
(CLAAANG)

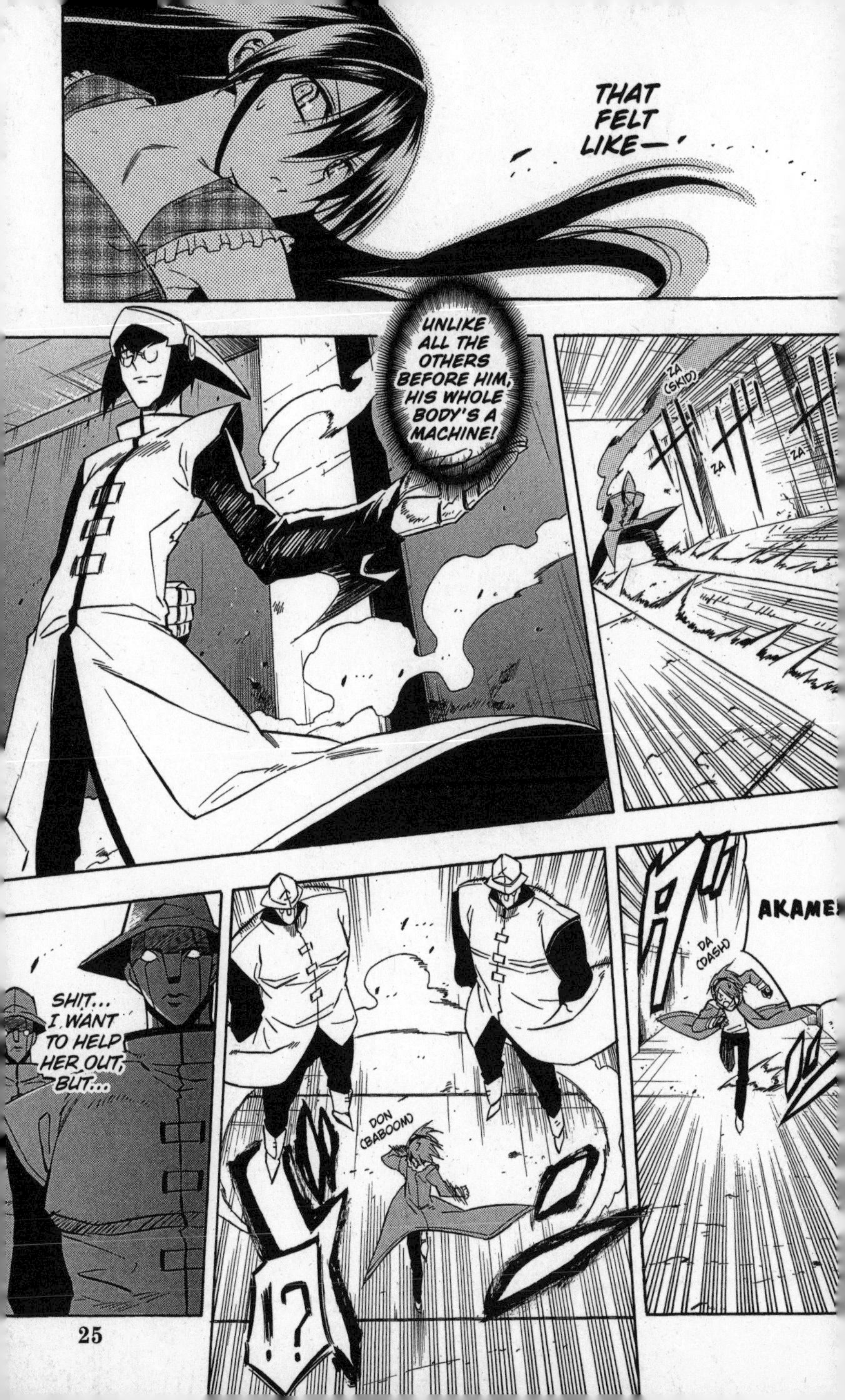
THAT FELT LIKE—
UNLIKE ALL THE OTHERS BEFORE HIM, HIS WHOLE BODY'S A MACHINE!
...
ZA (SKID)
ZA
ZA
...
SHIT... I WANT TO HELP HER OUT, BUT...
...
DON (BABOON)
!?
AKAME!
DA (DASH)

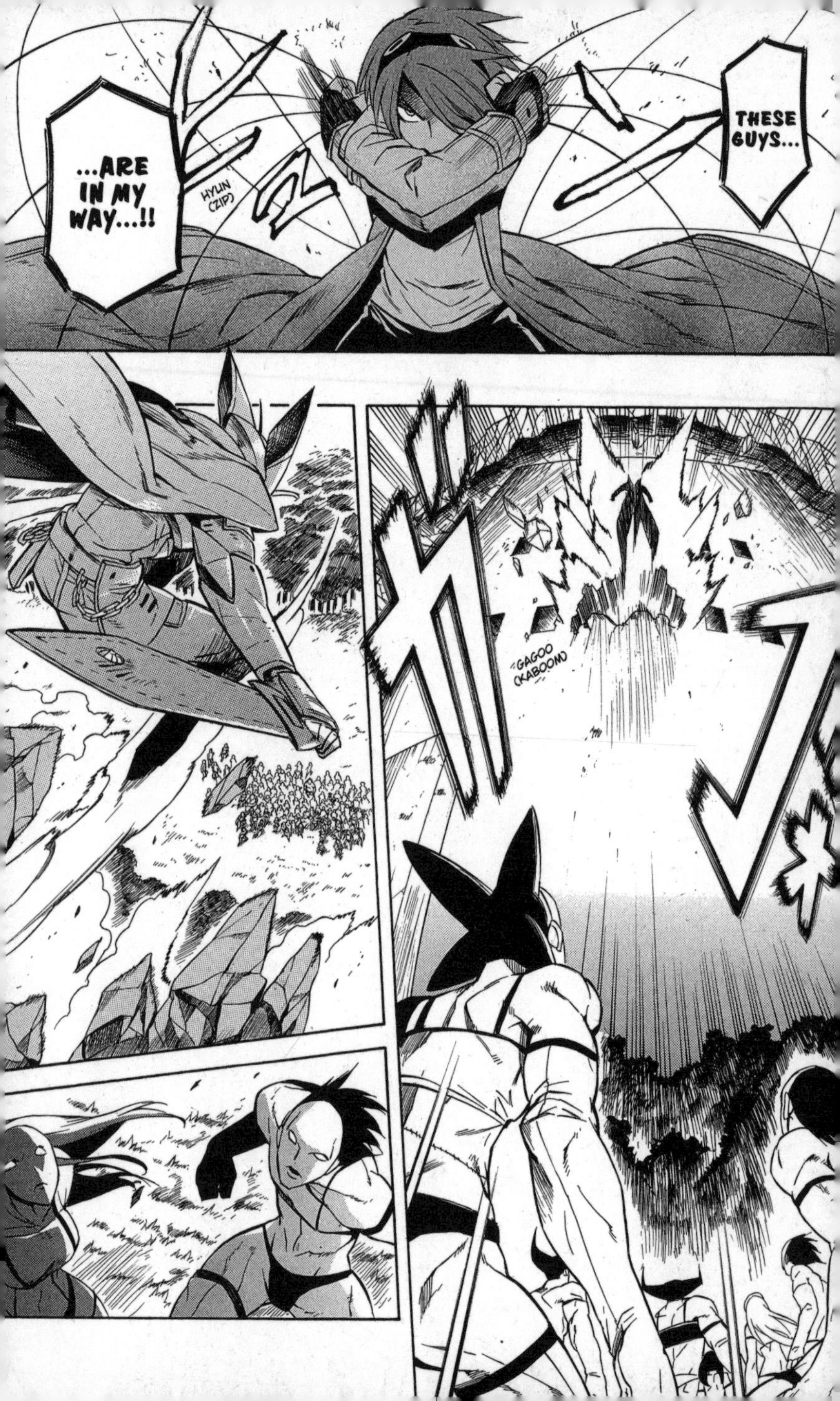
THESE GUYS...
...ARE IN MY WAY...!!
HYUN (ZIP)
GAGOO (KABOOM)

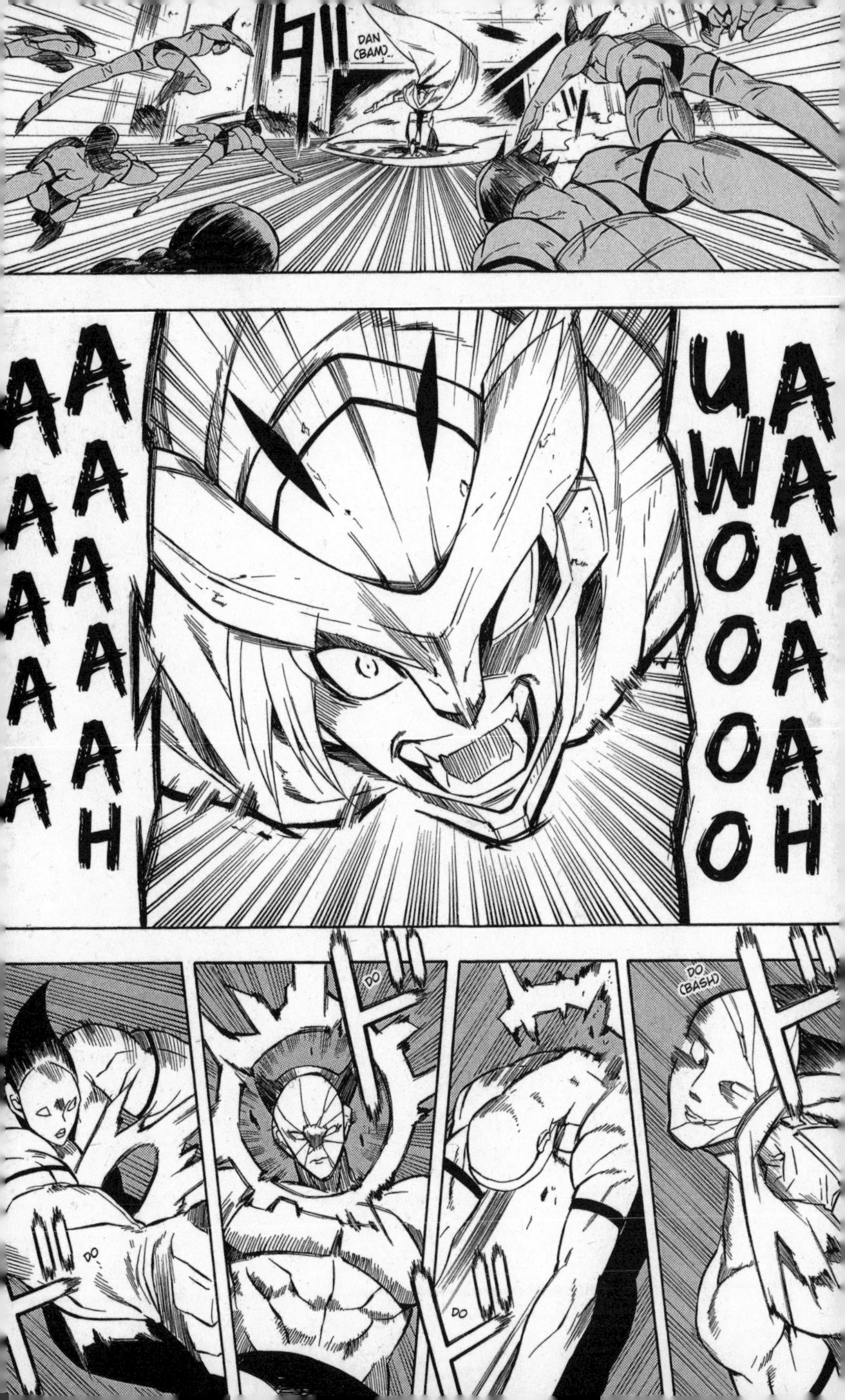
DAN (BAM)
UAWOOOOOOAAAAAAH
AAAAAAAAAAAAH
DO (BASH)
DO
DO
DO

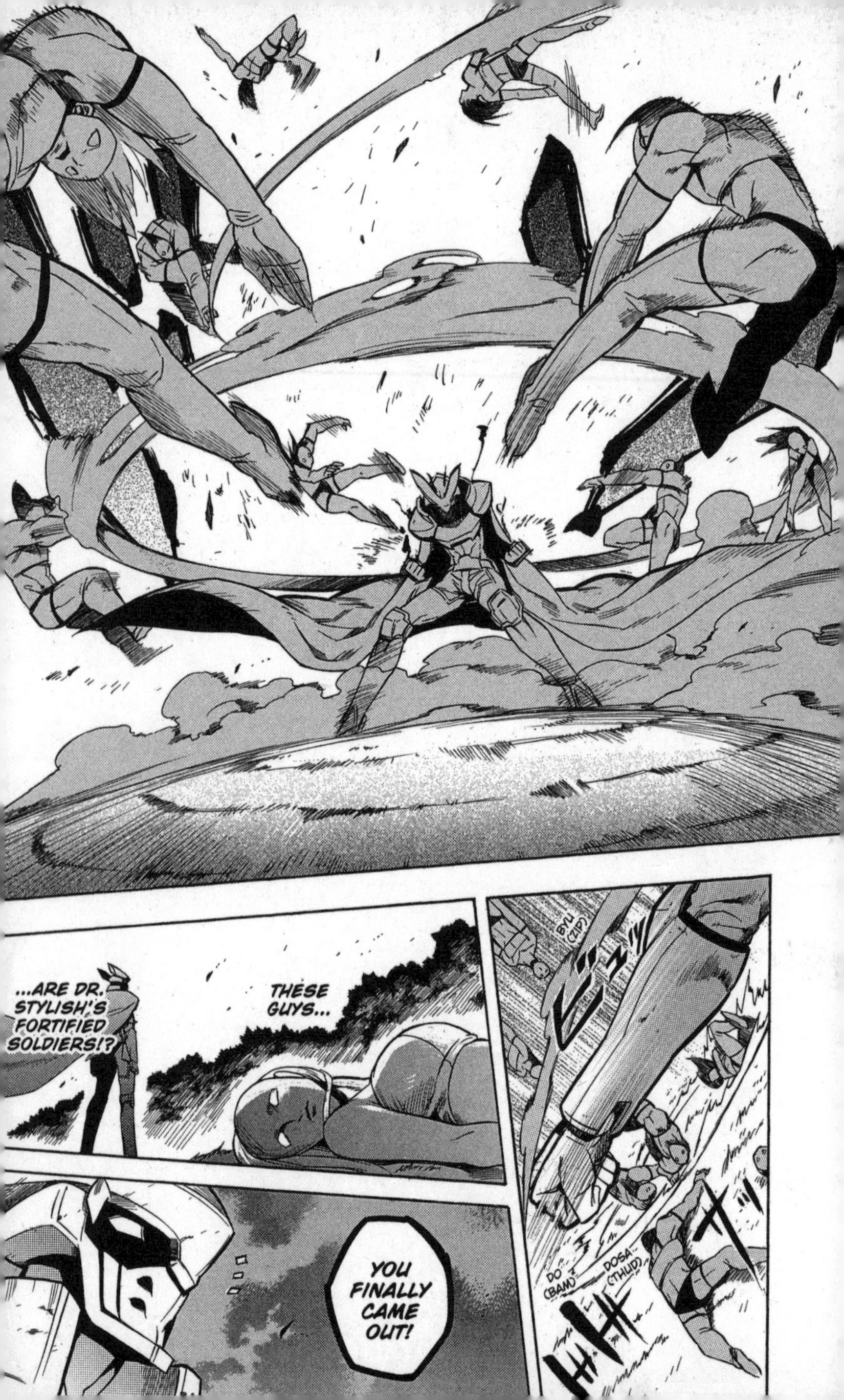
BYU (ZIP)
DO (BAM)
DOSA (THUD)
THESE GUYS...
...ARE DR. STYLISH'S FORTIFIED SOLDIERS!?
YOU FINALLY CAME OUT!

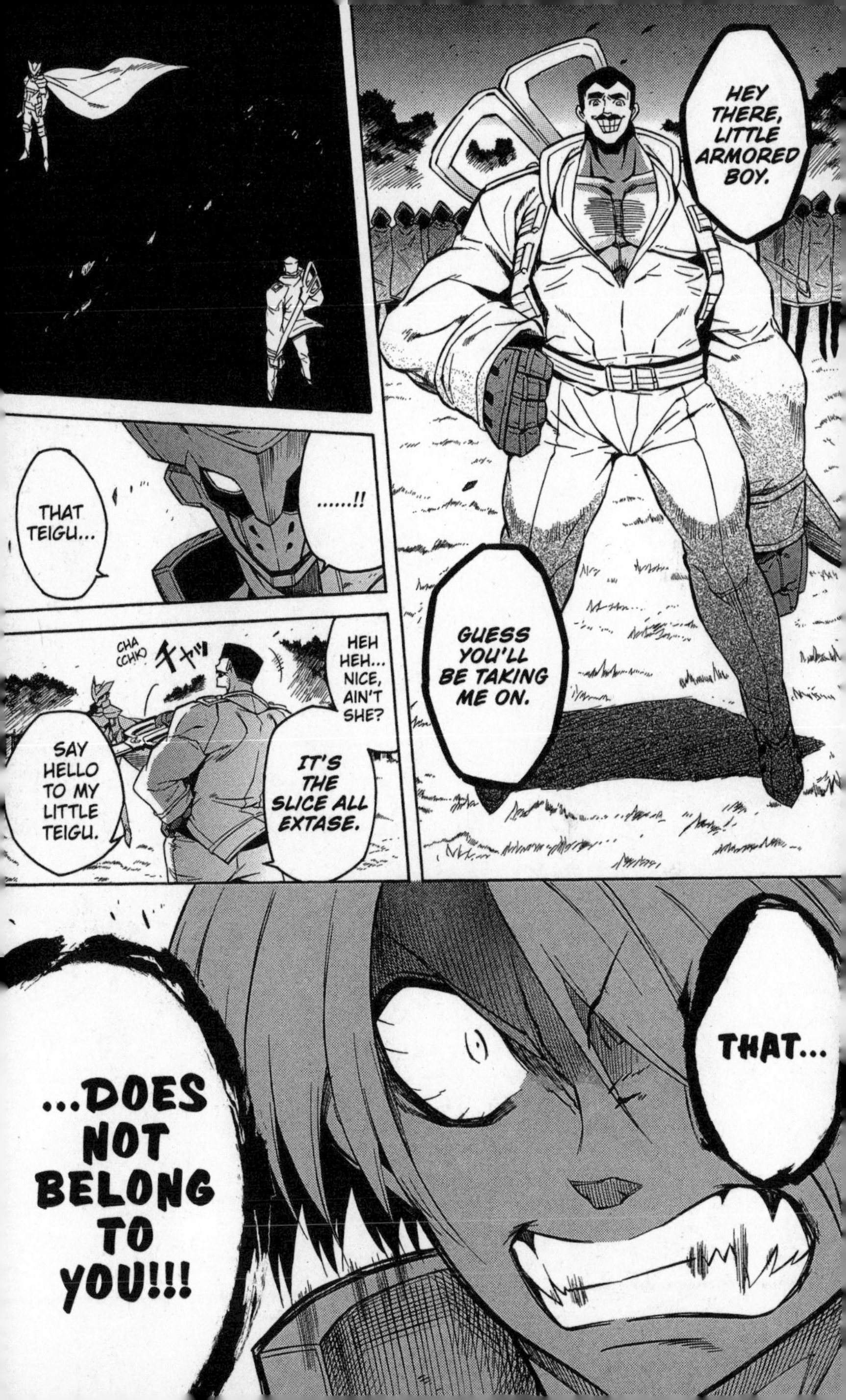
HEY THERE, LITTLE ARMORED BOY.
GUESS YOU'LL BE TAKING ME ON.
......!!
THAT TEIGU...
HEH HEH... NICE, AIN'T SHE?
チャッ
CHA (CHK)
IT'S THE SLICE ALL EXTASE.
SAY HELLO TO MY LITTLE TEIGU.
THAT...
...DOES NOT BELONG TO YOU!!!

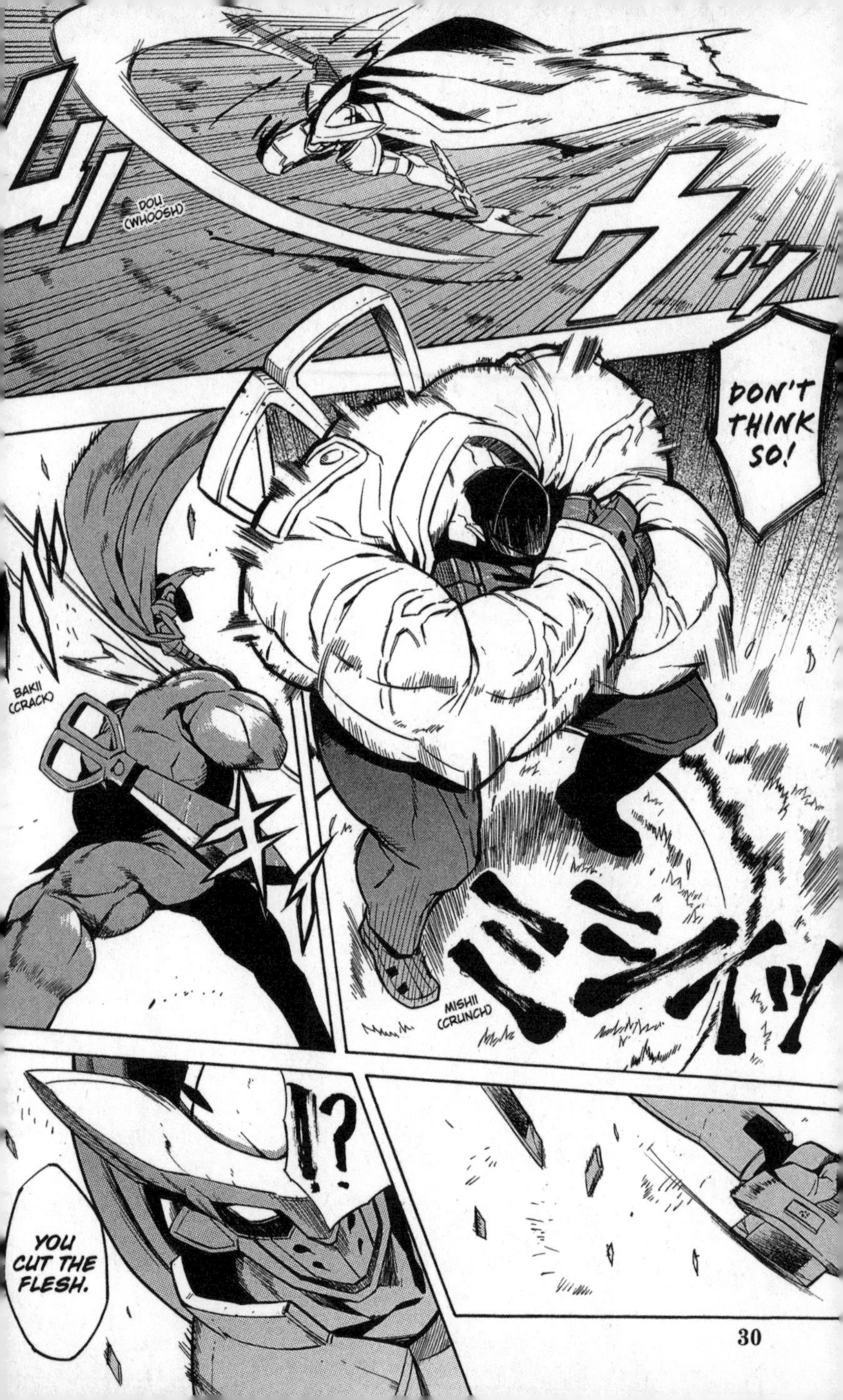
DOU (WHOOSH)
DON'T THINK SO!
BAKII (CRACK)
MISHII (CRUNCH)
!?
YOU CUT THE FLESH.

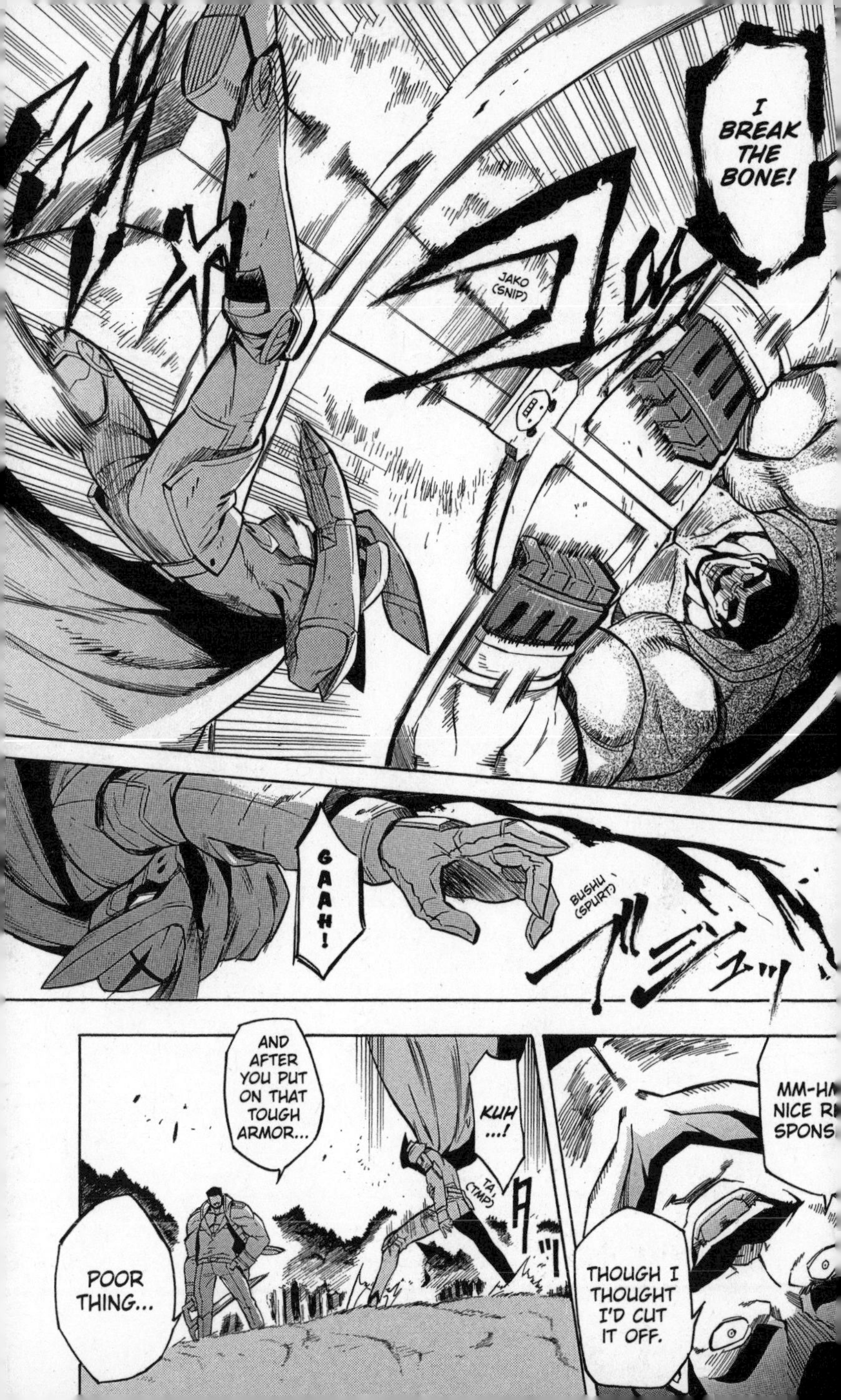
I BREAK THE BONE!
JAKO (SNIP)
BUSHU (SPURT)
GAAH!
MM-H NICE R SPONS
THOUGH I THOUGHT I'D CUT IT OFF.
AND AFTER YOU PUT ON THAT TOUGH ARMOR...
KUH ...!
TA! (TMP)
POOR THING...

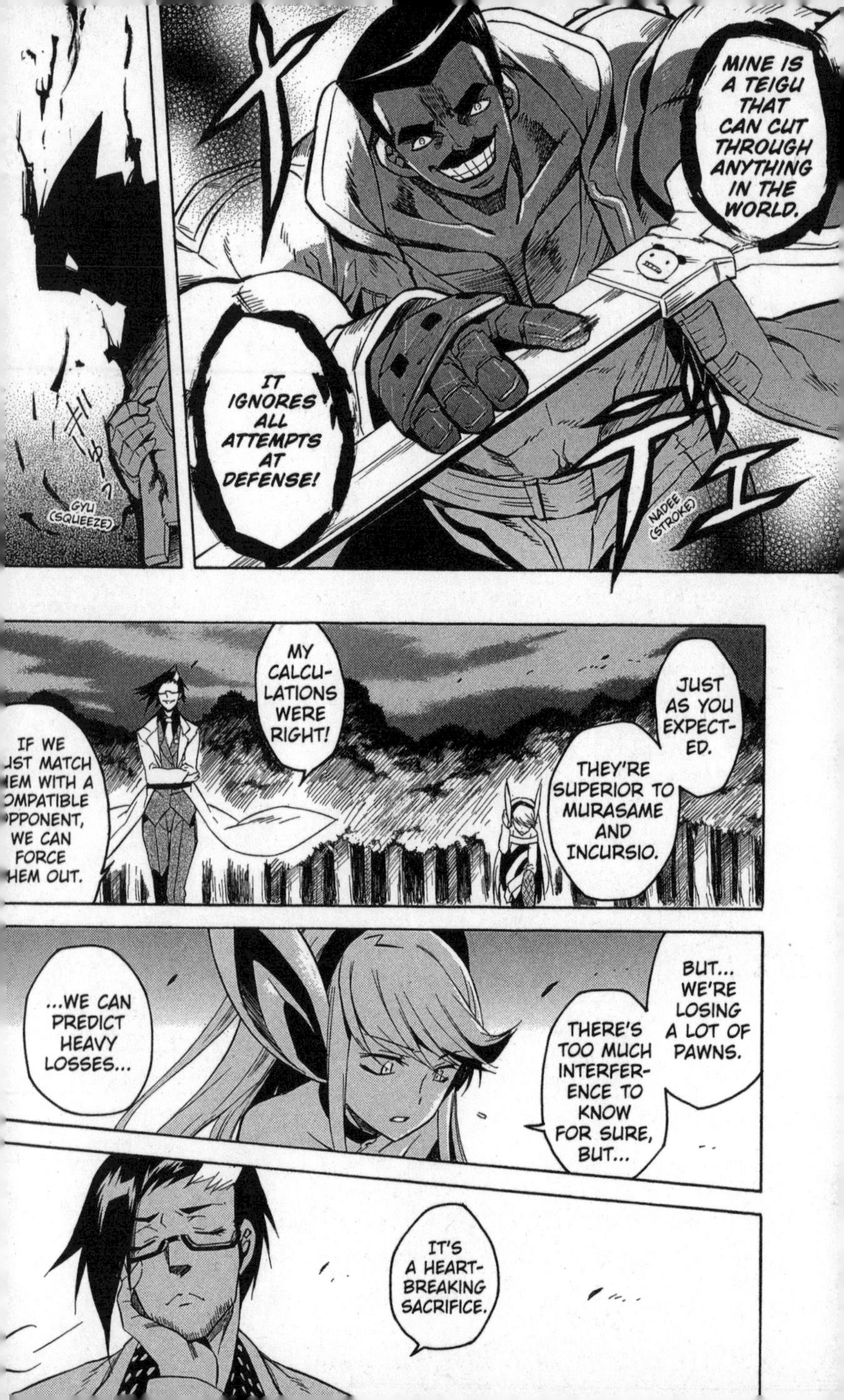
MINE IS A TEIGU THAT CAN CUT THROUGH ANYTHING IN THE WORLD.
IT IGNORES ALL ATTEMPTS AT DEFENSE!
NADEE (STROKE)
GYU (SQUEEZE)
JUST AS YOU EXPECT-ED.
THEY'RE SUPERIOR TO MURASAME AND INCURSIO.
MY CALCU-LATIONS WERE RIGHT!
IF WE UST MATCH HEM WITH A OMPATIBLE PPONENT, WE CAN FORCE HEM OUT.
BUT... WE'RE LOSING A LOT OF PAWNS.
THERE'S TOO MUCH INTERFER-ENCE TO KNOW FOR SURE, BUT...
...WE CAN PREDICT HEAVY LOSSES...
IT'S A HEART-BREAKING SACRIFICE.

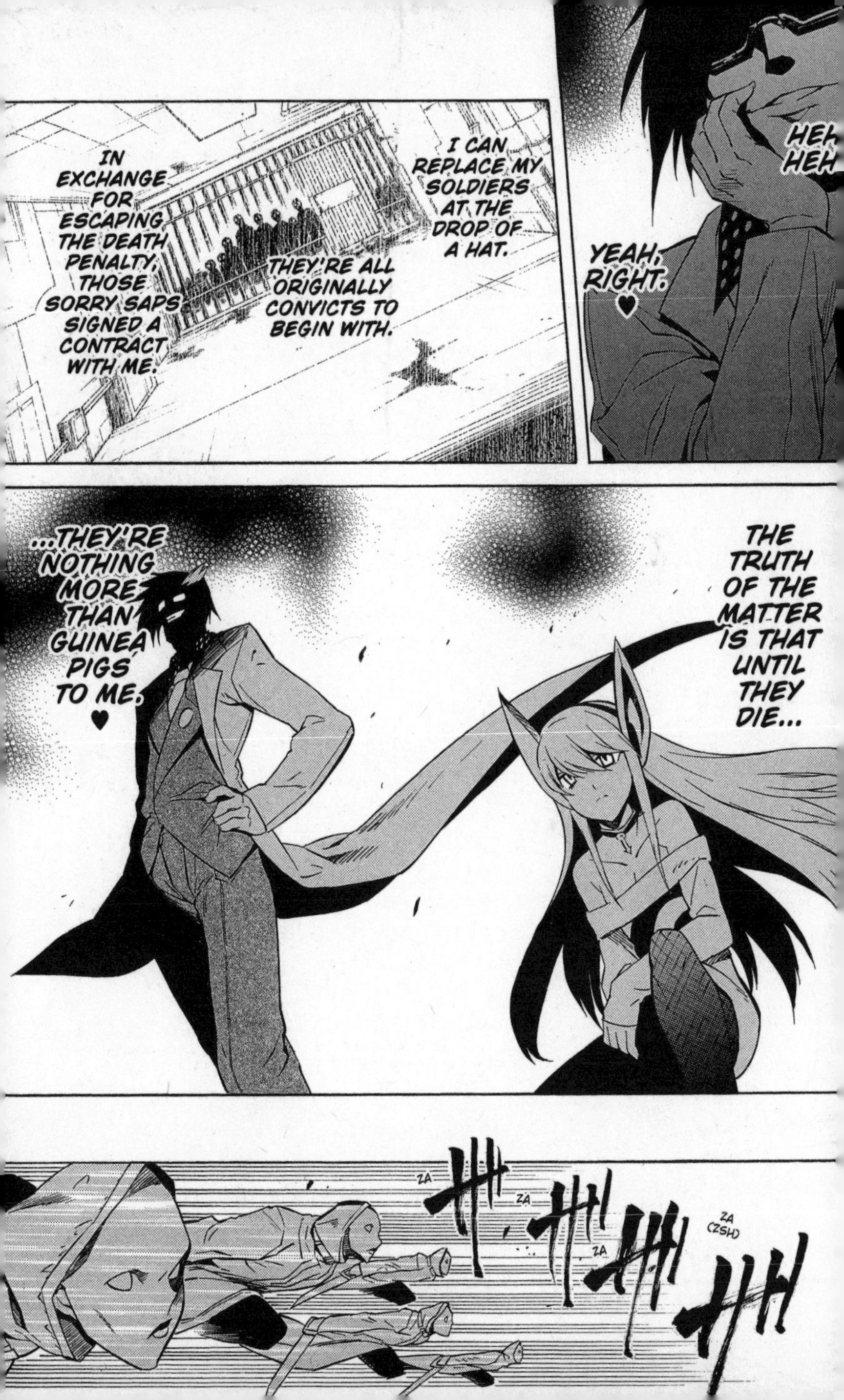
HEH HEH
YEAH, RIGHT. ♥
I CAN REPLACE MY SOLDIERS AT THE DROP OF A HAT.
THEY'RE ALL ORIGINALLY CONVICTS TO BEGIN WITH.
IN EXCHANGE FOR ESCAPING THE DEATH PENALTY, THOSE SORRY SAPS SIGNED A CONTRACT WITH ME.
THE TRUTH OF THE MATTER IS THAT UNTIL THEY DIE...
...THEY'RE NOTHING MORE THAN GUINEA PIGS TO ME. ♥
ZA
ZA
ZA
ZA (ZSH)

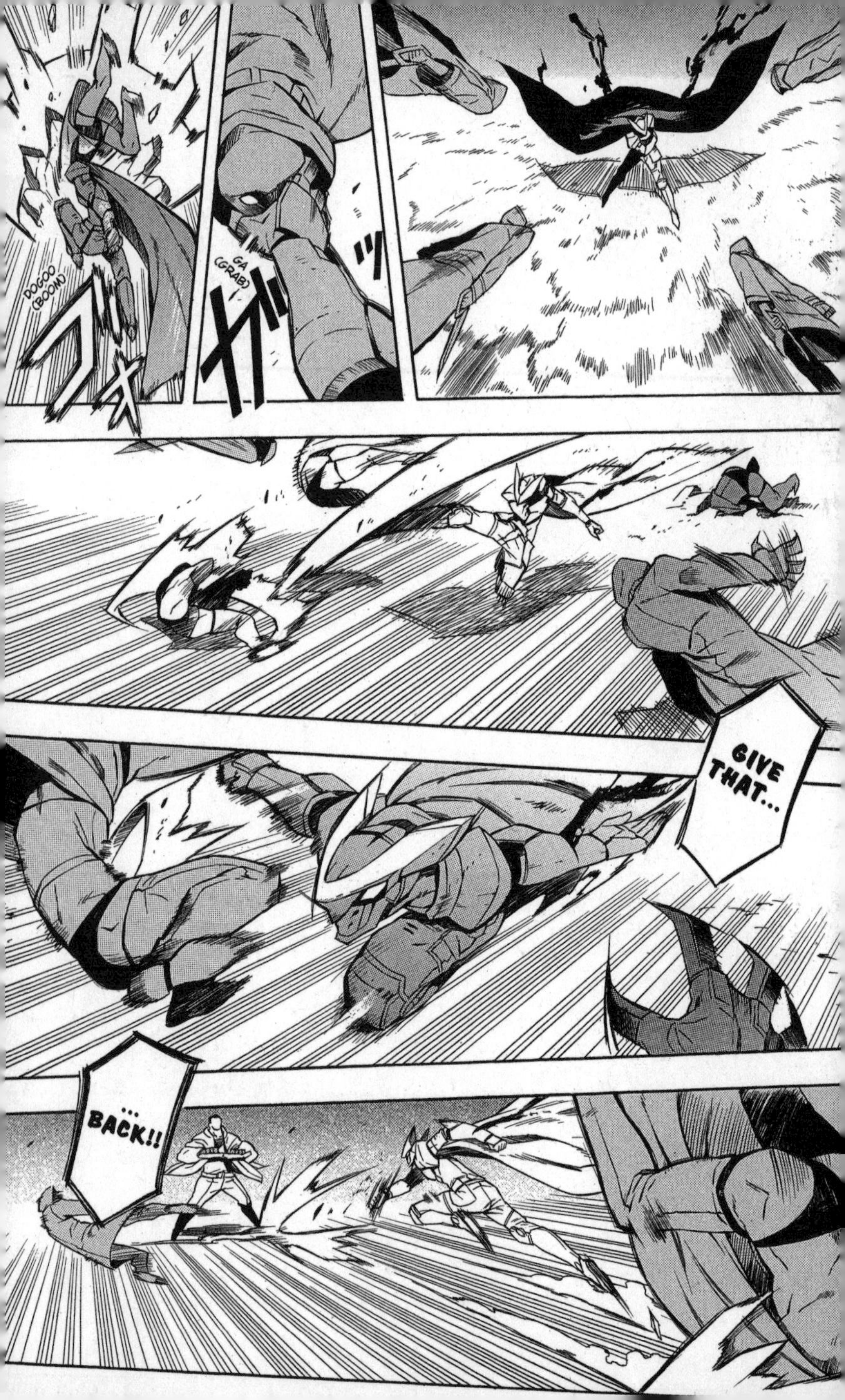

GA (GRAB)
DOGOO (BOOM)
GIVE THAT...
...BACK!!

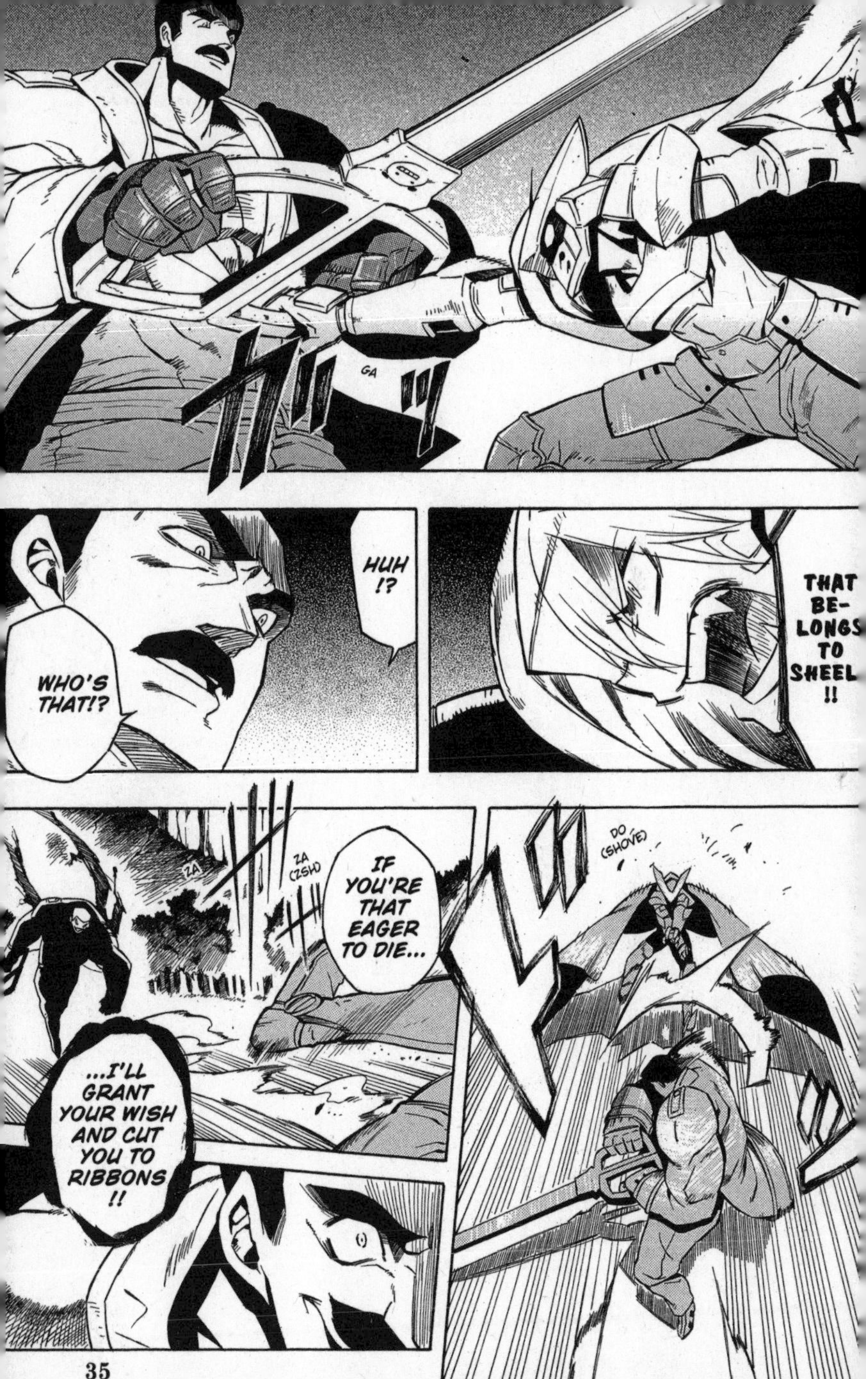
GA
THAT BE-LONGS TO SHEEL !!
HUH !?
WHO'S THAT!?
DO (SHOVE)
ZA (ZSH)
ZA
IF YOU'RE THAT EAGER TO DIE...
...I'LL GRANT YOUR WISH AND CUT YOU TO RIBBONS !!

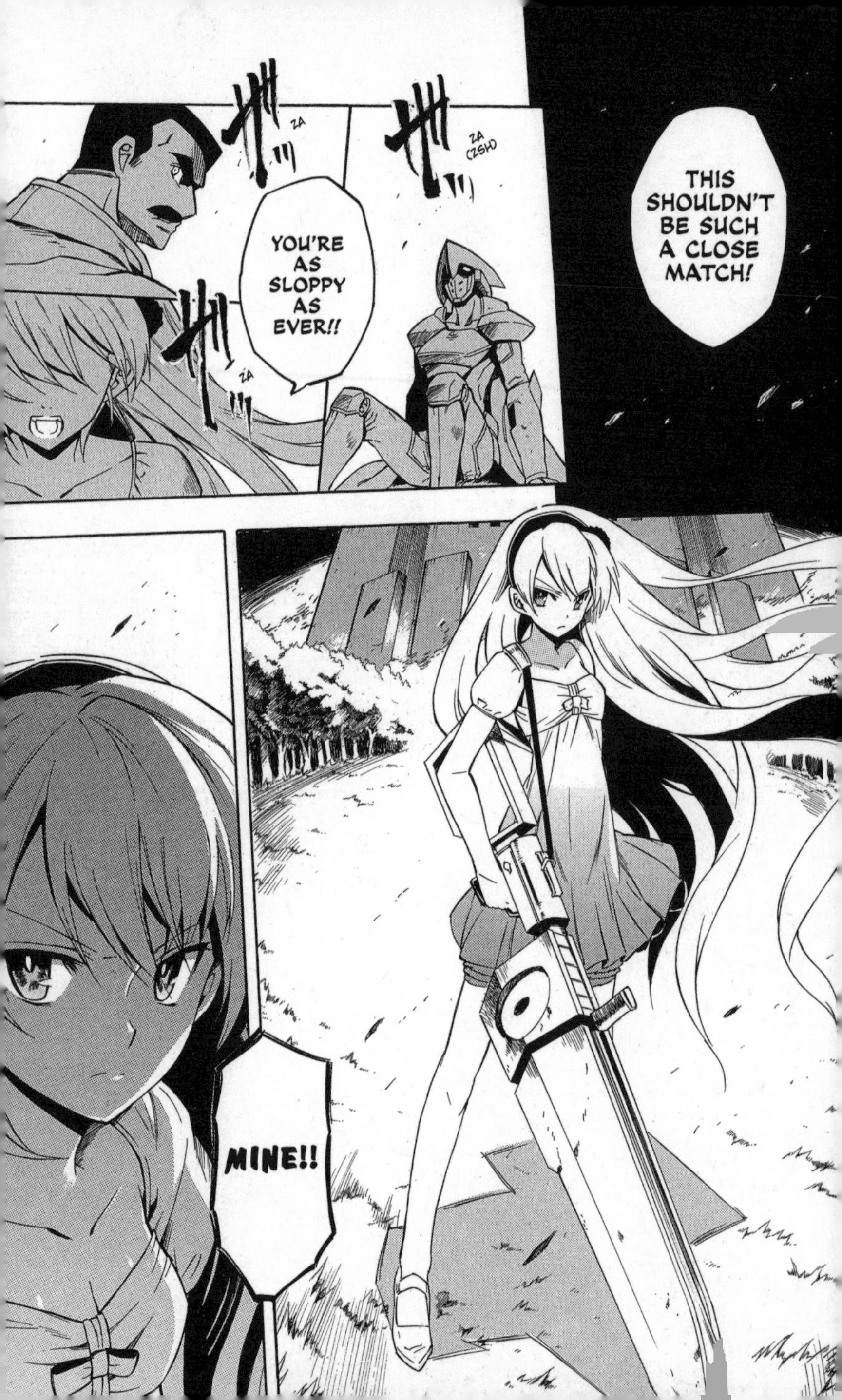
THIS SHOULDN'T BE SUCH A CLOSE MATCH!
ZA (ZSH)
YOU'RE AS SLOPPY AS EVER!!
ZA
ZA
MINE!!

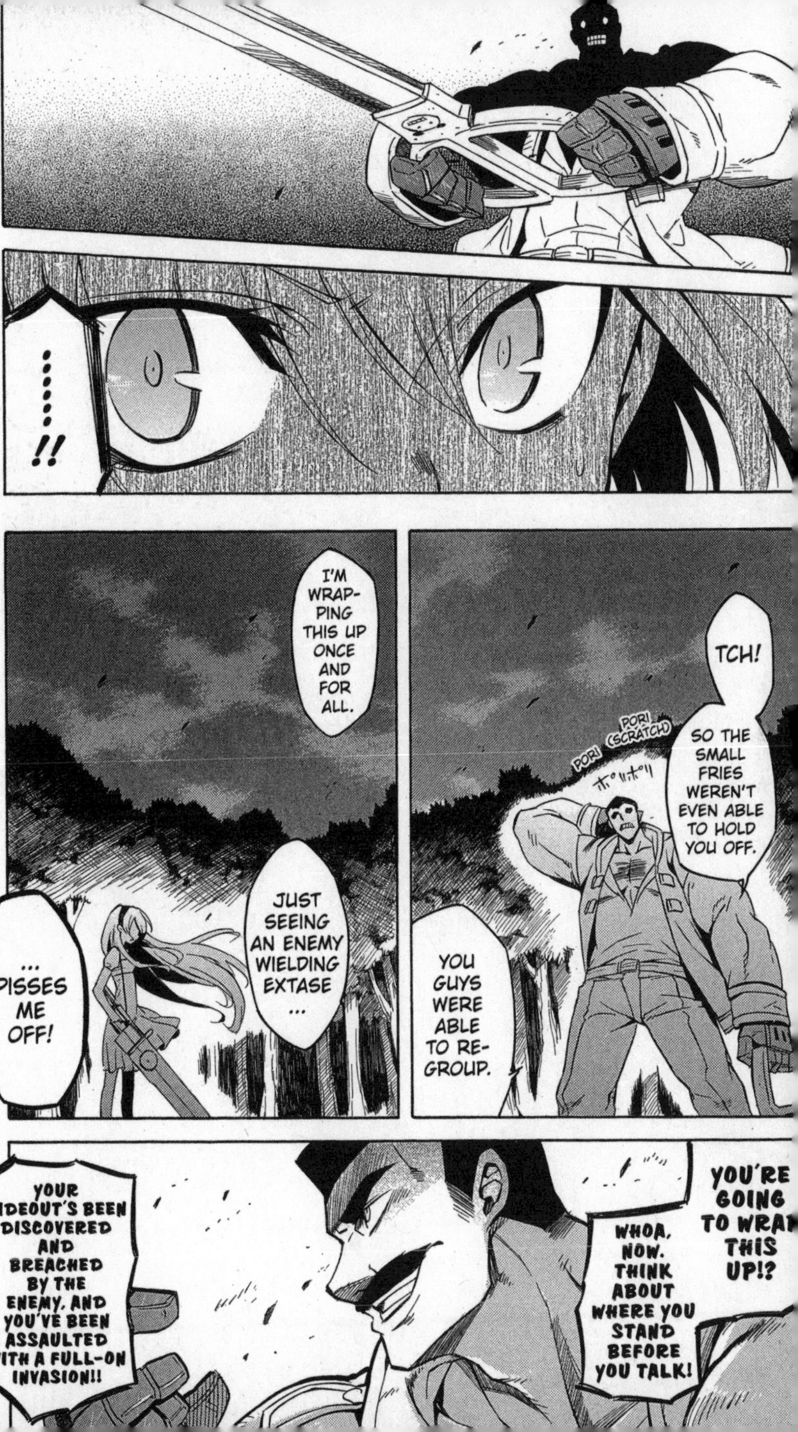
......!!
TCH!
SO THE SMALL FRIES WEREN'T EVEN ABLE TO HOLD YOU OFF.
PORI PORI (SCRATCH)
ポリポリ
YOU GUYS WERE ABLE TO RE-GROUP.
I'M WRAP-PING THIS UP ONCE AND FOR ALL.
JUST SEEING AN ENEMY WIELDING EXTASE ...
... PISSES ME OFF!
YOU'RE GOING TO WRA THIS UP!?
WHOA, NOW. THINK ABOUT WHERE YOU STAND BEFORE YOU TALK!
YOUR HIDEOUT'S BEEN DISCOVERED AND BREACHED BY THE ENEMY, AND YOU'VE BEEN ASSAULTED WITH A FULL-ON INVASION!!

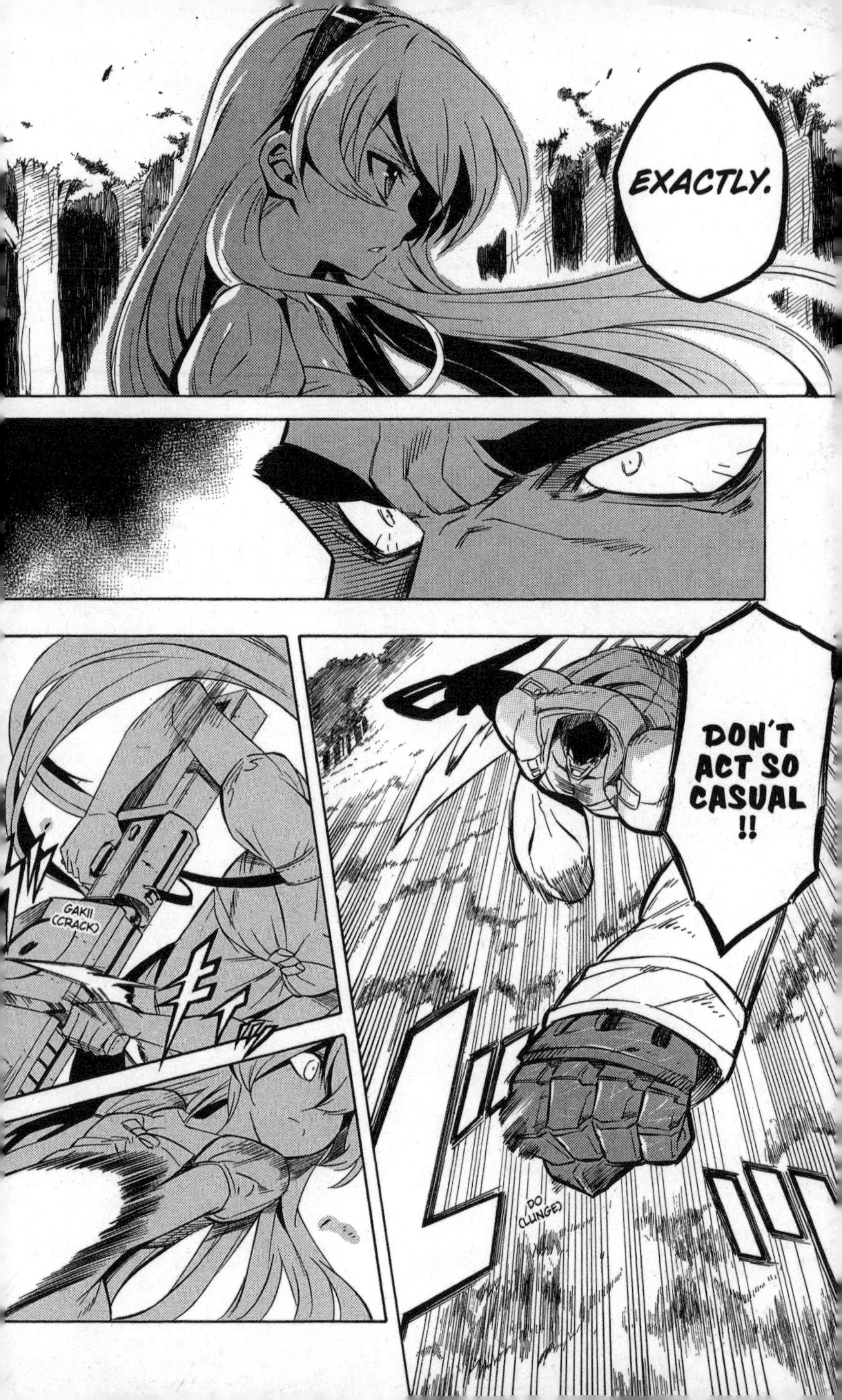
EXACTLY.
DON'T ACT SO CASUAL !!
GAKII (CRACK)
DO (LUNGE)

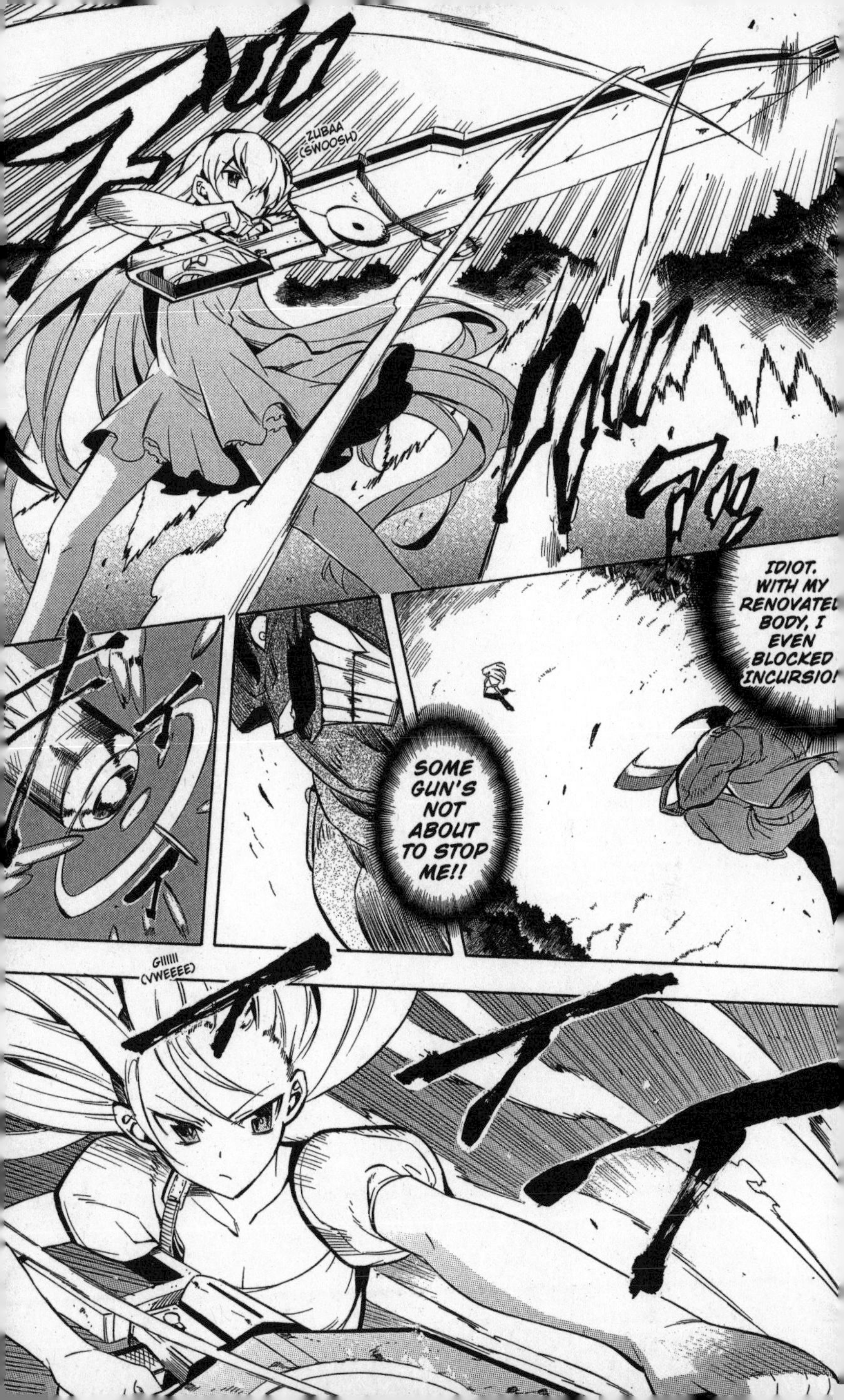
ZUBAA (SWOOSH)
IDIOT. WITH MY RENOVATED BODY, I EVEN BLOCKED INCURSIO!
SOME GUN'S NOT ABOUT TO STOP ME!!
GIIIIII (VWEEEE)

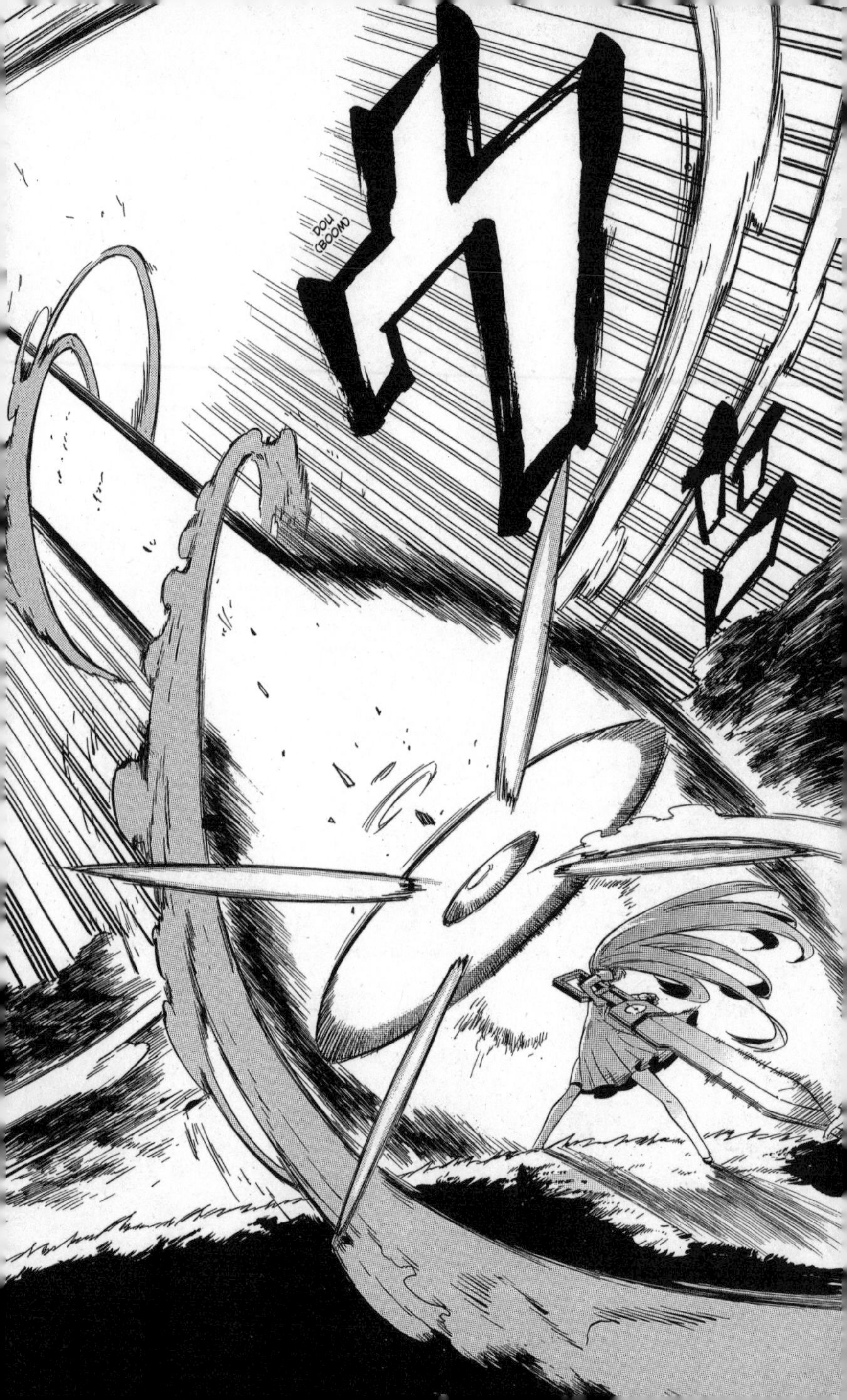
DOU (BOOM)

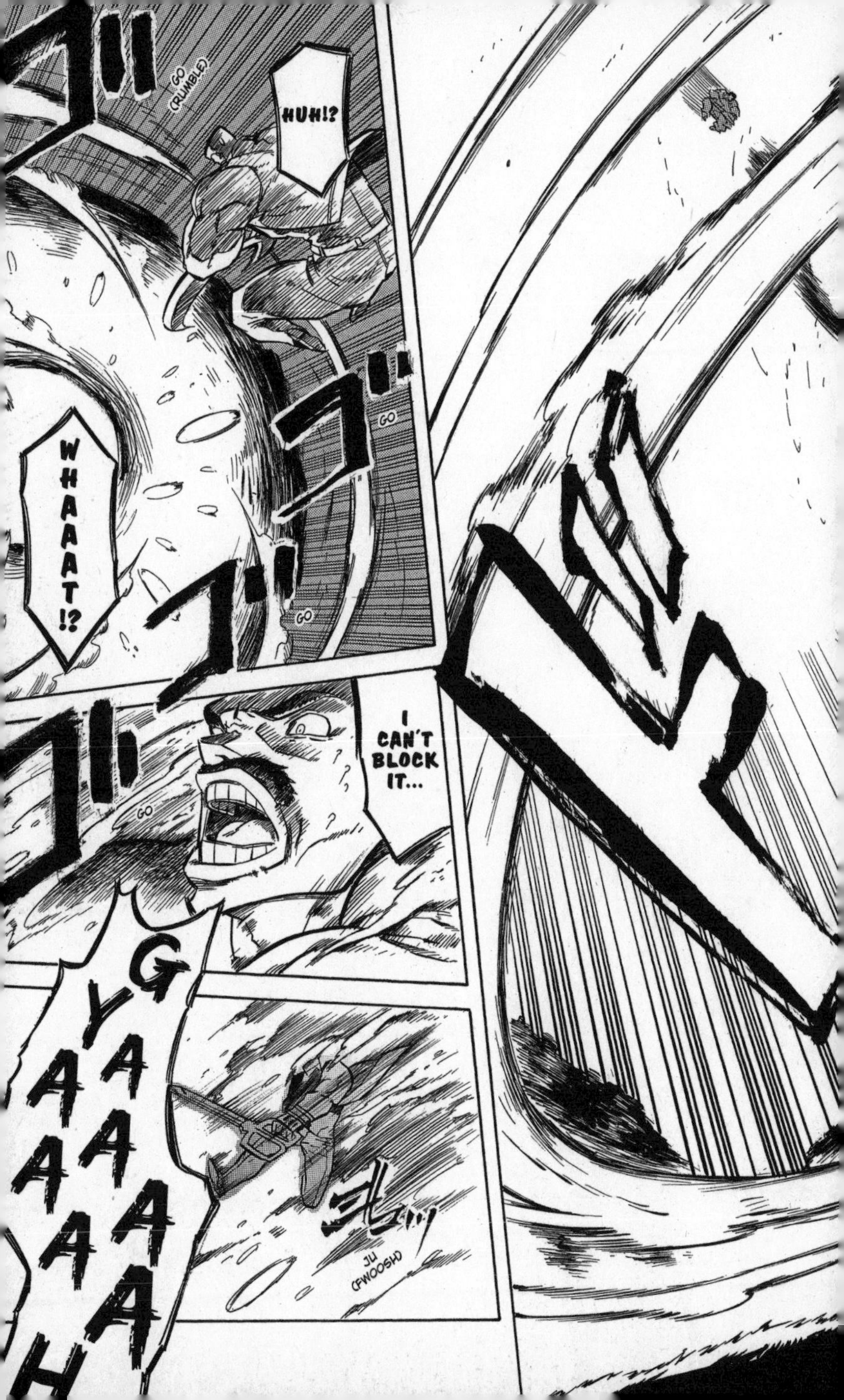

HUH!?
GO (RUMBLE)
GO
GO
WHAAAT!?
I CAN'T BLOCK IT...
GO
GYAAAAAAAH
JU (FWOOSH)

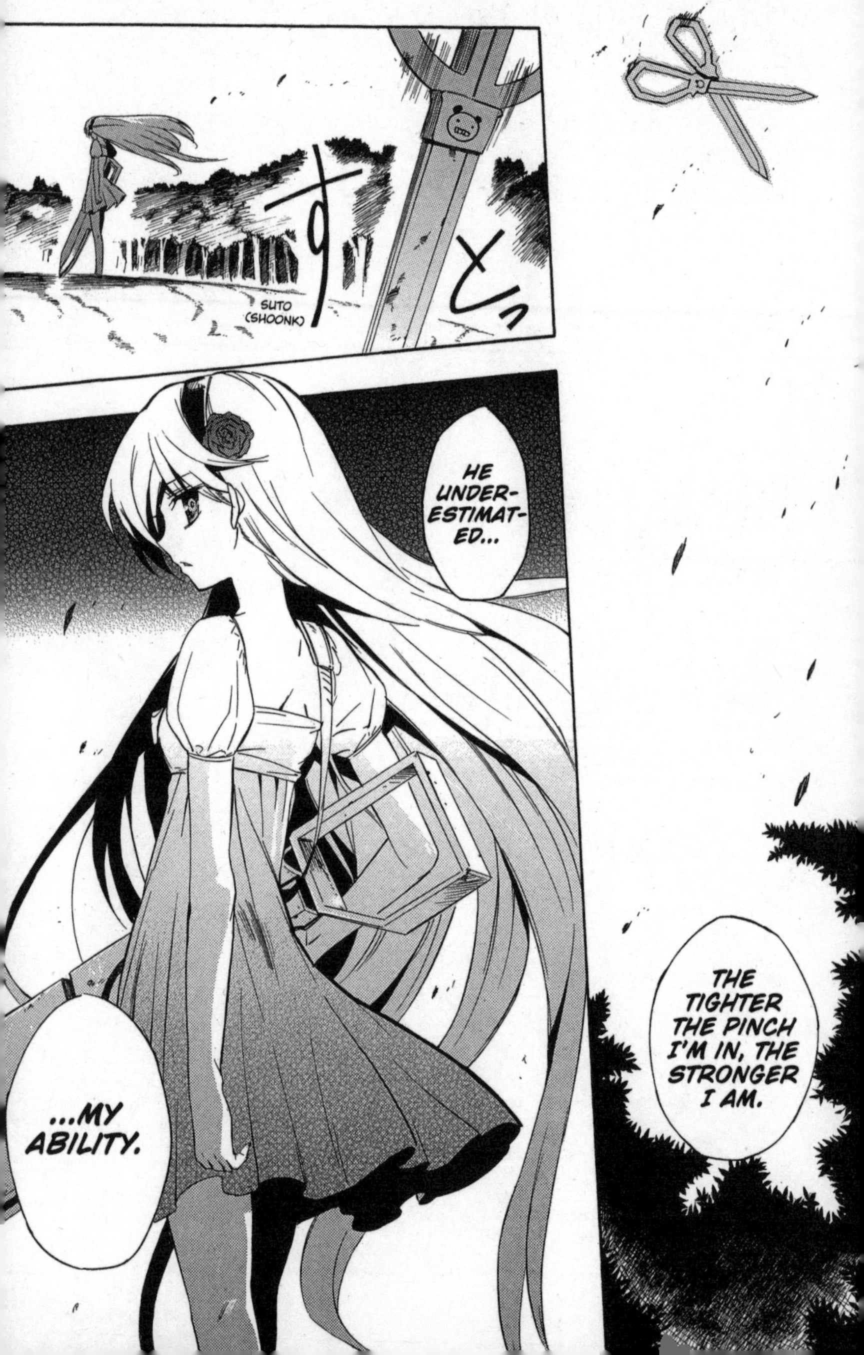
SUTO (SHOONK)
HE UNDER-ESTIMAT-ED...
...MY ABILITY.
THE TIGHTER THE PINCH I'M IN, THE STRONGER I AM.

[redacted]

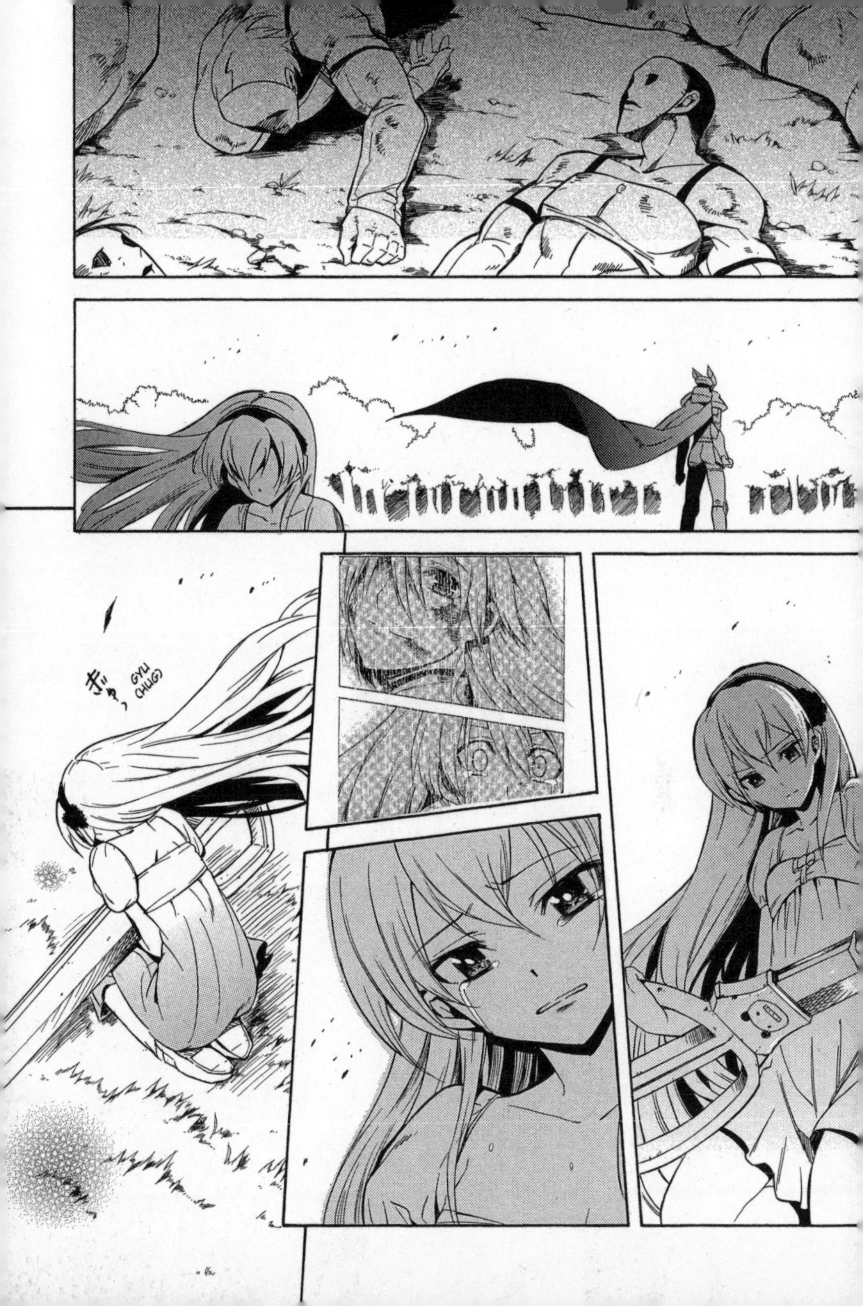
ぎゅっ
GYU (HUG)

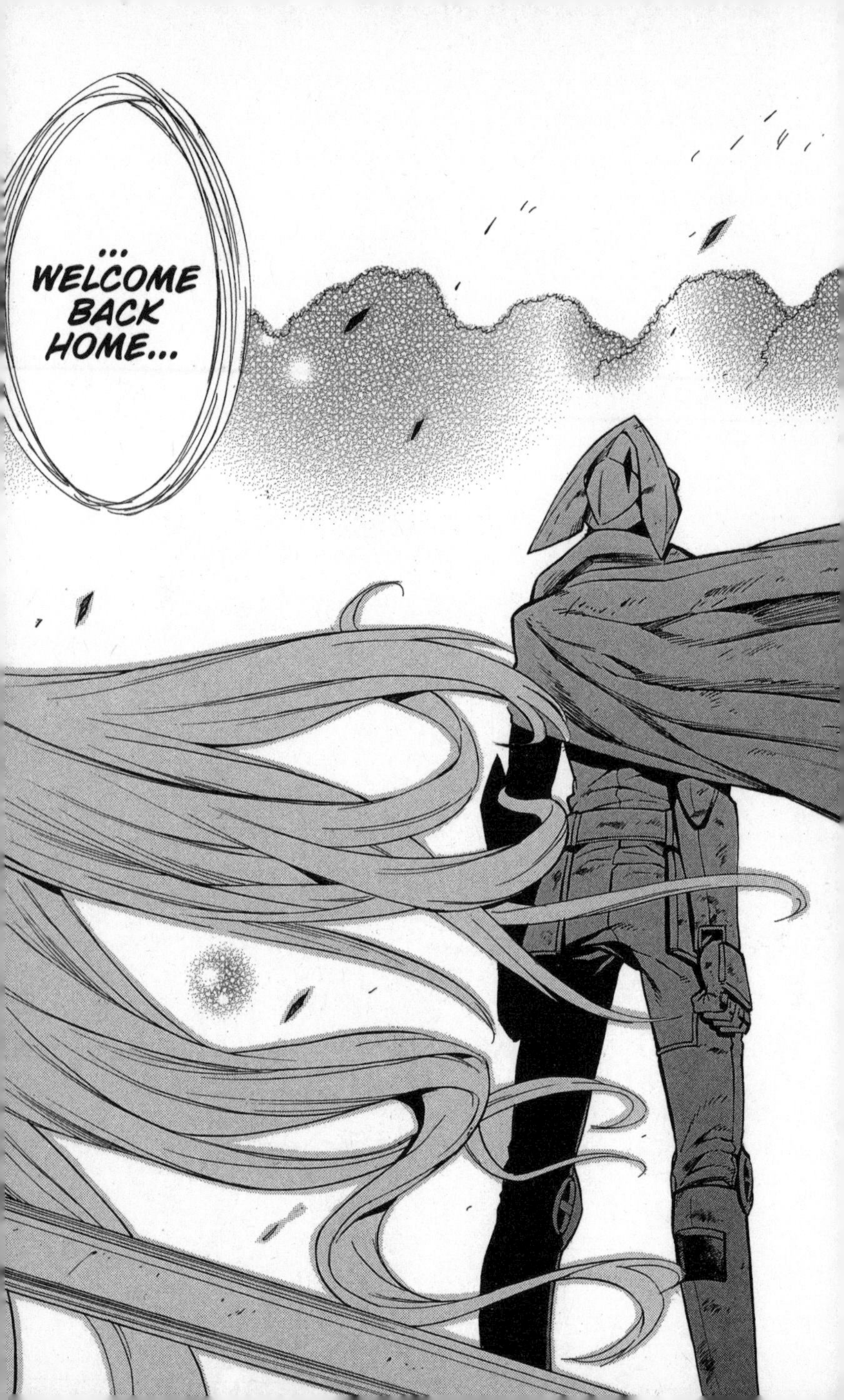
...WELCOME BACK HOME...

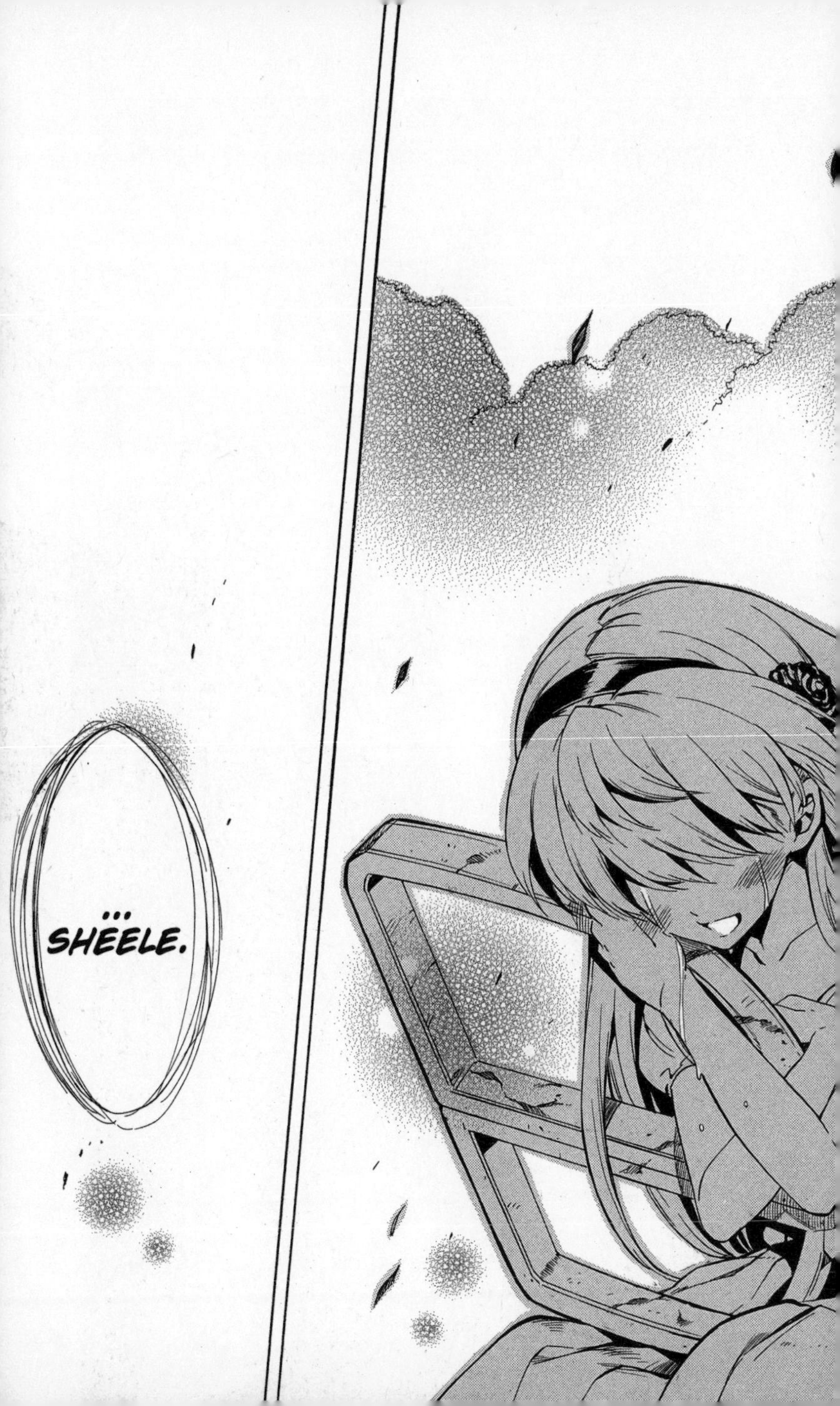
...
SHËELE.

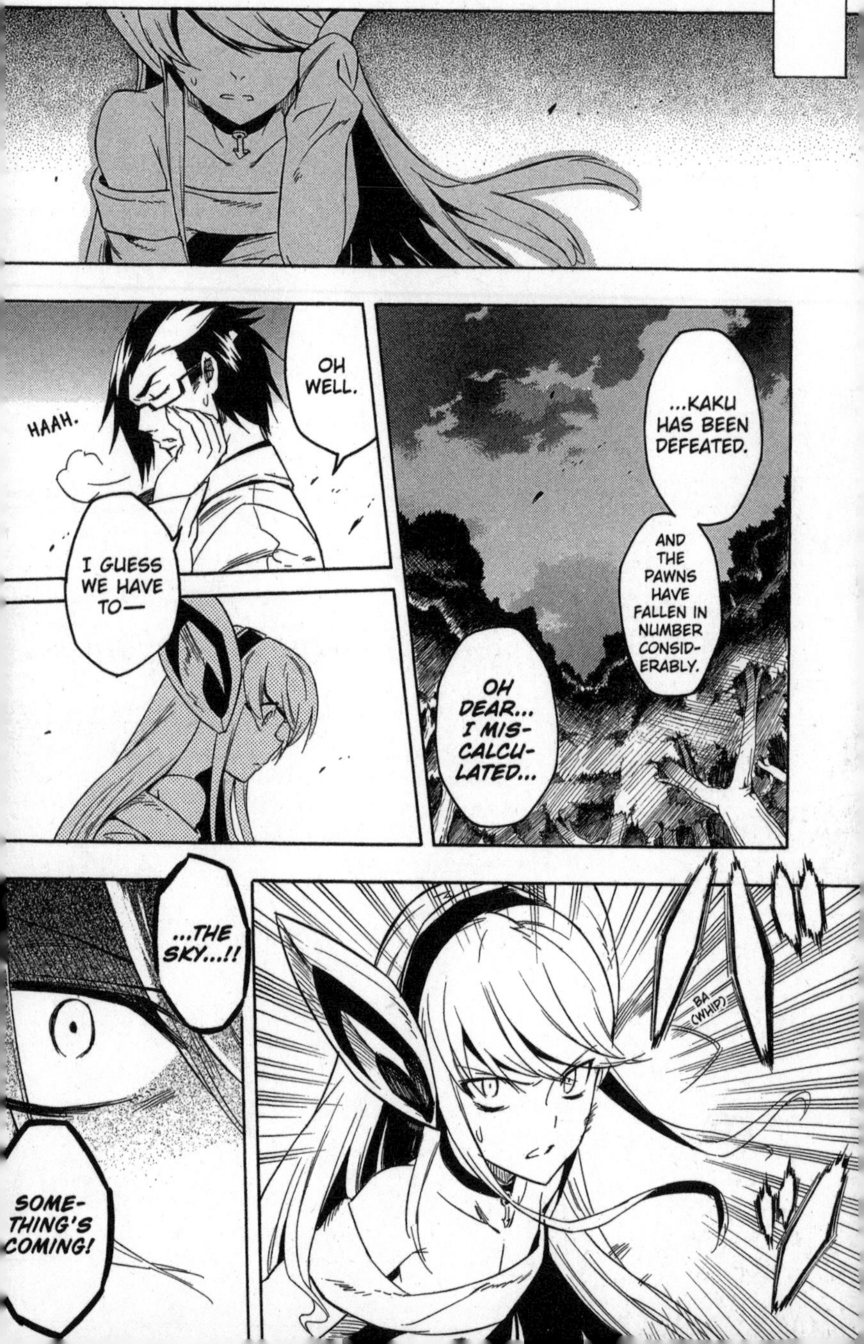
...KAKU HAS BEEN DEFEATED.
AND THE PAWNS HAVE FALLEN IN NUMBER CONSIDERABLY.
OH DEAR... I MISCALCULATED...
OH WELL.
HAAH.
I GUESS WE HAVE TO—
BA (WHIP)
...THE SKY...!!
SOMETHING'S COMING!

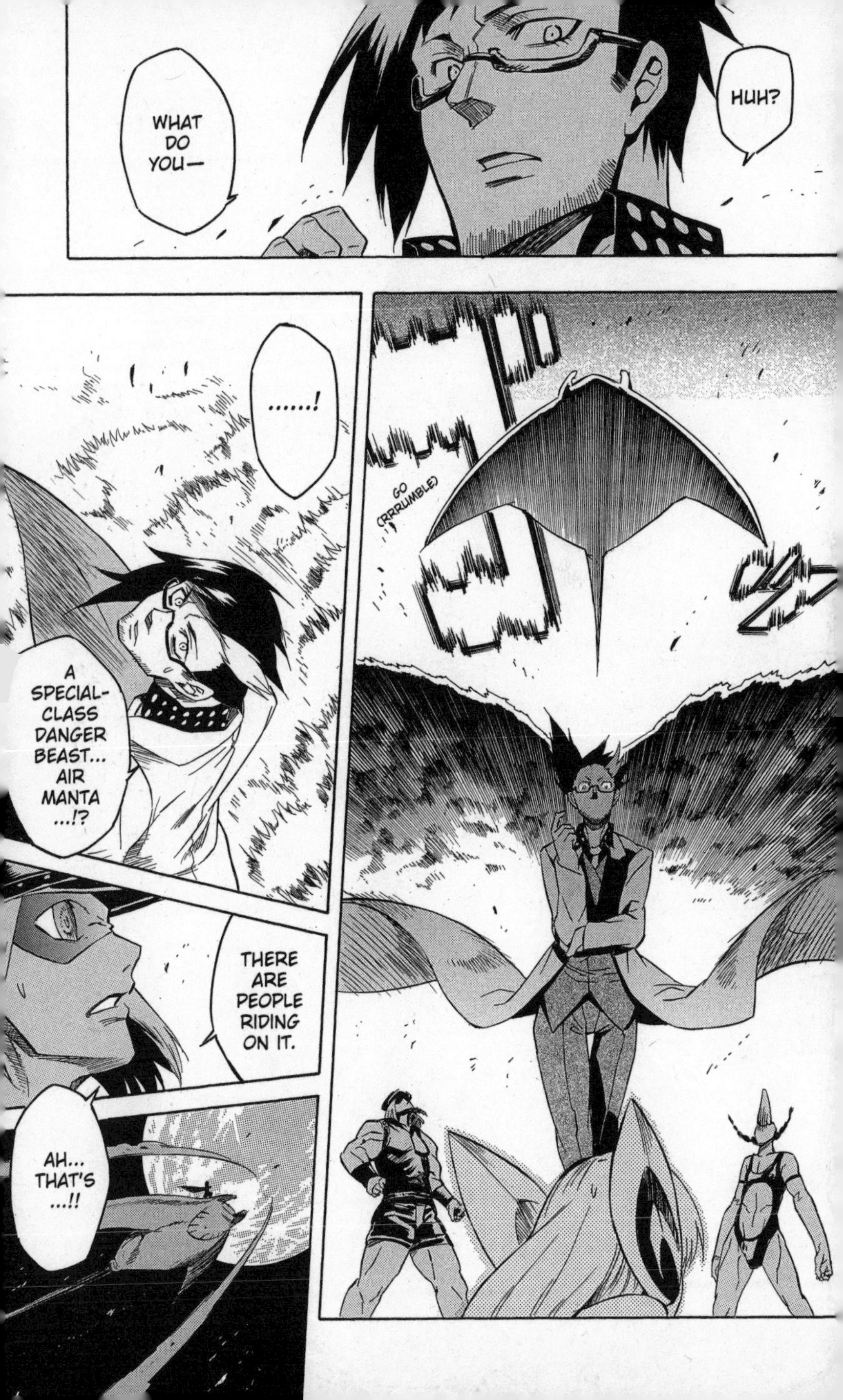

HUH?
WHAT DO YOU—
GO (RRRUMBLE)
......!
A SPECIAL-CLASS DANGER BEAST... AIR MANTA ...!?
THERE ARE PEOPLE RIDING ON IT.
AH... THAT'S ...!!

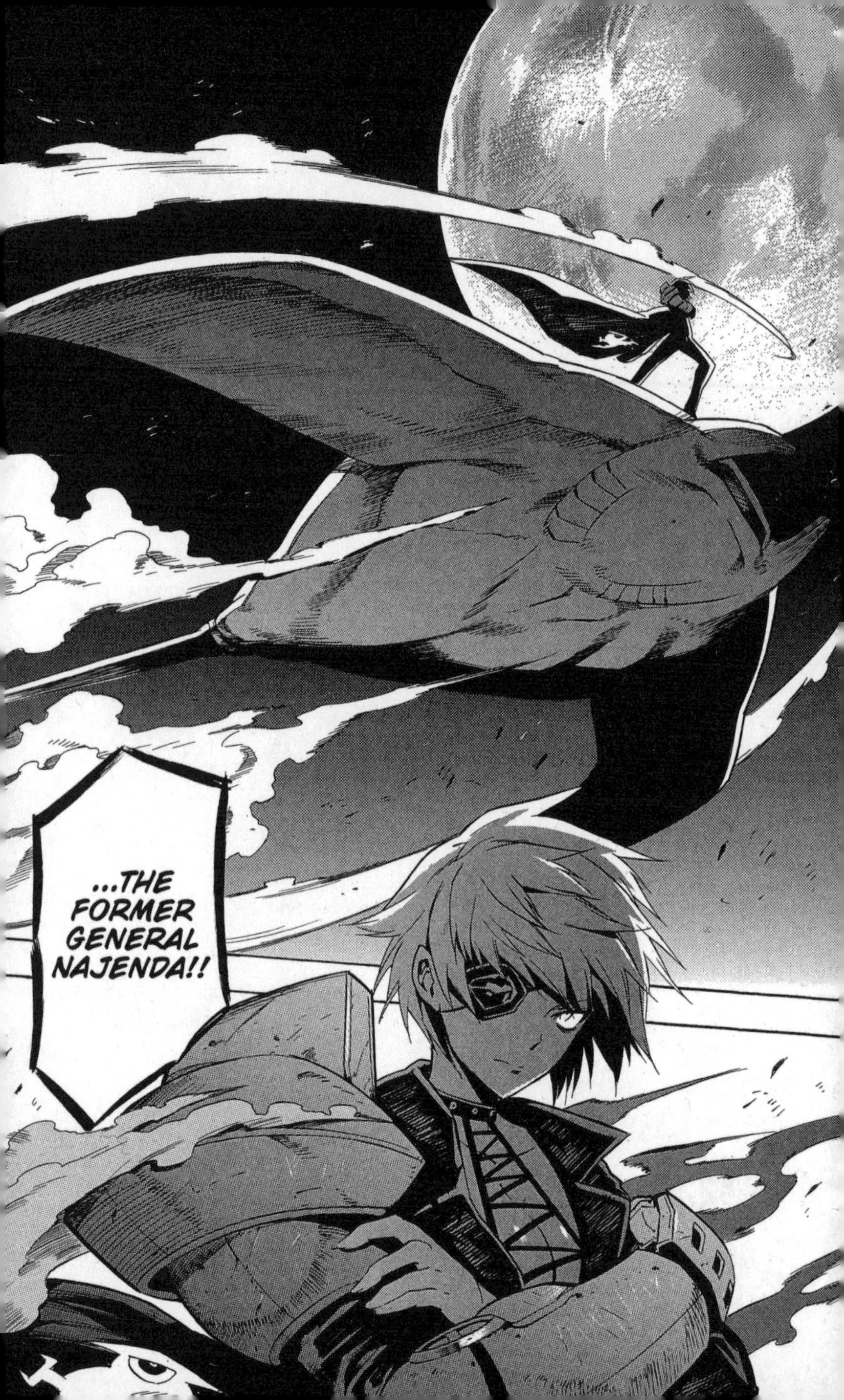
...THE FORMER GENERAL NAJENDA!!

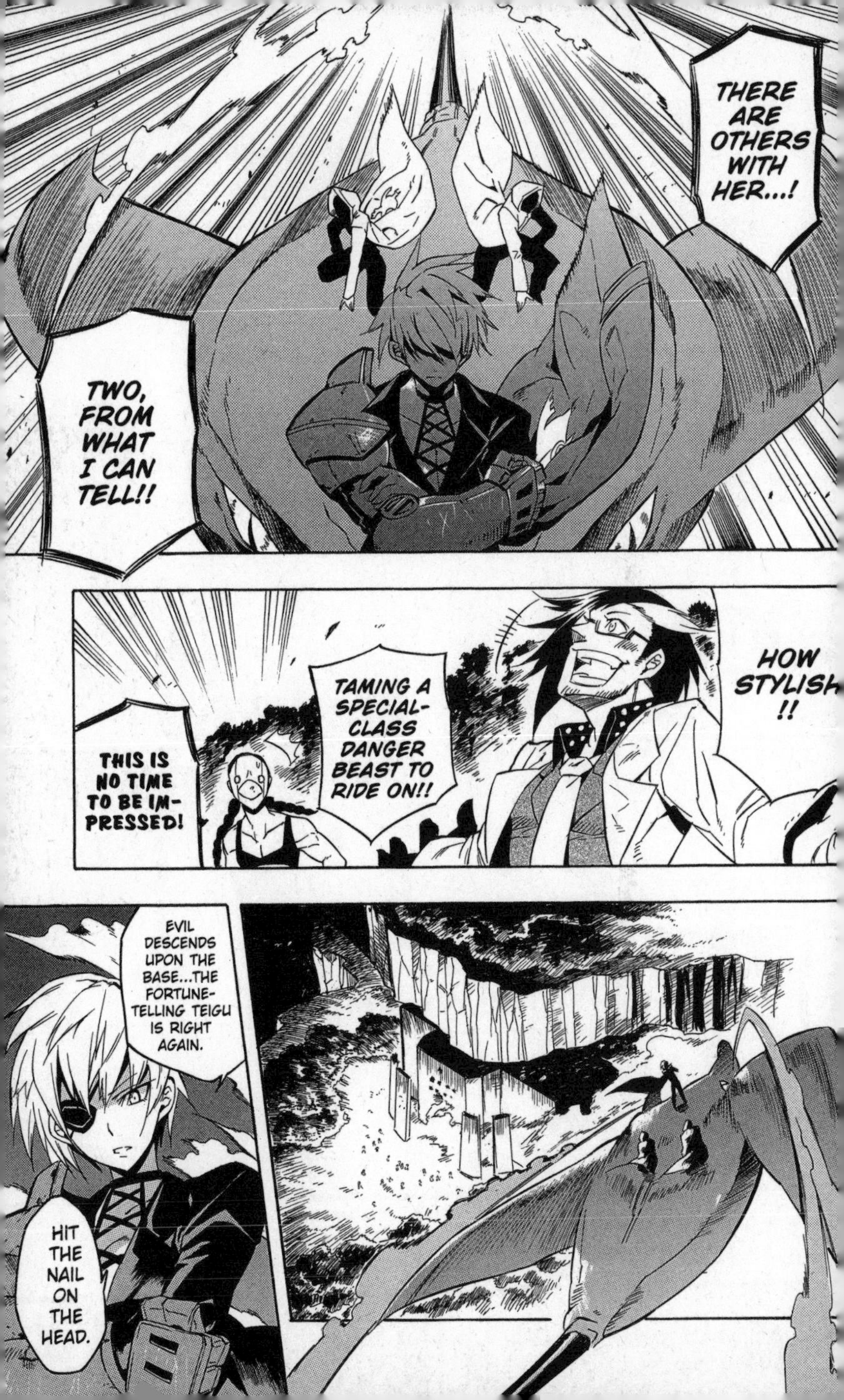
THERE ARE OTHERS WITH HER...!
TWO, FROM WHAT I CAN TELL!!
HOW STYLISH!!
TAMING A SPECIAL-CLASS DANGER BEAST TO RIDE ON!!
THIS IS NO TIME TO BE IM-PRESSED!
EVIL DESCENDS UPON THE BASE...THE FORTUNE-TELLING TEIGU IS RIGHT AGAIN.
HIT THE NAIL ON THE HEAD.

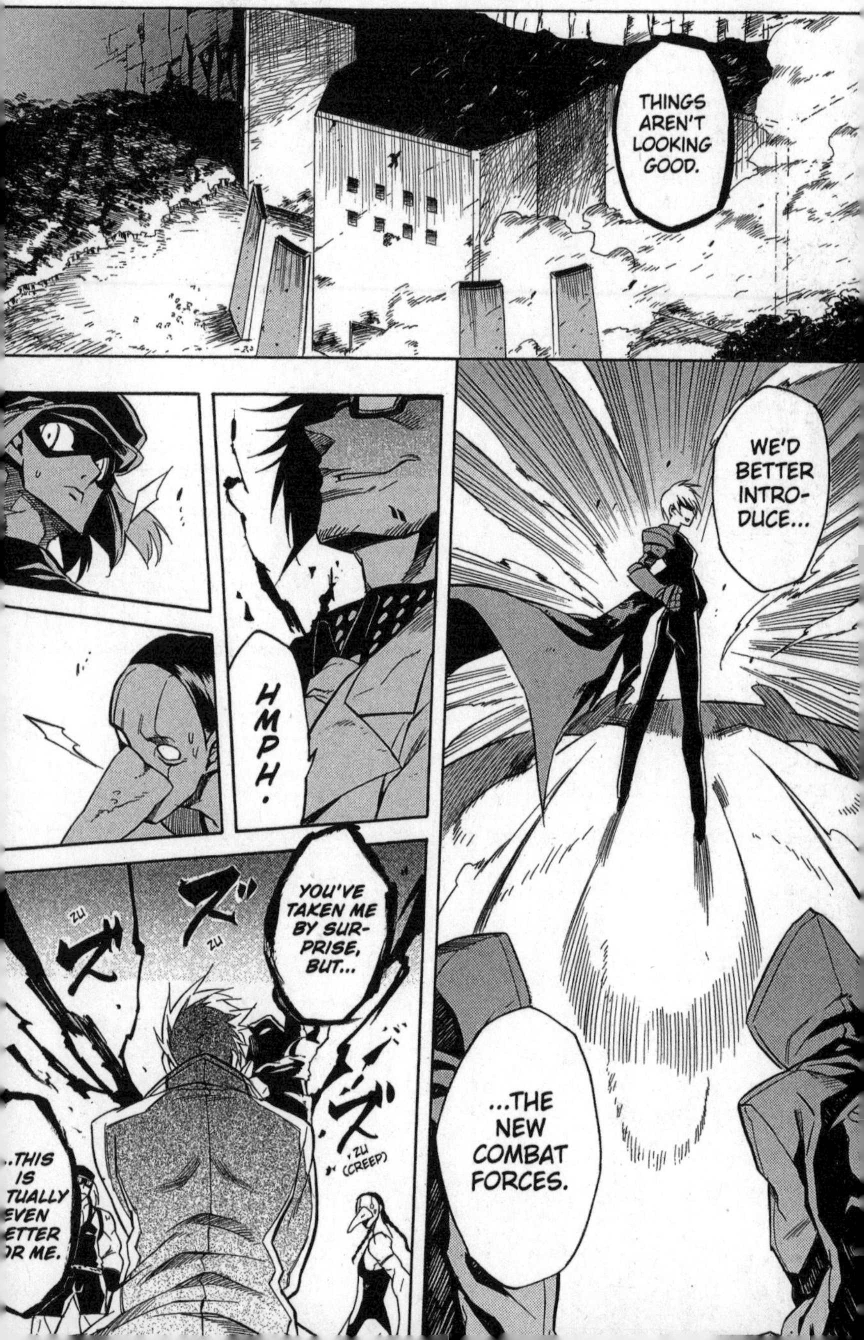
THINGS AREN'T LOOKING GOOD.
WE'D BETTER INTRODUCE...
...THE NEW COMBAT FORCES.
HMPH.
ZU
ZU
YOU'VE TAKEN ME BY SURPRISE, BUT...
ZU (CREEP)
..THIS IS TUALLY EVEN ETTER OR ME.

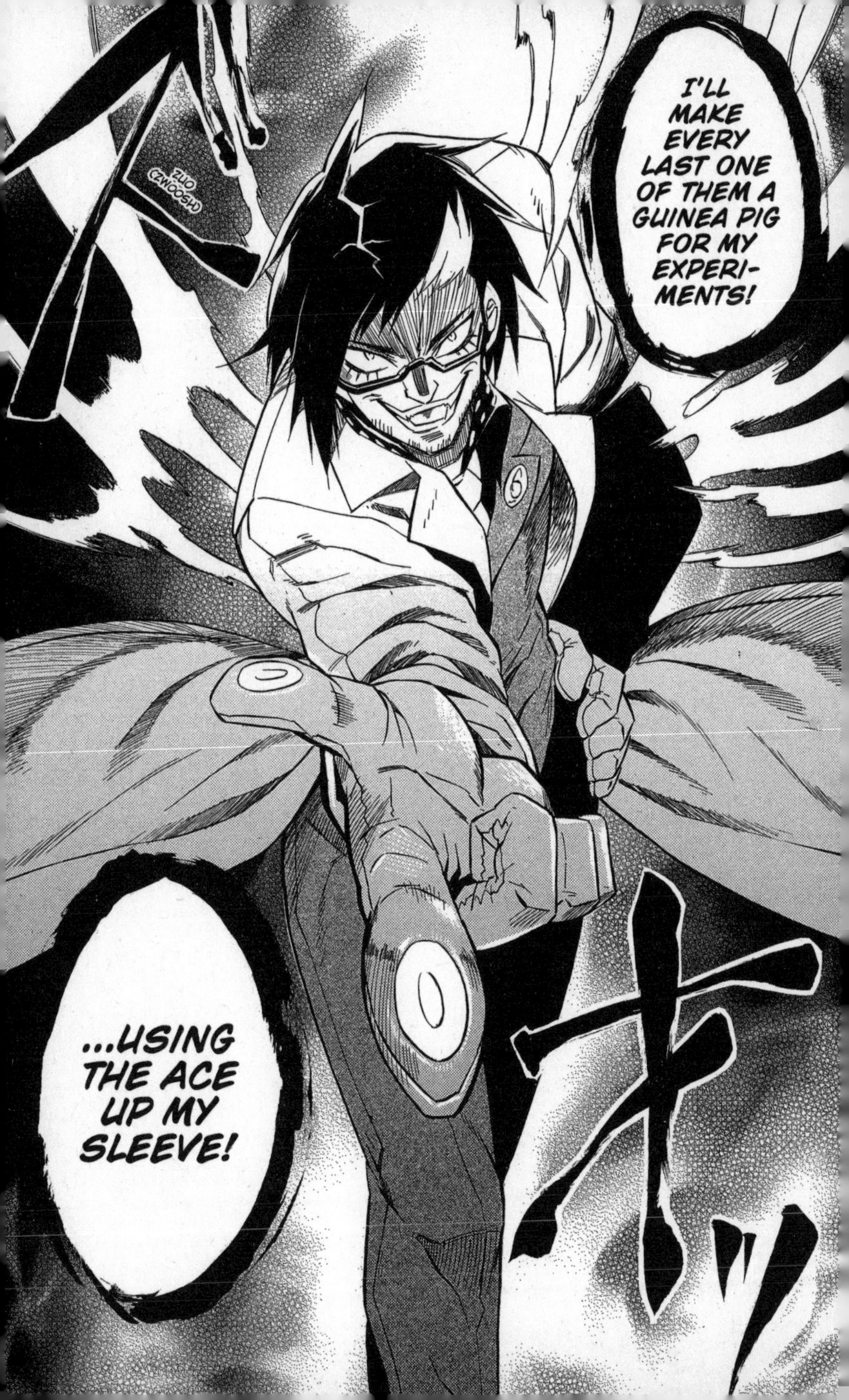
I'LL MAKE EVERY LAST ONE OF THEM A GUINEA PIG FOR MY EXPERI-MENTS!
...USING THE ACE UP MY SLEEVE!

Akame ga KILL!

Rough Sketches 1

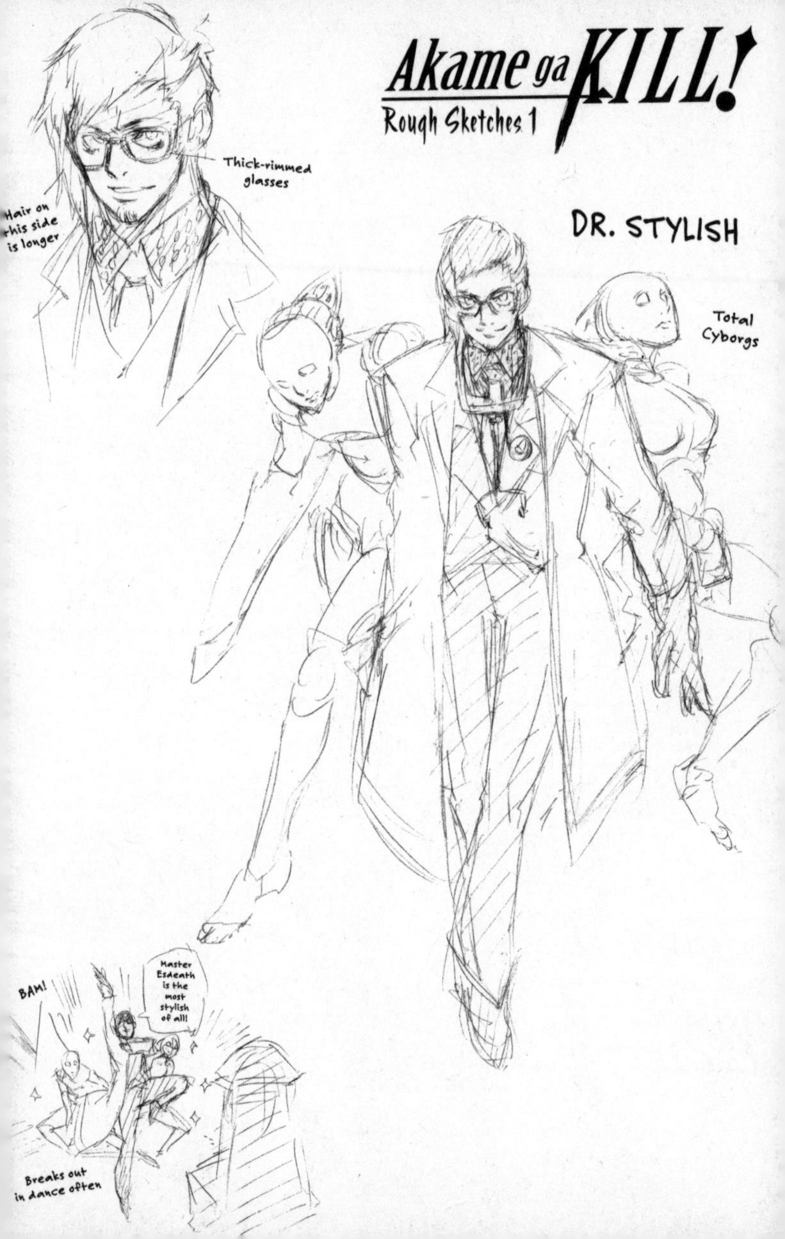
Thick-rimmed glasses
Hair on this side is longer
DR. STYLISH
Total Cyborgs
BAM!
Master Esdeath is the most stylish of all!
Breaks out in dance often

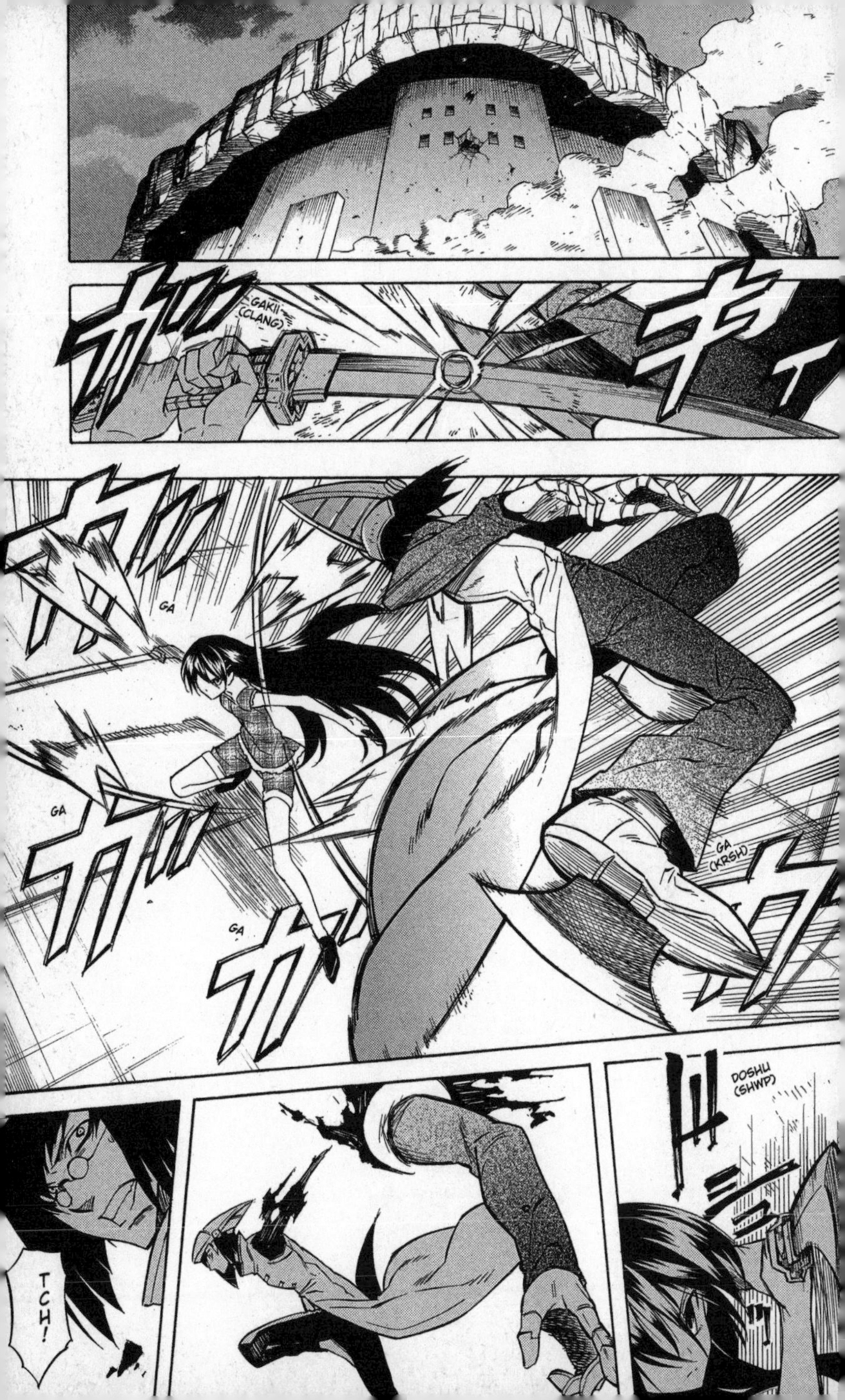
GAKII (CLANG)
GA
GA
GA
GA (KRSH)
DOSHU (SHWP)
TCH!

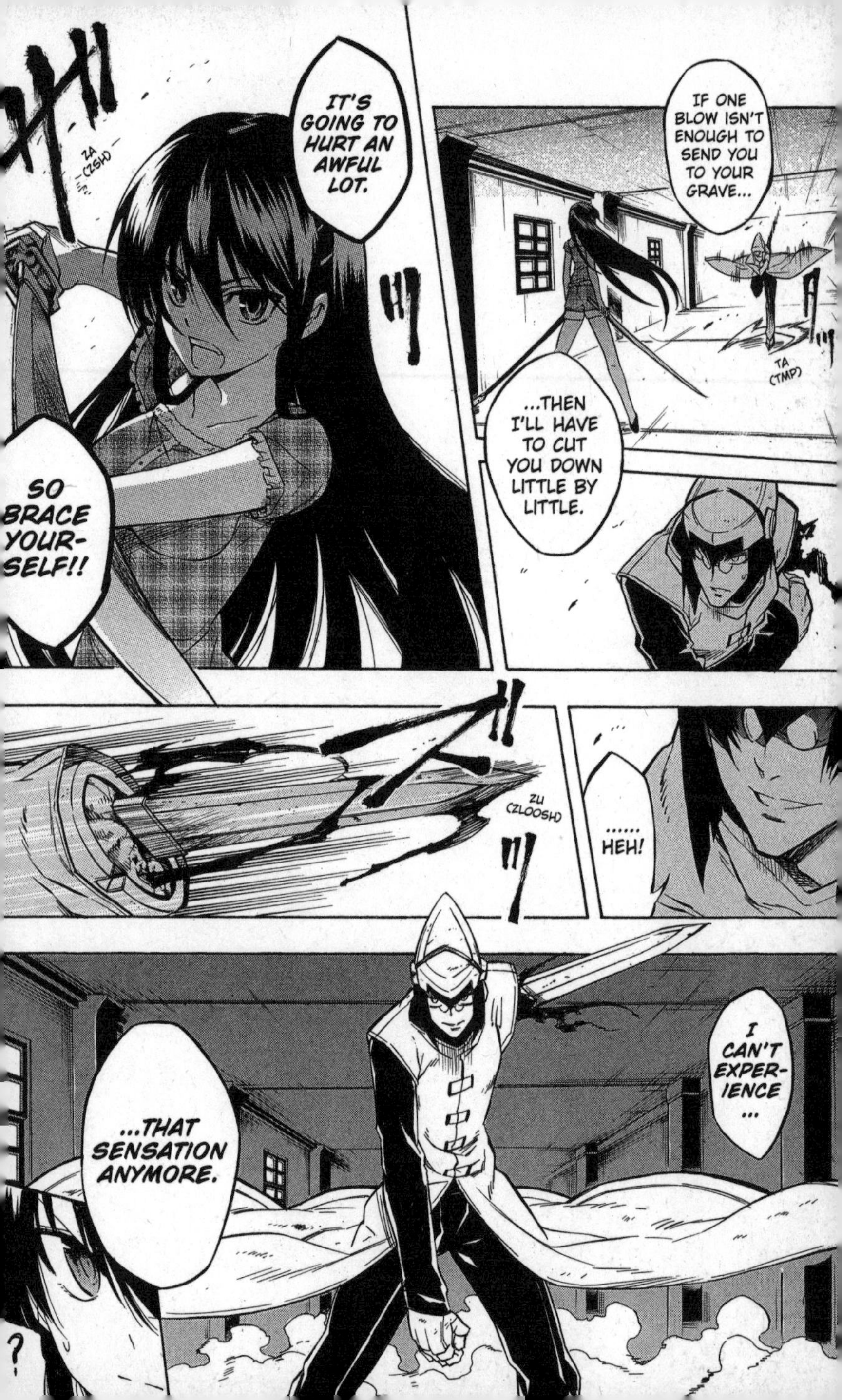
IF ONE BLOW ISN'T ENOUGH TO SEND YOU TO YOUR GRAVE...
TA (TMP)
...THEN I'LL HAVE TO CUT YOU DOWN LITTLE BY LITTLE.
IT'S GOING TO HURT AN AWFUL LOT.
ZA (ZSH)
SO BRACE YOURSELF!!
......HEH!
ZU (ZLOOSH)
I CAN'T EXPERIENCE...
...THAT SENSATION ANYMORE.
?

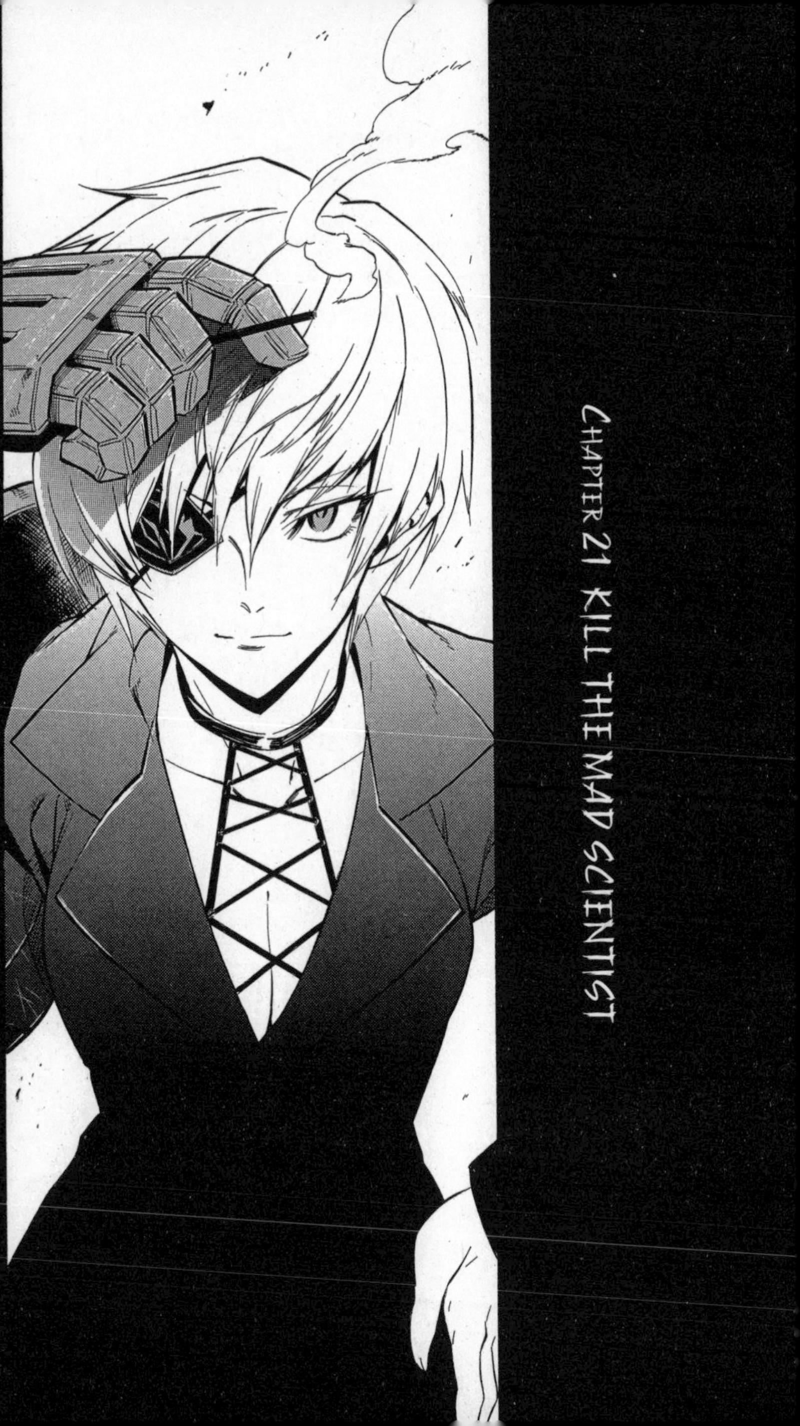

CHAPTER 21 KILL THE MAD SCIENTIST

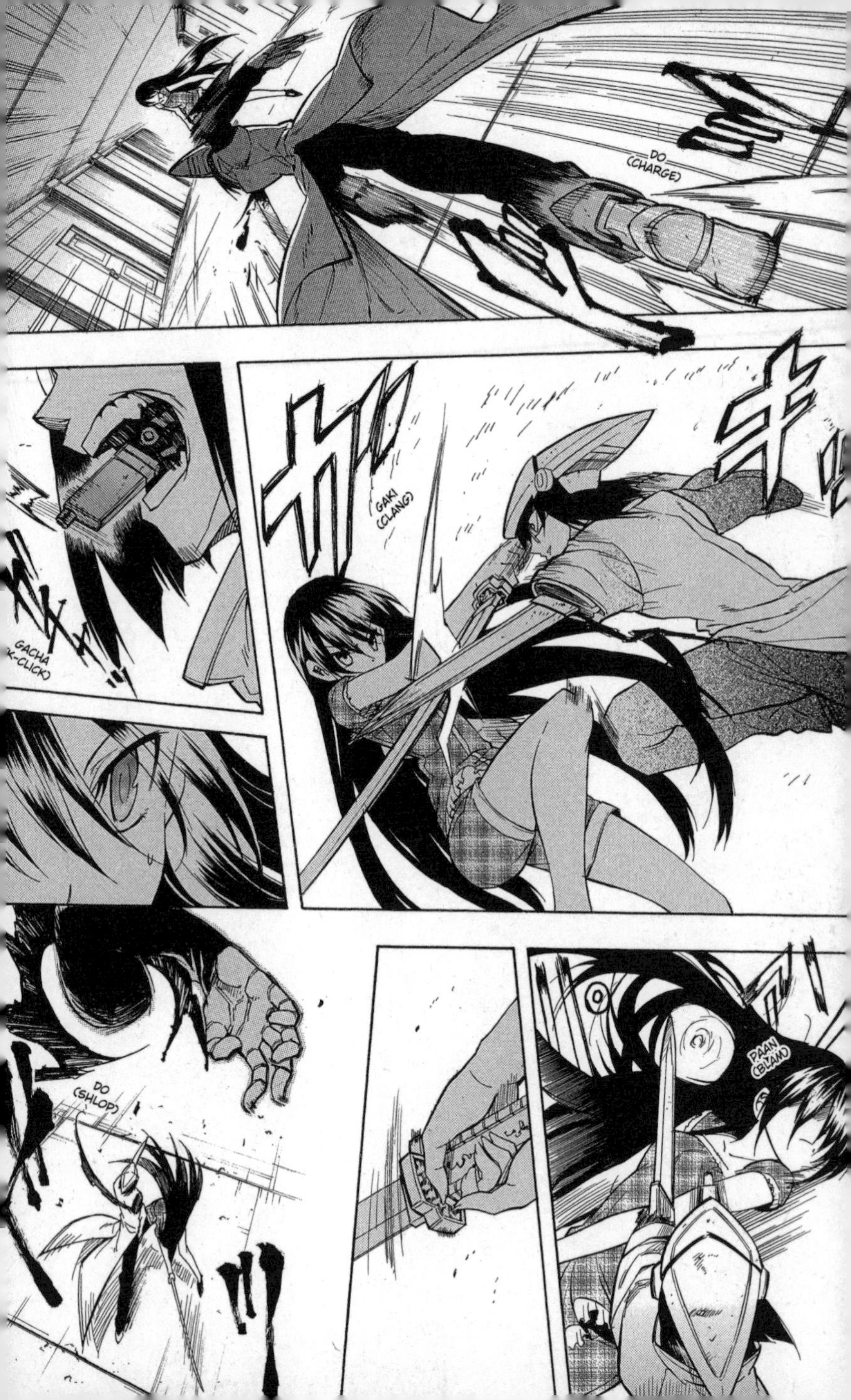
DO (CHARGE)
GAKI (CLANG)
GACHA (K-CLICK)
PAAN (BLAM)
DO (SHLOP)

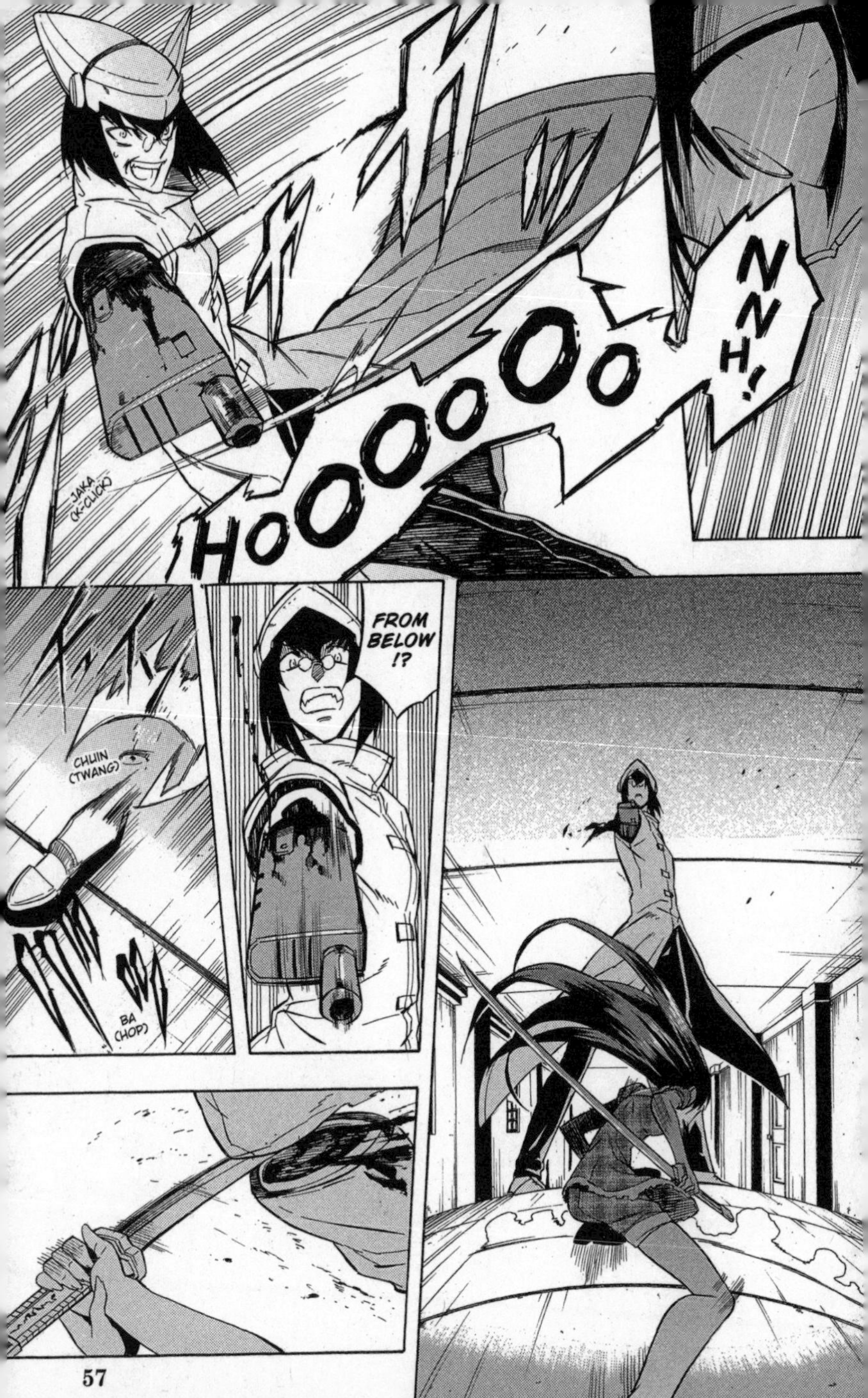

HOOOOOOOONNH!
JAKA (K-CLICK)
FROM BELOW !?
CHUIN (TWANG)
BA (HOP)

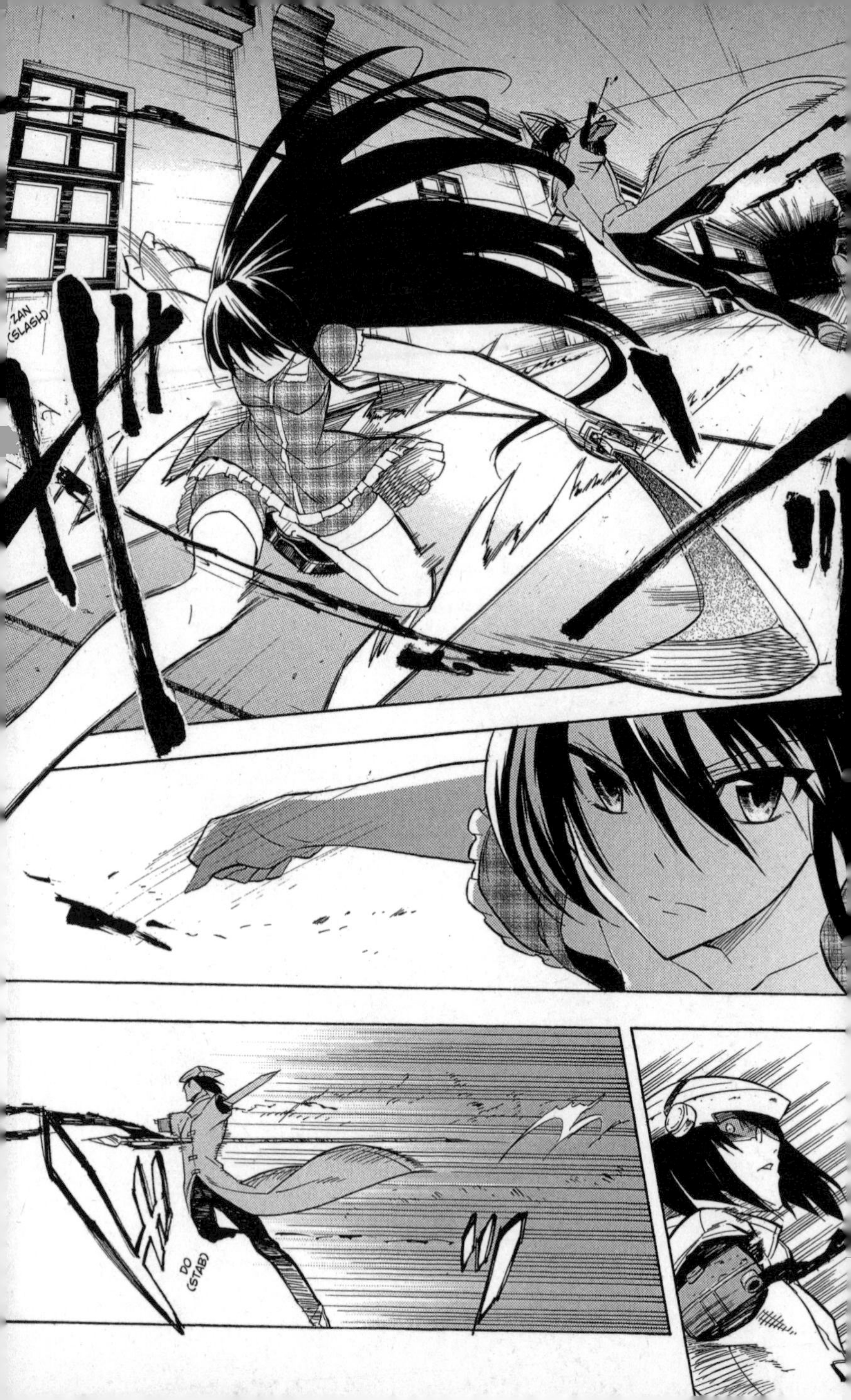
ZAN
(SLASH)
DO
(STAB)

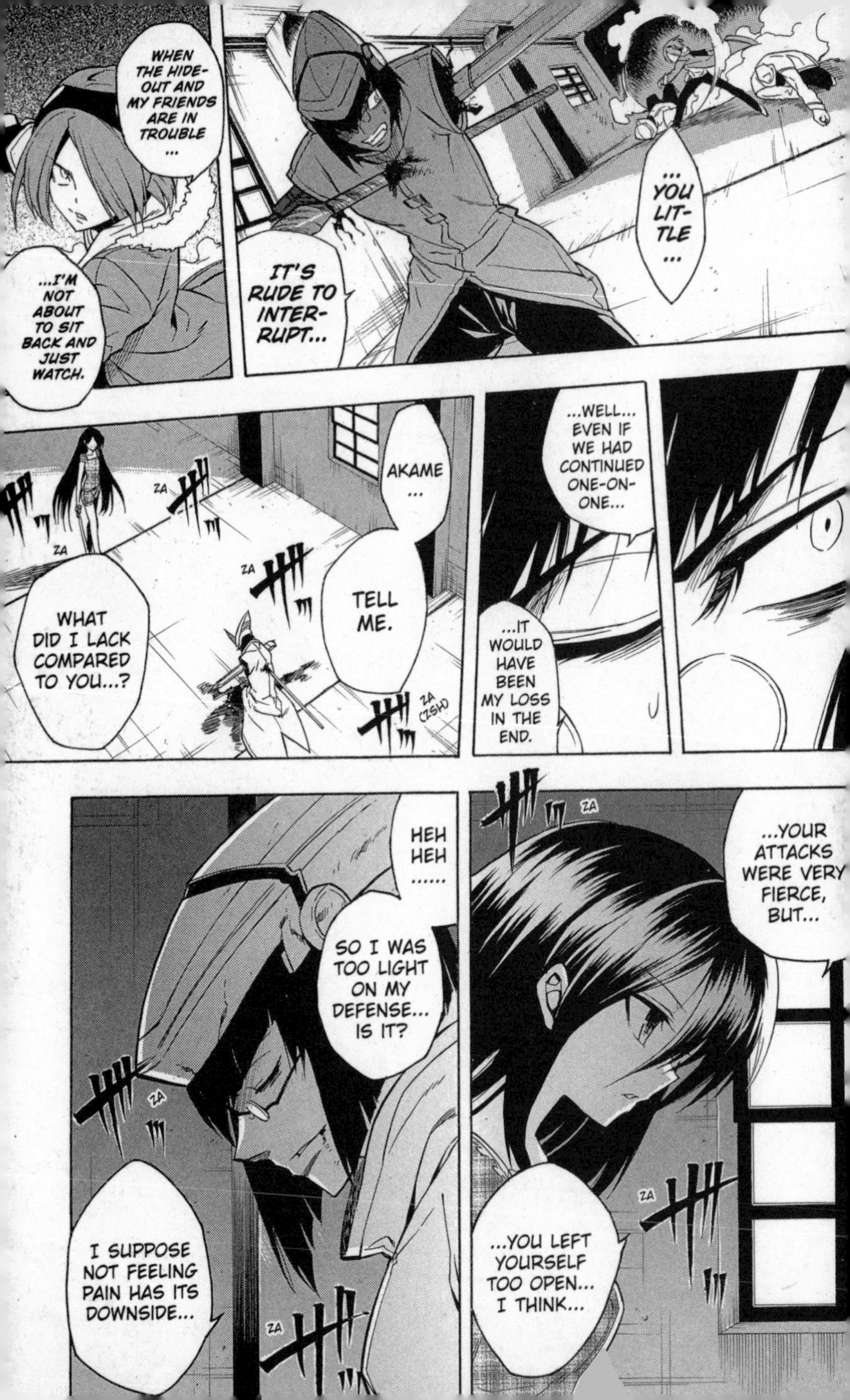
...YOU LITTLE...
IT'S RUDE TO INTERRUPT...
WHEN THE HIDEOUT AND MY FRIENDS ARE IN TROUBLE...
...I'M NOT ABOUT TO SIT BACK AND JUST WATCH.
...WELL... EVEN IF WE HAD CONTINUED ONE-ON-ONE...
...IT WOULD HAVE BEEN MY LOSS IN THE END.
AKAME...
TELL ME.
ZA (ZSH)
ZA
ZA
ZA
WHAT DID I LACK COMPARED TO YOU...?
ZA
...YOUR ATTACKS WERE VERY FIERCE, BUT...
ZA
...YOU LEFT YOURSELF TOO OPEN... I THINK...
HEH HEH ......
SO I WAS TOO LIGHT ON MY DEFENSE... IS IT?
ZA
ZA
I SUPPOSE NOT FEELING PAIN HAS ITS DOWNSIDE...

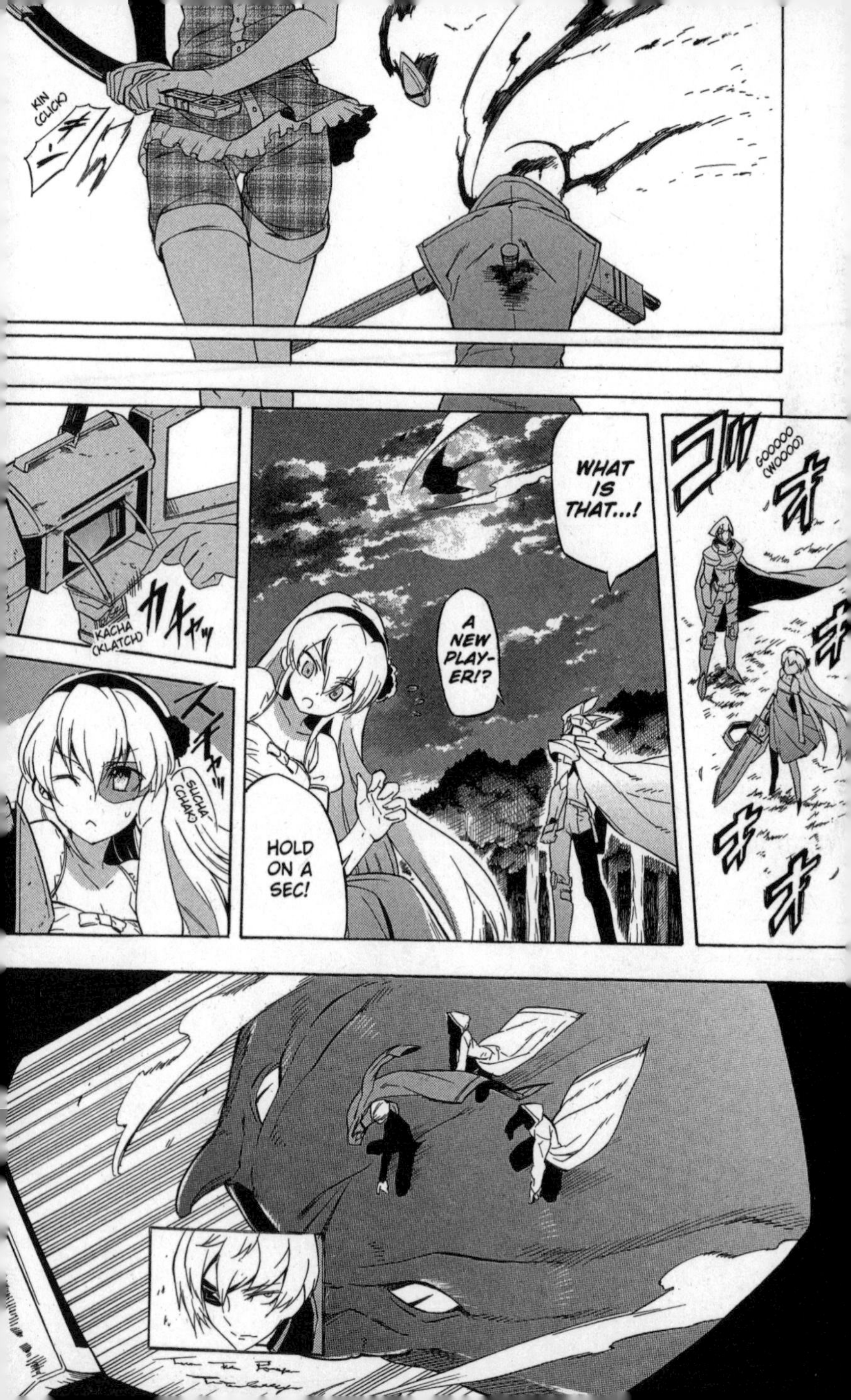
KIN (CLICK)
GOOOOO (WOOOO)
WHAT IS THAT...!
A NEW PLAYER!?
KACHA (KLATCH)
HOLD ON A SEC!
SUCHA (CHAK)

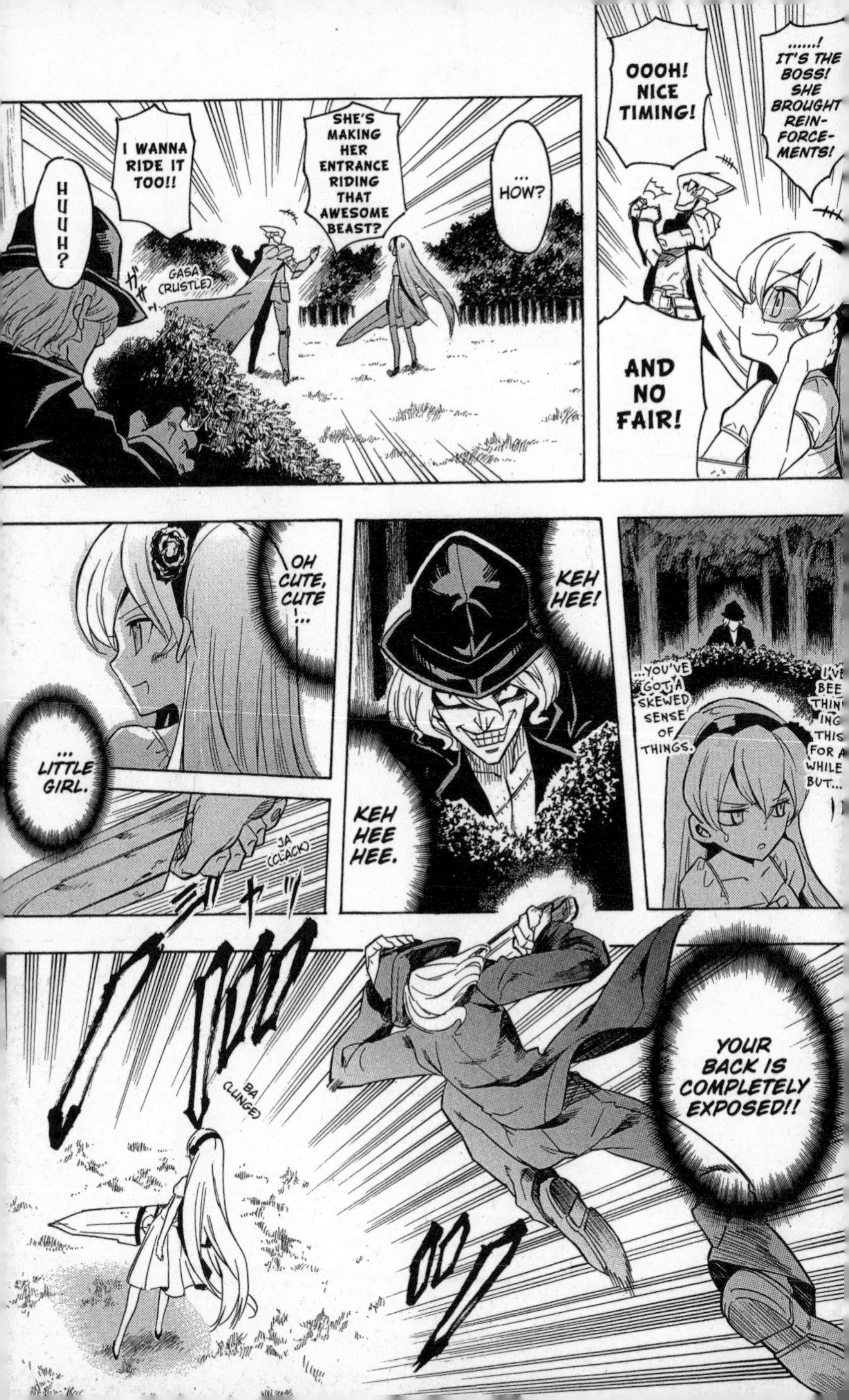
......! IT'S THE BOSS! SHE BROUGHT REIN-FORCE-MENTS!
OOOH! NICE TIMING!
AND NO FAIR!
... HOW?
SHE'S MAKING HER ENTRANCE RIDING THAT AWESOME BEAST?
I WANNA RIDE IT TOO!!
HUUH?
GASA (RUSTLE)
I'VE BEE THIN ING THIS FOR A WHILE BUT...
...YOU'VE GOT A SKEWED SENSE OF THINGS.
KEH HEE!
KEH HEE HEE.
OH CUTE, CUTE...
... LITTLE GIRL.
JA (CLACK)
YOUR BACK IS COMPLETELY EXPOSED!!
BA (LUNGE)

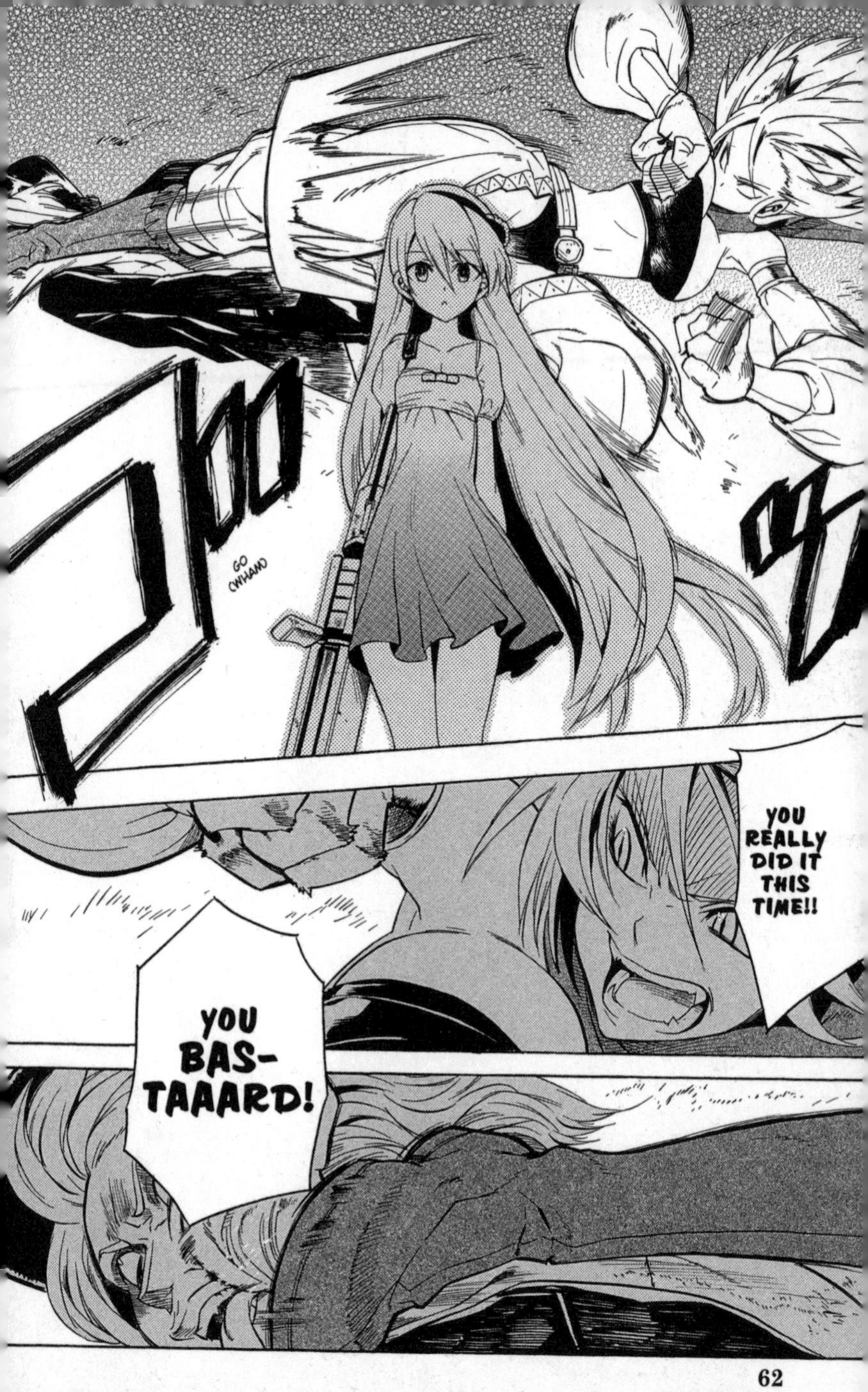
GO
(WHAM)
YOU REALLY DID IT THIS TIME!!
YOU BAS-TAAARD!

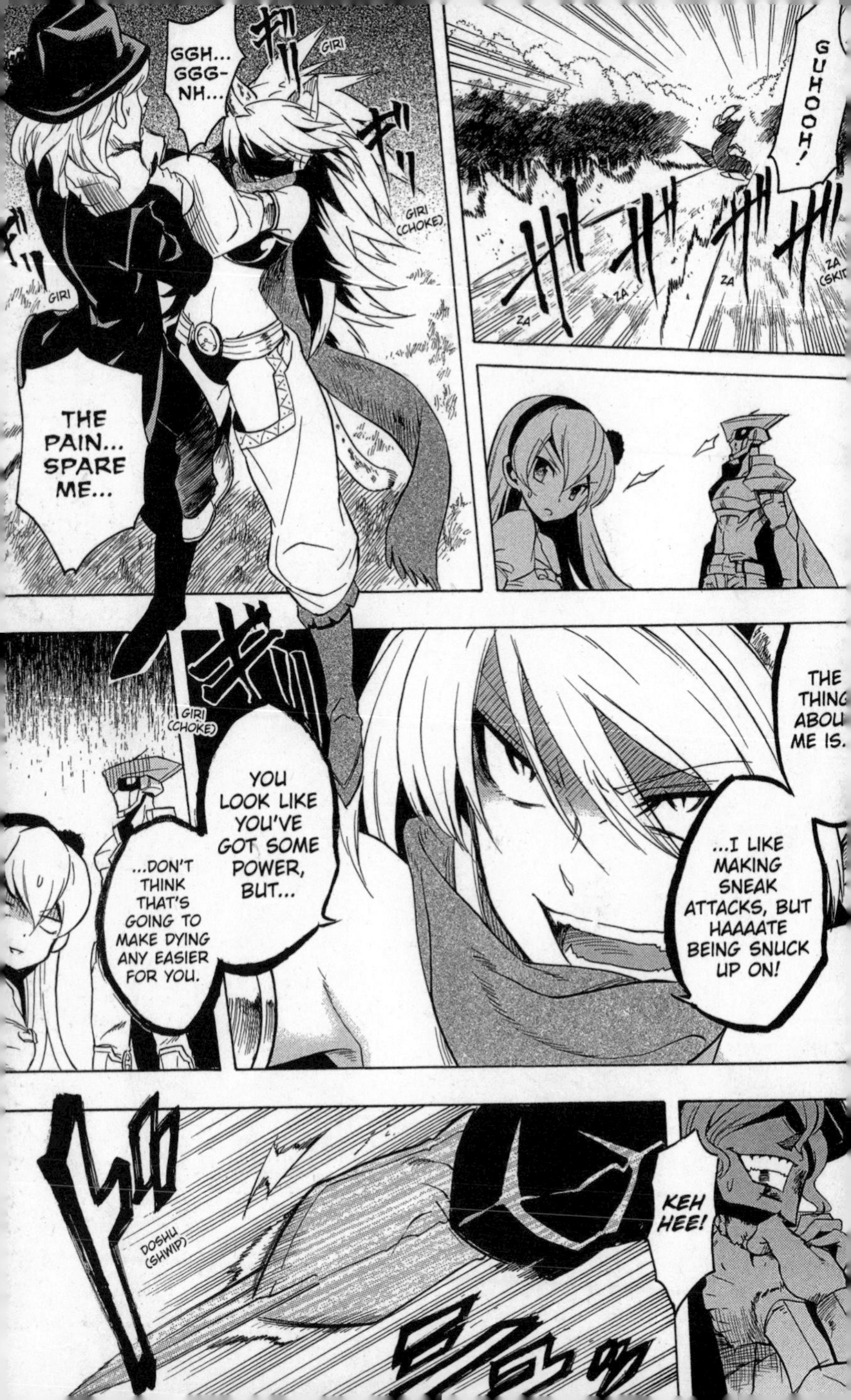
GUHOOOH!
ZA (SKID)
ZA
ZA
ZA
GGH... GGG-NH...
GIRI
GIRI (CHOKE)
GIRI
THE PAIN... SPARE ME...
THE THING ABOU ME IS.
...I LIKE MAKING SNEAK ATTACKS, BUT HAAAATE BEING SNUCK UP ON!
GIRI (CHOKE)
YOU LOOK LIKE YOU'VE GOT SOME POWER, BUT...
...DON'T THINK THAT'S GOING TO MAKE DYING ANY EASIER FOR YOU.
KEH HEE!
DOSHU (SHWIP)

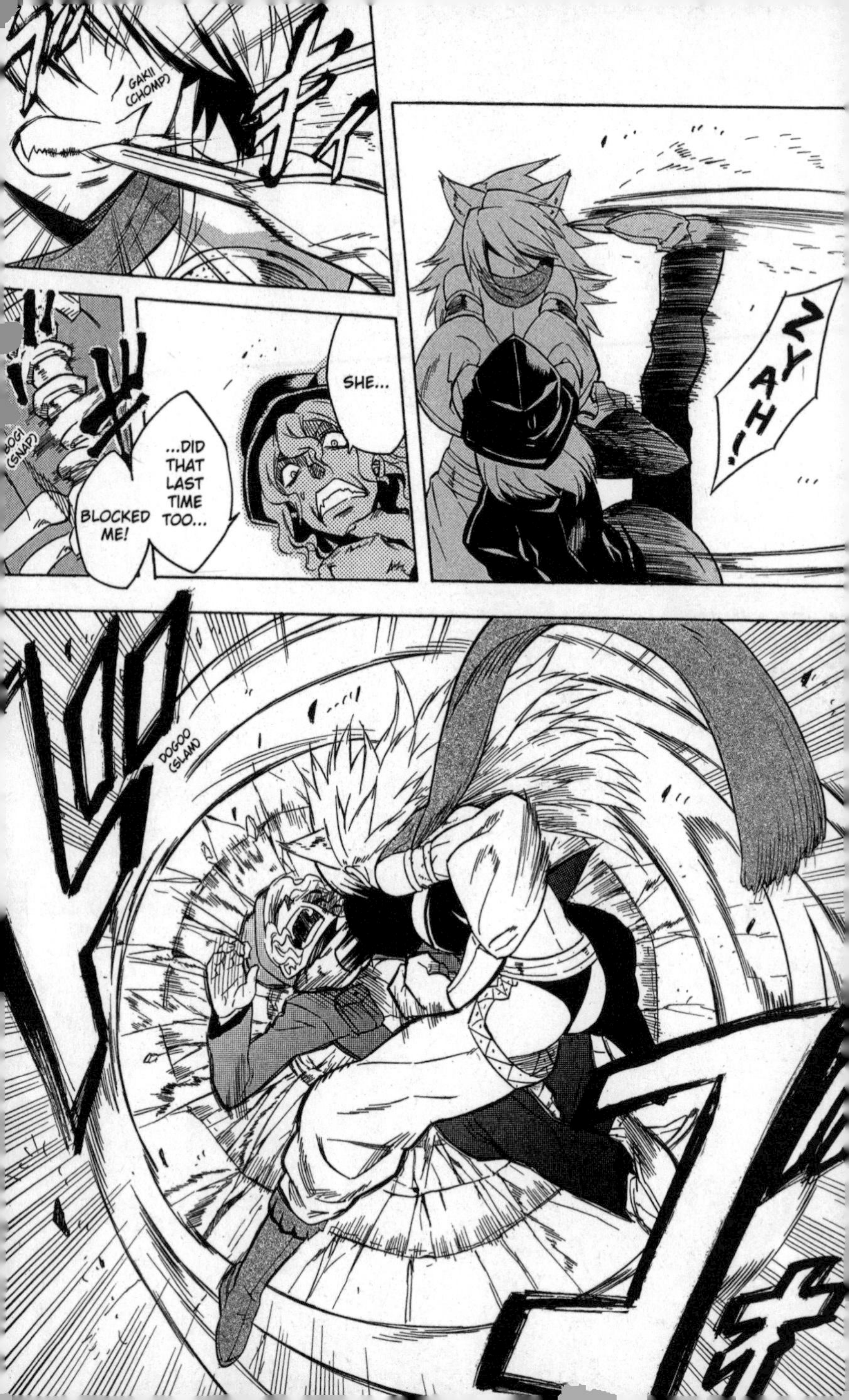

YAH!
GAKII (CHOMP)
SHE...
...DID THAT LAST TIME TOO...
BOGI (SNAP)
BLOCKED ME!
DOGOO (SLAM)

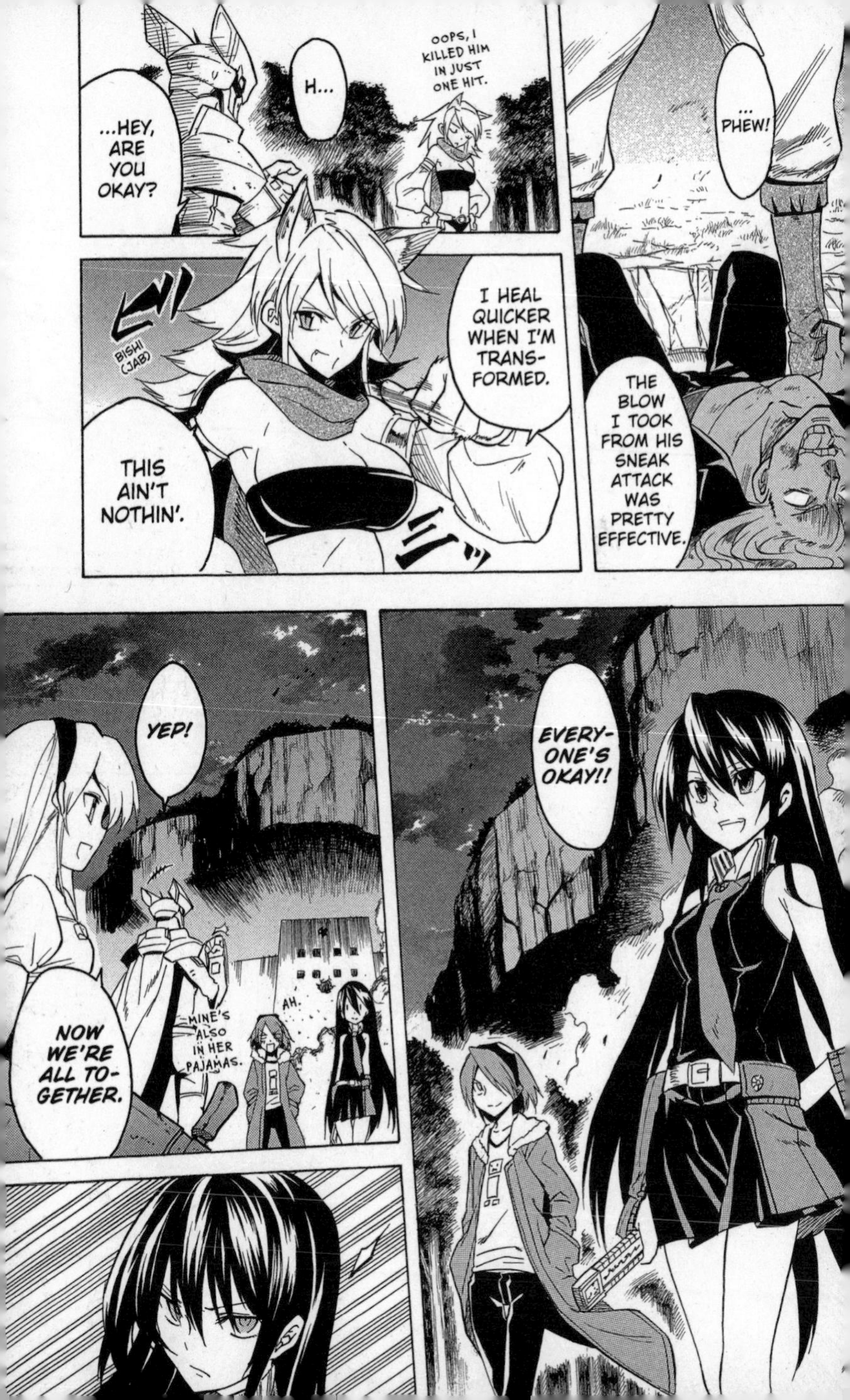
...PHEW!
THE BLOW I TOOK FROM HIS SNEAK ATTACK WAS PRETTY EFFECTIVE.
OOPS, I KILLED HIM IN JUST ONE HIT.
H...
...HEY, ARE YOU OKAY?
I HEAL QUICKER WHEN I'M TRANS-FORMED.
BISHI (JAB)
THIS AIN'T NOTHIN'.
EVERY-ONE'S OKAY!!
YEP!
AH.
MINE'S ALSO IN HER PAJAMAS.
NOW WE'RE ALL TO-GETHER.

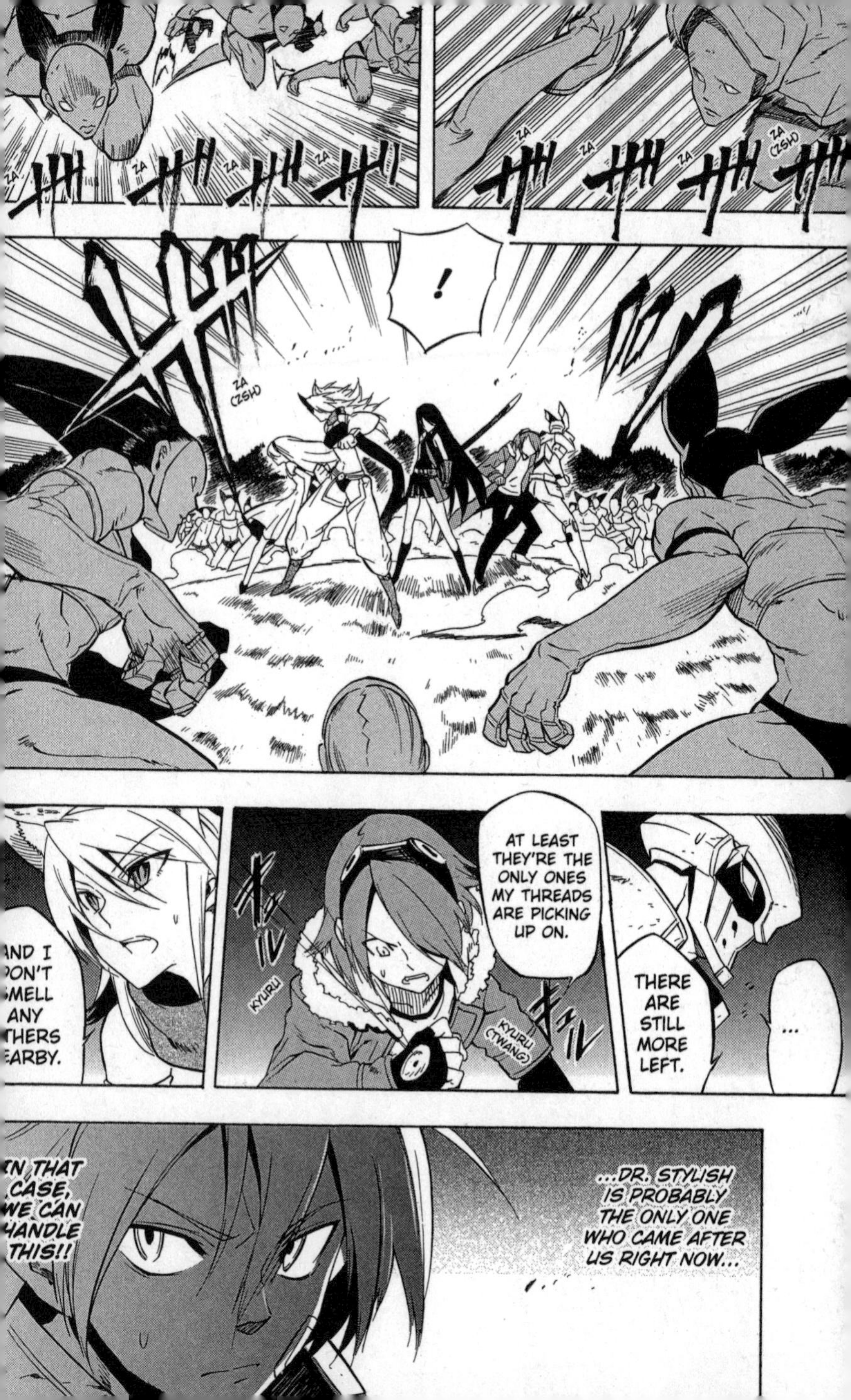
ZA
ZA
ZA
ZA (ZSH)
ZA
ZA
ZA
ZA
!
ZA (ZSH)
AT LEAST THEY'RE THE ONLY ONES MY THREADS ARE PICKING UP ON.
KYURU
KYURU (TWANG)
...
THERE ARE STILL MORE LEFT.
AND I DON'T SMELL ANY OTHERS NEARBY.
...DR. STYLISH IS PROBABLY THE ONLY ONE WHO CAME AFTER US RIGHT NOW...
IN THAT CASE, WE CAN HANDLE THIS!!

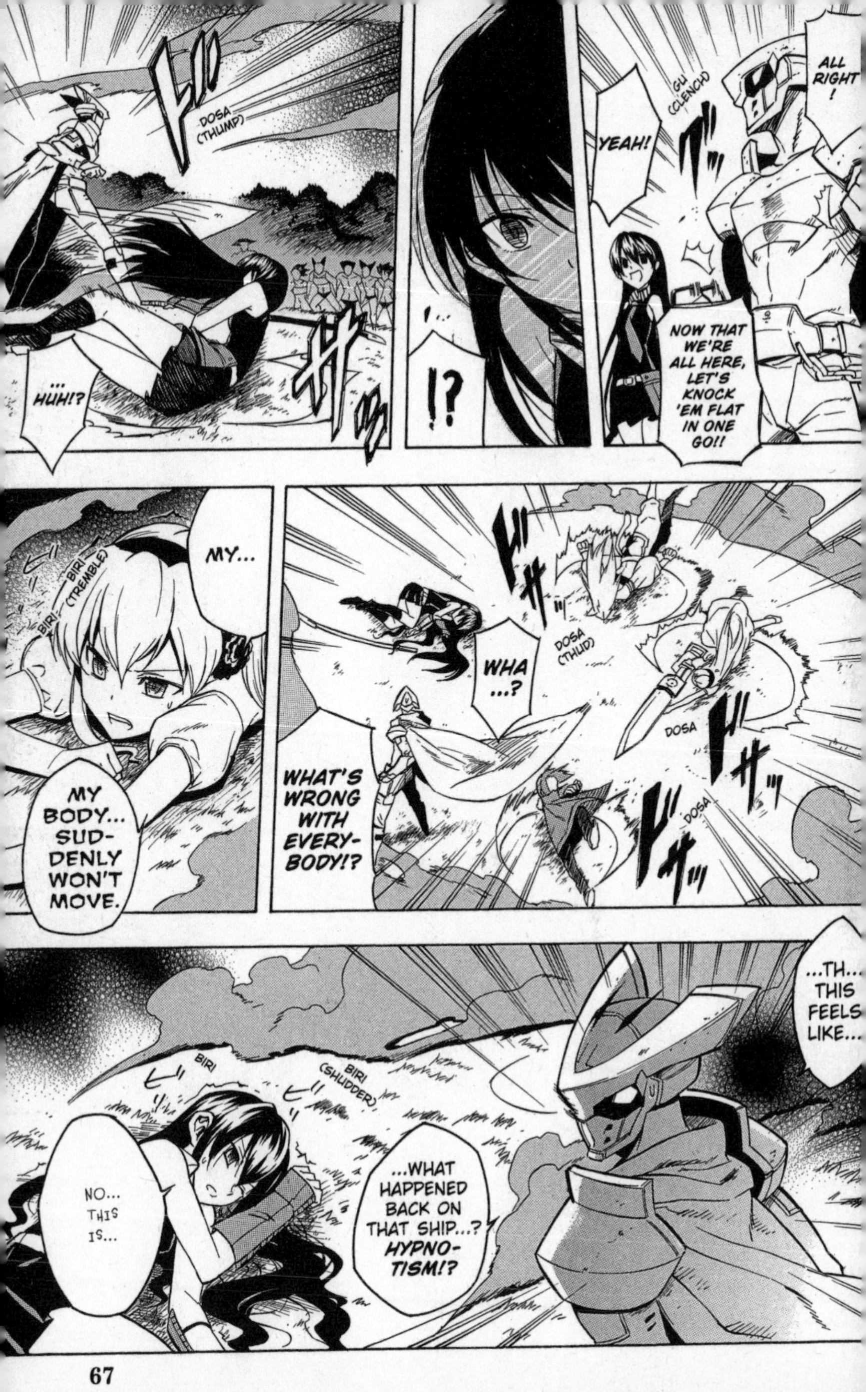
ALL RIGHT!
GU (CLENCH)
YEAH!
NOW THAT WE'RE ALL HERE, LET'S KNOCK 'EM FLAT IN ONE GO!!
!?
DOSA (THUMP)
...HUH!?
DOSA (THUD)
WHA...?
DOSA
DOSA
WHAT'S WRONG WITH EVERYBODY!?
BIRI BIRI (TREMBLE)
MY...
MY BODY... SUD-DENLY WON'T MOVE.
...TH... THIS FEELS LIKE...
...WHAT HAPPENED BACK ON THAT SHIP...? HYPNO-TISM!?
BIRI BIRI (SHUDDER)
NO... THIS IS...

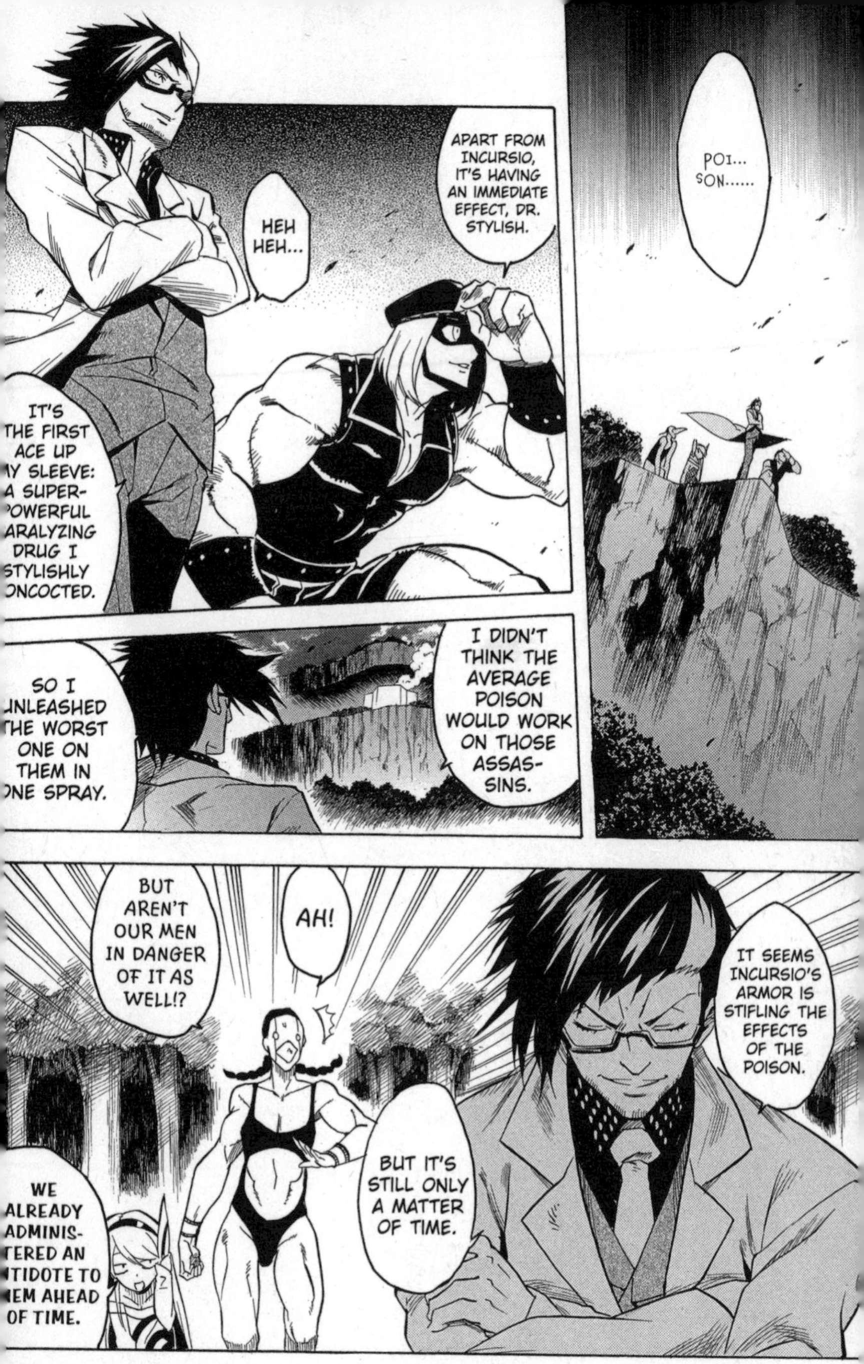
POI... SON......
APART FROM INCURSIO, IT'S HAVING AN IMMEDIATE EFFECT, DR. STYLISH.
HEH HEH...
IT'S THE FIRST ACE UP IY SLEEVE: A SUPER-POWERFUL ARALYZING DRUG I STYLISHLY ONCOCTED.
I DIDN'T THINK THE AVERAGE POISON WOULD WORK ON THOSE ASSAS-SINS.
SO I NLEASHED THE WORST ONE ON THEM IN ONE SPRAY.
IT SEEMS INCURSIO'S ARMOR IS STIFLING THE EFFECTS OF THE POISON.
BUT IT'S STILL ONLY A MATTER OF TIME.
AH!
BUT AREN'T OUR MEN IN DANGER OF IT AS WELL!?
WE ALREADY ADMINIS-TERED AN TIDOTE TO IEM AHEAD OF TIME.

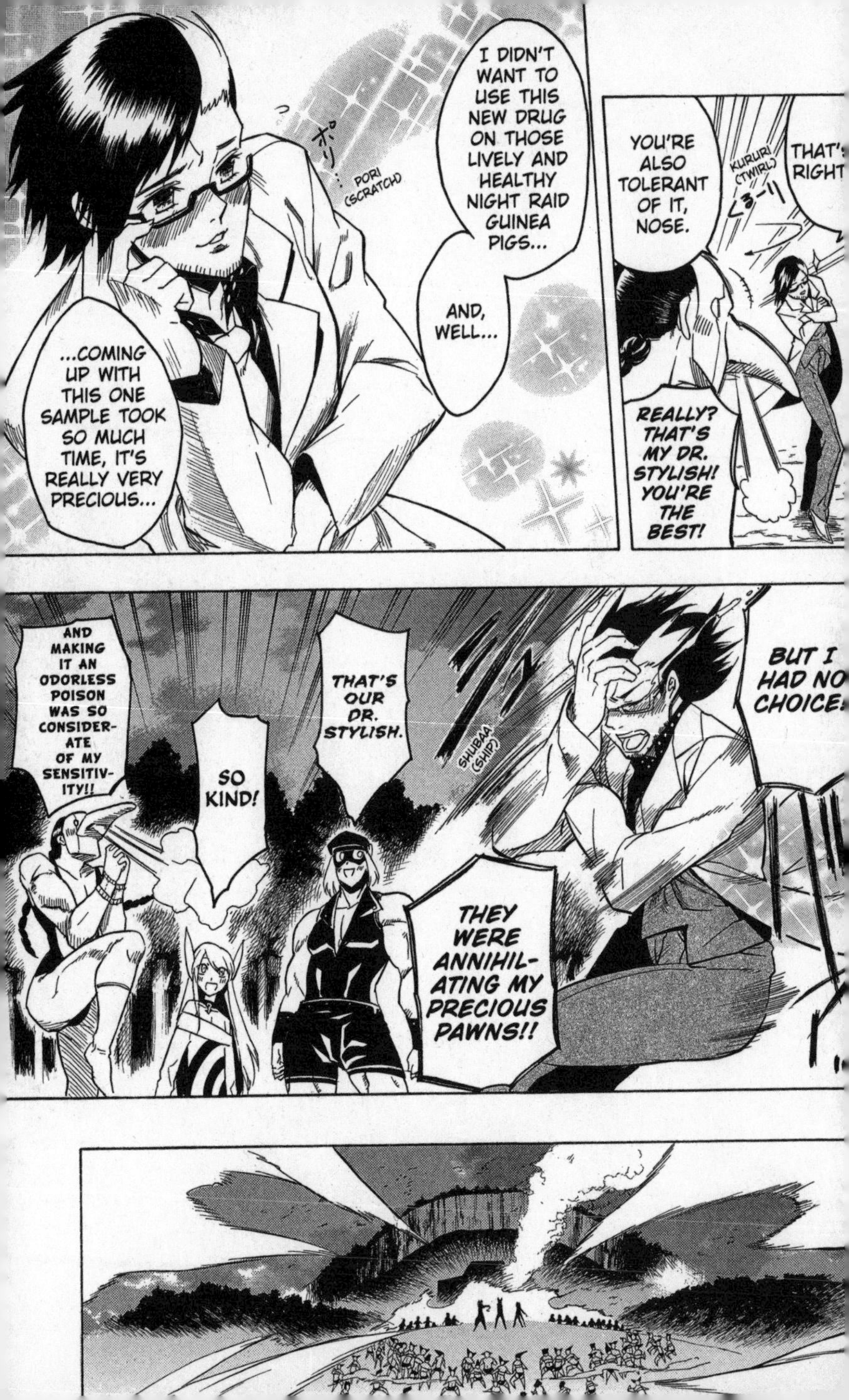
I DIDN'T WANT TO USE THIS NEW DRUG ON THOSE LIVELY AND HEALTHY NIGHT RAID GUINEA PIGS...
AND, WELL...
ポリ
PORI (SCRATCH)
...COMING UP WITH THIS ONE SAMPLE TOOK SO MUCH TIME, IT'S REALLY VERY PRECIOUS...
THAT'S RIGHT
KURURI (TWIRL)
くるーり
YOU'RE ALSO TOLERANT OF IT, NOSE.
REALLY? THAT'S MY DR. STYLISH! YOU'RE THE BEST!
BUT I HAD NO CHOICE!
THEY WERE ANNIHIL-ATING MY PRECIOUS PAWNS!!
SHUBAA (SHIP)
THAT'S OUR DR. STYLISH.
SO KIND!
AND MAKING IT AN ODORLESS POISON WAS SO CONSIDER-ATE OF MY SENSITIV-ITY!!

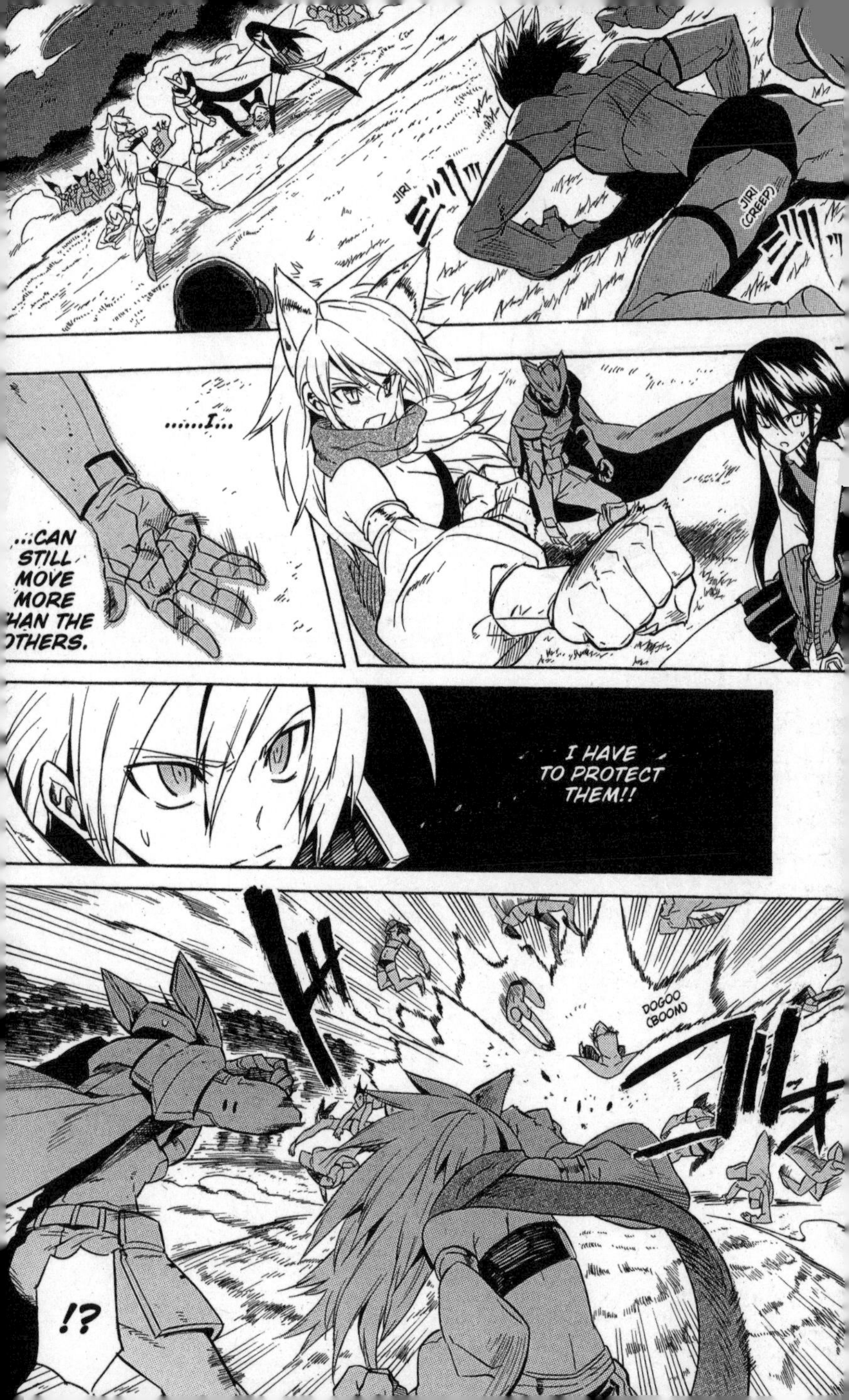
JIRI (CREEP)
JIRI
......I...
...CAN STILL MOVE MORE THAN THE OTHERS.
I HAVE TO PROTECT THEM!!
DOGOO (BOOM)
!?

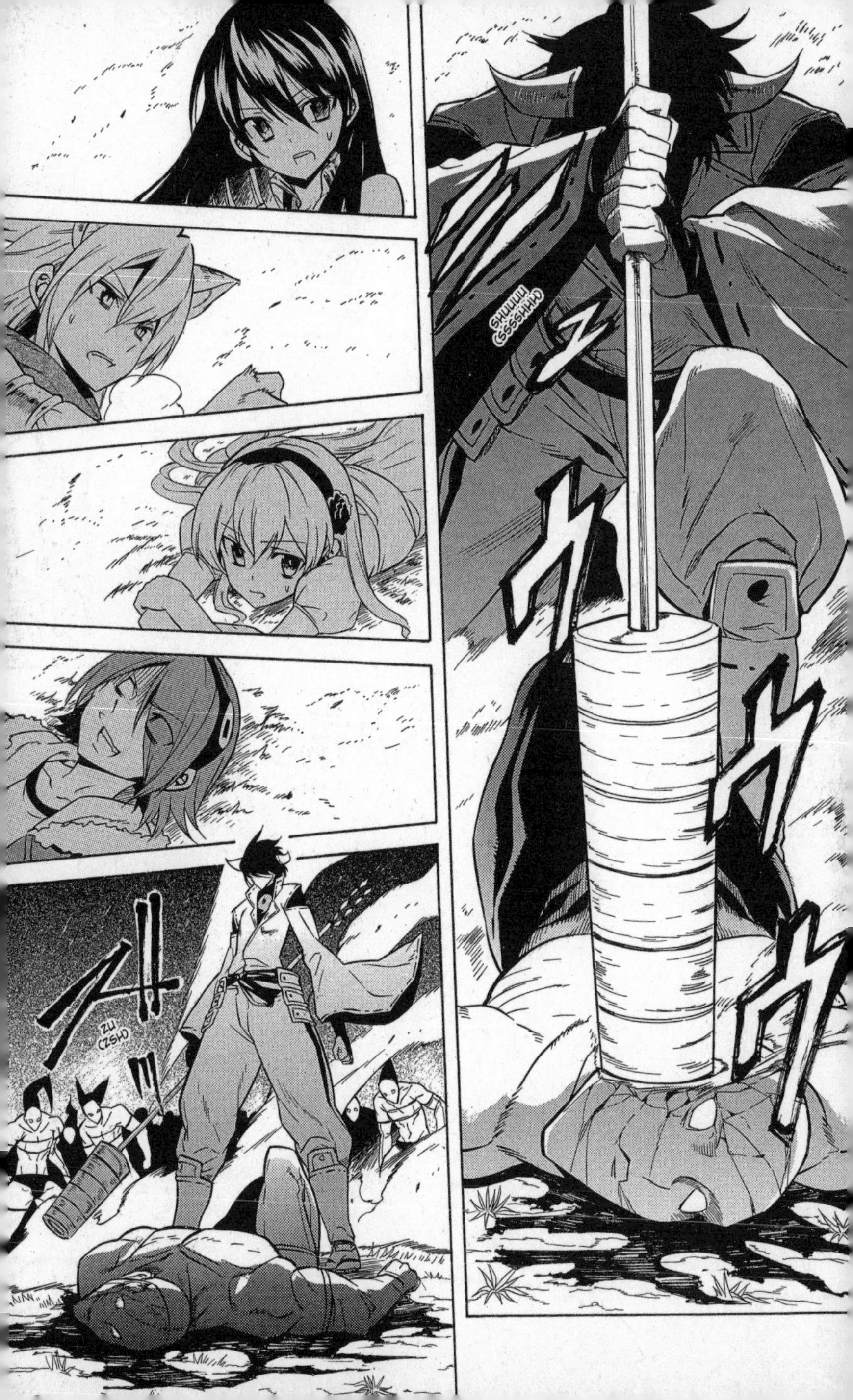
SHUUUU
(SSSSHHH)
ZU
(CZSH)

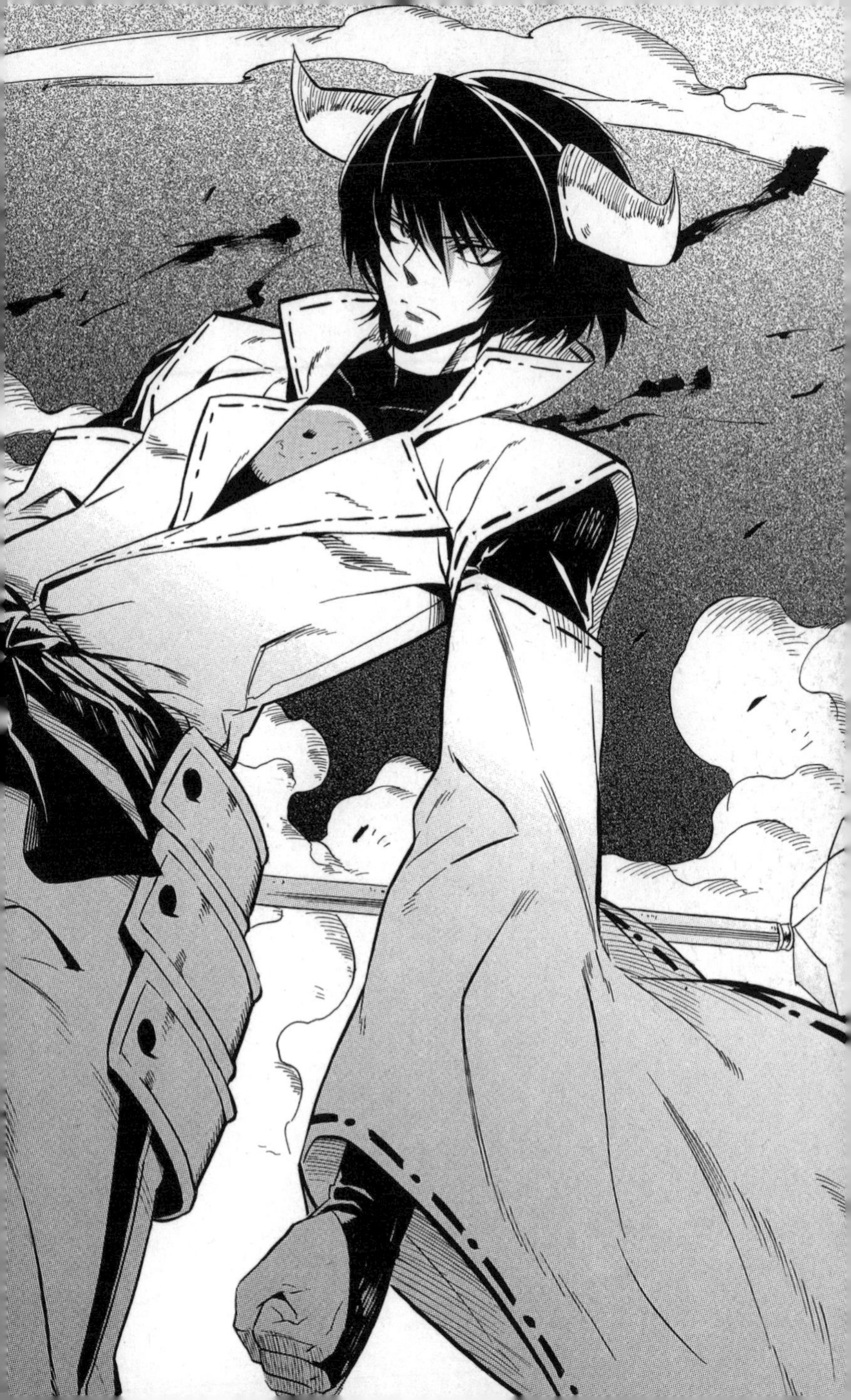

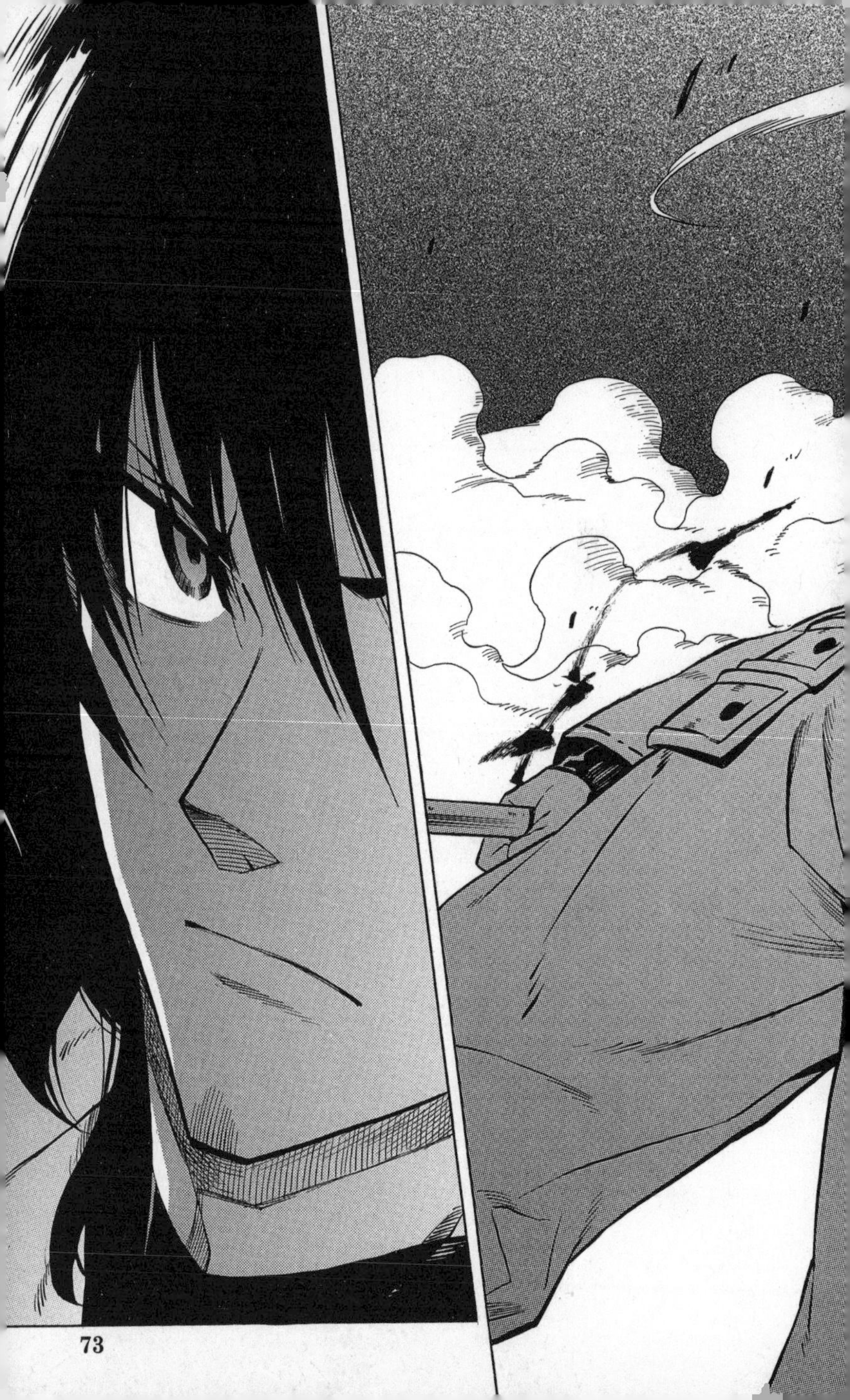

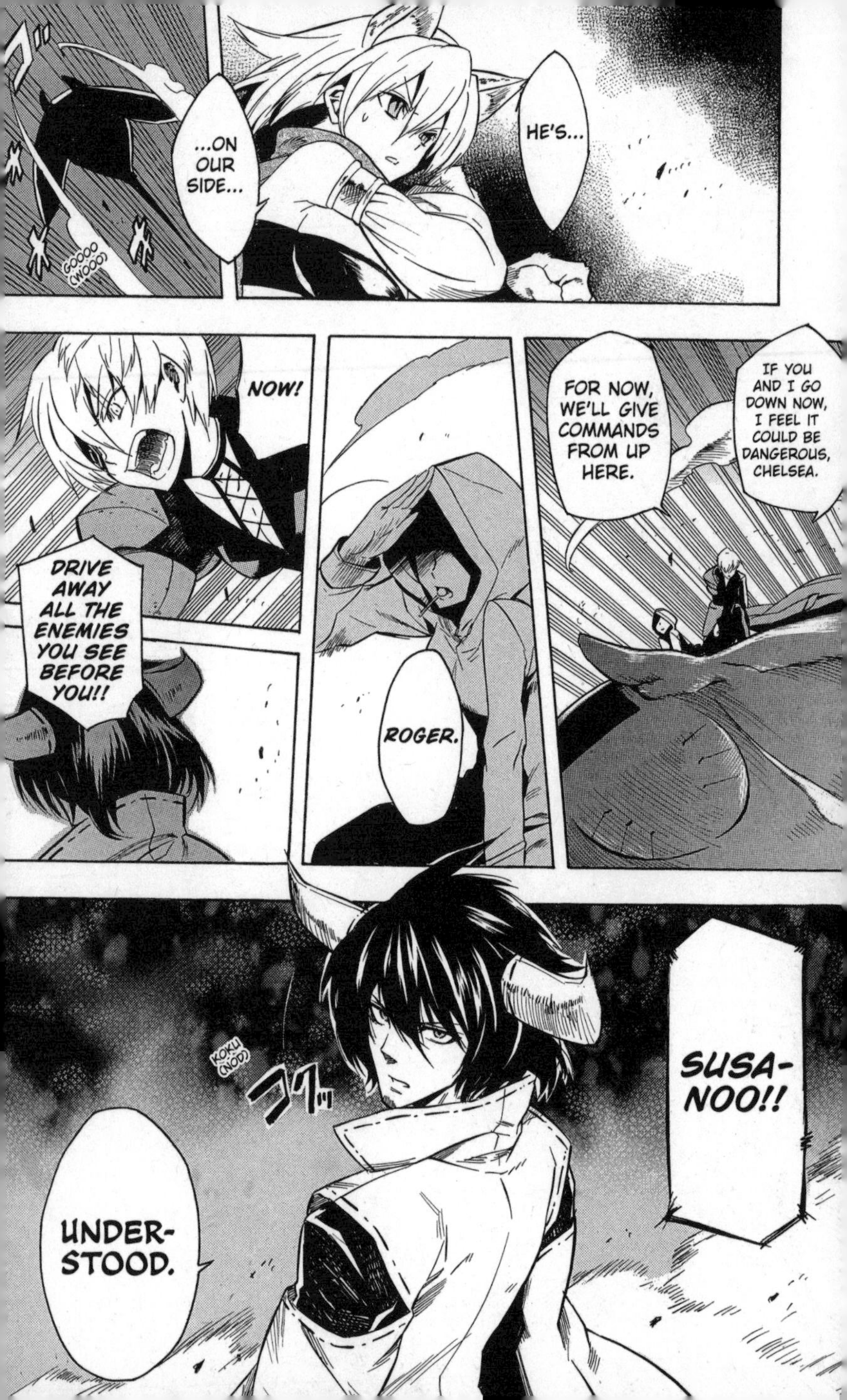
HE'S...
...ON OUR SIDE...
GOOOO (WOOO)
IF YOU AND I GO DOWN NOW, I FEEL IT COULD BE DANGEROUS, CHELSEA.
FOR NOW, WE'LL GIVE COMMANDS FROM UP HERE.
ROGER.
NOW!
DRIVE AWAY ALL THE ENEMIES YOU SEE BEFORE YOU!!
SUSA-NOO!!
KOKU (NOD)
UNDER-STOOD.

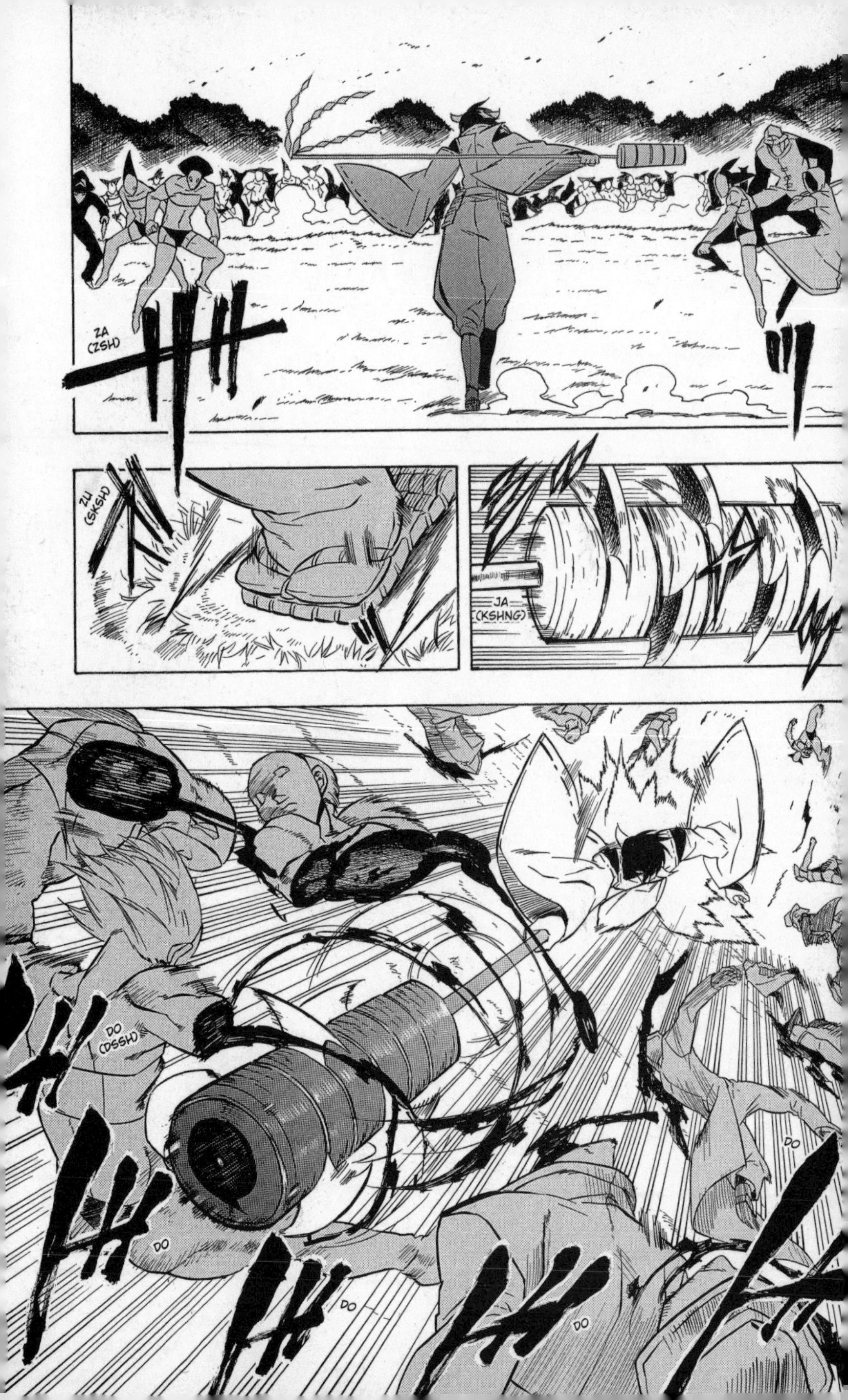
ZA
(ZSH)
ZU
(SKSH)
JA
(KSHNG)
DO
(DSSH)
DO
DO
DO
DO

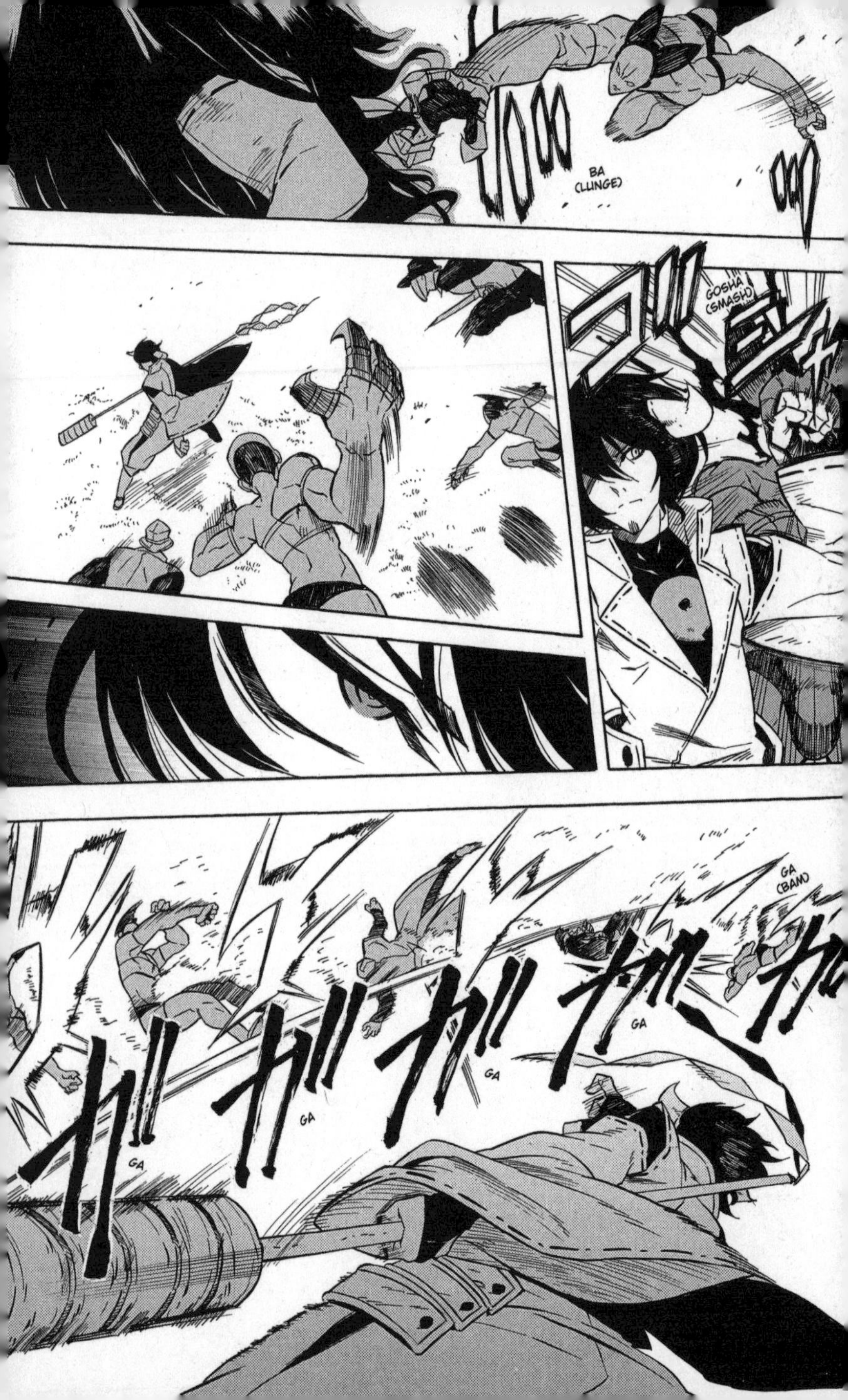
BA
(LUNGE)
GOSHA
(SMASH)
GA
(BAM)
GA
GA
GA
GA

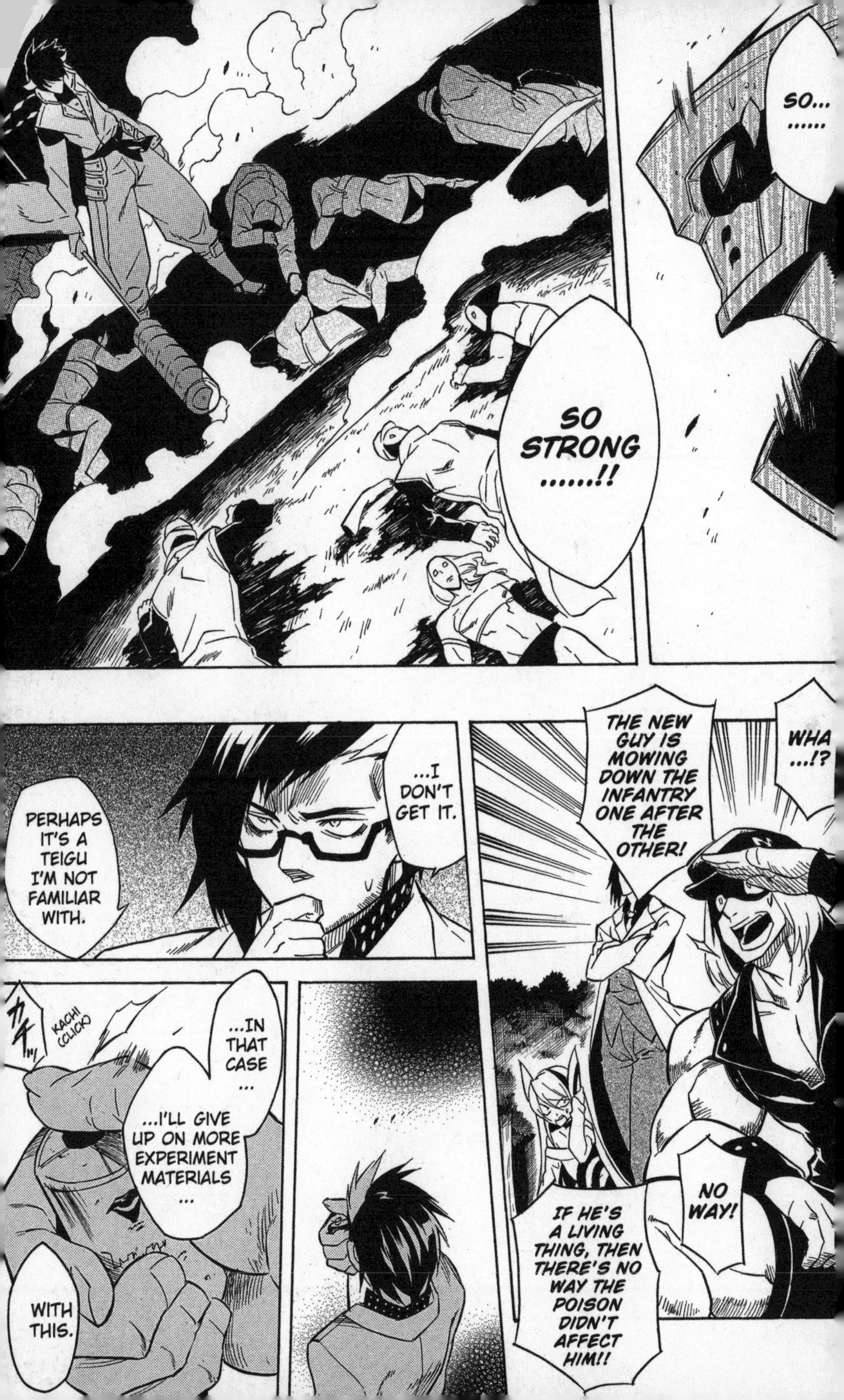

SO... ......
SO STRONG ......!!
WHA ...!?
THE NEW GUY IS MOWING DOWN THE INFANTRY ONE AFTER THE OTHER!
...I DON'T GET IT.
PERHAPS IT'S A TEIGU I'M NOT FAMILIAR WITH.
NO WAY!
IF HE'S A LIVING THING, THEN THERE'S NO WAY THE POISON DIDN'T AFFECT HIM!!
...IN THAT CASE ...
...I'LL GIVE UP ON MORE EXPERIMENT MATERIALS ...
KACHI (CLICK)
WITH THIS.

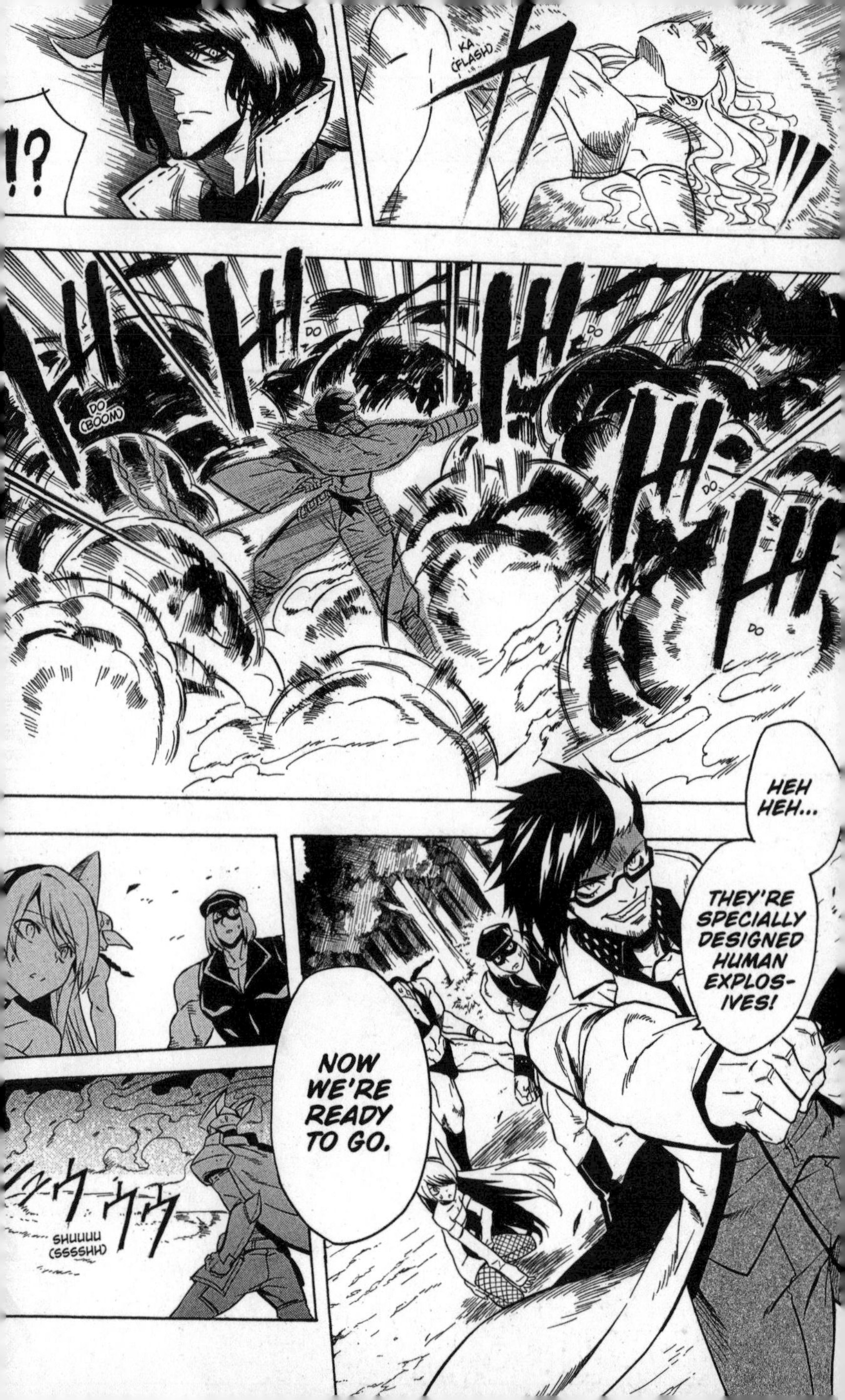

KA (FLASH)
!!
!?
DO
DO
DO (BOOM)
DO
DO
HEH HEH...
THEY'RE SPECIALLY DESIGNED HUMAN EXPLOSIVES!
NOW WE'RE READY TO GO.
SHUUUU (SSSSHH)

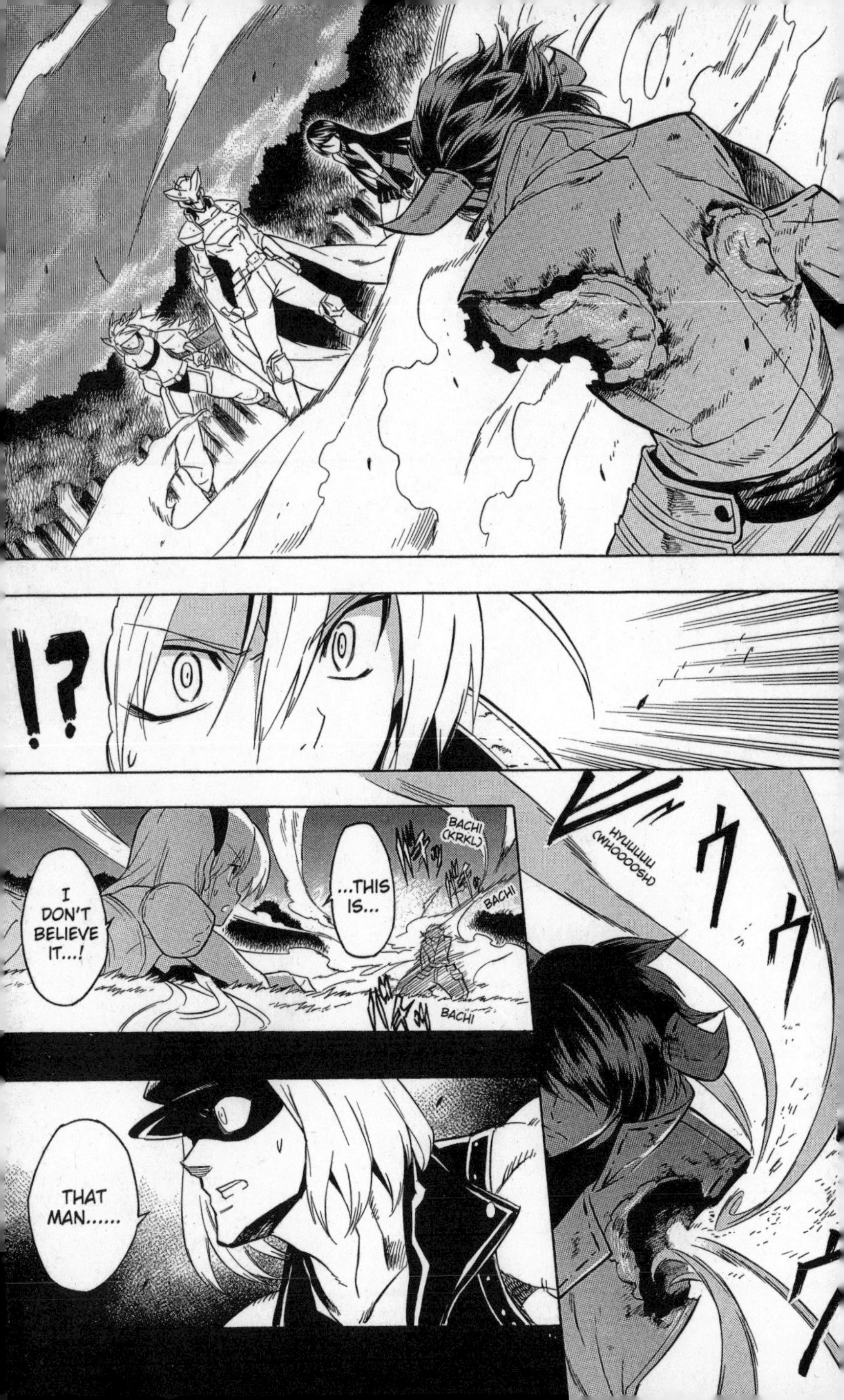
!?
HYUUUUU (WHOOOOSH)
BACHI (KRKL)
BACHI
BACHI
...THIS IS...
I DON'T BELIEVE IT...!
THAT MAN......

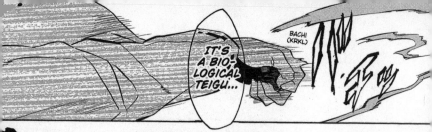

IT'S A BIOLOGICAL TEIGU...

BACHI (KRKL)

DON (BADUM)

A HUMANOID TEIGU!!

ZAN (ZSH)

WH...

WHAT?

......

JIIII (STAAARE)

80

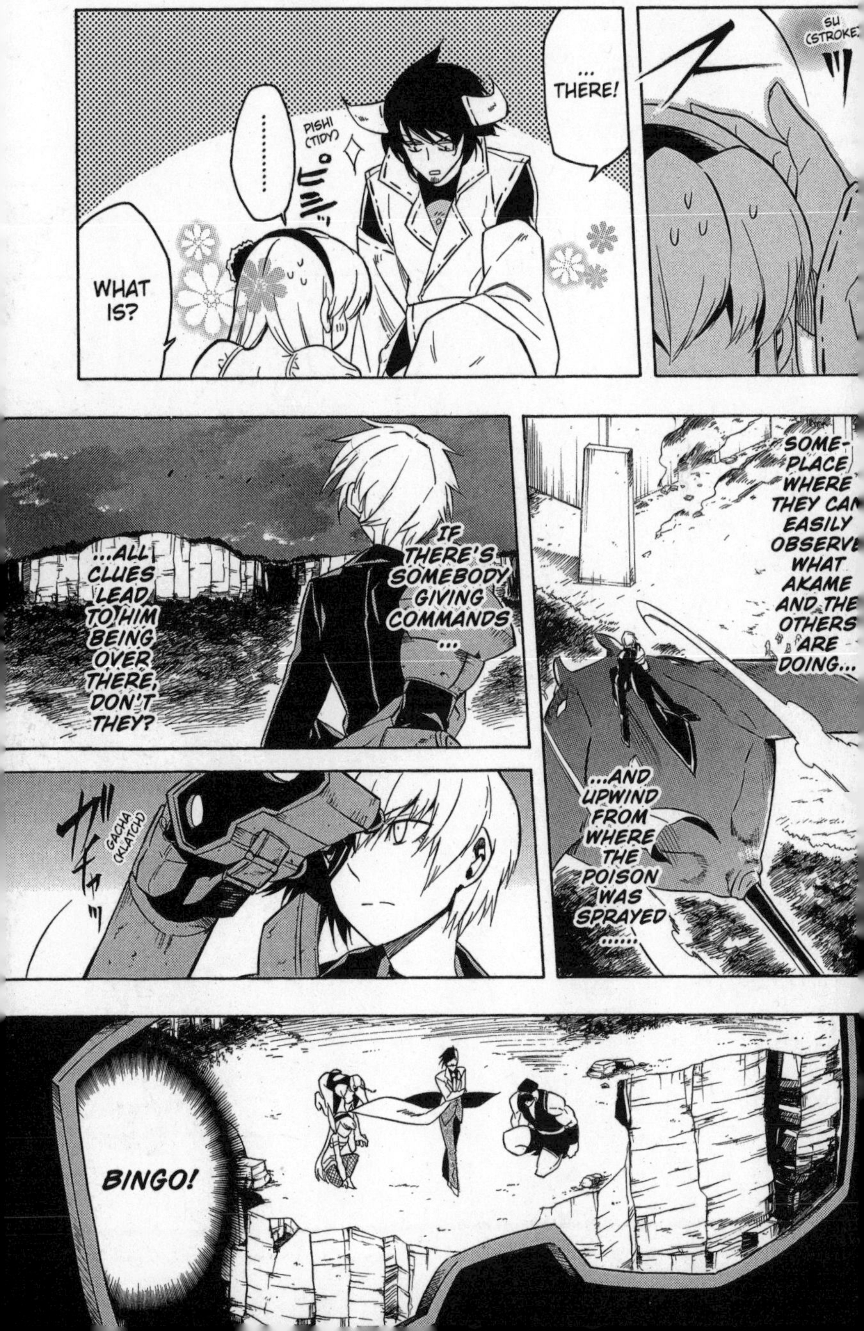
SU (STROKE)
...THERE!
PISHI (TIDY)
......
WHAT IS?
SOME-PLACE WHERE THEY CAN EASILY OBSERVE WHAT AKAME AND THE OTHERS ARE DOING...
IF THERE'S SOMEBODY GIVING COMMANDS...
...ALL CLUES LEAD TO HIM BEING OVER THERE, DON'T THEY?
...AND UPWIND FROM WHERE THE POISON WAS SPRAYED......
GACHA (KLATCH)
BINGO!

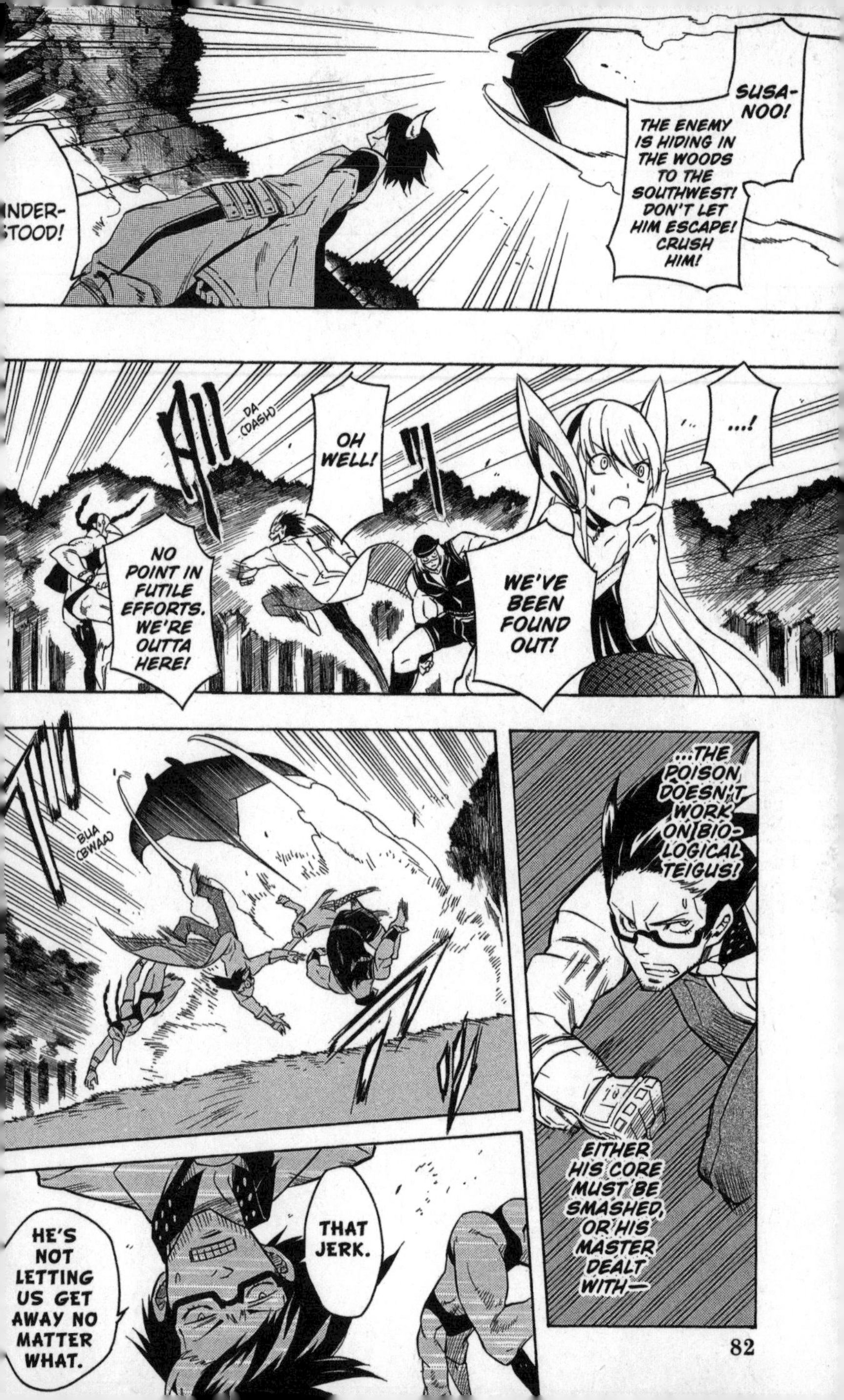
SUSA-NOO!
THE ENEMY IS HIDING IN THE WOODS TO THE SOUTHWEST! DON'T LET HIM ESCAPE! CRUSH HIM!
NDER-STOOD!
...!
WE'VE BEEN FOUND OUT!
OH WELL!
DA (DASH)
NO POINT IN FUTILE EFFORTS. WE'RE OUTTA HERE!
...THE POISON DOESN'T WORK ON BIO-LOGICAL TEIGUS!
EITHER HIS CORE MUST BE SMASHED, OR HIS MASTER DEALT WITH—
BUA (BWAA)
THAT JERK.
HE'S NOT LETTING US GET AWAY NO MATTER WHAT.

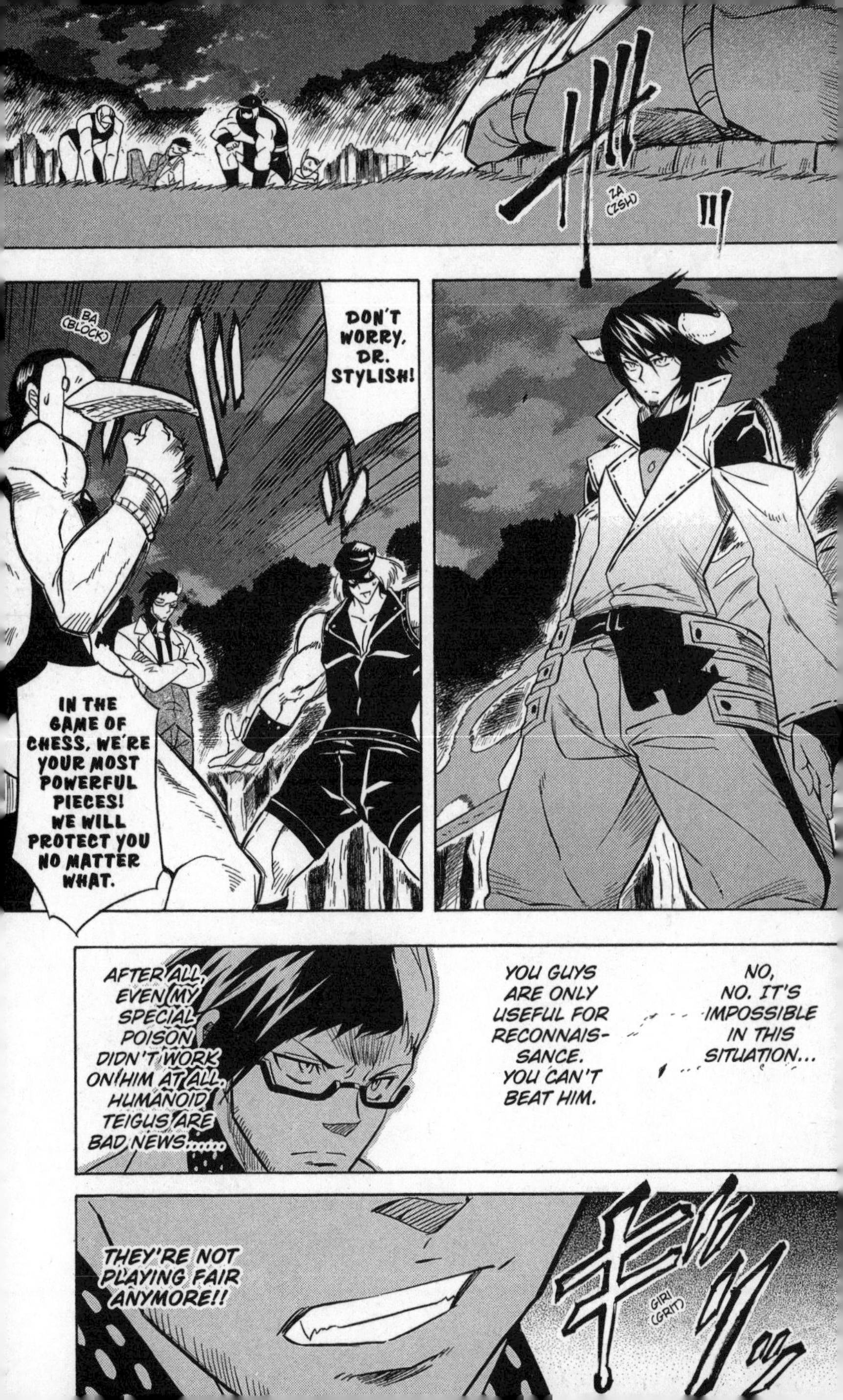
ZA (ZSH)
BA (BLOCK)
DON'T WORRY, DR. STYLISH!
IN THE GAME OF CHESS, WE'RE YOUR MOST POWERFUL PIECES! WE WILL PROTECT YOU NO MATTER WHAT.
NO, NO. IT'S IMPOSSIBLE IN THIS SITUATION...
YOU GUYS ARE ONLY USEFUL FOR RECONNAIS-SANCE. YOU CAN'T BEAT HIM.
AFTER ALL, EVEN MY SPECIAL POISON DIDN'T WORK ON HIM AT ALL. HUMANOID TEIGUS ARE BAD NEWS......
GIRI (GRIT)
THEY'RE NOT PLAYING FAIR ANYMORE!!

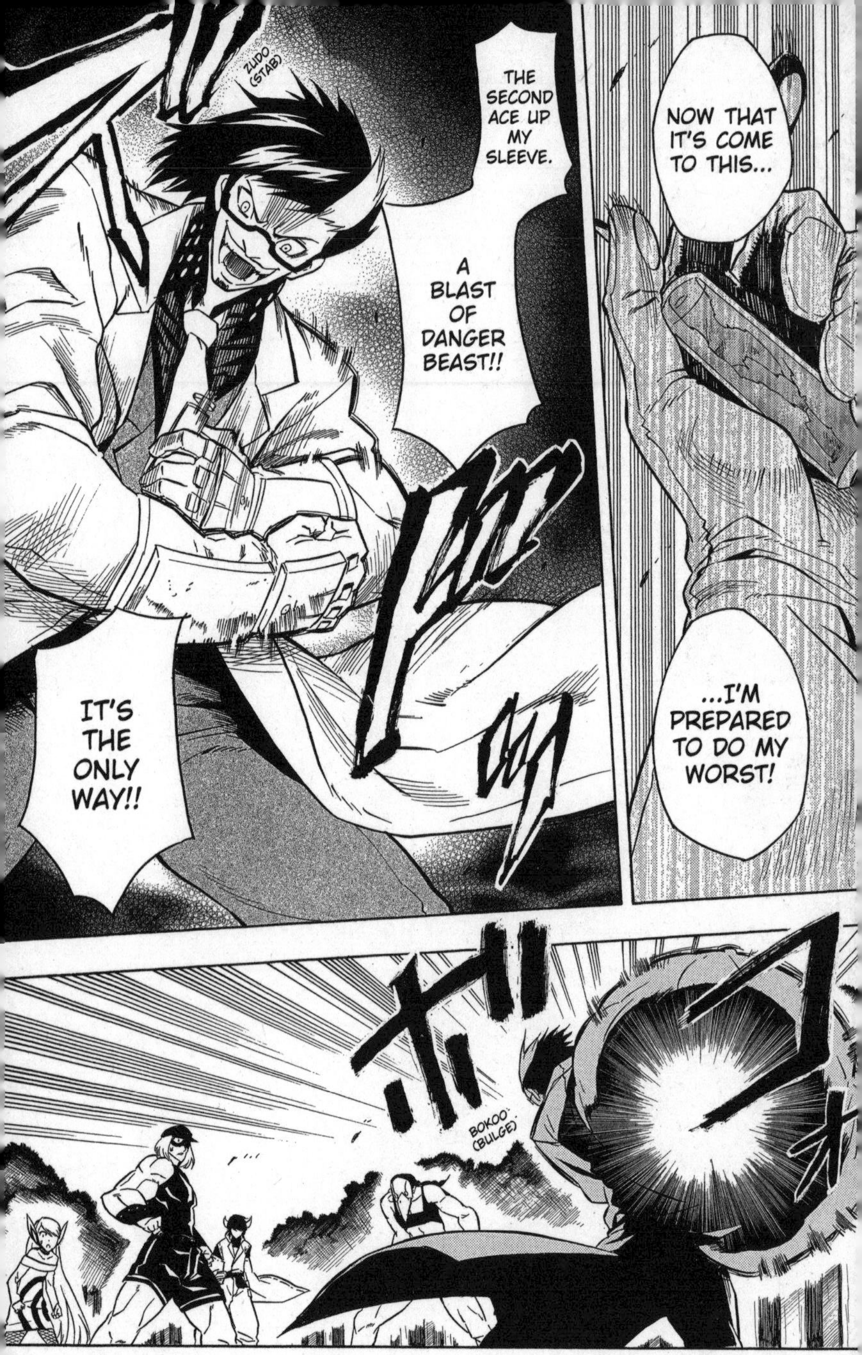
NOW THAT IT'S COME TO THIS...
...I'M PREPARED TO DO MY WORST!
THE SECOND ACE UP MY SLEEVE.
A BLAST OF DANGER BEAST!!
ZUDO (STAB)
IT'S THE ONLY WAY!!
BOKOO (BULGE)

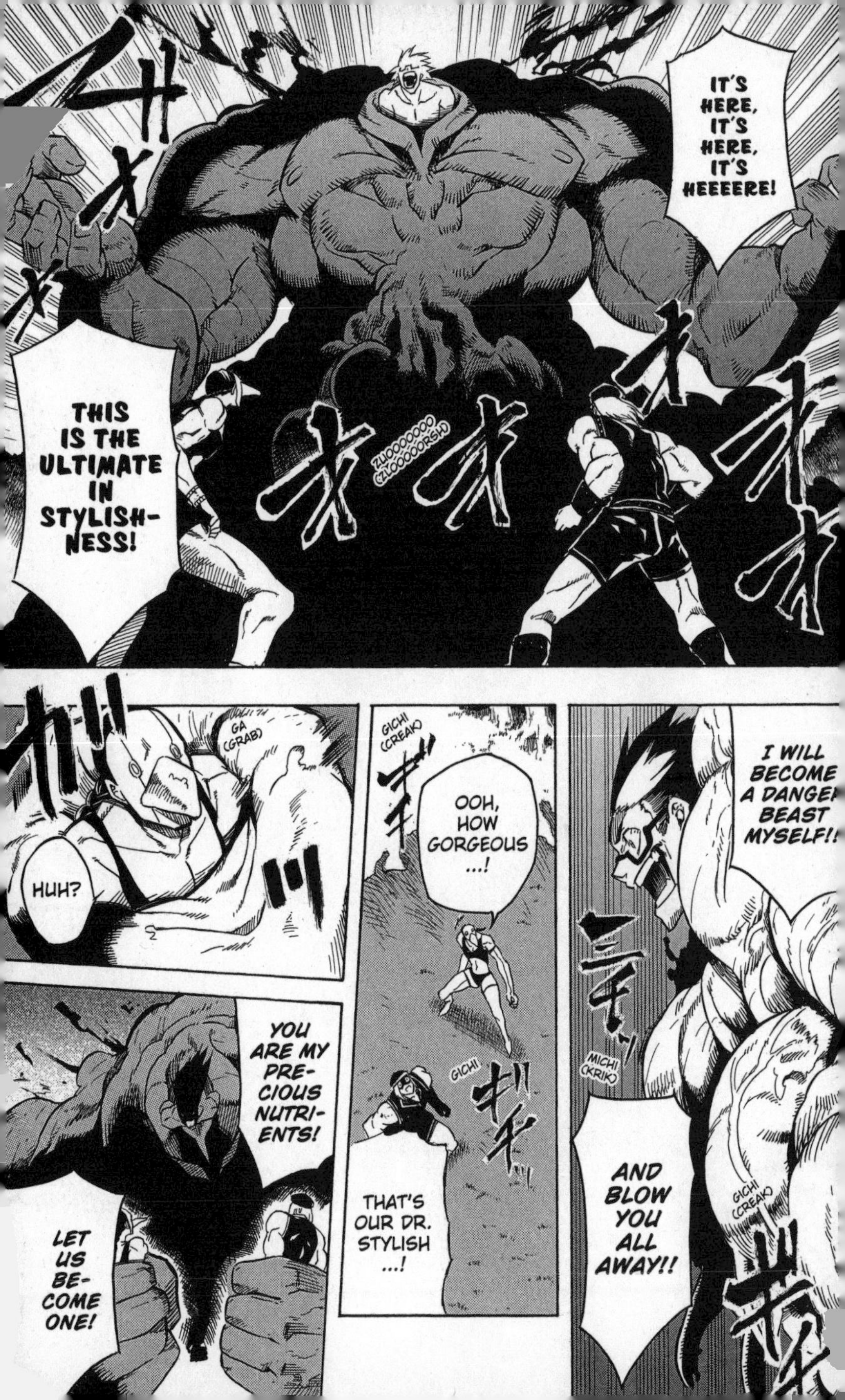

IT'S HERE, IT'S HERE, IT'S HEEEERE!
ZUOOOOOOO (ZUOOOOORSH)
THIS IS THE ULTIMATE IN STYLISHNESS!
I WILL BECOME A DANGER BEAST MYSELF!!
MICHI (KRIK)
AND BLOW YOU ALL AWAY!!
GICHI (CREAK)
GICHI (CREAK)
OOH, HOW GORGEOUS ...!
GICHI
THAT'S OUR DR. STYLISH ...!
GA (GRAB)
HUH?
YOU ARE MY PRECIOUS NUTRIENTS!
LET US BECOME ONE!

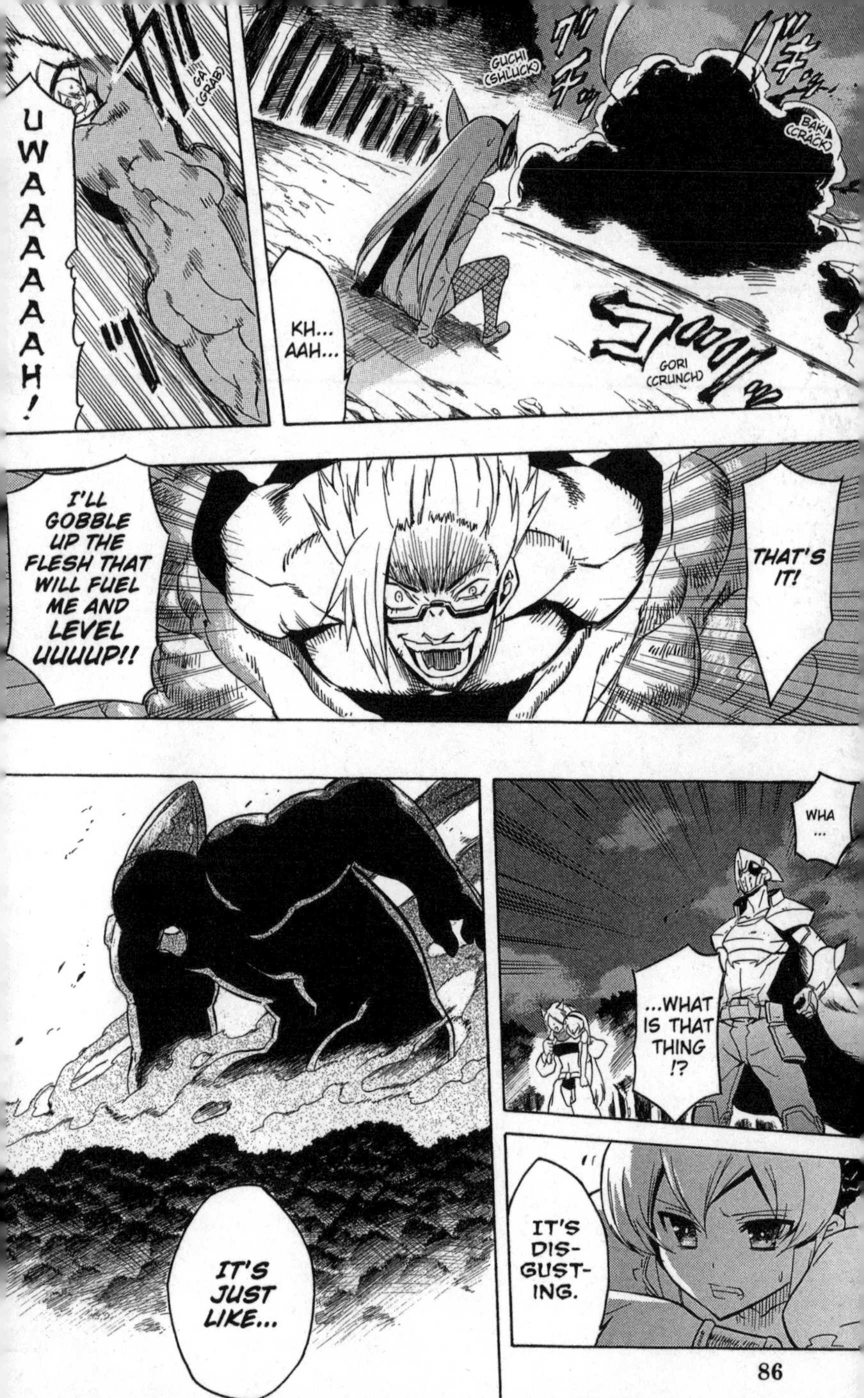
GUCHI (SHLUCK)
BAKI (CRACK)
GORI (CRUNCH)
KH... AAH...
GA (GRAB)
UWAAAAAAAAH!
THAT'S IT!
I'LL GOBBLE UP THE FLESH THAT WILL FUEL ME AND LEVEL UUUUP!!
WHA...
...WHAT IS THAT THING!?
IT'S DIS-GUST-ING.
IT'S JUST LIKE...

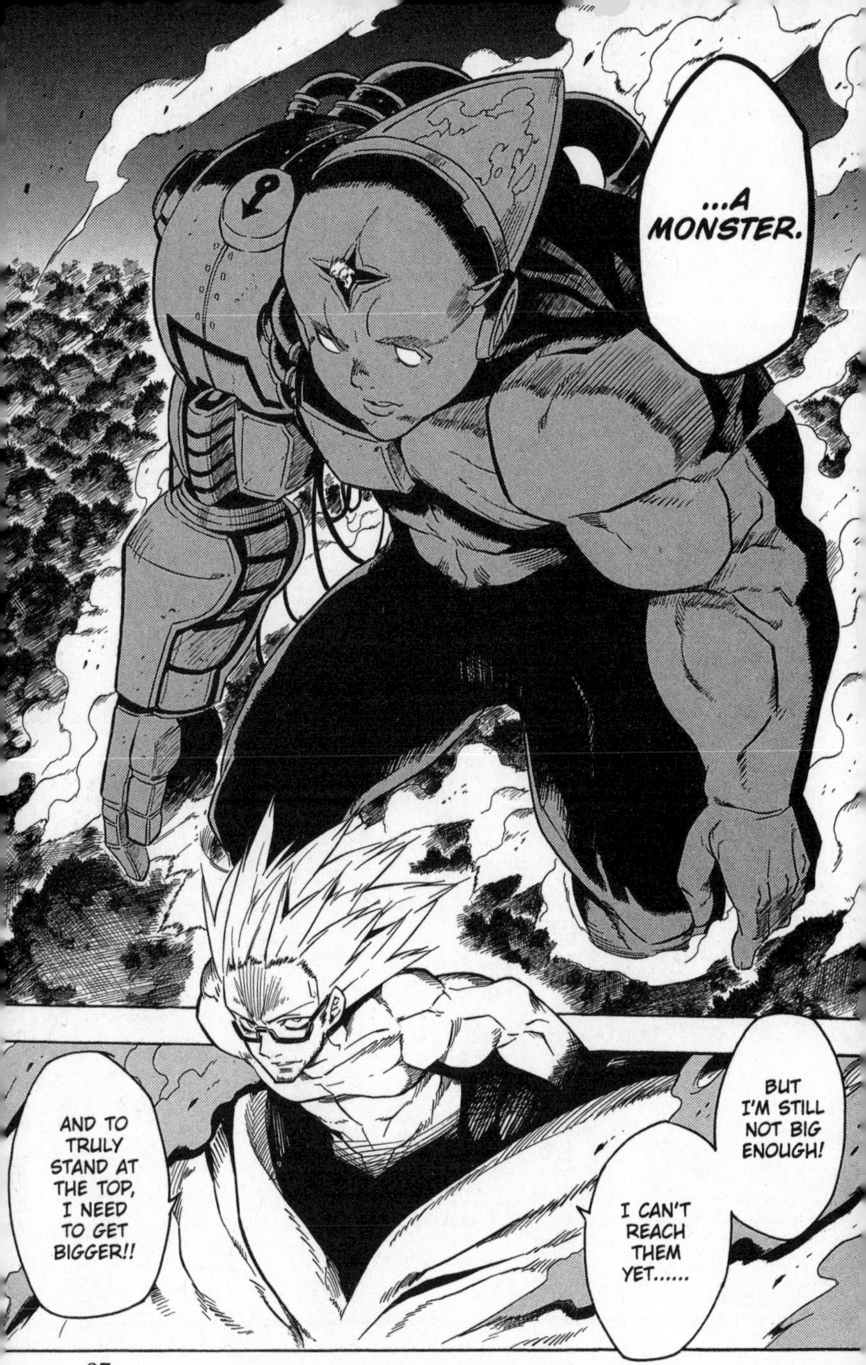
...A MONSTER.
BUT I'M STILL NOT BIG ENOUGH!
I CAN'T REACH THEM YET......
AND TO TRULY STAND AT THE TOP, I NEED TO GET BIGGER!!

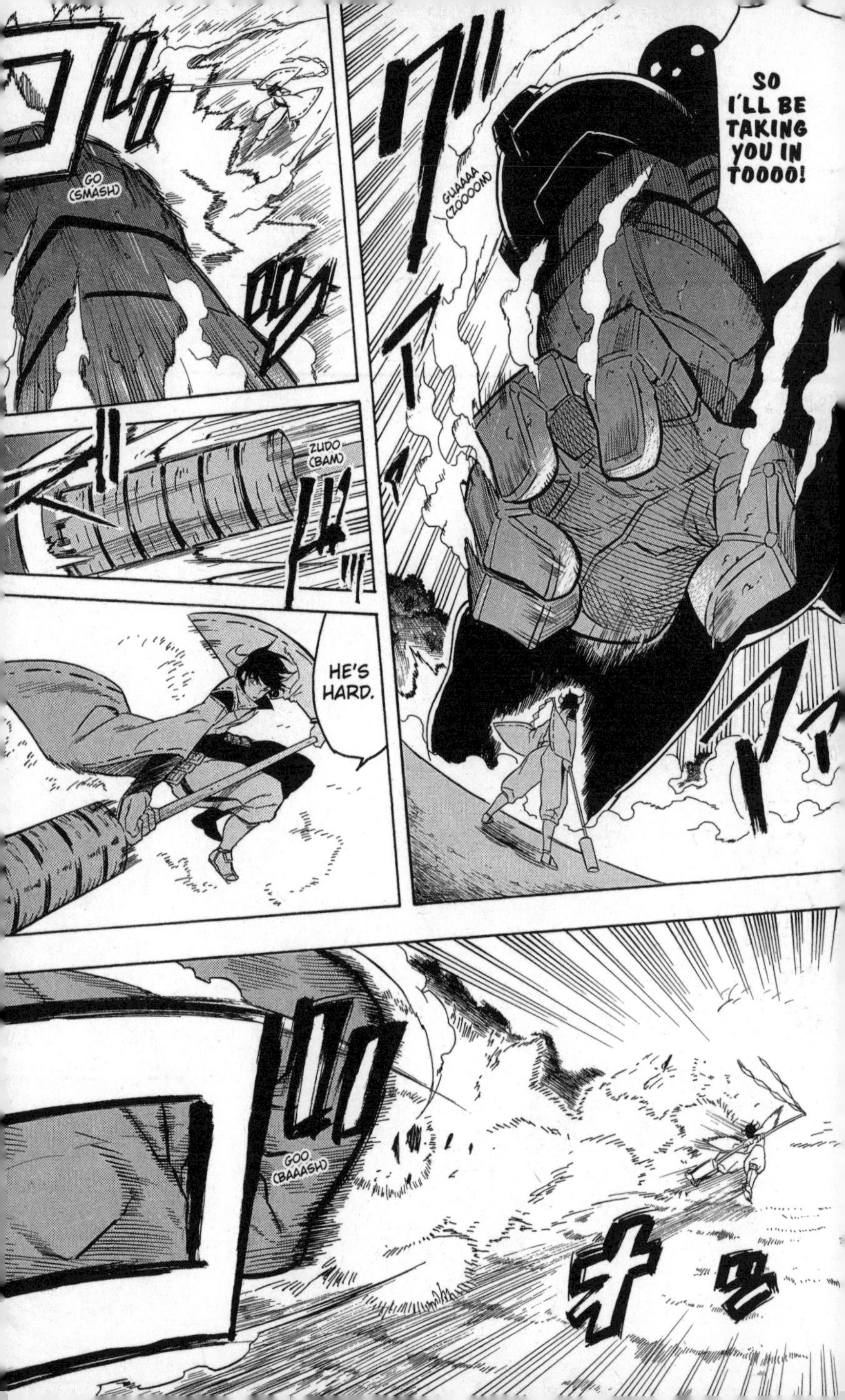
SO I'LL BE TAKING YOU IN TOOOO!
GUAAAA (ZOOOOM)
GO (SMASH)
ZUDO (BAM)
HE'S HARD.
GOO (BAAASH)

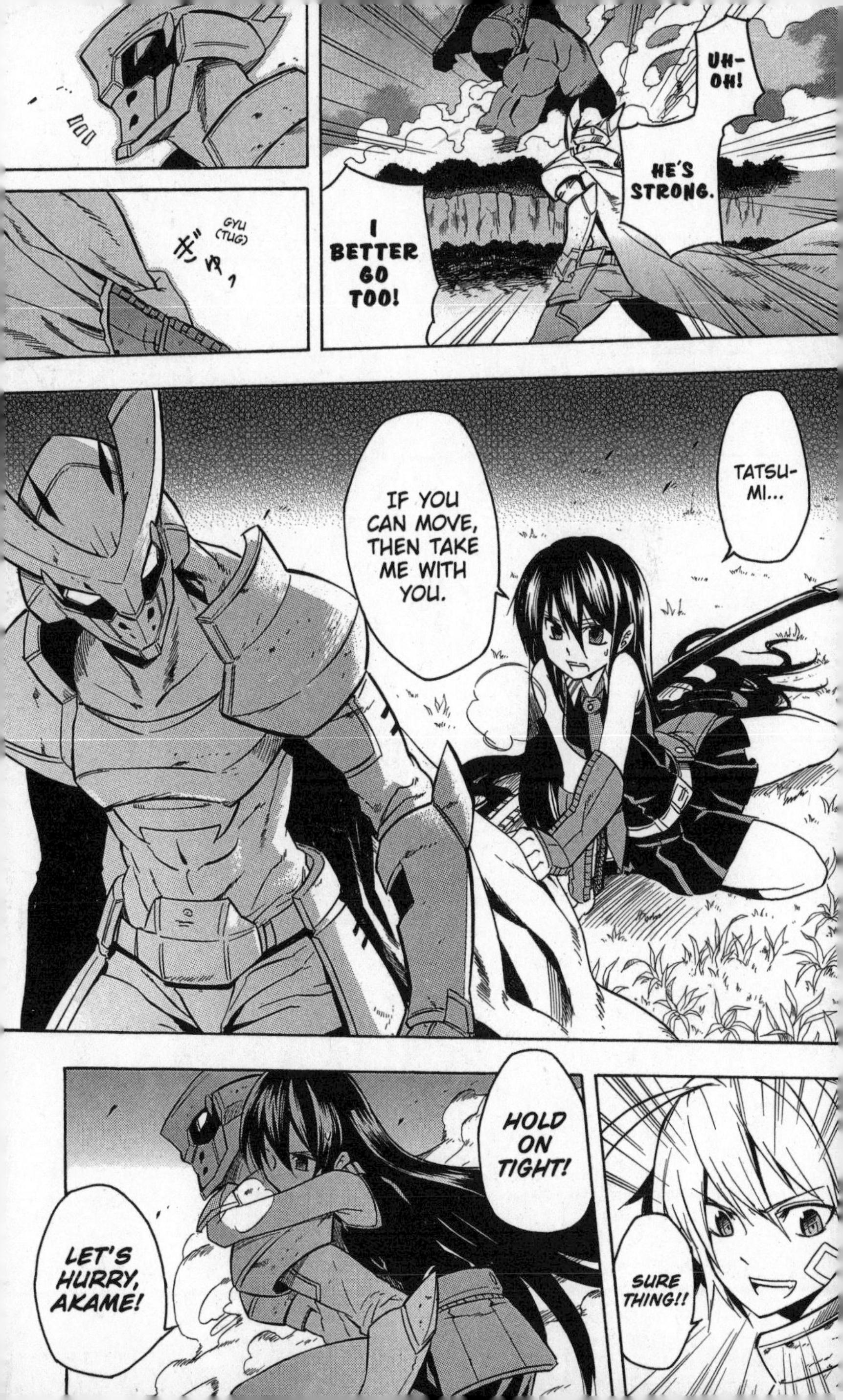
UH-OH!
HE'S STRONG.
I BETTER GO TOO!
GYU (TUG)
ぎゅっ
TATSUMI...
IF YOU CAN MOVE, THEN TAKE ME WITH YOU.
SURE THING!!
HOLD ON TIGHT!
LET'S HURRY, AKAME!

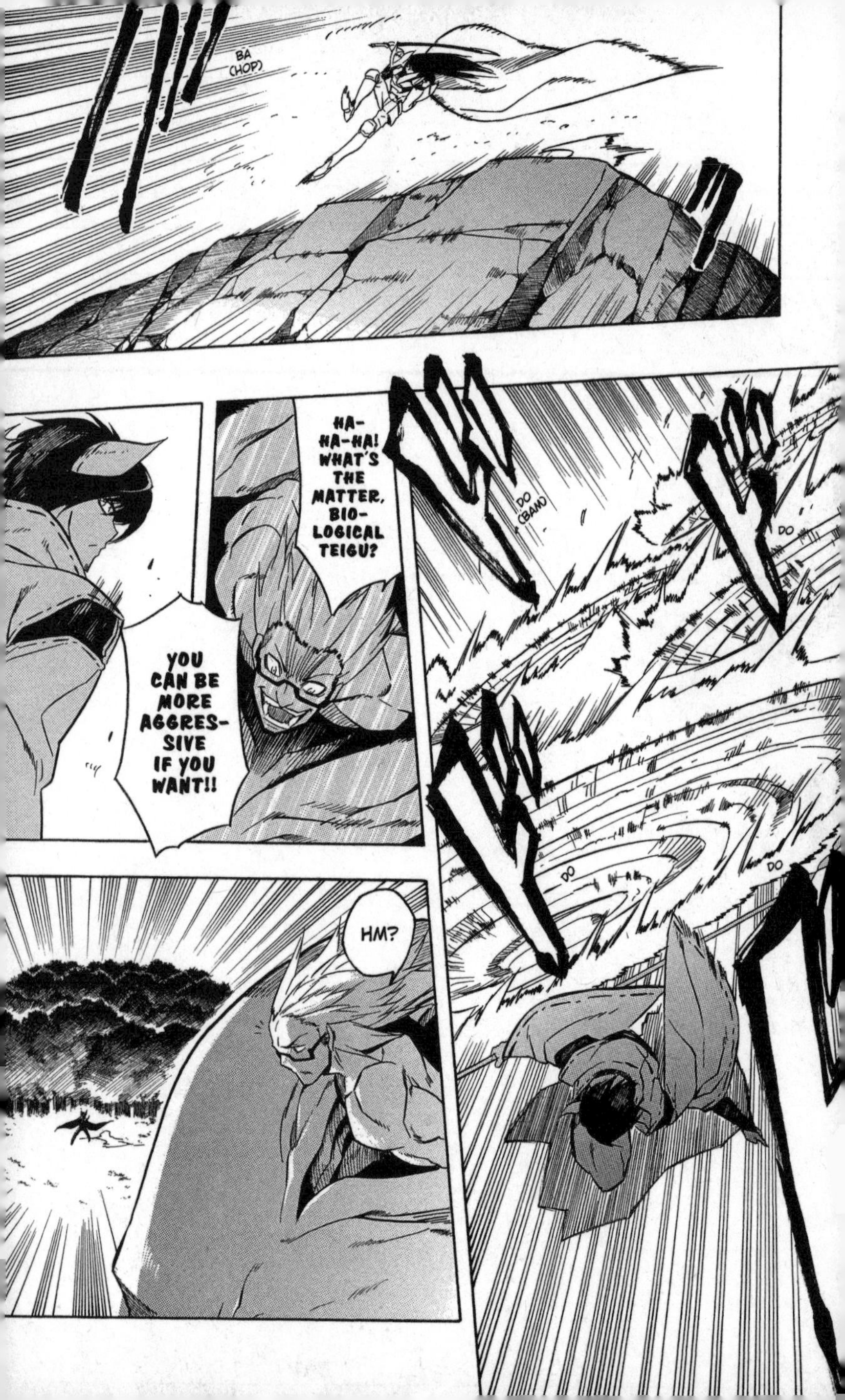
BA (HOP)
DO (BAM)
DO
DO
DO
HA-HA-HA! WHAT'S THE MATTER, BIOLOGICAL TEIGU?
YOU CAN BE MORE AGGRESSIVE IF YOU WANT!!
HM?

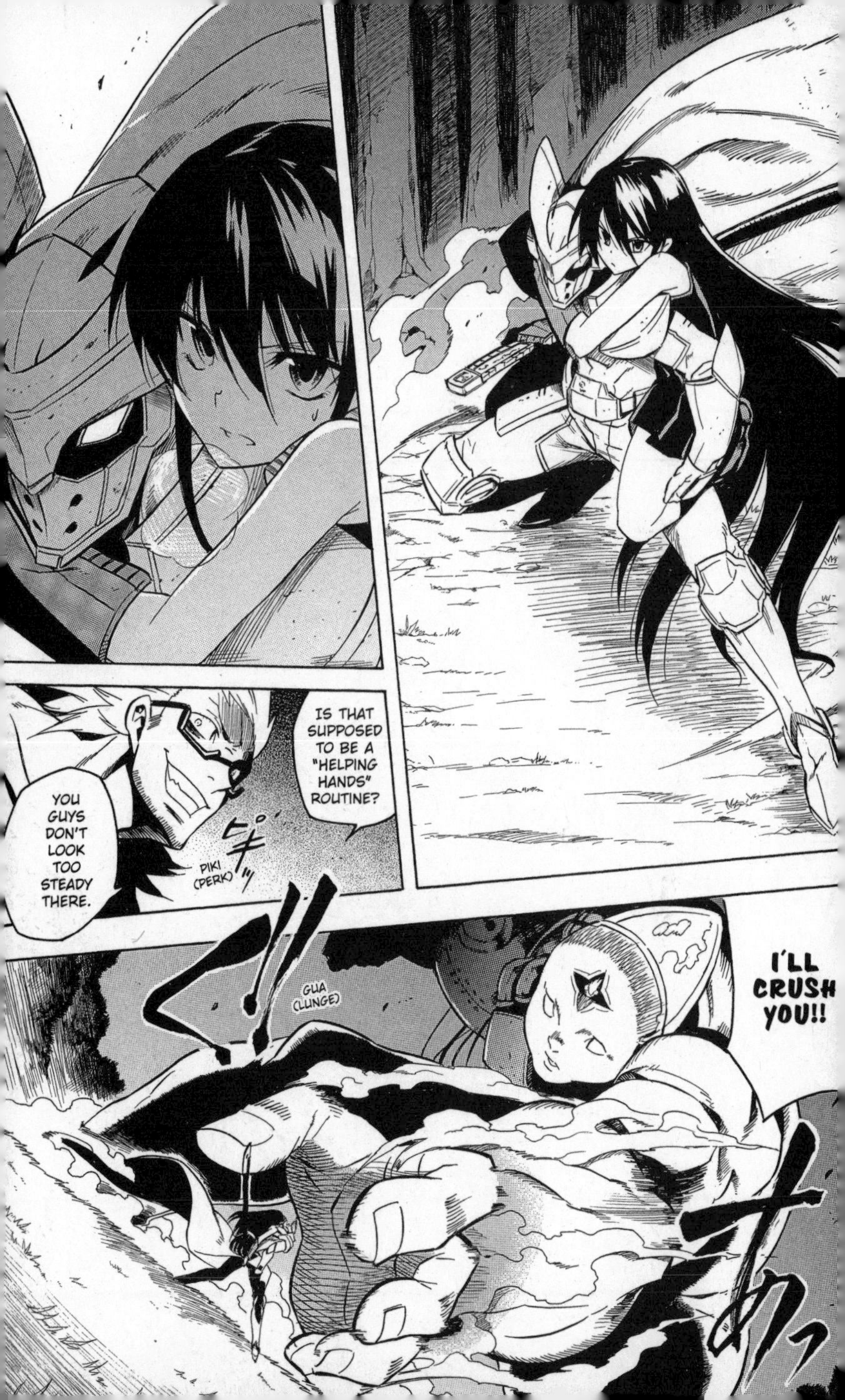
IS THAT SUPPOSED TO BE A "HELPING HANDS" ROUTINE?
YOU GUYS DON'T LOOK TOO STEADY THERE.
PIKI (PERK)
I'LL CRUSH YOU!!
GUA (LUNGE)

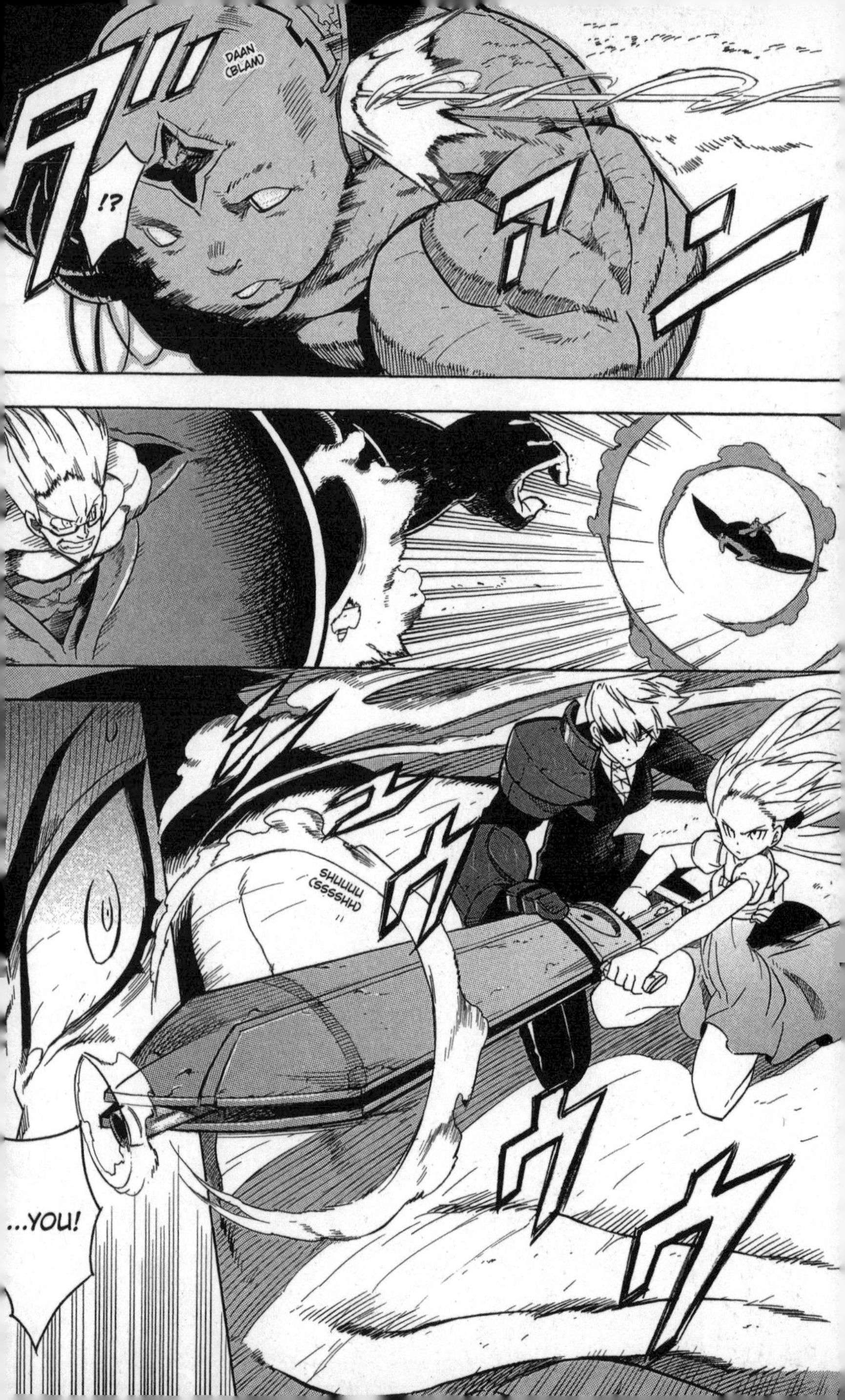
DAAN (BLAM)
!?
SHUUUUU
(SSSSHH)
...YOU!

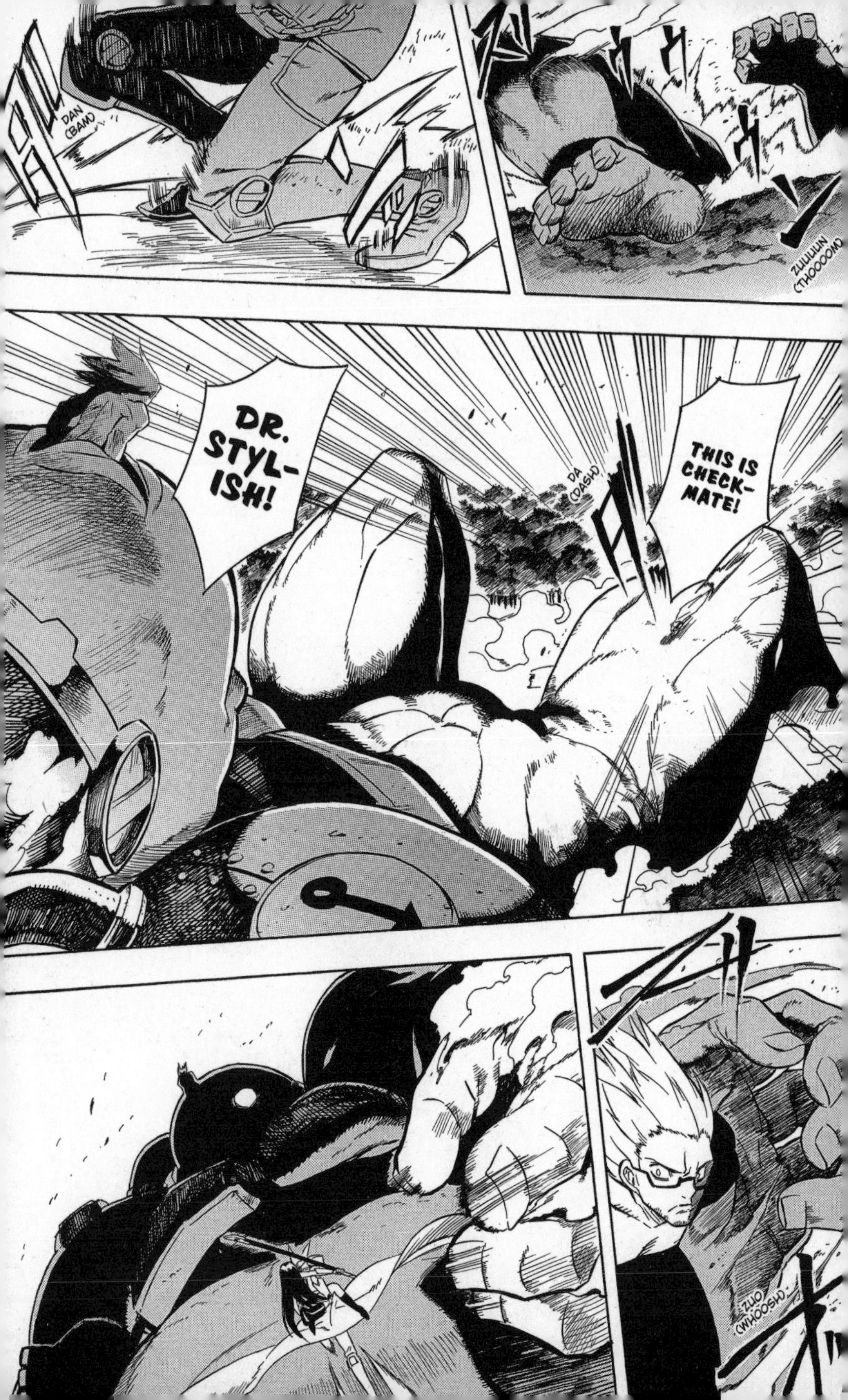
ZUUUUUN (THOOOOOM)
DAN (BAM)
THIS IS CHECKMATE!
DA (DASH)
DR. STYLISH!
ZUO (WHOOSH)

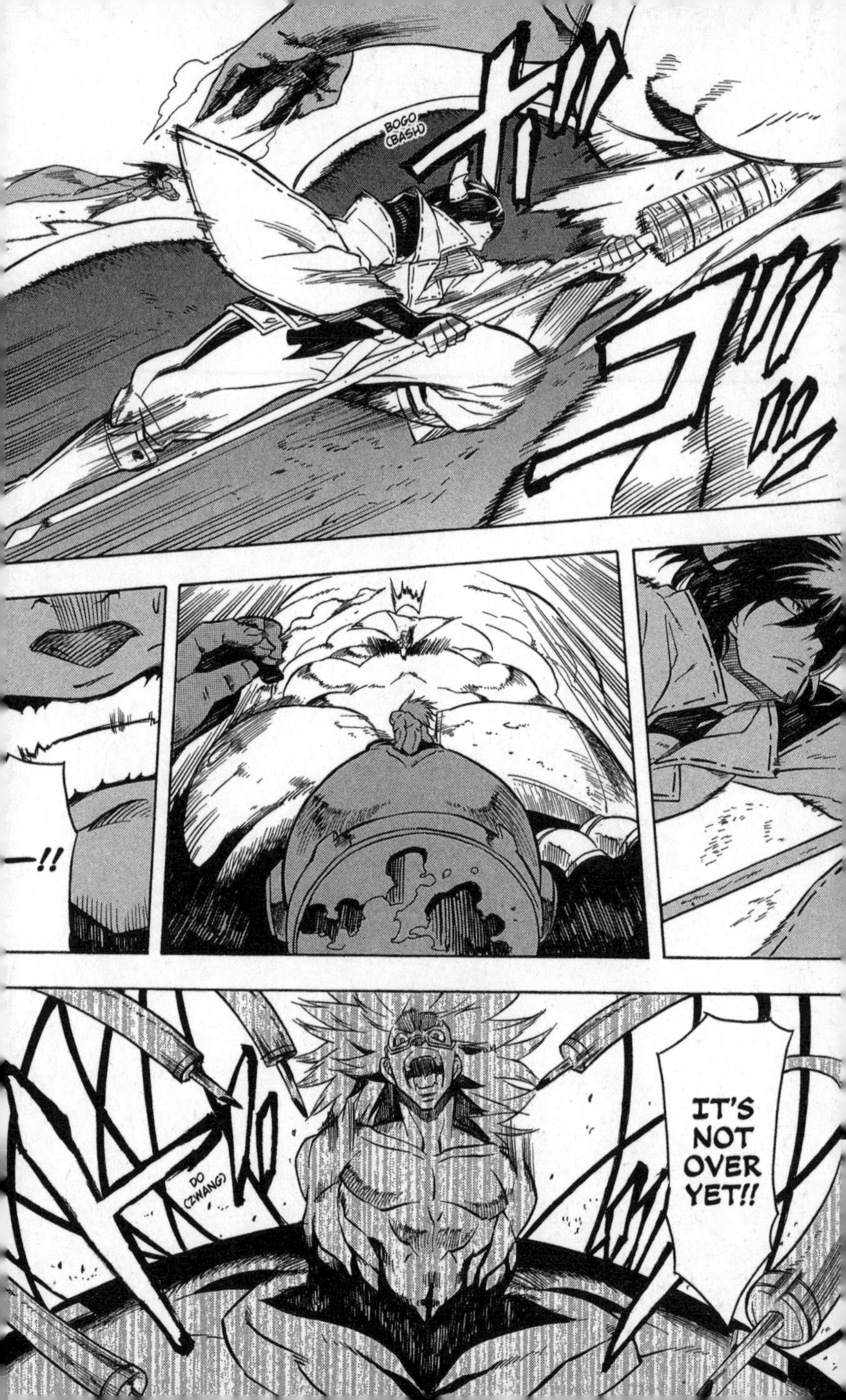
BOGO (BASH)
—!!
IT'S NOT OVER YET!!
DO (ZWANG)

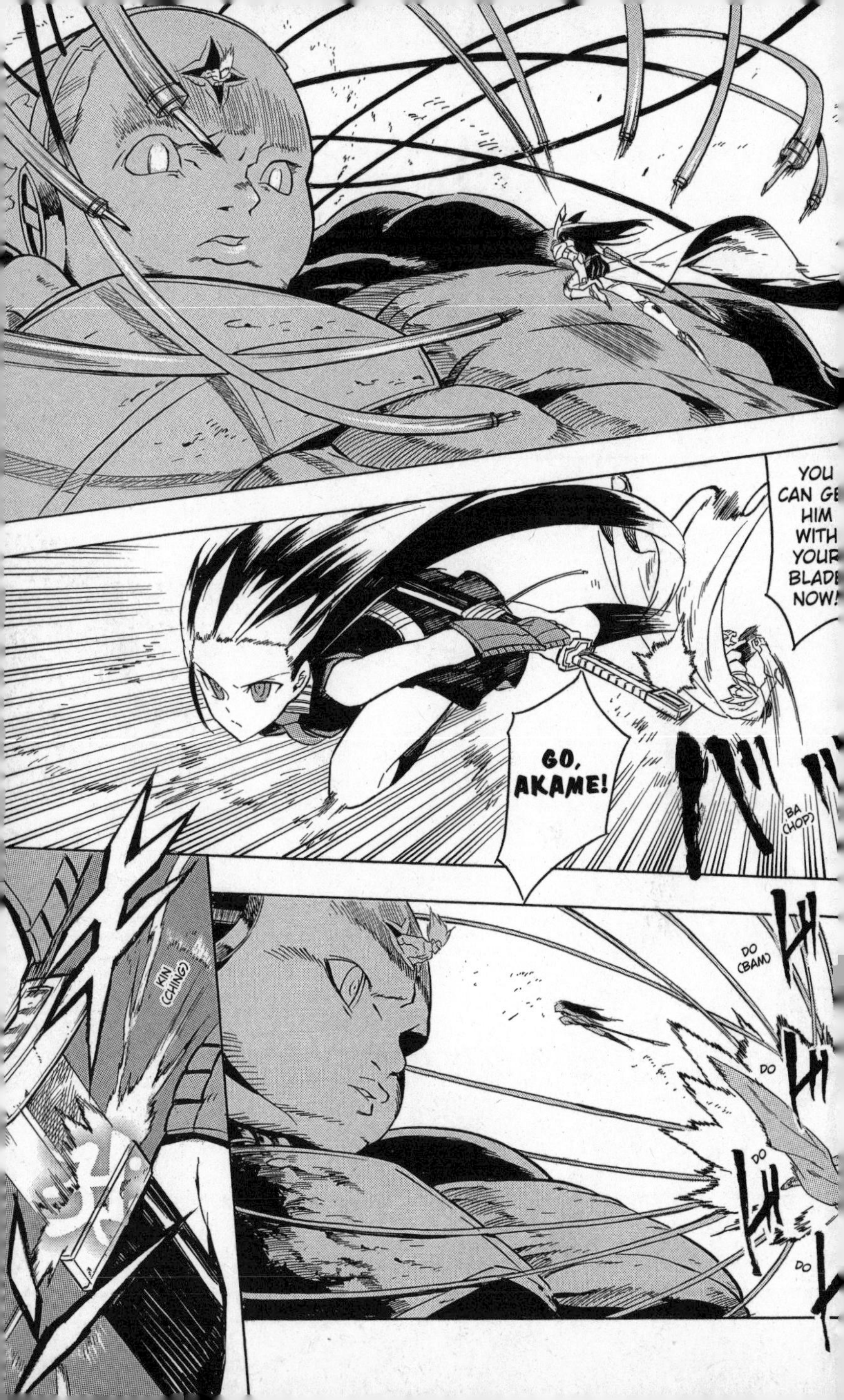

YOU CAN GET HIM WITH YOUR BLADE NOW!
GO, AKAME!
BA (HOP)
KIN (CHING)
DO (BAM)
DO
DO
DO

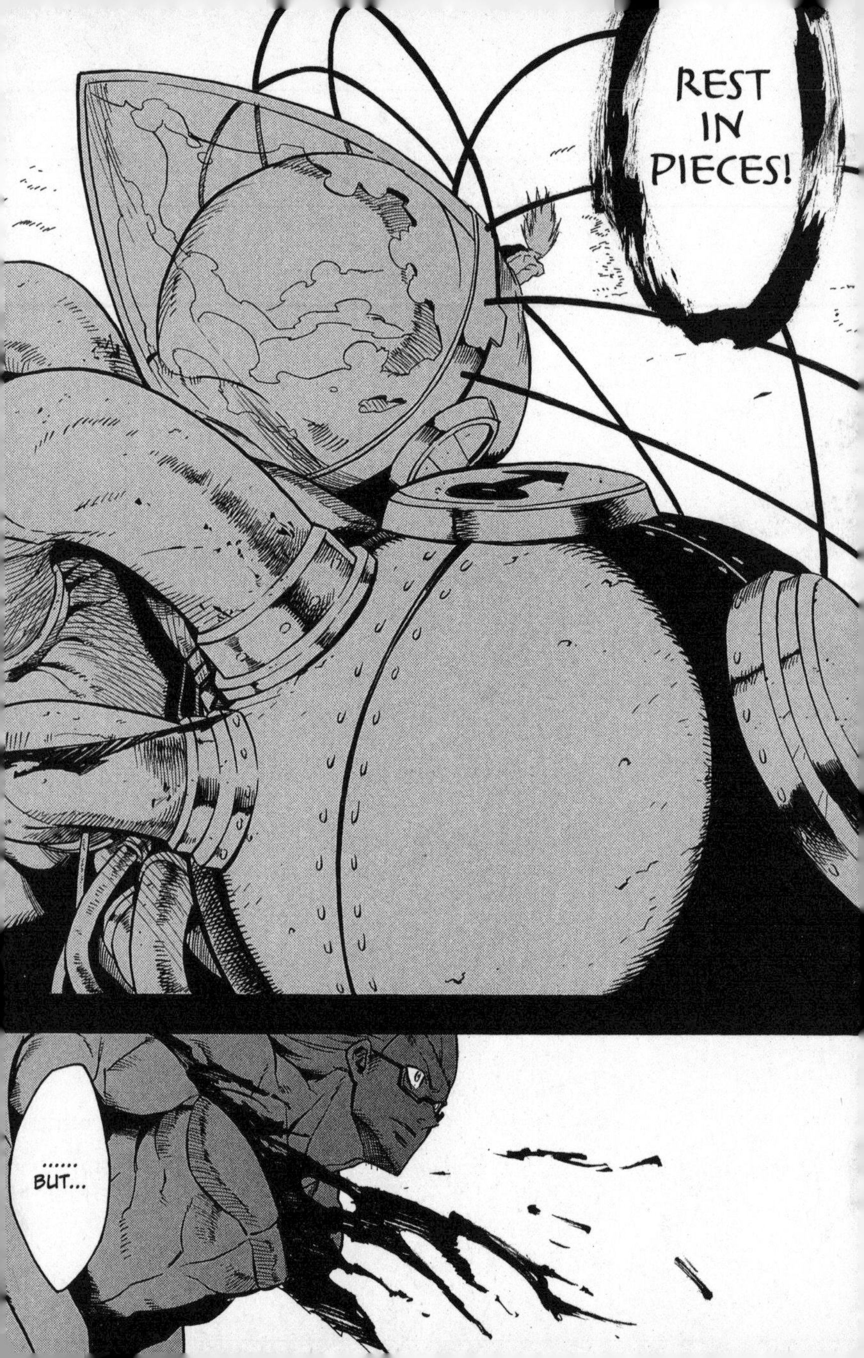
REST IN PIECES!
...... BUT...

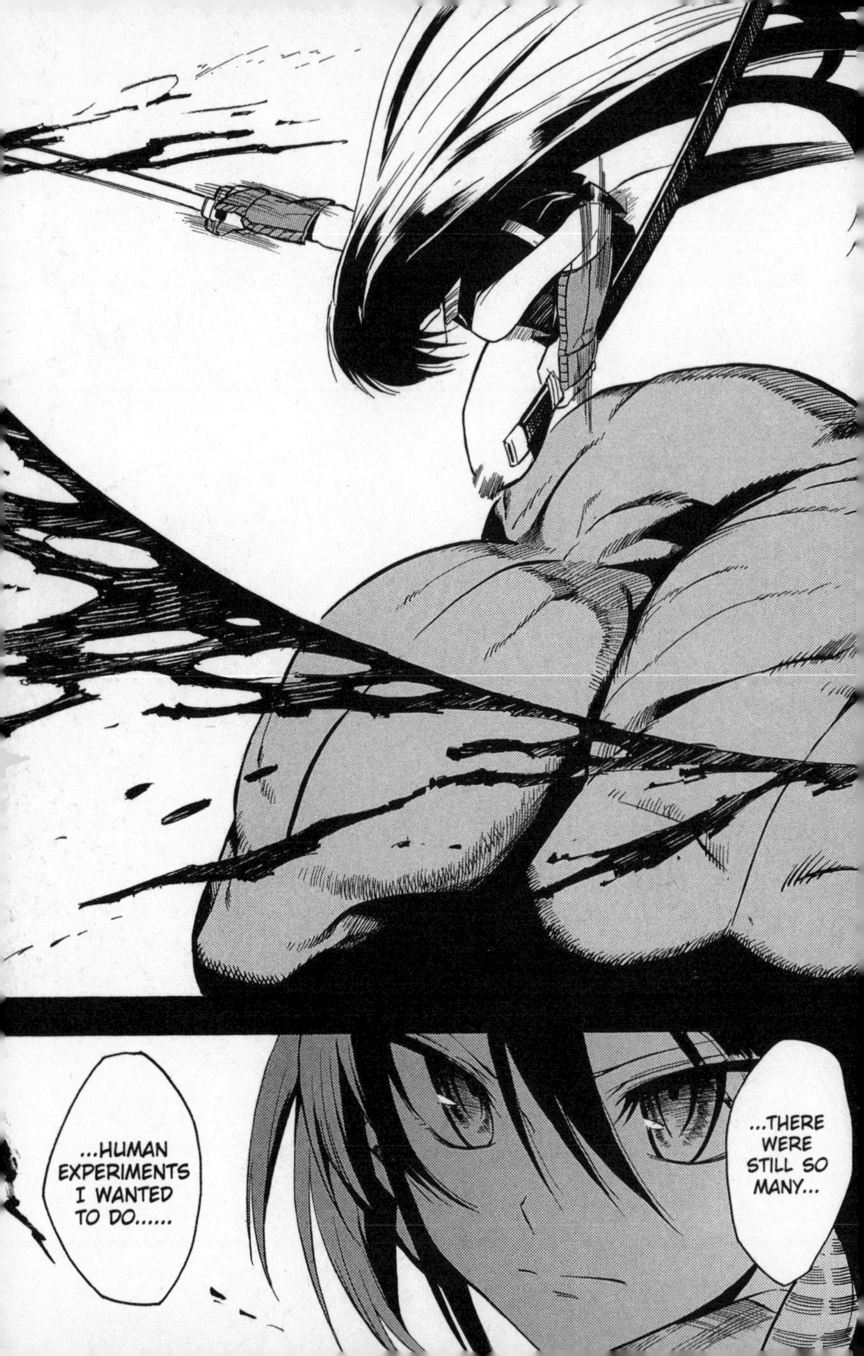
...THERE WERE STILL SO MANY...
...HUMAN EXPERIMENTS I WANTED TO DO......

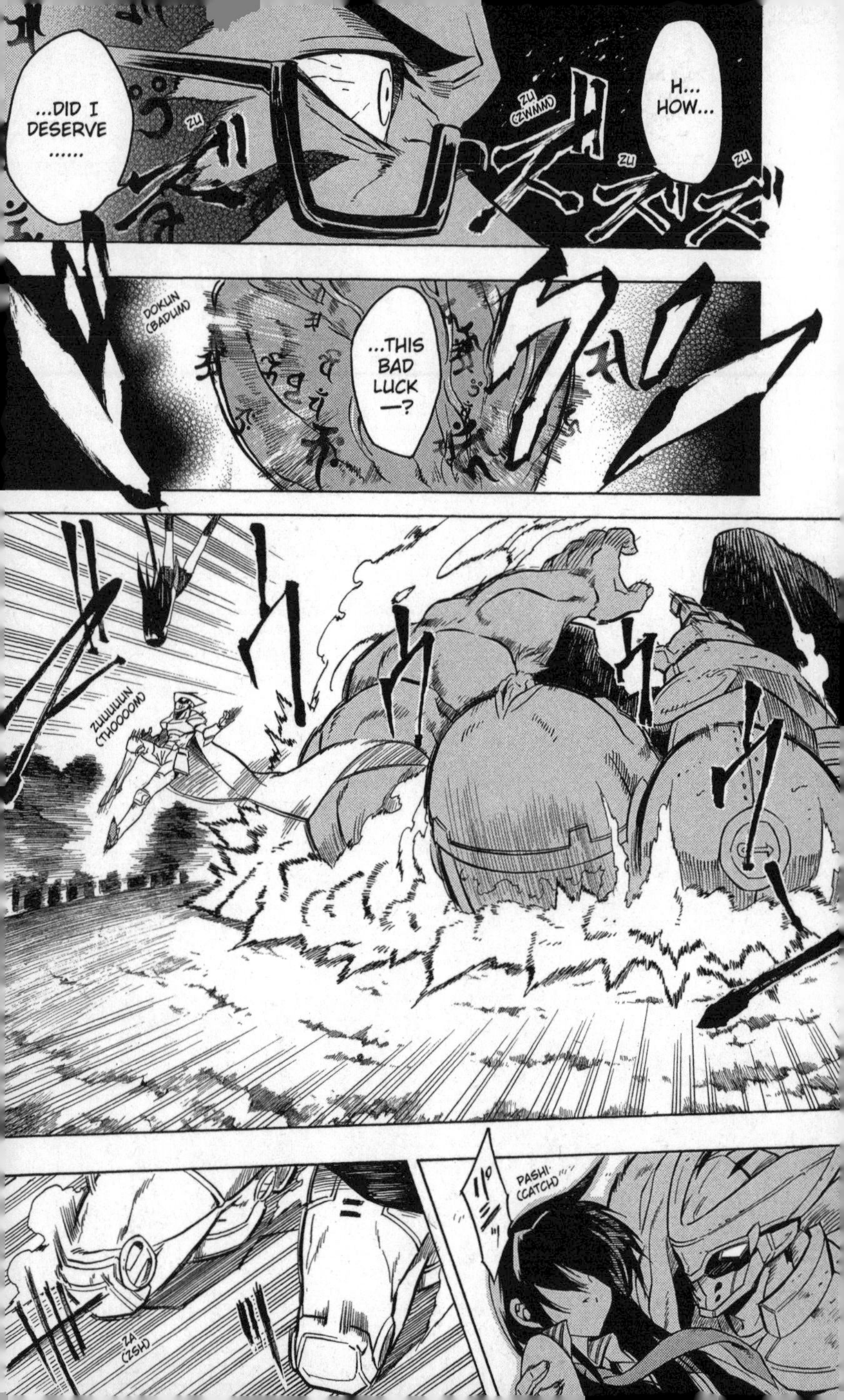
H... HOW...
ZU ZU
ZU (ZWMM)
ZU
...DID I DESERVE ......
...THIS BAD LUCK—?
DOKUN (BADUM)
ZUUUUUN (THOOOOM)
PASHI (CATCH)
ZA (ZSH)

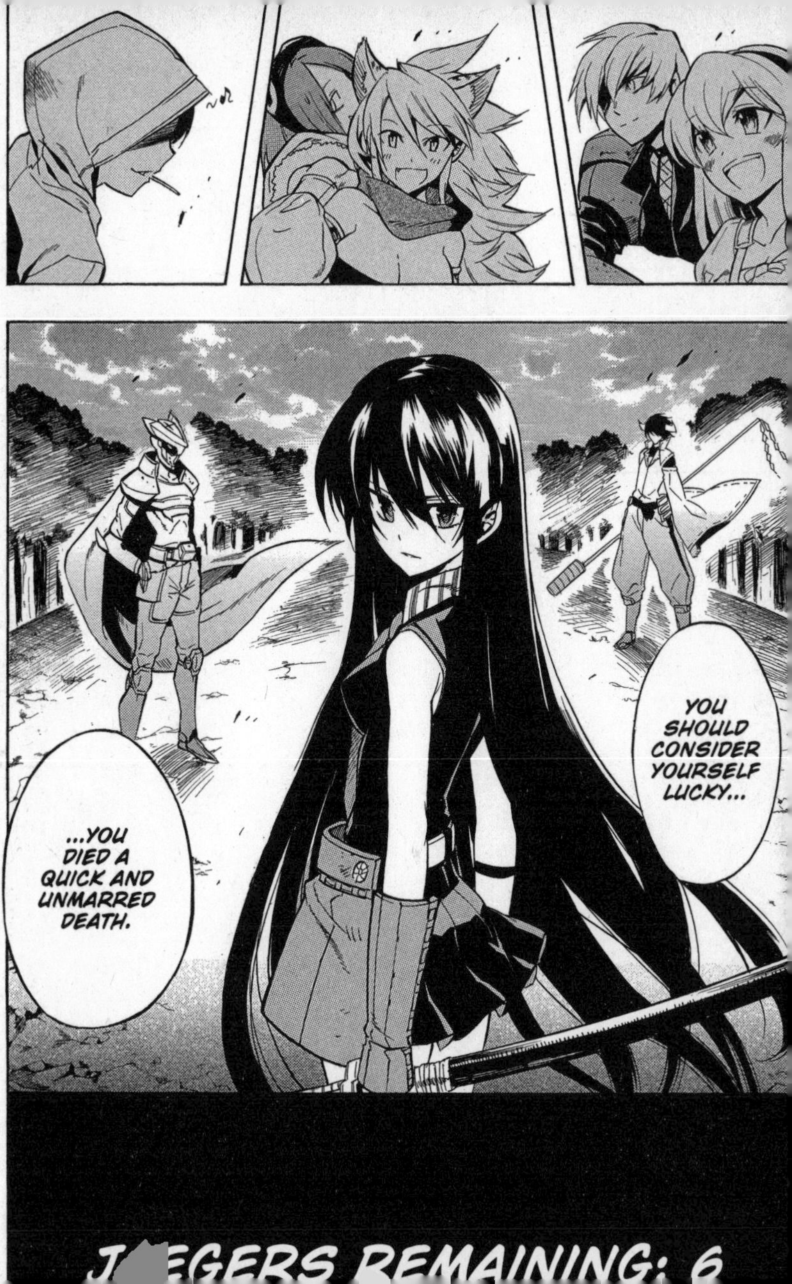

YOU SHOULD CONSIDER YOURSELF LUCKY...
...YOU DIED A QUICK AND UNMARRED DEATH.
J EGERS REMAINING: 6

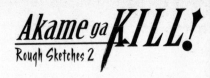

Akame ga KILL!

Rough Sketches 2

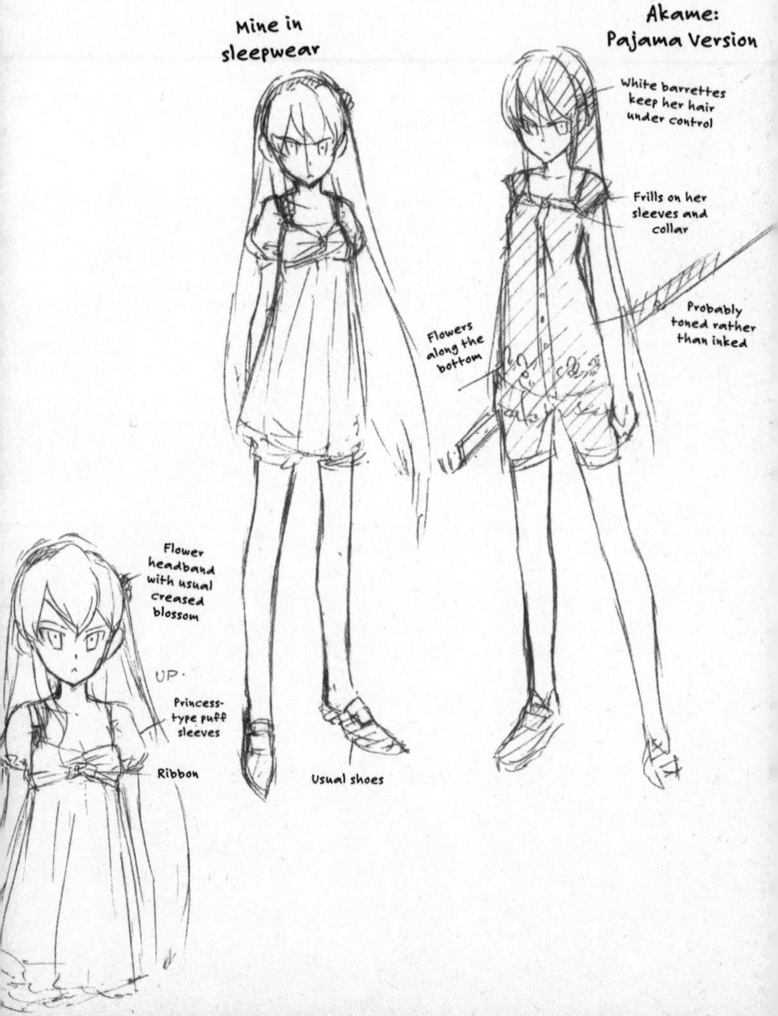

Mine in sleepwear
Akame: Pajama Version
White barrettes keep her hair under control
Frills on her sleeves and collar
Probably toned rather than inked
Flowers along the bottom
Flower headband with usual creased blossom
UP.
Princess-type puff sleeves
Ribbon
Usual shoes

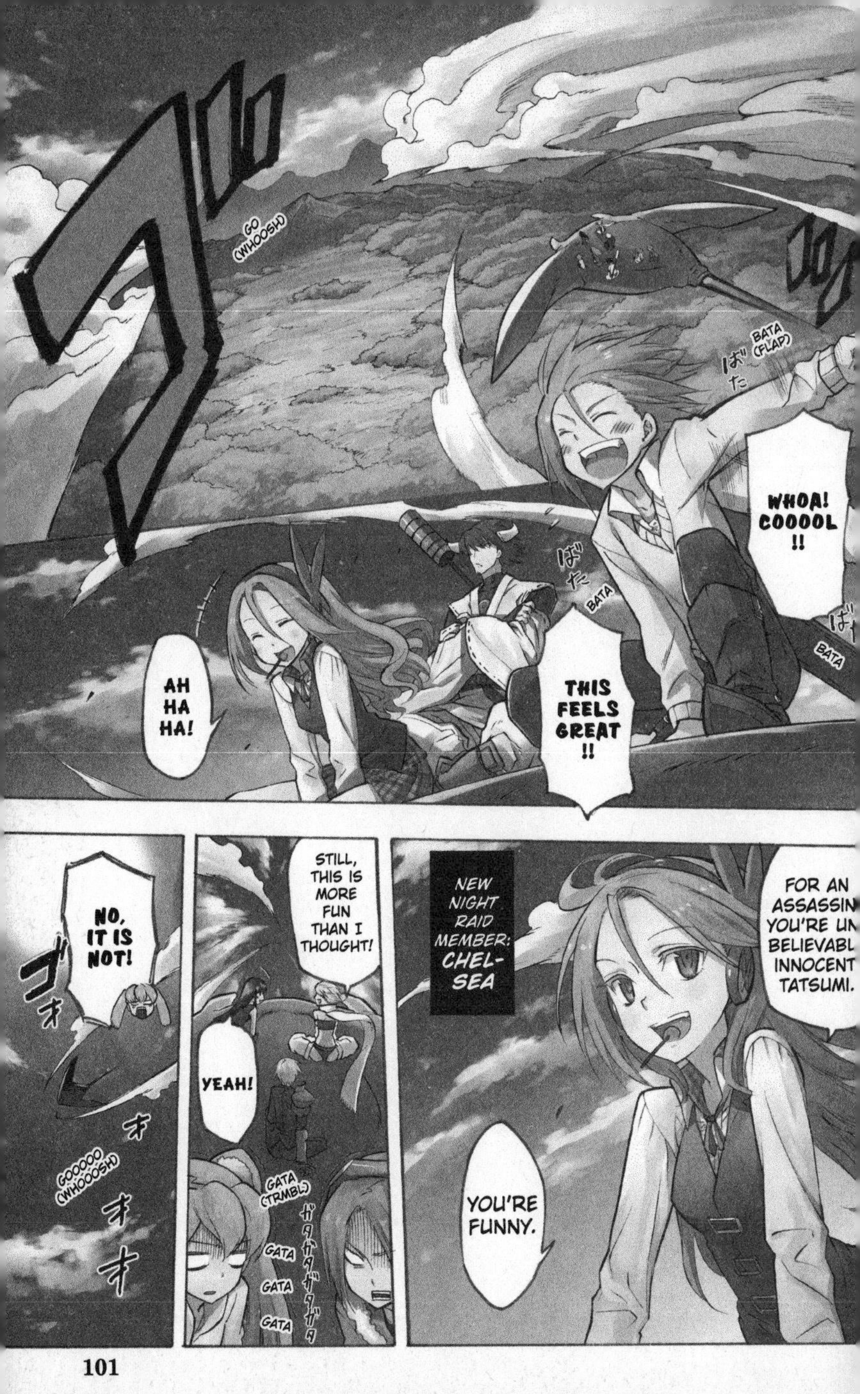
GO (WHOOSH)
BATA (FLAP)
WHOA! COOOOL!!
BATA
BATA
THIS FEELS GREAT!!
AH HA HA!
FOR AN ASSASSIN YOU'RE UN BELIEVABL INNOCENT TATSUMI.
NEW NIGHT RAID MEMBER: CHEL-SEA
YOU'RE FUNNY.
STILL, THIS IS MORE FUN THAN I THOUGHT!
YEAH!
GATA (TRMBL)
GATA
GATA
GATA
NO, IT IS NOT!
GOOOOO (WHOOOSH)

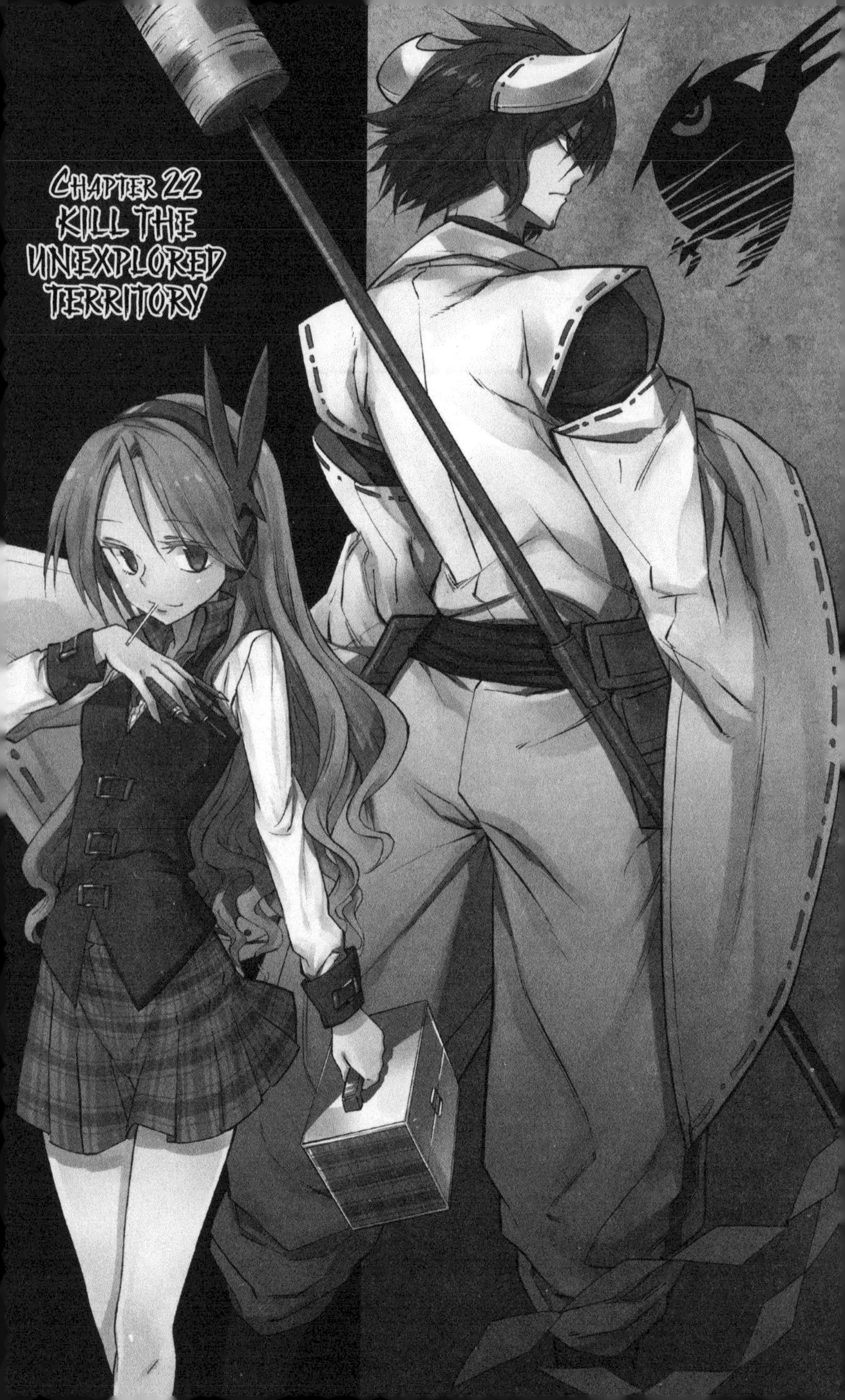
Chapter 22
Kill the Unexplored Territory

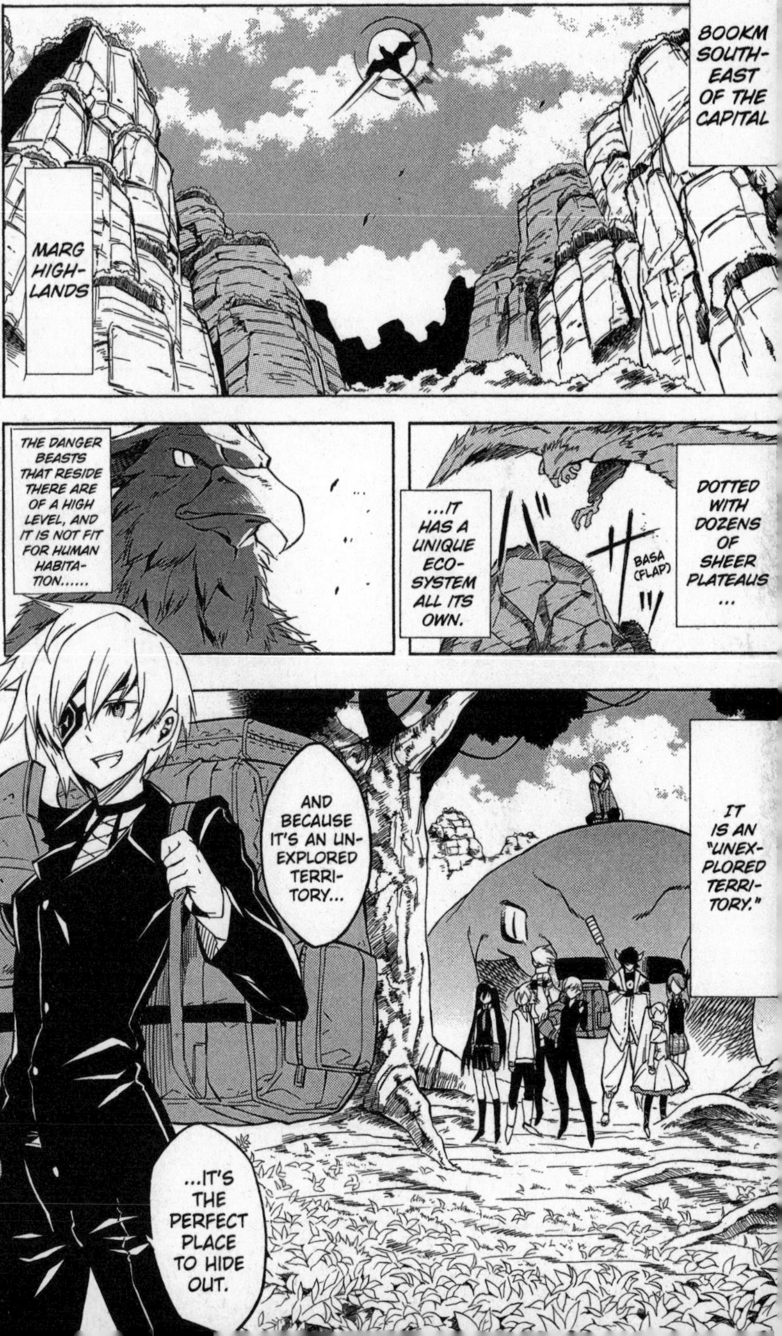
800KM SOUTH-EAST OF THE CAPITAL
MARG HIGH-LANDS
DOTTED WITH DOZENS OF SHEER PLATEAUS ...
BASA (FLAP)
...IT HAS A UNIQUE ECO-SYSTEM ALL ITS OWN.
THE DANGER BEASTS THAT RESIDE THERE ARE OF A HIGH LEVEL, AND IT IS NOT FIT FOR HUMAN HABITA-TION......
IT IS AN "UNEX-PLORED TERRI-TORY."
AND BECAUSE IT'S AN UN-EXPLORED TERRI-TORY...
...IT'S THE PERFECT PLACE TO HIDE OUT.

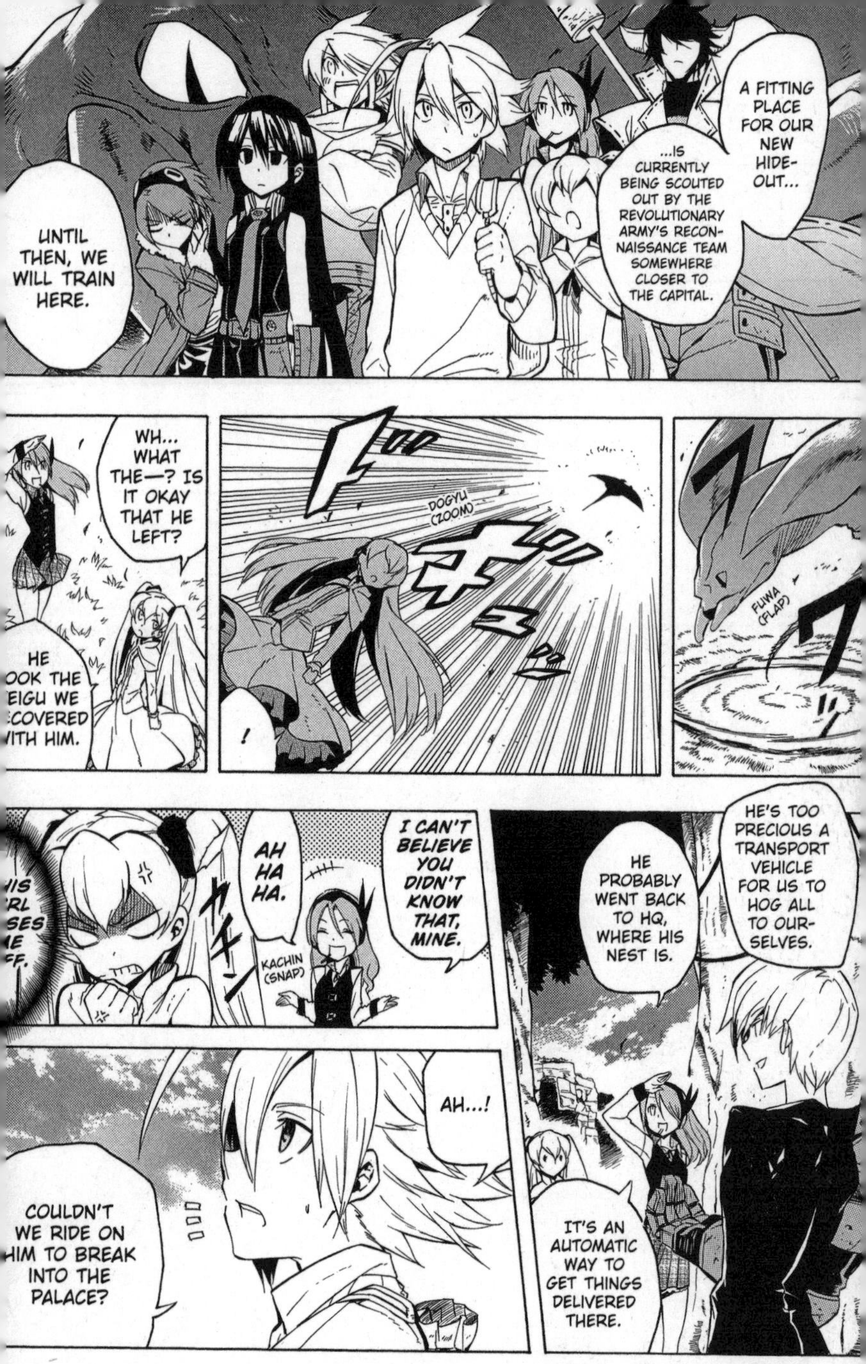
A FITTING PLACE FOR OUR NEW HIDE-OUT...
...IS CURRENTLY BEING SCOUTED OUT BY THE REVOLUTIONARY ARMY'S RECONNAISSANCE TEAM SOMEWHERE CLOSER TO THE CAPITAL.
UNTIL THEN, WE WILL TRAIN HERE.
FUWA (FLAP)
DOGYU (ZOOM)
!
WH... WHAT THE—? IS IT OKAY THAT HE LEFT?
HE OOK THE EIGU WE ECOVERED ITH HIM.
HE'S TOO PRECIOUS A TRANSPORT VEHICLE FOR US TO HOG ALL TO OURSELVES.
HE PROBABLY WENT BACK TO HQ, WHERE HIS NEST IS.
IT'S AN AUTOMATIC WAY TO GET THINGS DELIVERED THERE.
I CAN'T BELIEVE YOU DIDN'T KNOW THAT, MINE.
KACHIN (SNAP)
AH HA HA.
AH...!
COULDN'T WE RIDE ON IIM TO BREAK INTO THE PALACE?

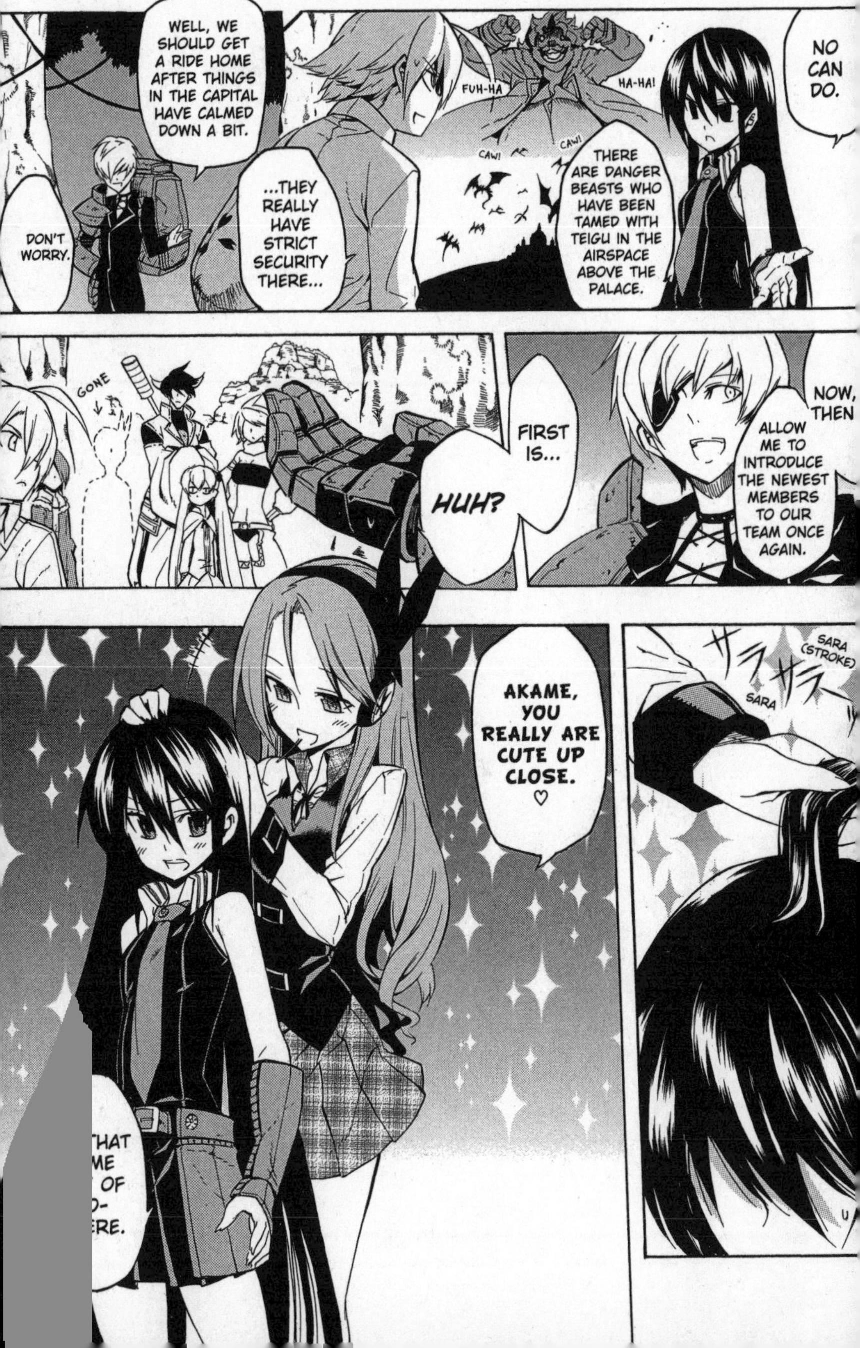
NO CAN DO.
THERE ARE DANGER BEASTS WHO HAVE BEEN TAMED WITH TEIGU IN THE AIRSPACE ABOVE THE PALACE.
CAW!
CAW!
FUH-HA
HA-HA!
...THEY REALLY HAVE STRICT SECURITY THERE...
WELL, WE SHOULD GET A RIDE HOME AFTER THINGS IN THE CAPITAL HAVE CALMED DOWN A BIT.
DON'T WORRY.
NOW, THEN
ALLOW ME TO INTRODUCE THE NEWEST MEMBERS TO OUR TEAM ONCE AGAIN.
FIRST IS...
HUH?
GONE
SARA (STROKE)
SARA
AKAME, YOU REALLY ARE CUTE UP CLOSE. ♡
THAT
ME
OF
ERE.

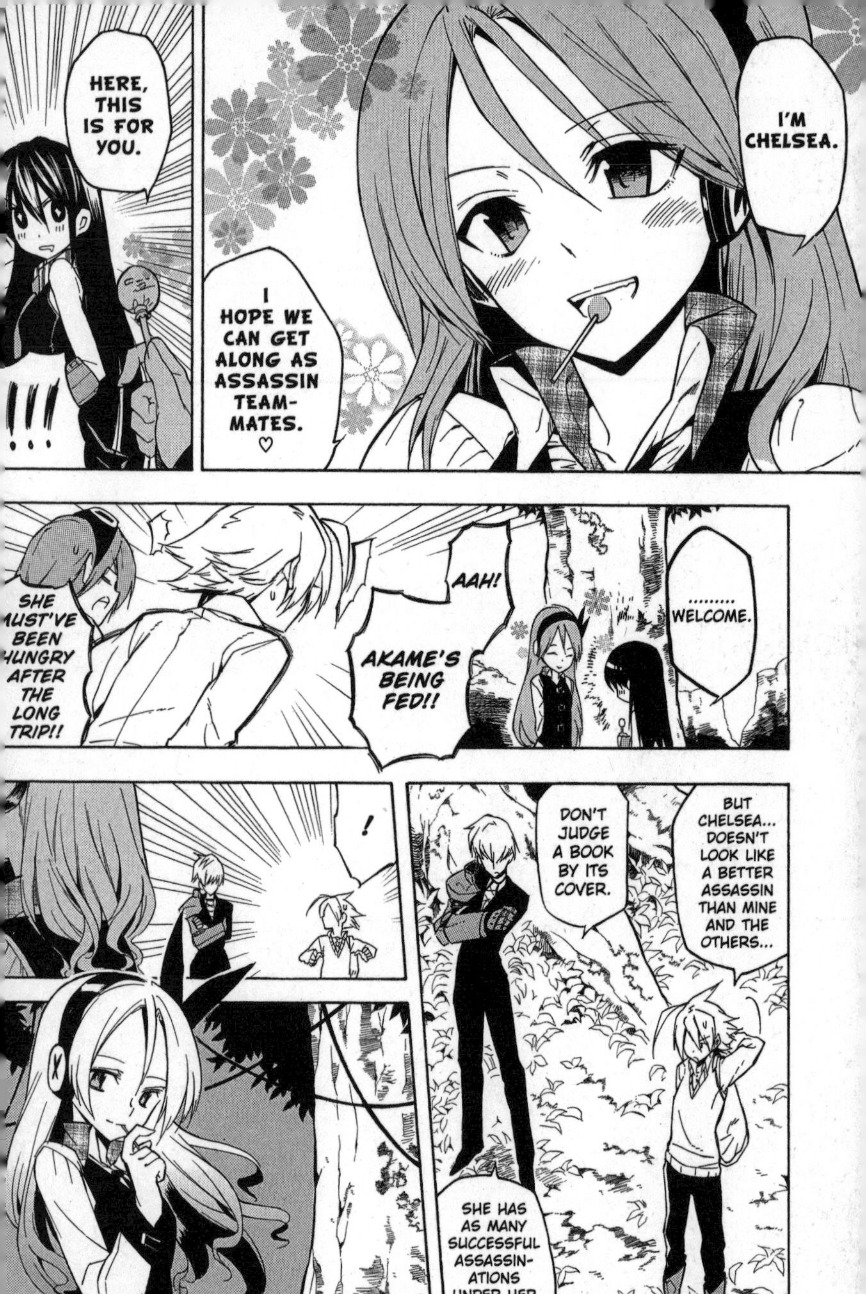
I'M CHELSEA.
I HOPE WE CAN GET ALONG AS ASSASSIN TEAM-MATES. ♡
HERE, THIS IS FOR YOU.
!!!...
.... WELCOME.
AAH!
AKAME'S BEING FED!!
SHE MUST'VE BEEN HUNGRY AFTER THE LONG TRIP!!
BUT CHELSEA... DOESN'T LOOK LIKE A BETTER ASSASSIN THAN MINE AND THE OTHERS...
DON'T JUDGE A BOOK BY ITS COVER.
SHE HAS AS MANY SUCCESSFUL ASSASSIN-ATIONS UNDER HER BELT AS AKAME.
!

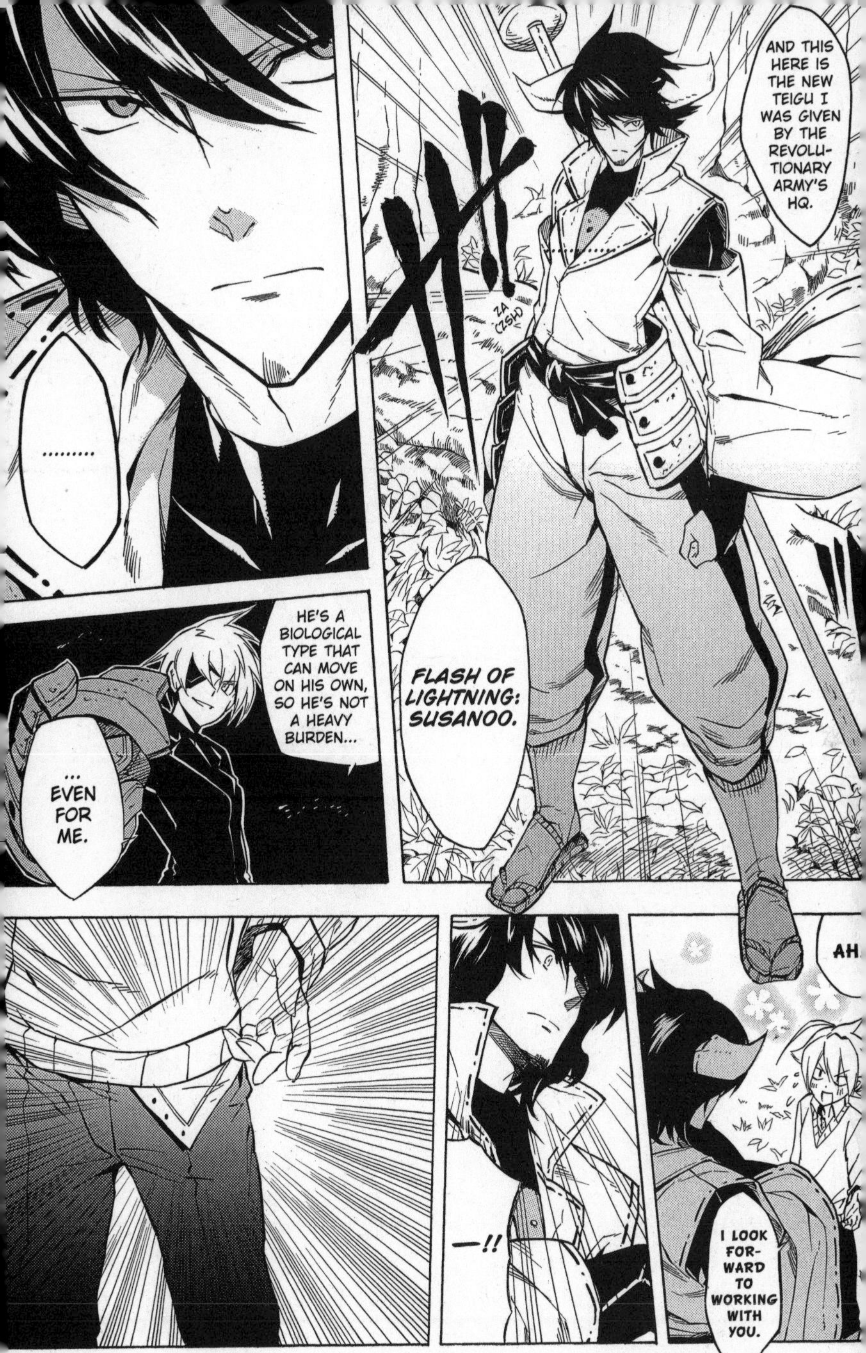

AND THIS HERE IS THE NEW TEIGU I WAS GIVEN BY THE REVOLUTIONARY ARMY'S HQ.
FLASH OF LIGHTNING: SUSANOO.
....
HE'S A BIOLOGICAL TYPE THAT CAN MOVE ON HIS OWN, SO HE'S NOT A HEAVY BURDEN...
... EVEN FOR ME.
AH.
I LOOK FORWARD TO WORKING WITH YOU.
—!!

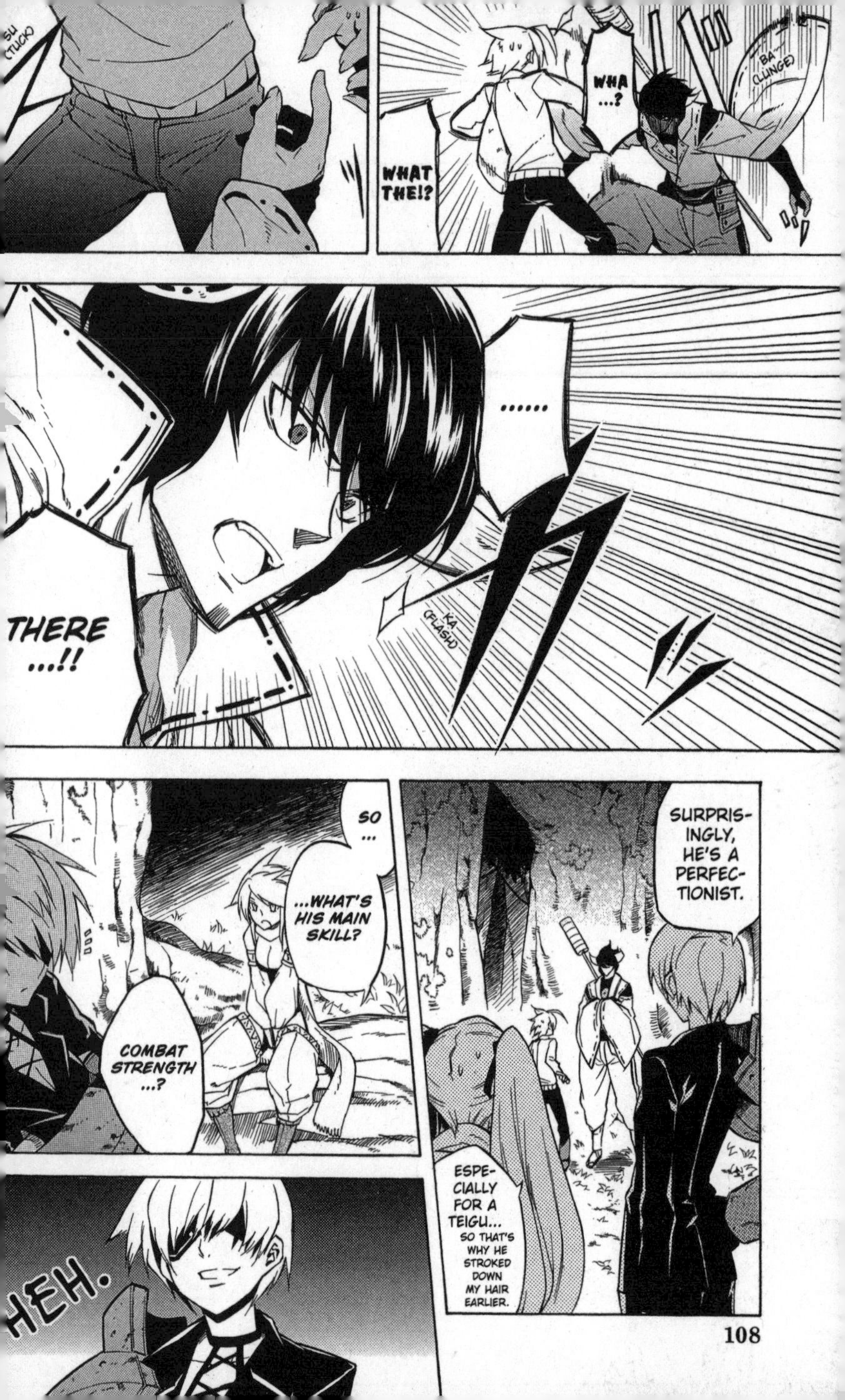
BA- (LUNGE)
WHA ...?
WHAT THE!?
SU (TUCK)
......
KA (FLASH)
THERE ...!!
SURPRIS-INGLY, HE'S A PERFEC-TIONIST.
ESPE-CIALLY FOR A TEIGU...
SO THAT'S WHY HE STROKED DOWN MY HAIR EARLIER.
SO ...
...WHAT'S HIS MAIN SKILL?
COMBAT STRENGTH ...?
HEH.

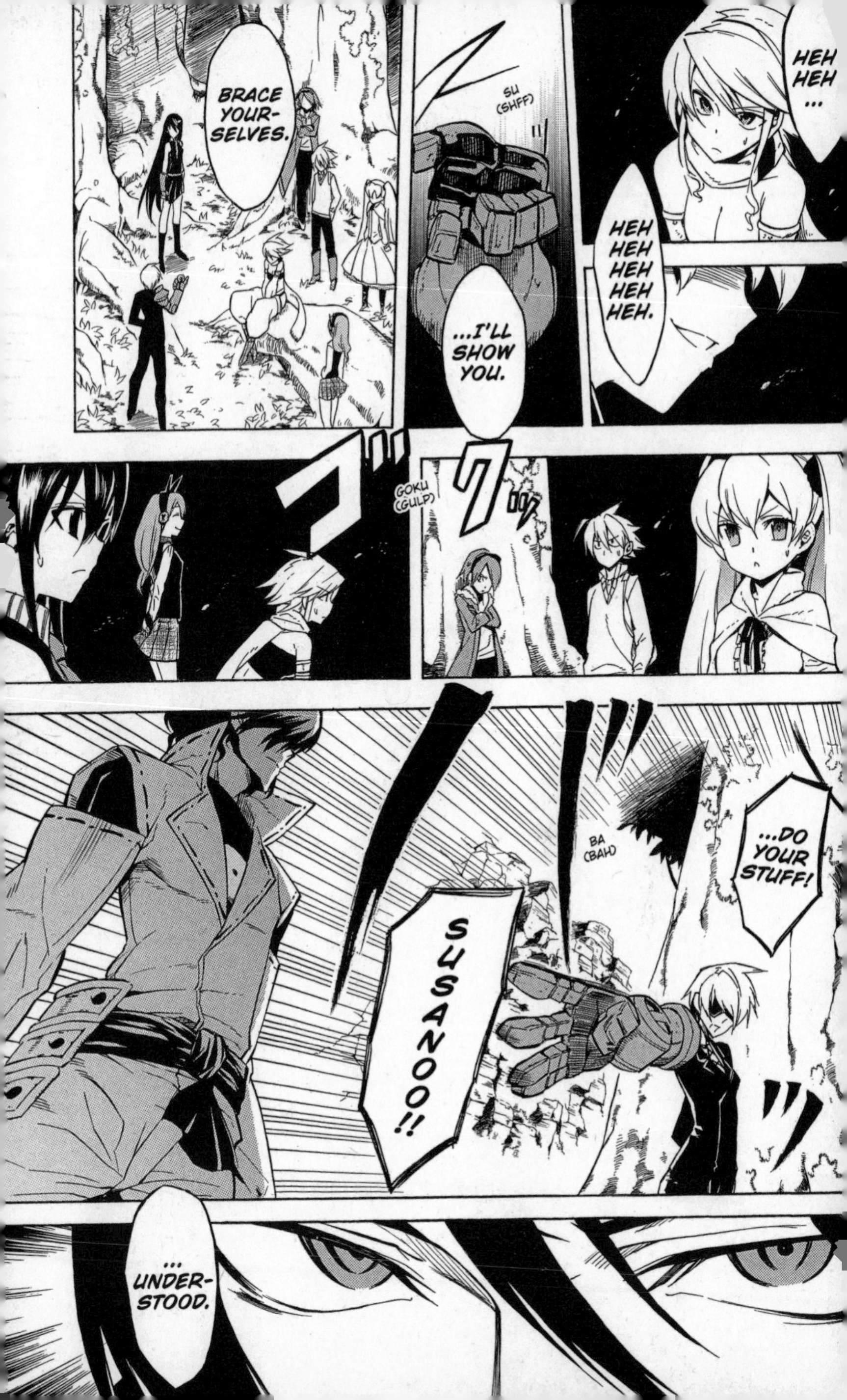

HEH HEH ...
HEH HEH HEH HEH HEH.
SU (SHFF)
...I'LL SHOW YOU.
BRACE YOUR-SELVES.
GOKU (GULP)
...DO YOUR STUFF!
BA (BAH)
SUSANOO!!
... UNDER-STOOD.

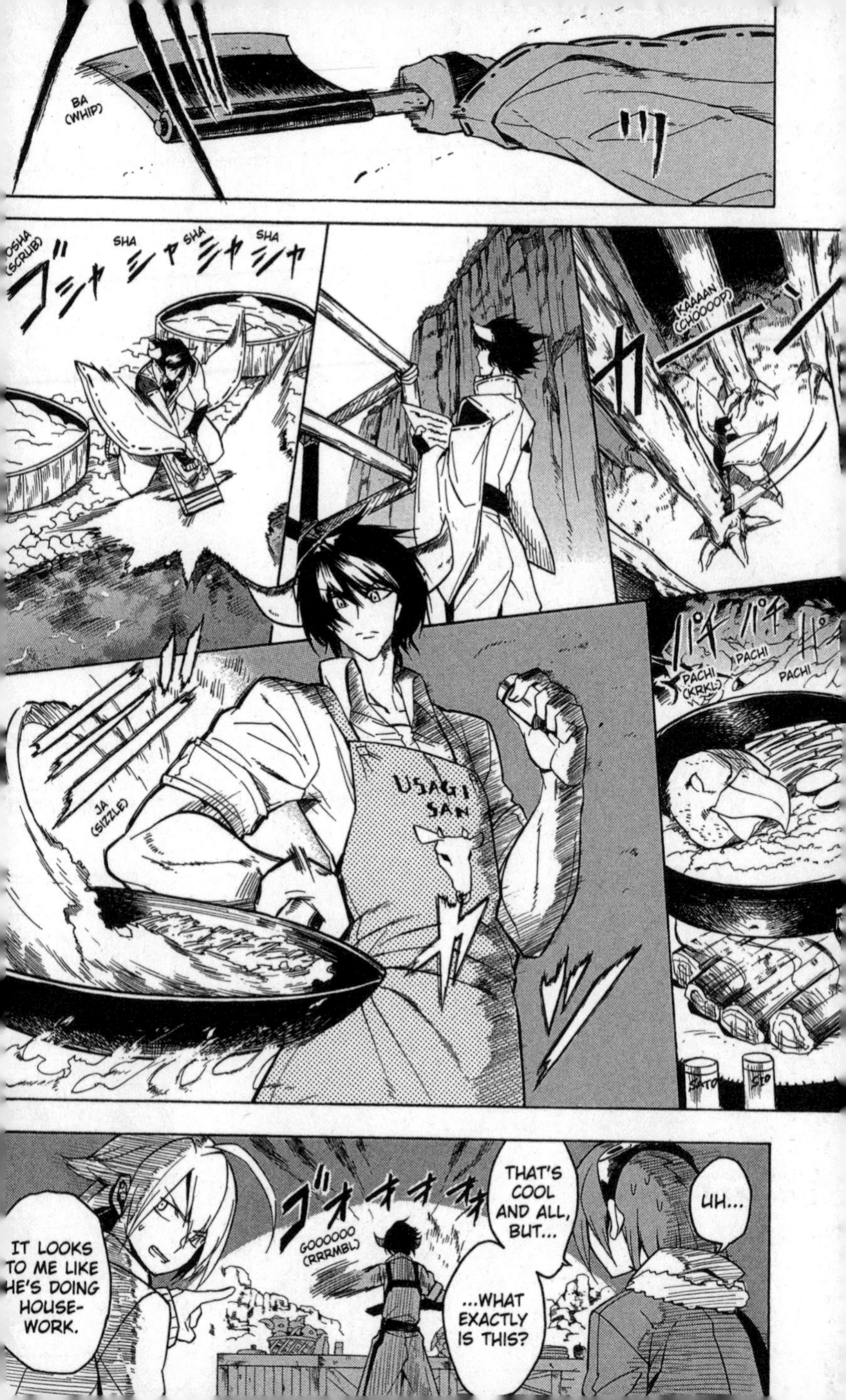

BA
(WHIP)
KAAAAN
(CHOOOOP)
GOSHA
(SCRUB)
SHA
SHA
SHA
PACHI
(KRKL)
PACHI
PACHI
JA
(SIZZLE)
USAGI SAN
SATO
SIO
UH...
THAT'S COOL AND ALL, BUT...
...WHAT EXACTLY IS THIS?
GOOOOOO
(RRRMBL)
IT LOOKS TO ME LIKE HE'S DOING HOUSE-WORK.

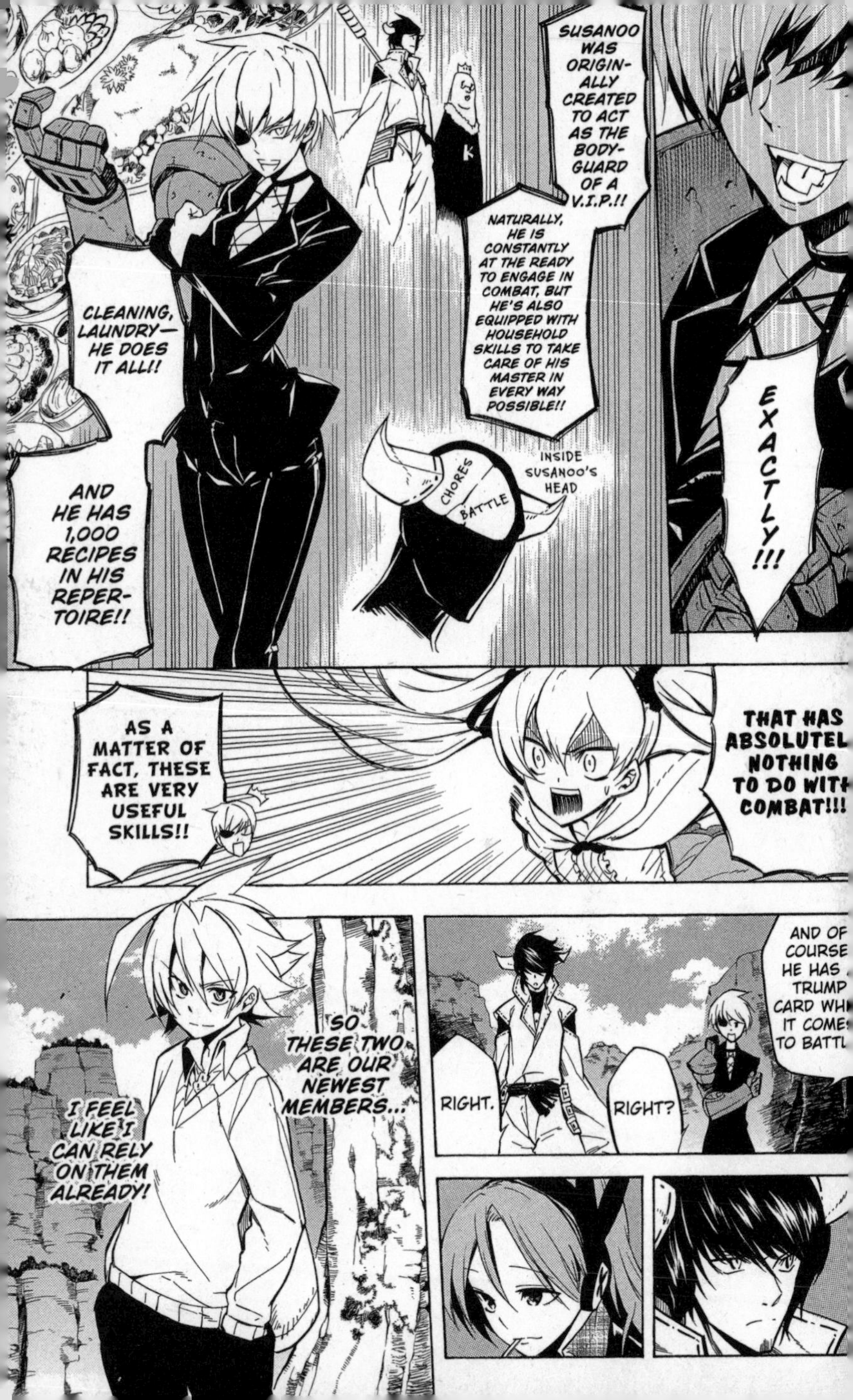
SUSANOO WAS ORIGIN-ALLY CREATED TO ACT AS THE BODY-GUARD OF A V.I.P.!!
NATURALLY, HE IS CONSTANTLY AT THE READY TO ENGAGE IN COMBAT, BUT HE'S ALSO EQUIPPED WITH HOUSEHOLD SKILLS TO TAKE CARE OF HIS MASTER IN EVERY WAY POSSIBLE!!
EXACTLY!!!
CLEANING, LAUNDRY— HE DOES IT ALL!!
INSIDE SUSANOO'S HEAD
CHORES
BATTLE
AND HE HAS 1,000 RECIPES IN HIS REPER-TOIRE!!
THAT HAS ABSOLUTEL NOTHING TO DO WIT COMBAT!!!
AS A MATTER OF FACT, THESE ARE VERY USEFUL SKILLS!!
AND OF COURSE HE HAS TRUMP CARD WH IT COMES TO BATTL
RIGHT?
RIGHT.
SO THESE TWO ARE OUR NEWEST MEMBERS...
I FEEL LIKE I CAN RELY ON THEM ALREADY!

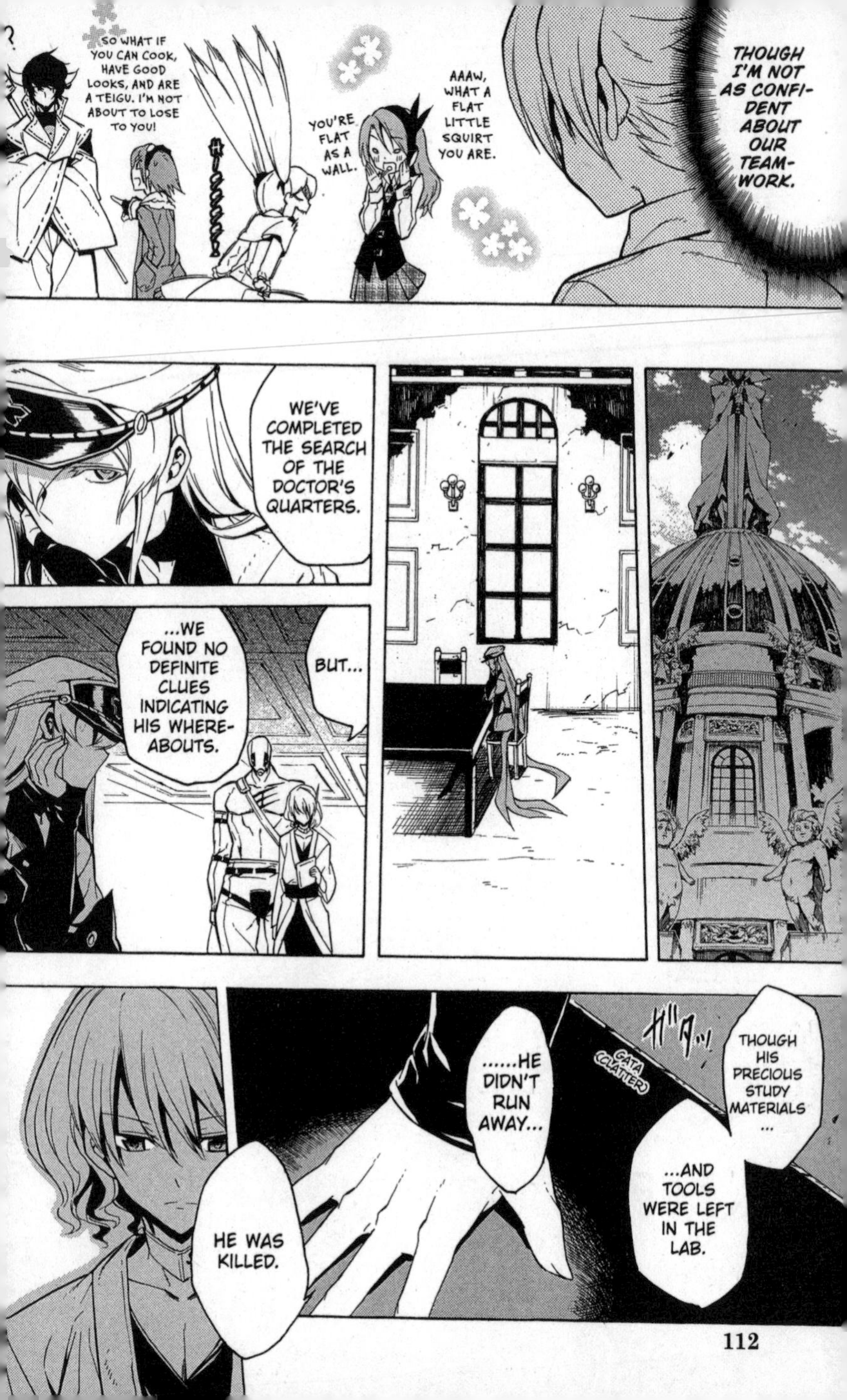
THOUGH I'M NOT AS CONFIDENT ABOUT OUR TEAMWORK.
AAAW, WHAT A FLAT LITTLE SQUIRT YOU ARE.
YOU'RE FLAT AS A WALL.
SO WHAT IF YOU CAN COOK, HAVE GOOD LOOKS, AND ARE A TEIGU. I'M NOT ABOUT TO LOSE TO YOU!
WE'VE COMPLETED THE SEARCH OF THE DOCTOR'S QUARTERS.
BUT...
...WE FOUND NO DEFINITE CLUES INDICATING HIS WHEREABOUTS.
THOUGH HIS PRECIOUS STUDY MATERIALS ...
...AND TOOLS WERE LEFT IN THE LAB.
GATA (CLATTER)
......HE DIDN'T RUN AWAY...
HE WAS KILLED.

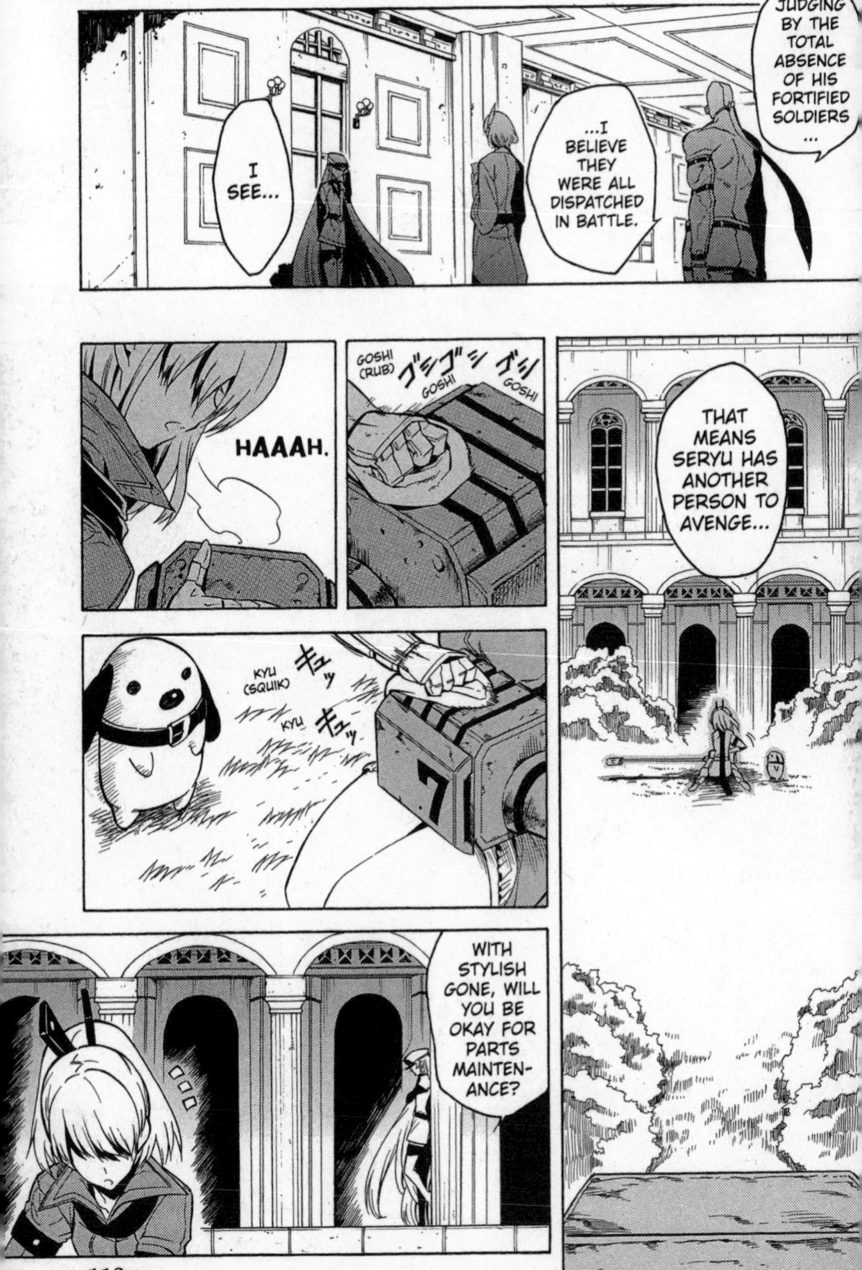
JUDGING BY THE TOTAL ABSENCE OF HIS FORTIFIED SOLDIERS...
...I BELIEVE THEY WERE ALL DISPATCHED IN BATTLE.
I SEE...
THAT MEANS SERYU HAS ANOTHER PERSON TO AVENGE...
GOSHI (RUB)
ゴシゴシ
GOSHI
ゴシ
GOSHI
HAAAH.
キュッ
KYU (SQUIK)
キュッ
KYU
WITH STYLISH GONE, WILL YOU BE OKAY FOR PARTS MAINTENANCE?

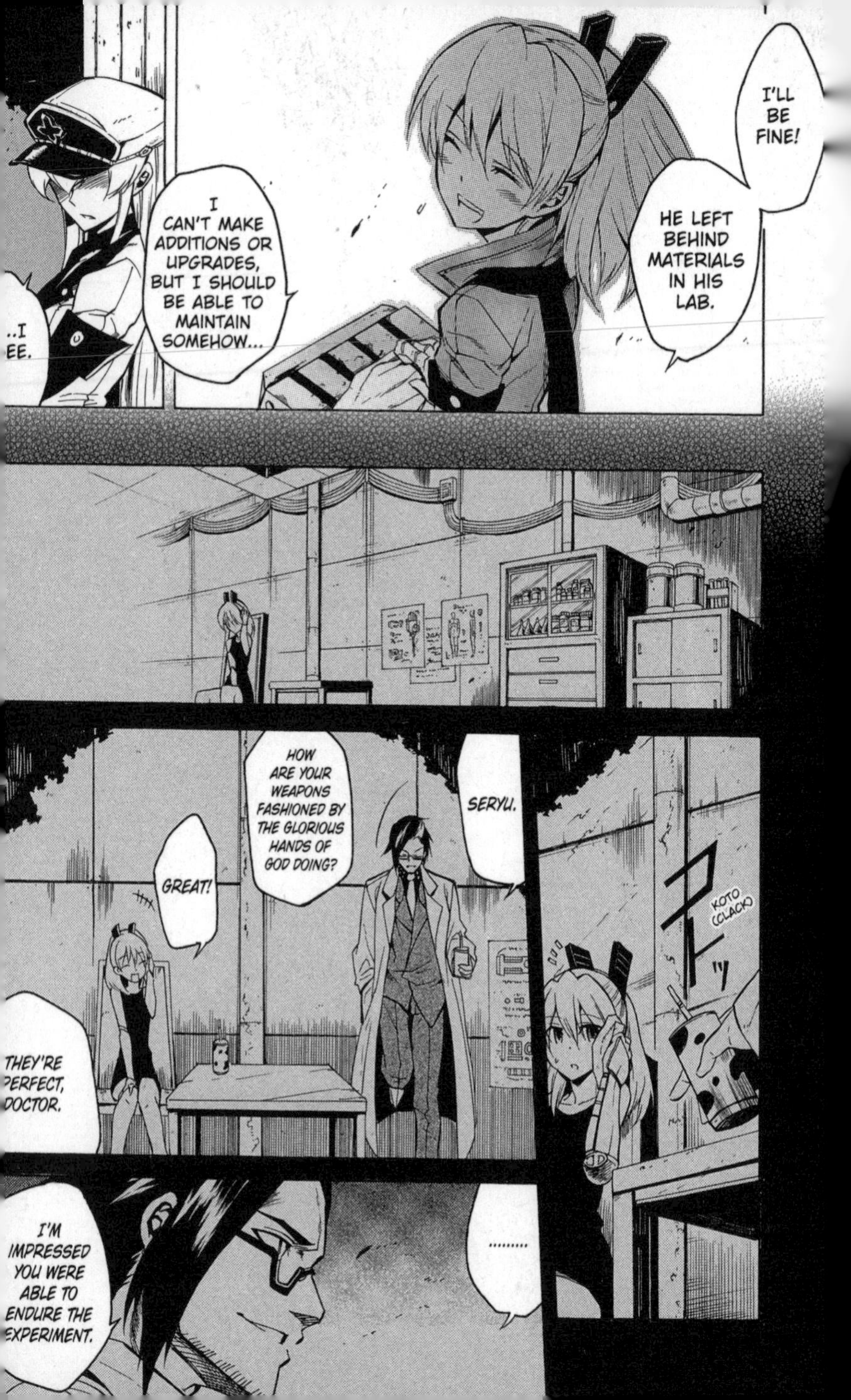
I'LL BE FINE!
HE LEFT BEHIND MATERIALS IN HIS LAB.
I CAN'T MAKE ADDITIONS OR UPGRADES, BUT I SHOULD BE ABLE TO MAINTAIN SOMEHOW...
..I EE.
KOTO (CLACK)
SERYU.
HOW ARE YOUR WEAPONS FASHIONED BY THE GLORIOUS HANDS OF GOD DOING?
GREAT!
THEY'RE ERFECT, DOCTOR.
....
I'M IMPRESSED YOU WERE ABLE TO ENDURE THE EXPERIMENT.

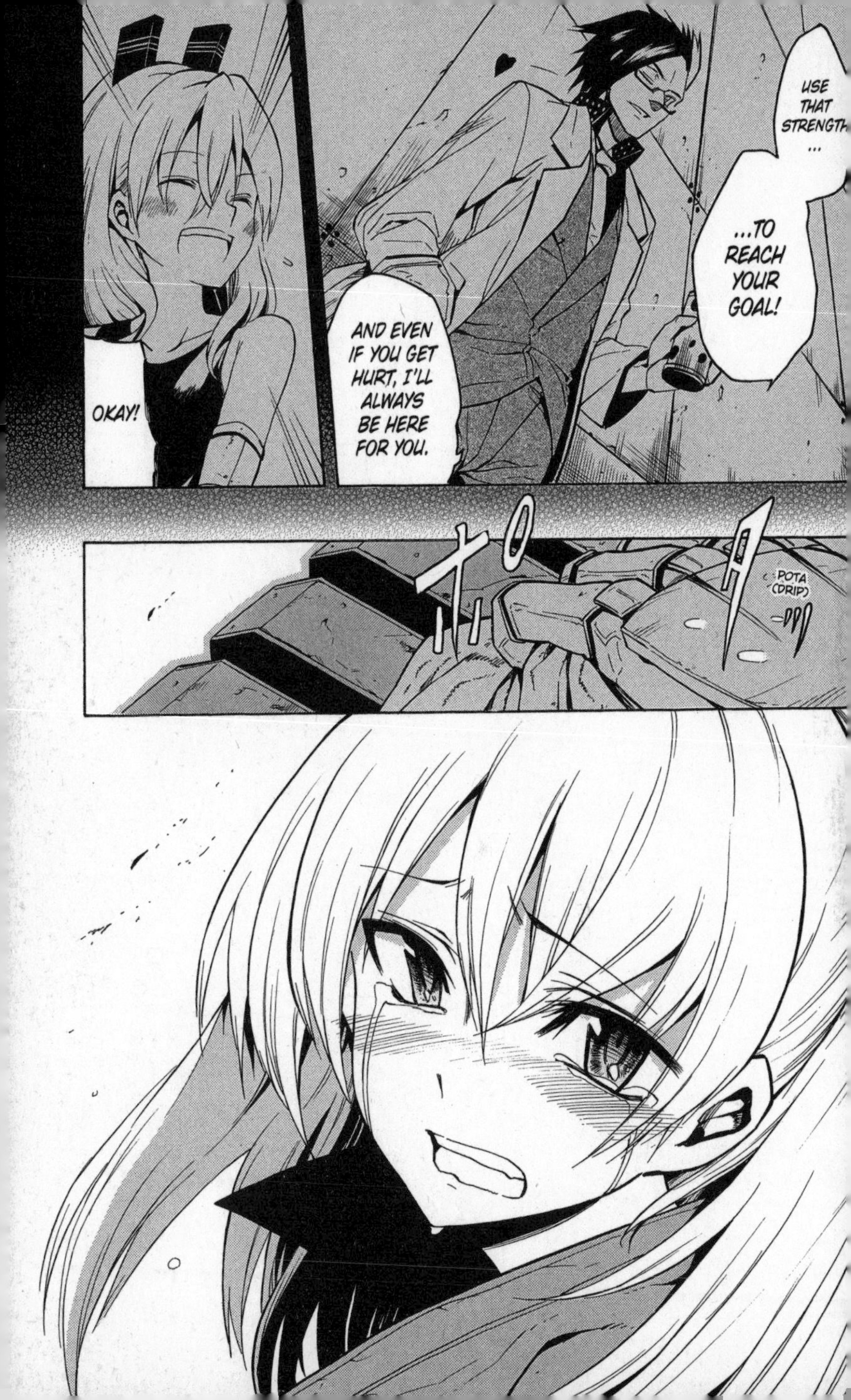
USE THAT STRENGTH...
...TO REACH YOUR GOAL!
AND EVEN IF YOU GET HURT, I'LL ALWAYS BE HERE FOR YOU.
OKAY!
POTA (DRIP)

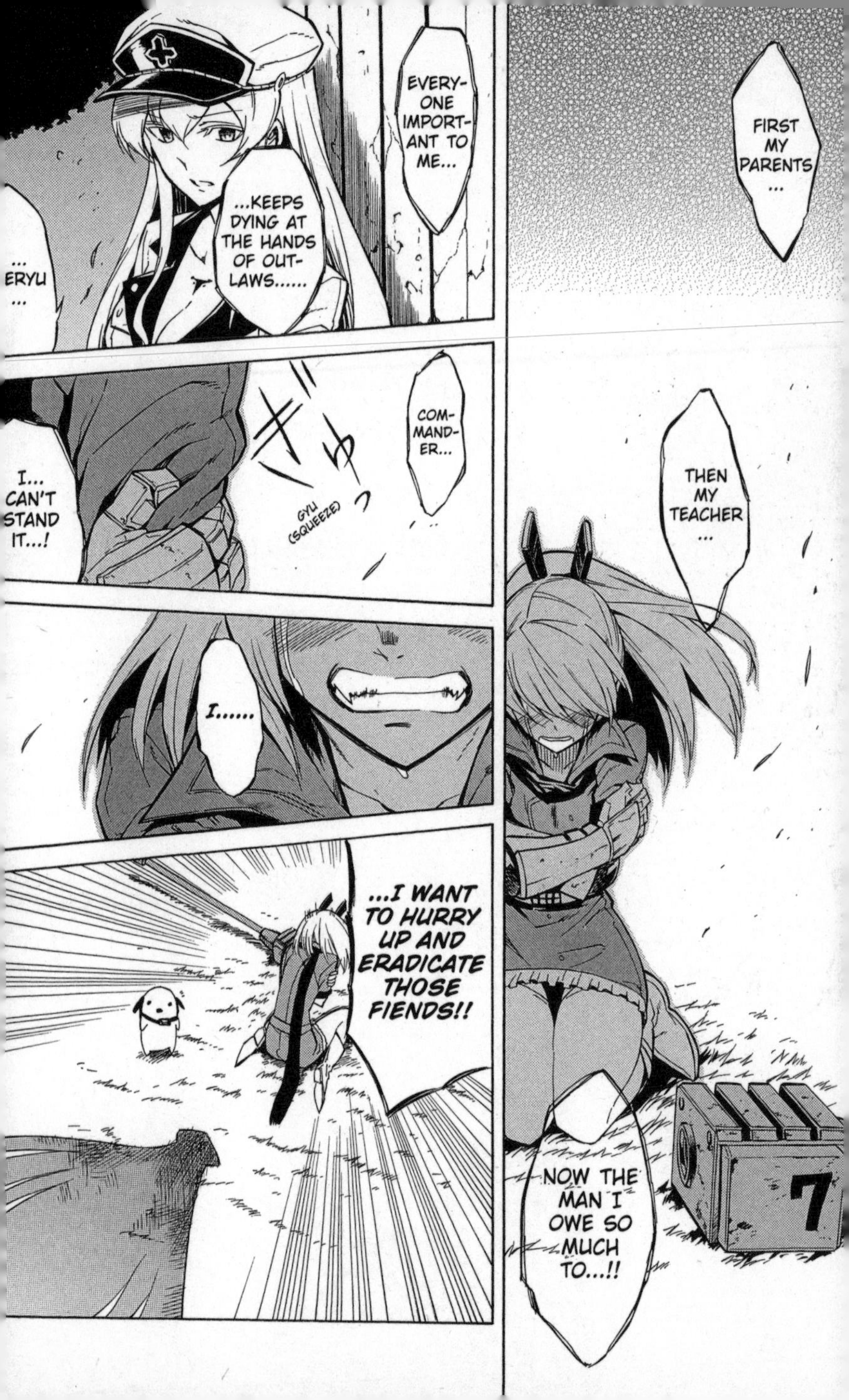
FIRST MY PARENTS...
EVERYONE IMPORTANT TO ME...
...KEEPS DYING AT THE HANDS OF OUTLAWS......
...ERYU...
THEN MY TEACHER...
NOW THE MAN I OWE SO MUCH TO...!!
COMMANDER...
GYU (SQUEEZE)
I... CAN'T STAND IT...!
I......
...I WANT TO HURRY UP AND ERADICATE THOSE FIENDS!!

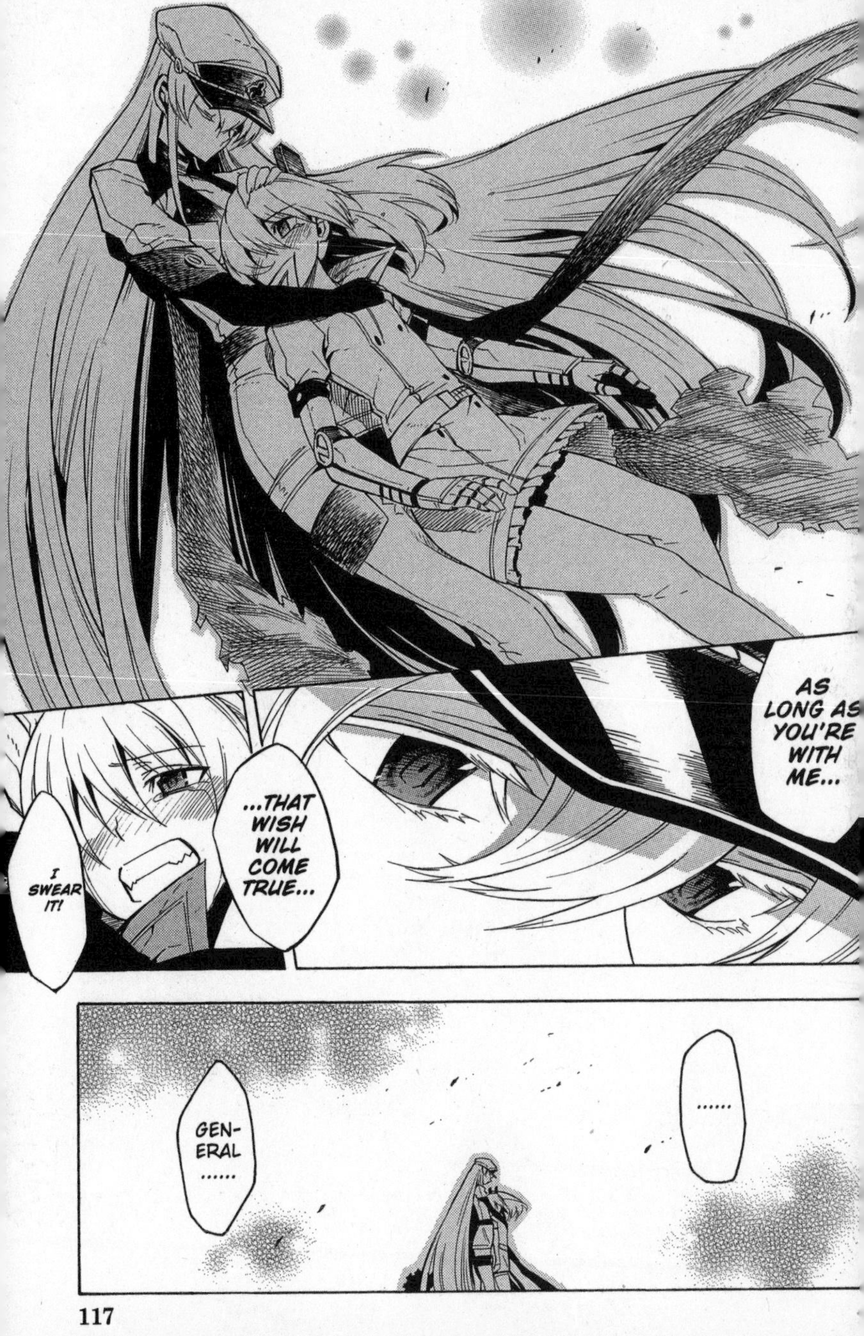
AS LONG AS YOU'RE WITH ME...
...THAT WISH WILL COME TRUE...
I SWEAR IT!
......
GEN-ERAL......

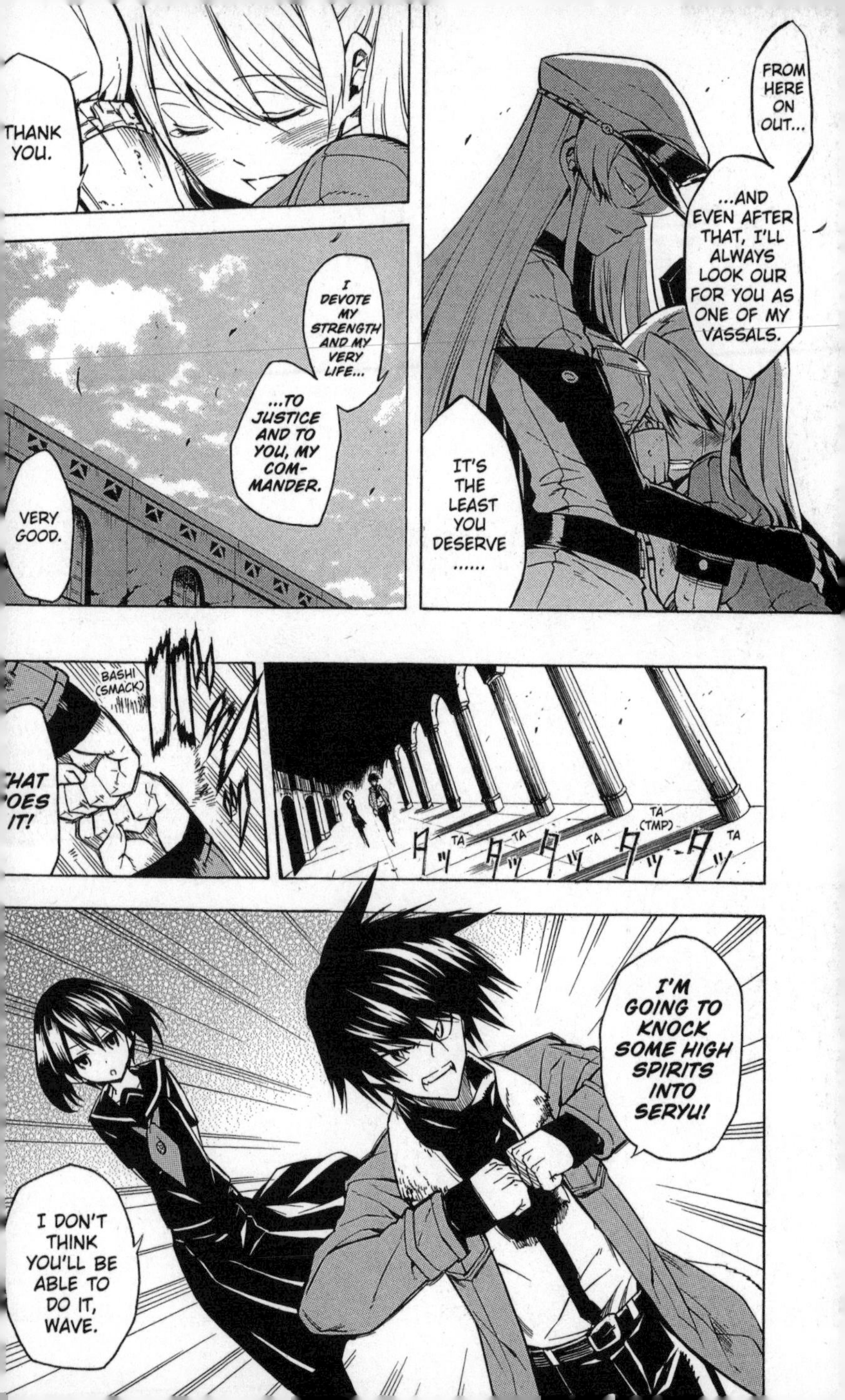
FROM HERE ON OUT...
...AND EVEN AFTER THAT, I'LL ALWAYS LOOK OUR FOR YOU AS ONE OF MY VASSALS.
IT'S THE LEAST YOU DESERVE ......
THANK YOU.
I DEVOTE MY STRENGTH AND MY VERY LIFE...
...TO JUSTICE AND TO YOU, MY COMMANDER.
VERY GOOD.
TA
TA (TMP)
TA
TA
TA
BASHI (SMACK)
I'M GOING TO KNOCK SOME HIGH SPIRITS INTO SERYU!
I DON'T THINK YOU'LL BE ABLE TO DO IT, WAVE.

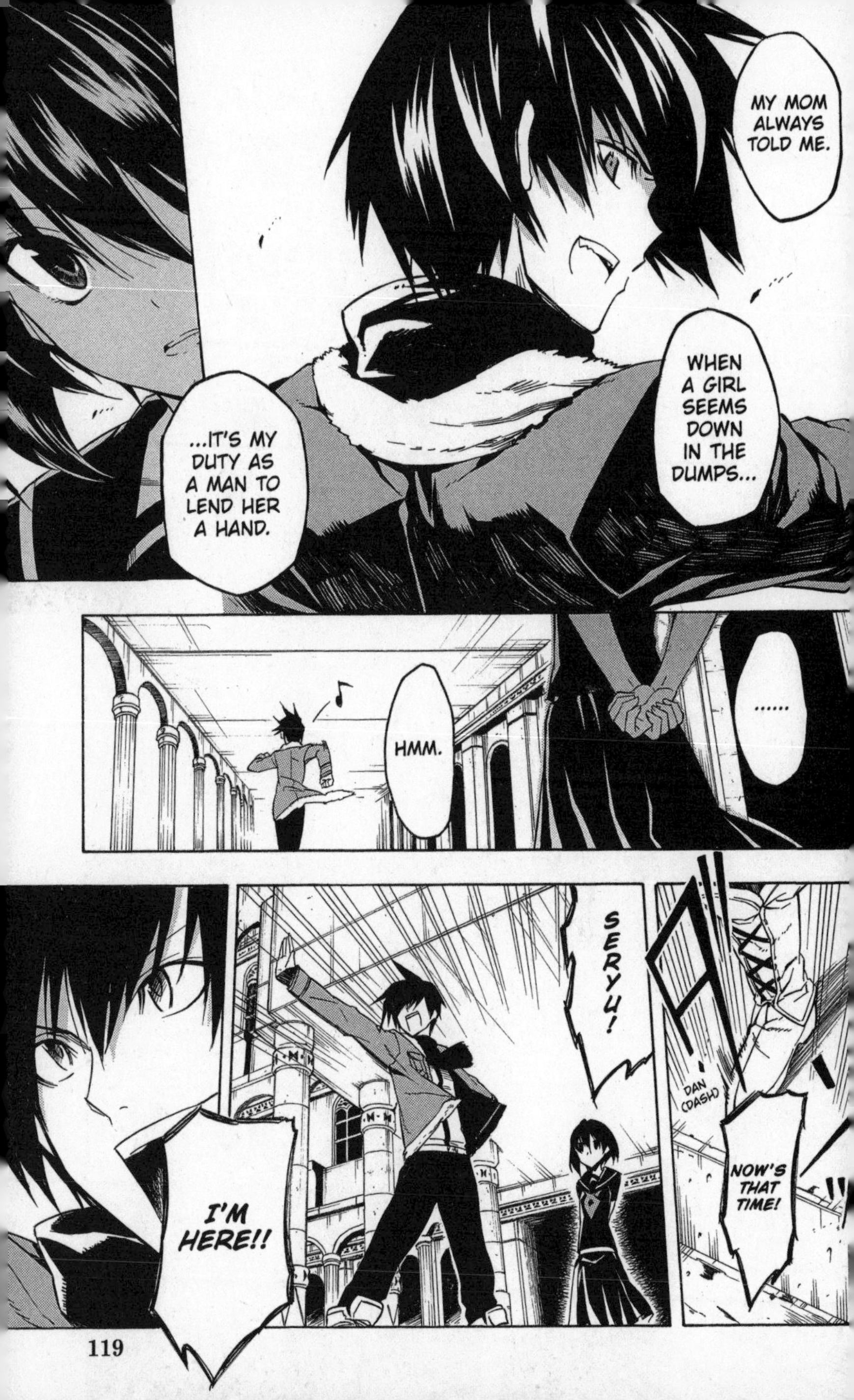
MY MOM ALWAYS TOLD ME.
WHEN A GIRL SEEMS DOWN IN THE DUMPS...
...IT'S MY DUTY AS A MAN TO LEND HER A HAND.
......
HMM.
DAN (DASH)
NOW'S THAT TIME!
SERYU!
I'M HERE!!

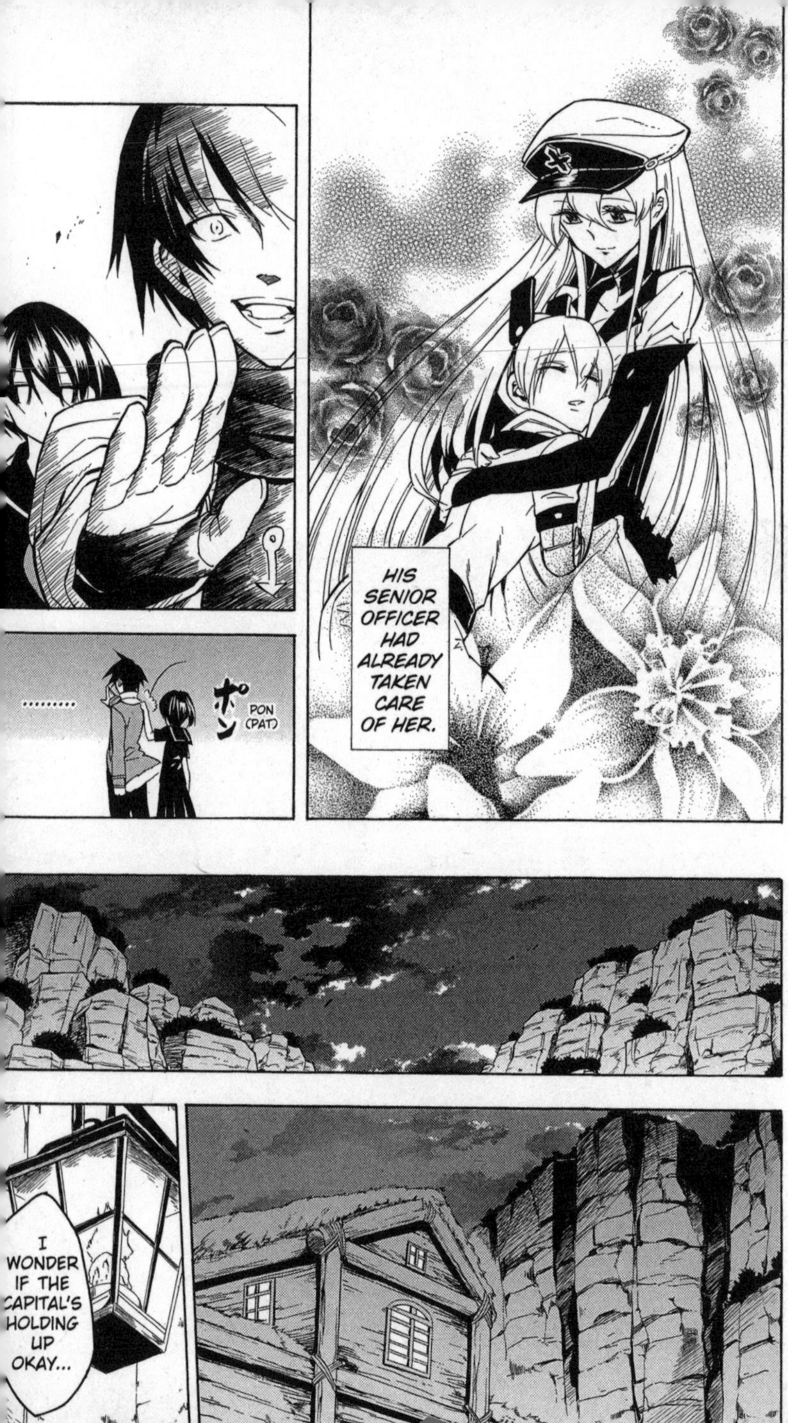

HIS SENIOR OFFICER HAD ALREADY TAKEN CARE OF HER.
...!!
....
ポン
PON (PAT)
I WONDER IF THE CAPITAL'S HOLDING UP OKAY...

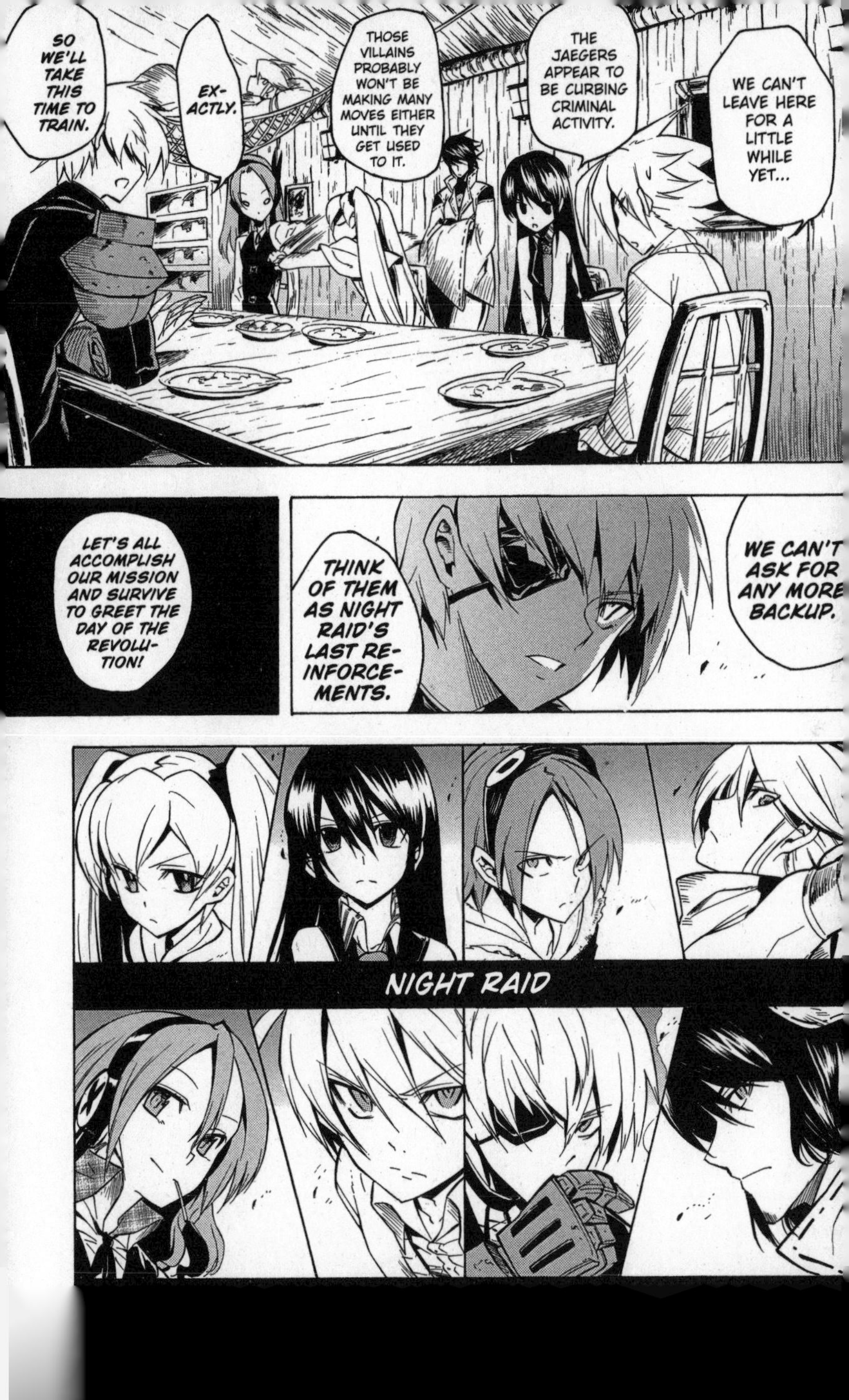
WE CAN'T LEAVE HERE FOR A LITTLE WHILE YET...
THE JAEGERS APPEAR TO BE CURBING CRIMINAL ACTIVITY.
THOSE VILLAINS PROBABLY WON'T BE MAKING MANY MOVES EITHER UNTIL THEY GET USED TO IT.
EX-ACTLY.
SO WE'LL TAKE THIS TIME TO TRAIN.
WE CAN'T ASK FOR ANY MORE BACKUP.
THINK OF THEM AS NIGHT RAID'S LAST RE-INFORCE-MENTS.
LET'S ALL ACCOMPLISH OUR MISSION AND SURVIVE TO GREET THE DAY OF THE REVOLU-TION!
NIGHT RAID

Akame ga KILL!
Rough Sketches 3

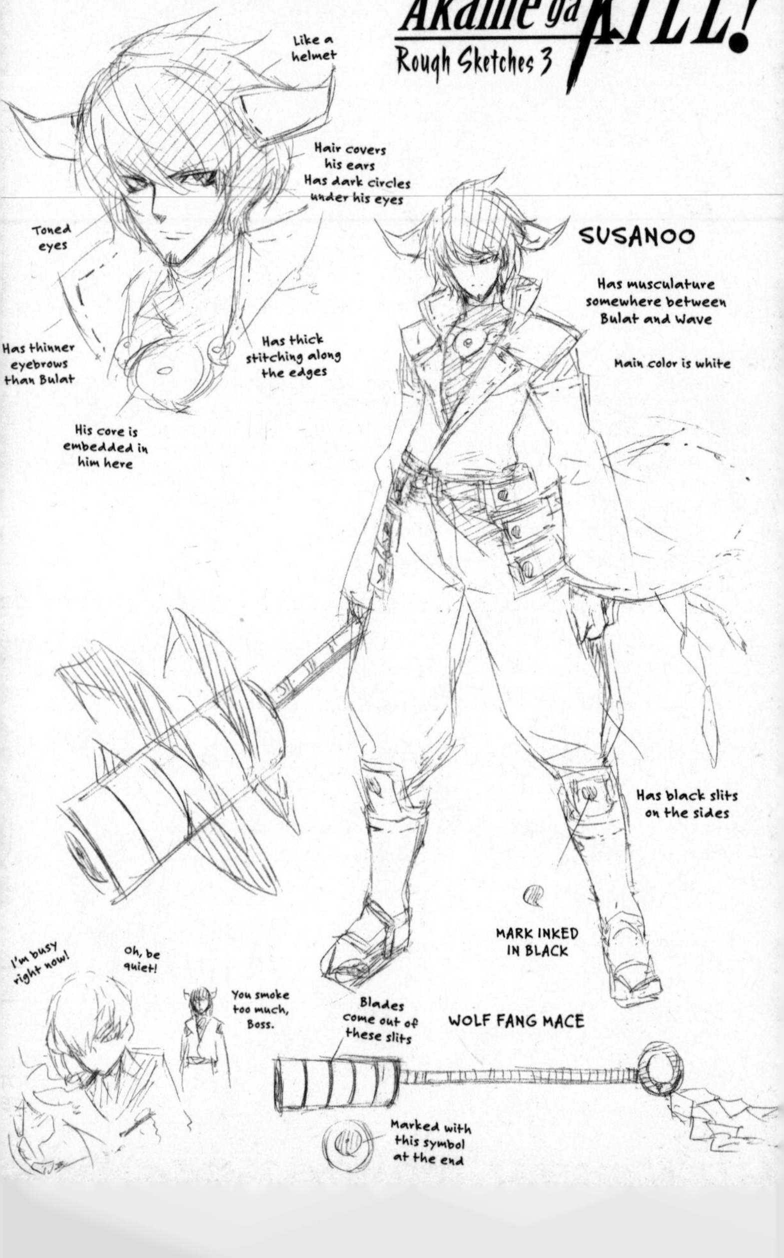
Like a helmet
Hair covers his ears
Has dark circles under his eyes
Toned eyes
Has thinner eyebrows than Bulat
Has thick stitching along the edges
His core is embedded in him here
SUSANOO
Has musculature somewhere between Bulat and Wave
Main color is white
Has black slits on the sides
MARK INKED IN BLACK
I'm busy right now!
Oh, be quiet!
You smoke too much, Boss.
Blades come out of these slits
WOLF FANG MACE
Marked with this symbol at the end

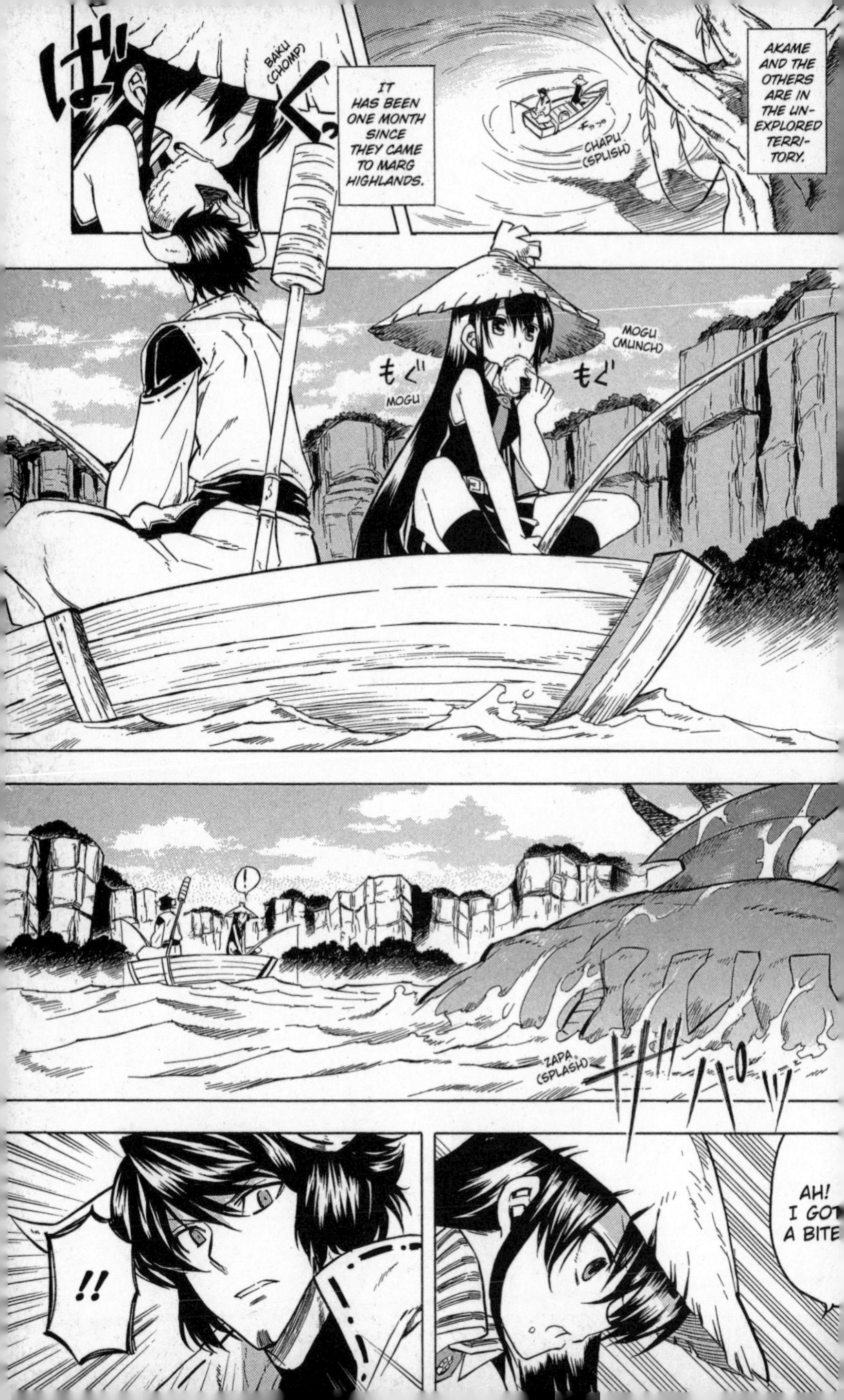
AKAME AND THE OTHERS ARE IN THE UN-EXPLORED TERRITORY.
CHAPU (SPLISH)
IT HAS BEEN ONE MONTH SINCE THEY CAME TO MARG HIGHLANDS.
BAKU (CHOMP)
もぐ
MOGU (MUNCH)
もぐ
MOGU
!
ZAPA (SPLASH)
AH! I GOT A BITE
!!

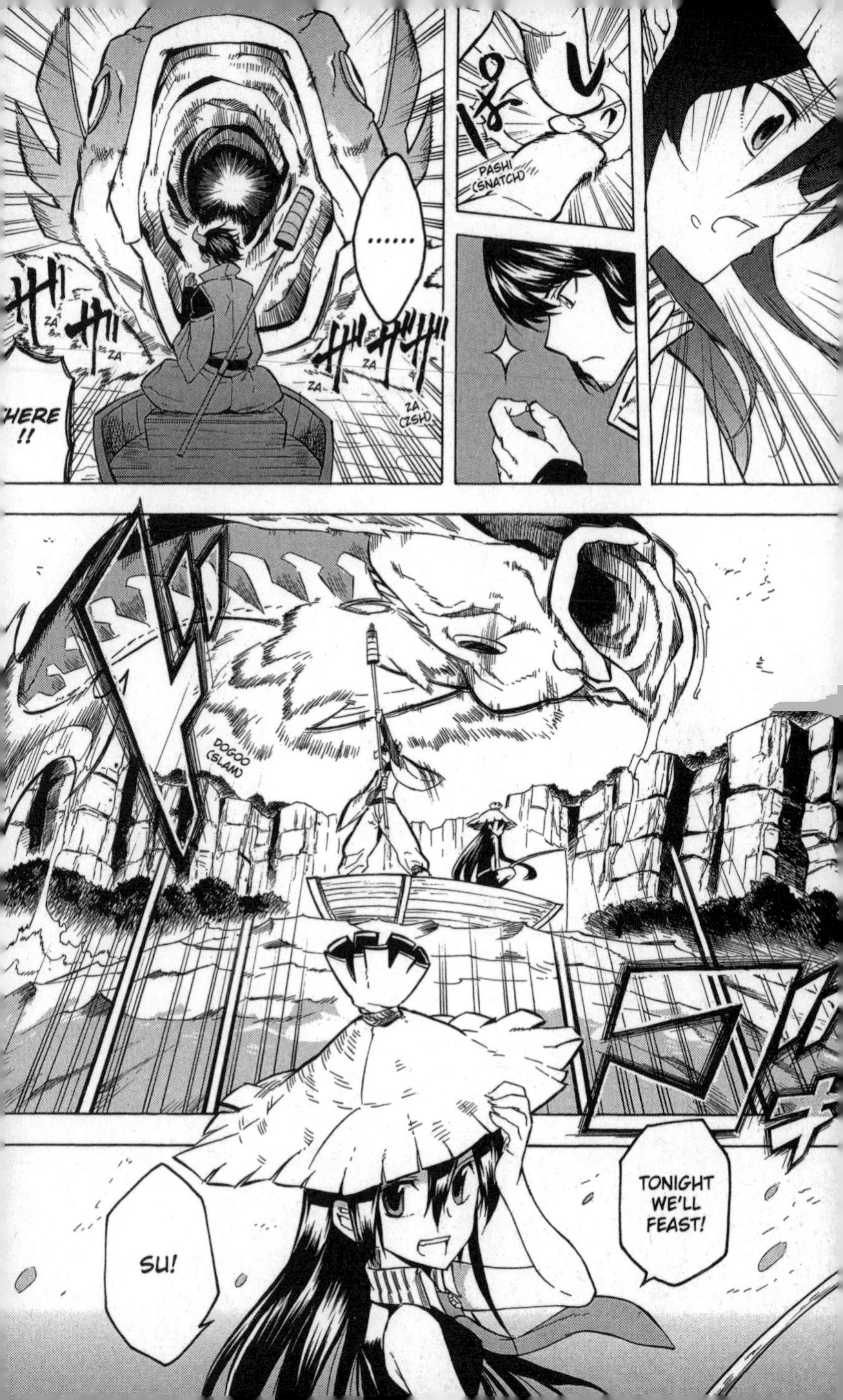

PASHI (SNATCH)
......
ZA
ZA
ZA
ZA
ZA (ZSH)
HERE !!
DOGOO (SLAM)
TONIGHT WE'LL FEAST!
SU!

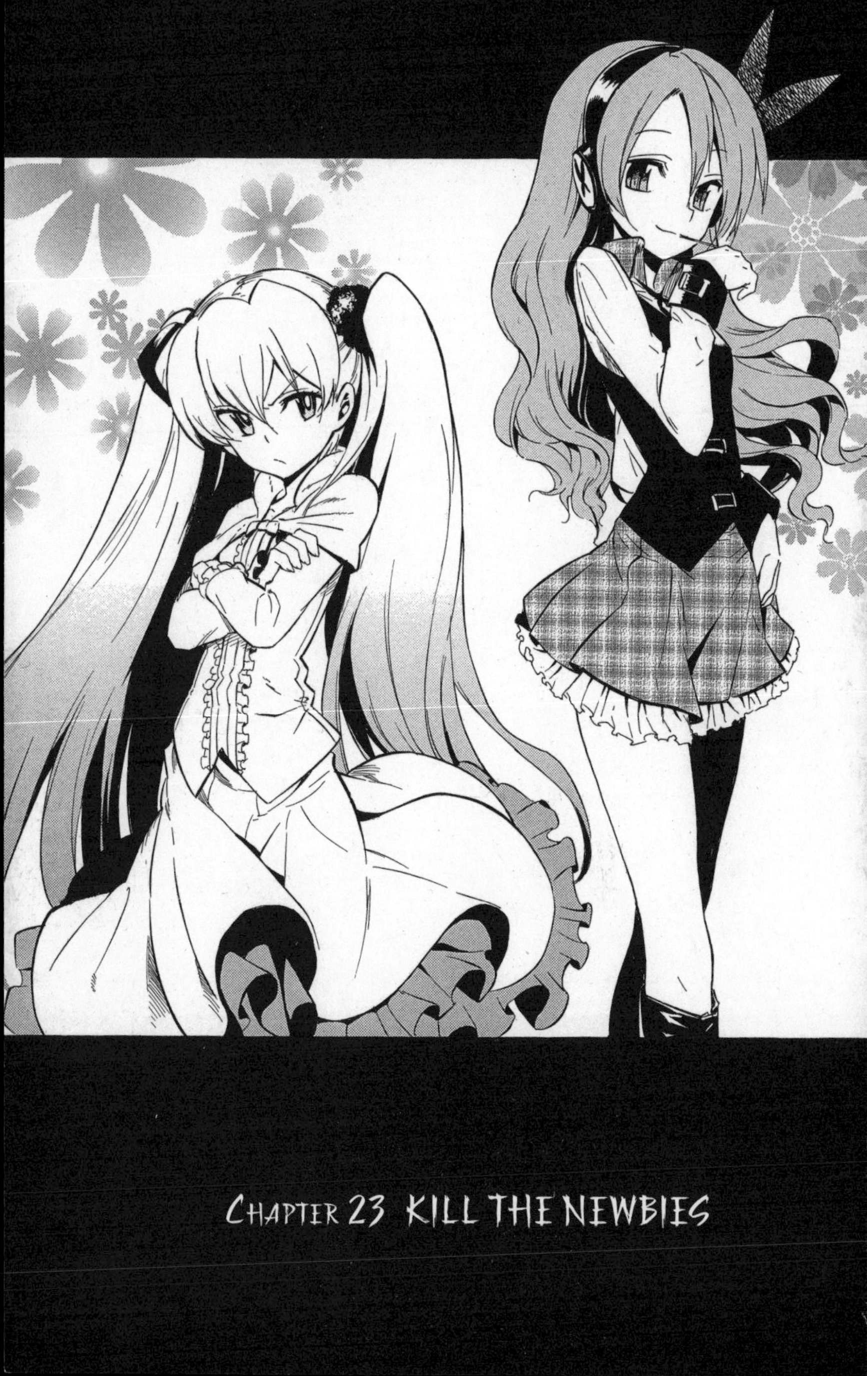

CHAPTER 23 KILL THE NEWBIES

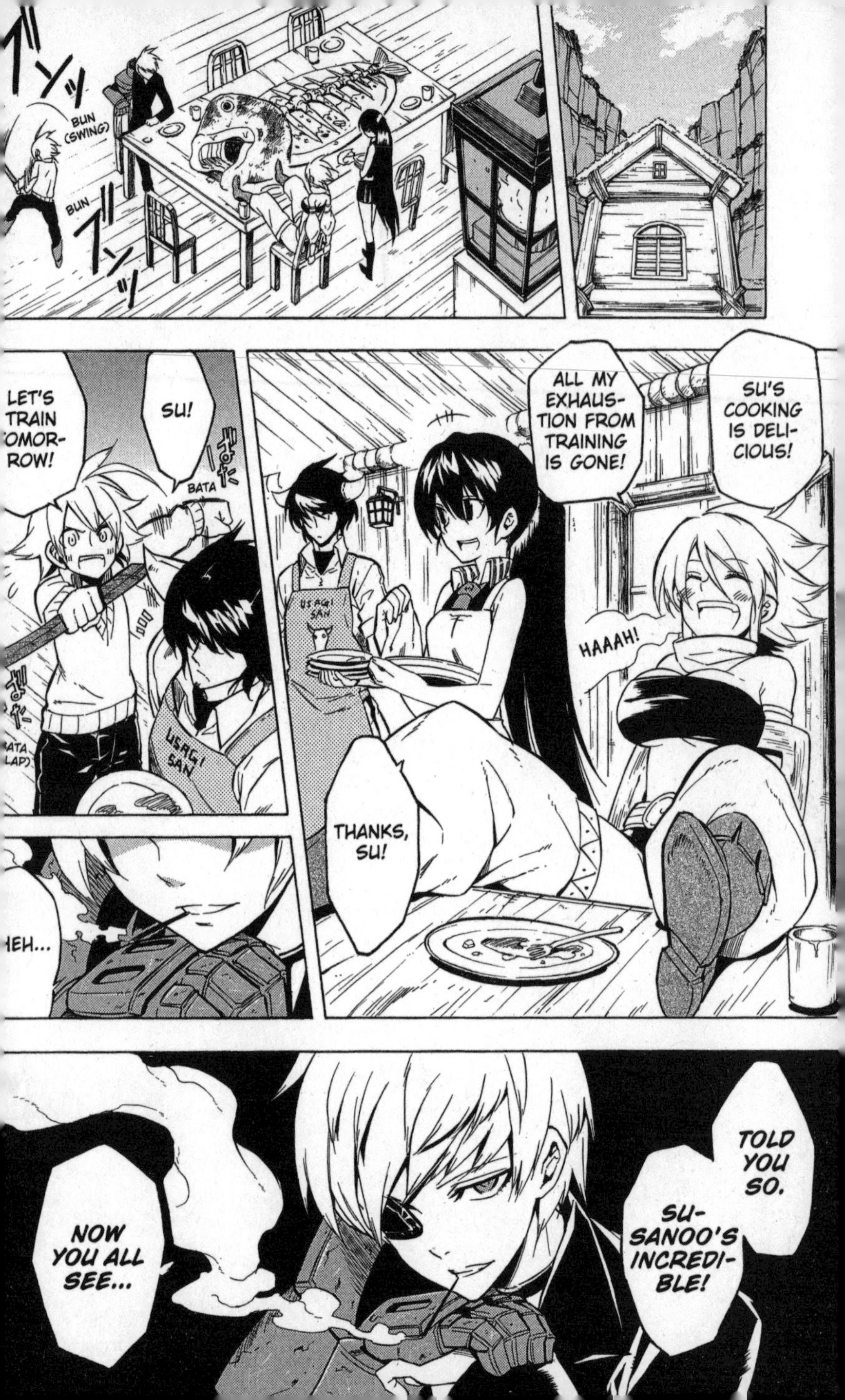

BUN (SWING)
BUN
SU'S COOKING IS DELICIOUS!
ALL MY EXHAUSTION FROM TRAINING IS GONE!
HAAAH!
SU!
BATA
LET'S TRAIN TOMORROW!
BATA
THANKS, SU!
HEH...
TOLD YOU SO.
SU-SANOO'S INCREDIBLE!
NOW YOU ALL SEE...

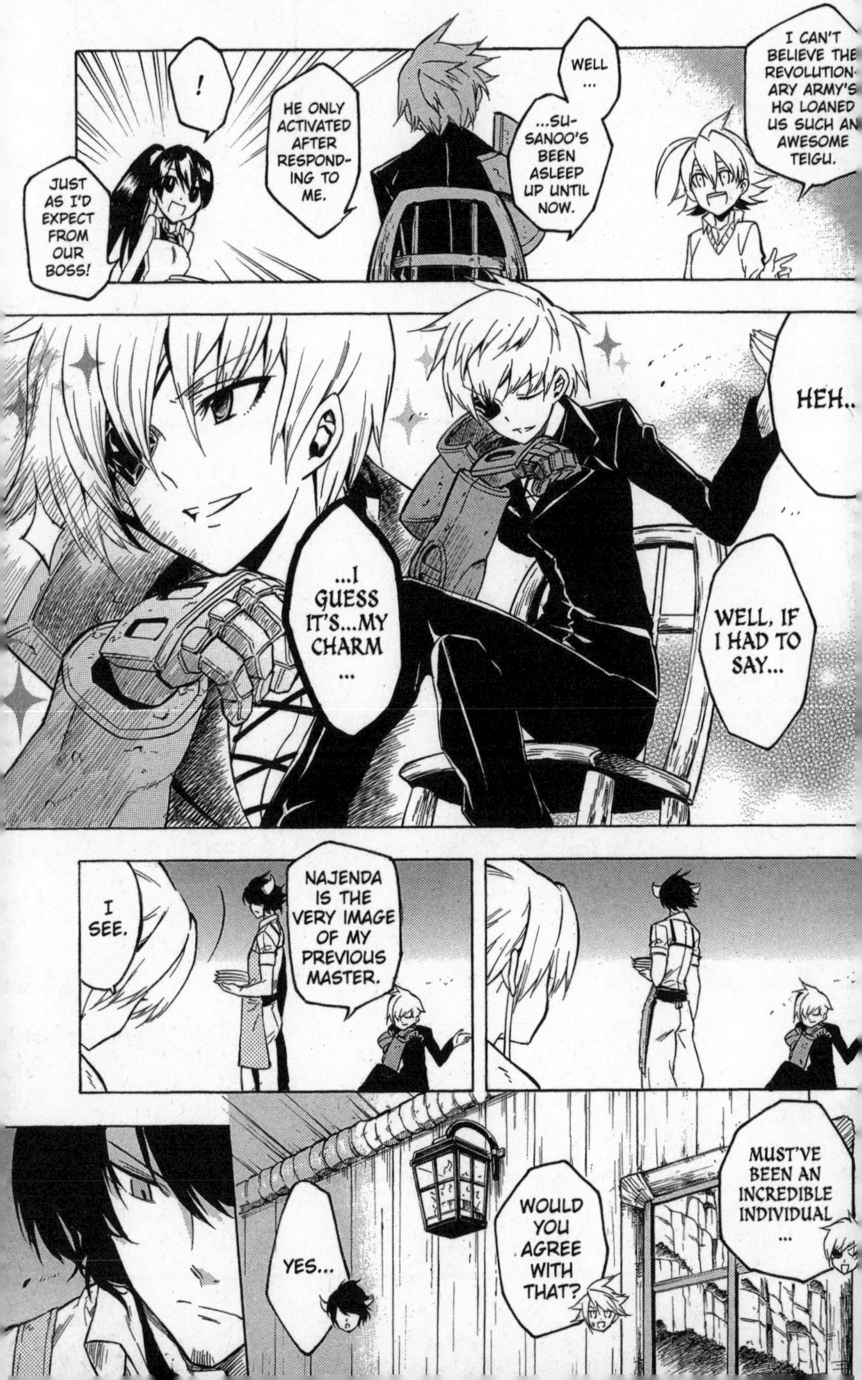

I CAN'T BELIEVE THE REVOLUTIONARY ARMY'S HQ LOANED US SUCH AN AWESOME TEIGU.
WELL...
...SUSANOO'S BEEN ASLEEP UP UNTIL NOW.
HE ONLY ACTIVATED AFTER RESPONDING TO ME.
!
JUST AS I'D EXPECT FROM OUR BOSS!
HEH...
WELL, IF I HAD TO SAY...
...I GUESS IT'S...MY CHARM...
NAJENDA IS THE VERY IMAGE OF MY PREVIOUS MASTER.
I SEE.
MUST'VE BEEN AN INCREDIBLE INDIVIDUAL...
WOULD YOU AGREE WITH THAT?
YES...

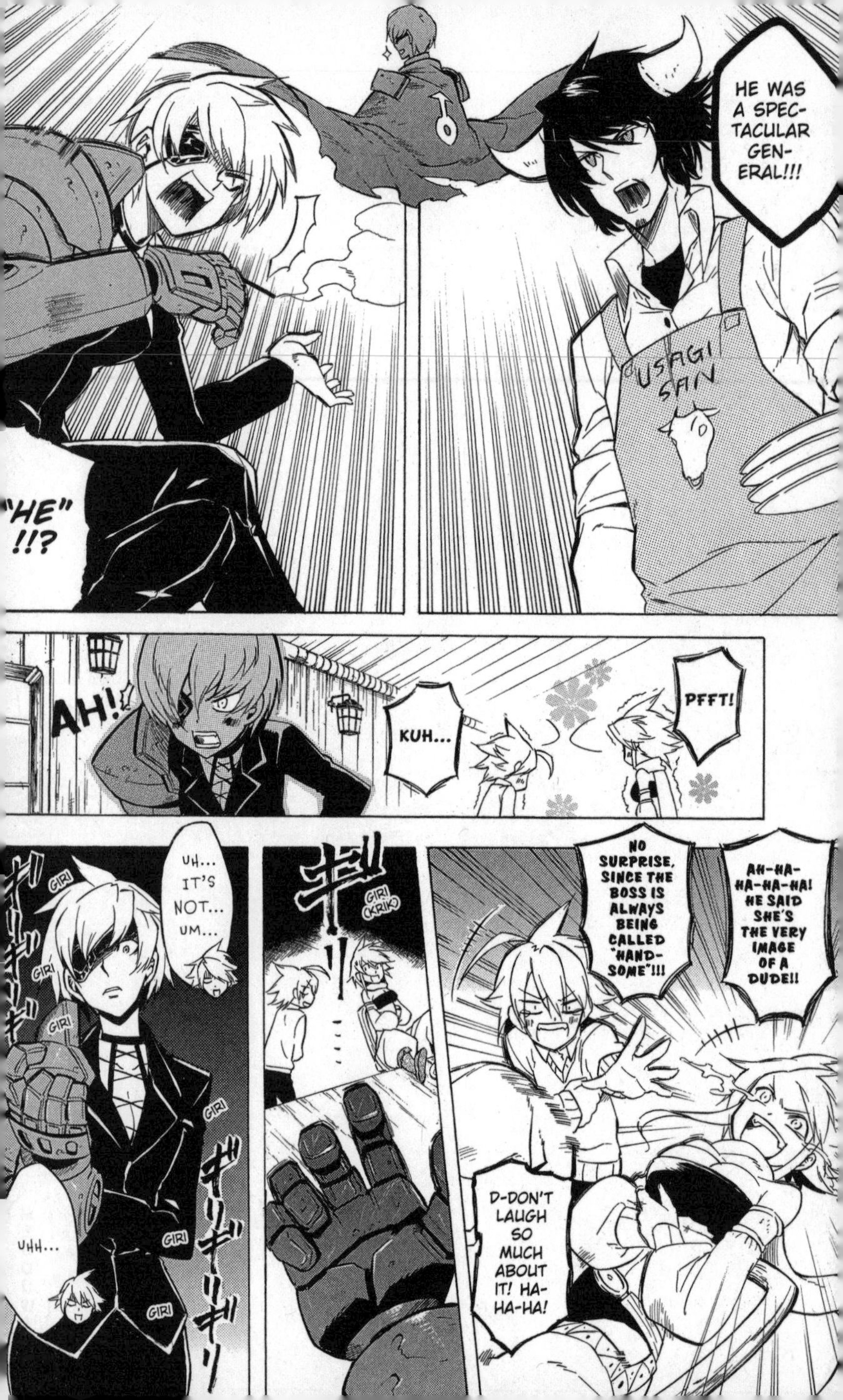
HE WAS A SPECTACULAR GENERAL!!!
"HE" !!?
USAGI SAN
AH!
PFFT!
KUH...
NO SURPRISE, SINCE THE BOSS IS ALWAYS BEING CALLED "HANDSOME"!!!
AH-HA-HA-HA-HA! HE SAID SHE'S THE VERY IMAGE OF A DUDE!!
UH... IT'S NOT... UM...
GIRI (KRIK)
GIRI
UHH...
D-DON'T LAUGH SO MUCH ABOUT IT! HA-HA-HA!

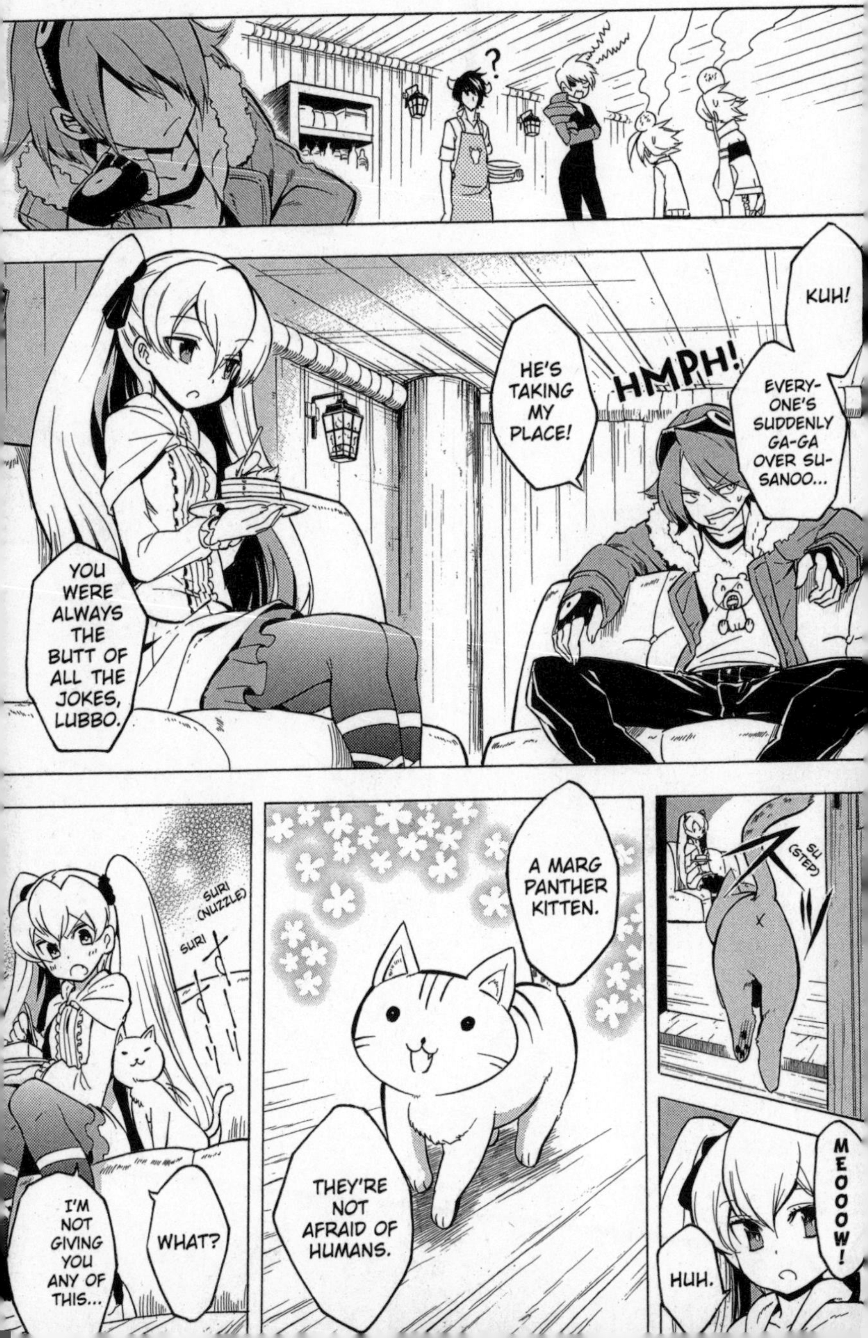
?
KUH!
EVERY-ONE'S SUDDENLY GA-GA OVER SU-SANOO...
HMPH!
HE'S TAKING MY PLACE!
YOU WERE ALWAYS THE BUTT OF ALL THE JOKES, LUBBO.
SU (STEP)
MEOOOW!
HUH.
A MARG PANTHER KITTEN.
THEY'RE NOT AFRAID OF HUMANS.
SURI (NUZZLE)
SURI
WHAT?
I'M NOT GIVING YOU ANY OF THIS...

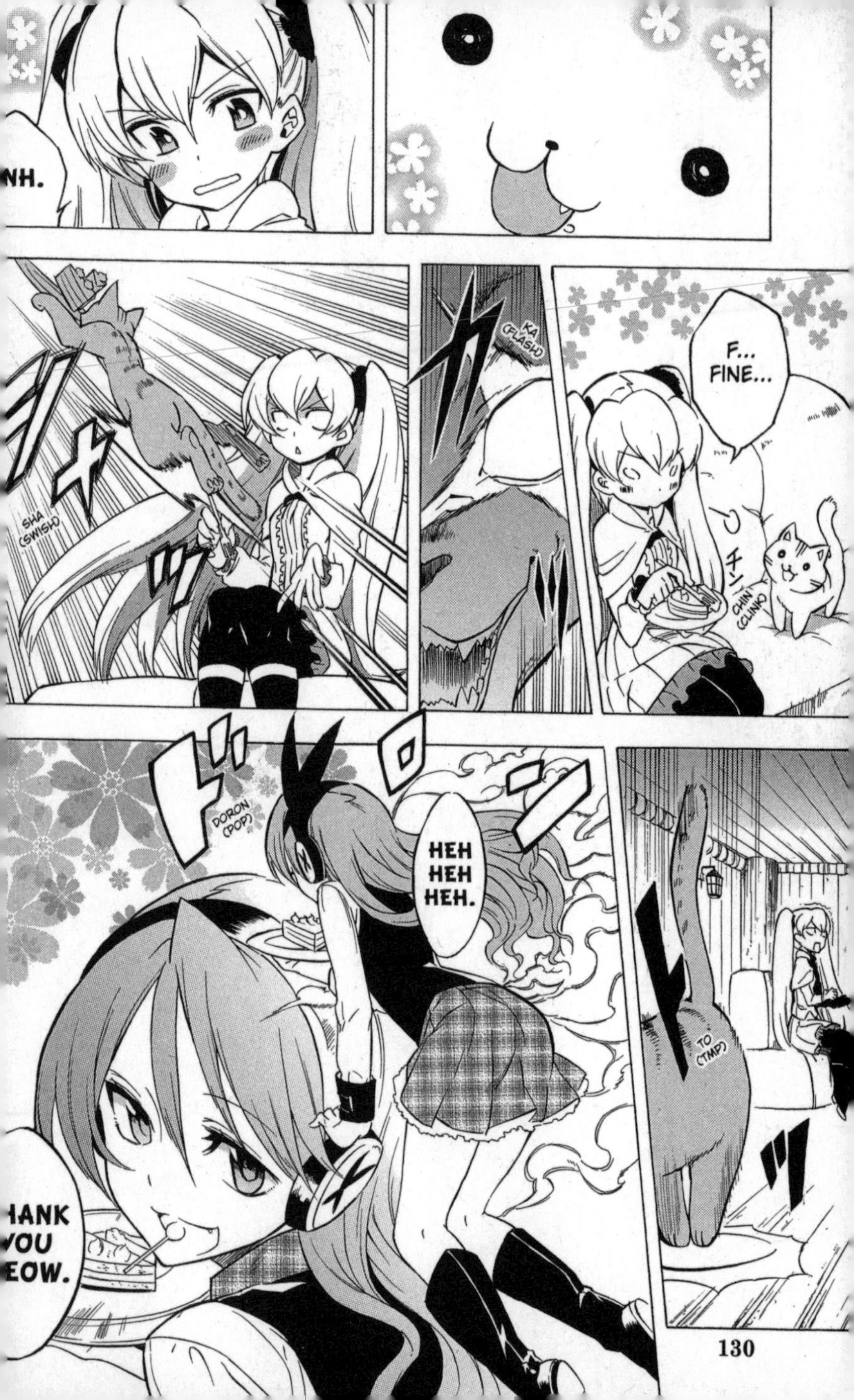
NH.
F... FINE...
チン
CHIN (CLINK)
KA (FLASH)
SHA (SWISH)
TO (TMP)
DORON (POP)
HEH HEH HEH.
HANK YOU EOW.

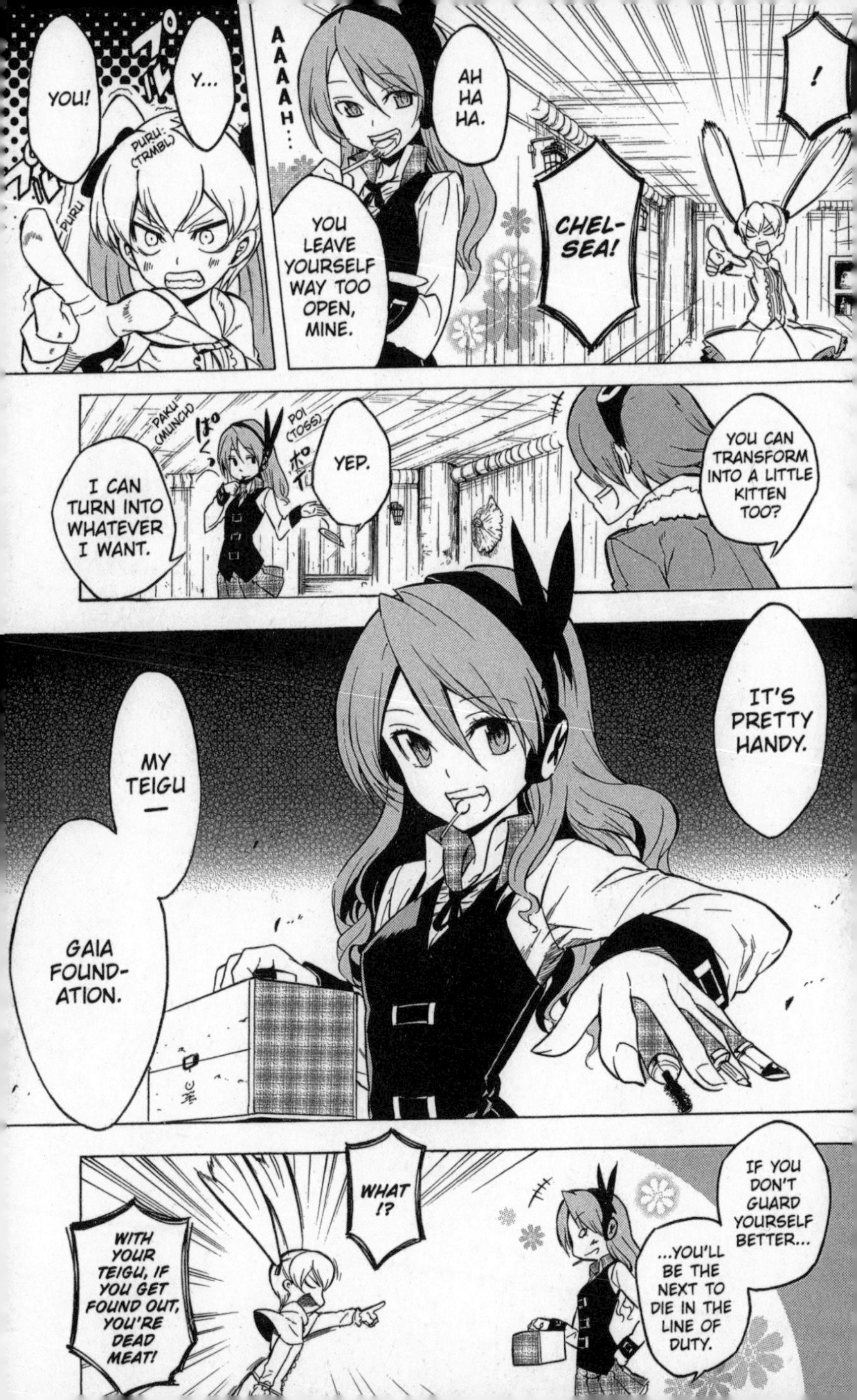
!
CHEL-SEA!
AH HA HA.
AAAAAH...
YOU LEAVE YOURSELF WAY TOO OPEN, MINE.
Y...
YOU!
PURU (TRMBL)
PURU
YOU CAN TRANSFORM INTO A LITTLE KITTEN TOO?
POI (TOSS)
YEP.
PAKU (MUNCH)
I CAN TURN INTO WHATEVER I WANT.
IT'S PRETTY HANDY.
MY TEIGU —
GAIA FOUND-ATION.
IF YOU DON'T GUARD YOURSELF BETTER...
...YOU'LL BE THE NEXT TO DIE IN THE LINE OF DUTY.
WHAT !?
WITH YOUR TEIGU, IF YOU GET FOUND OUT, YOU'RE DEAD MEAT!

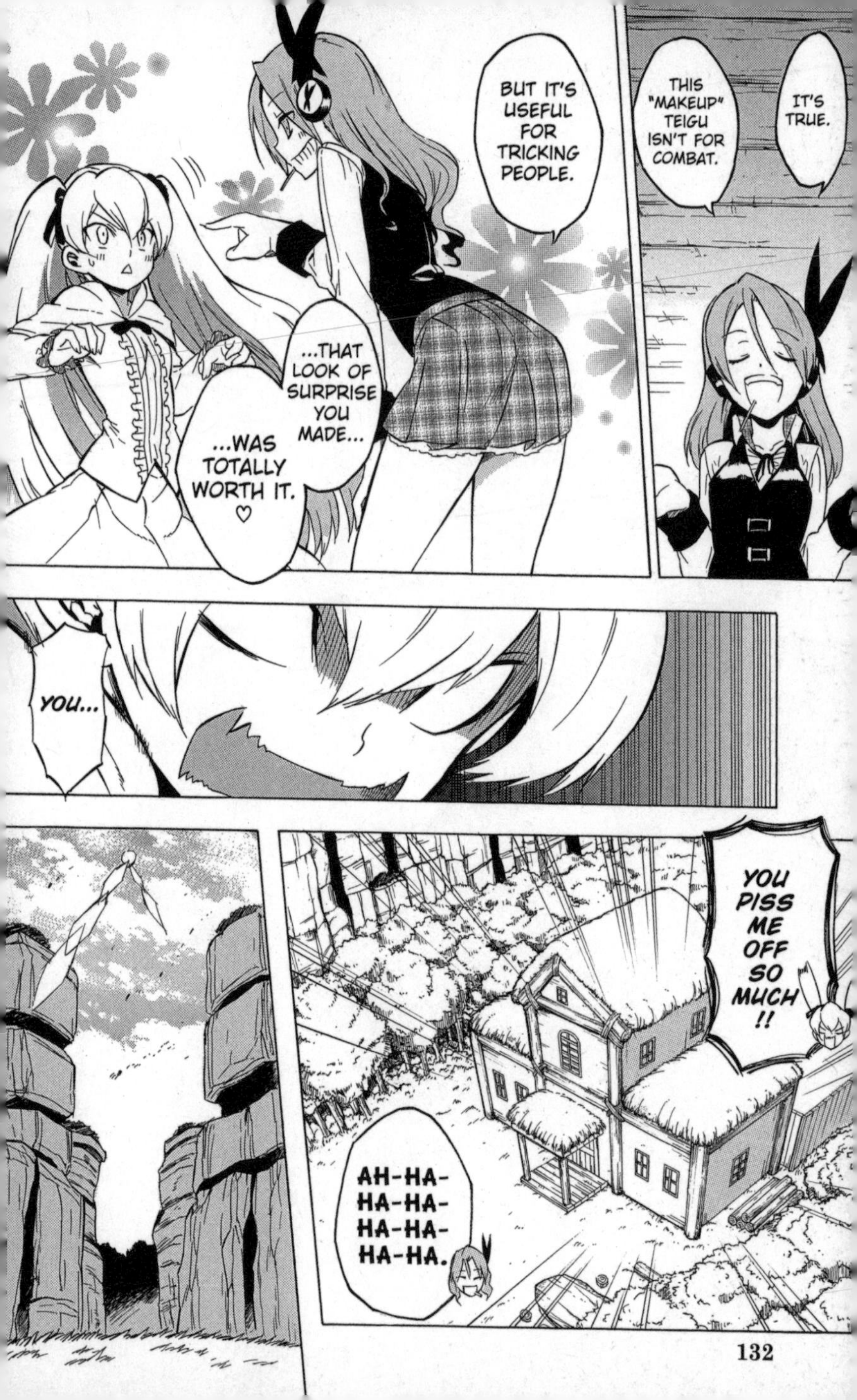

IT'S TRUE.
THIS "MAKEUP" TEIGU ISN'T FOR COMBAT.
BUT IT'S USEFUL FOR TRICKING PEOPLE.
...THAT LOOK OF SURPRISE YOU MADE...
...WAS TOTALLY WORTH IT. ♡
YOU...
YOU PISS ME OFF SO MUCH!!
AH-HA-HA-HA-HA-HA-HA-HA.

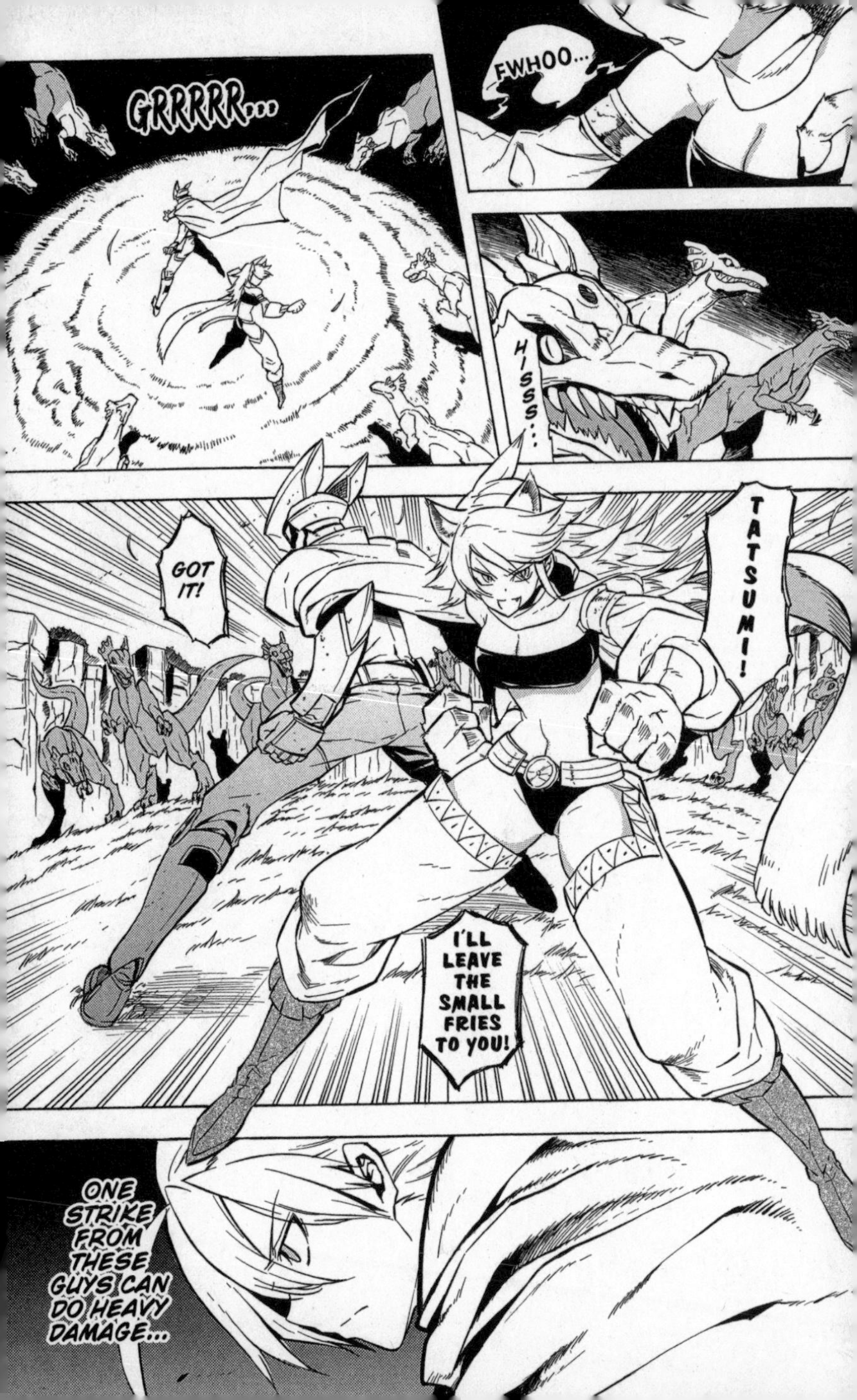
FWHOO...
GRRRRR...
HISS...
TATSUMI!
GOT IT!
I'LL LEAVE THE SMALL FRIES TO YOU!
ONE STRIKE FROM THESE GUYS CAN DO HEAVY DAMAGE...

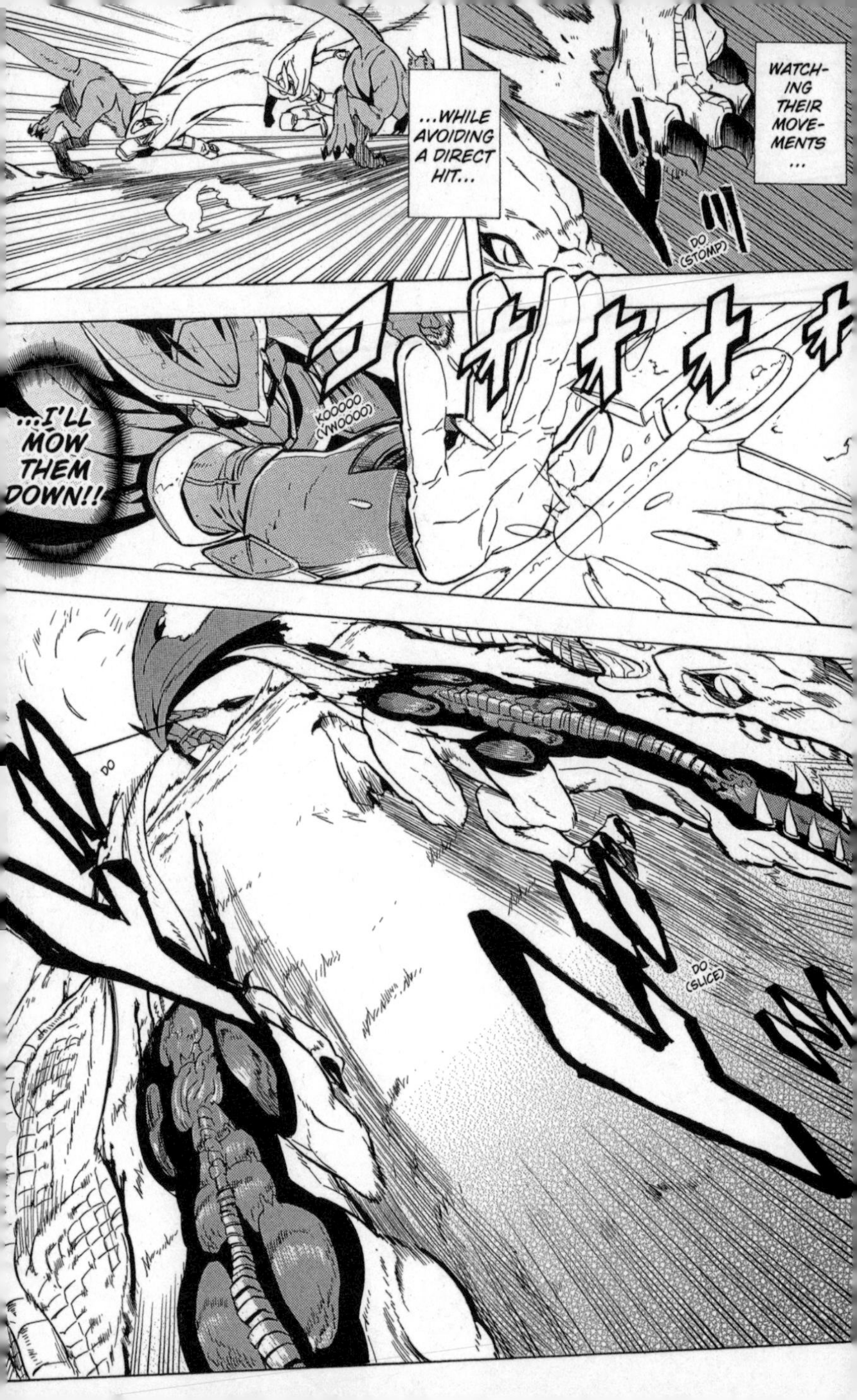
WATCHING THEIR MOVEMENTS...
...WHILE AVOIDING A DIRECT HIT...
DO (STOMP)
KOOOOO (VWOOOO)
...I'LL MOW THEM DOWN!!
DO (SLICE)
DO

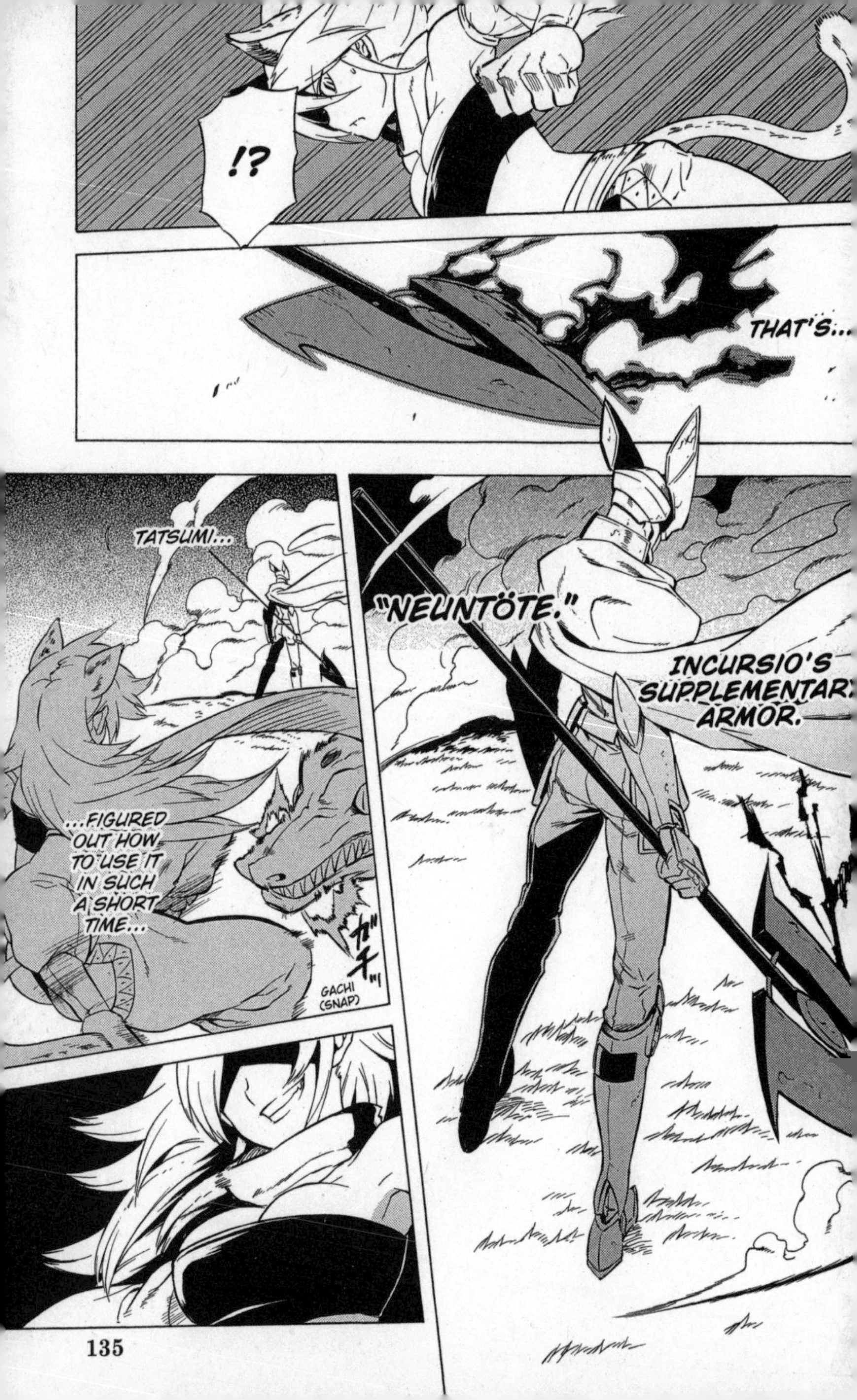
!?
THAT'S...
"NEUNTÖTE."
INCURSIO'S SUPPLEMENTARY ARMOR.
TATSUMI...
...FIGURED OUT HOW TO USE IT IN SUCH A SHORT TIME...
GACHI (SNAP)

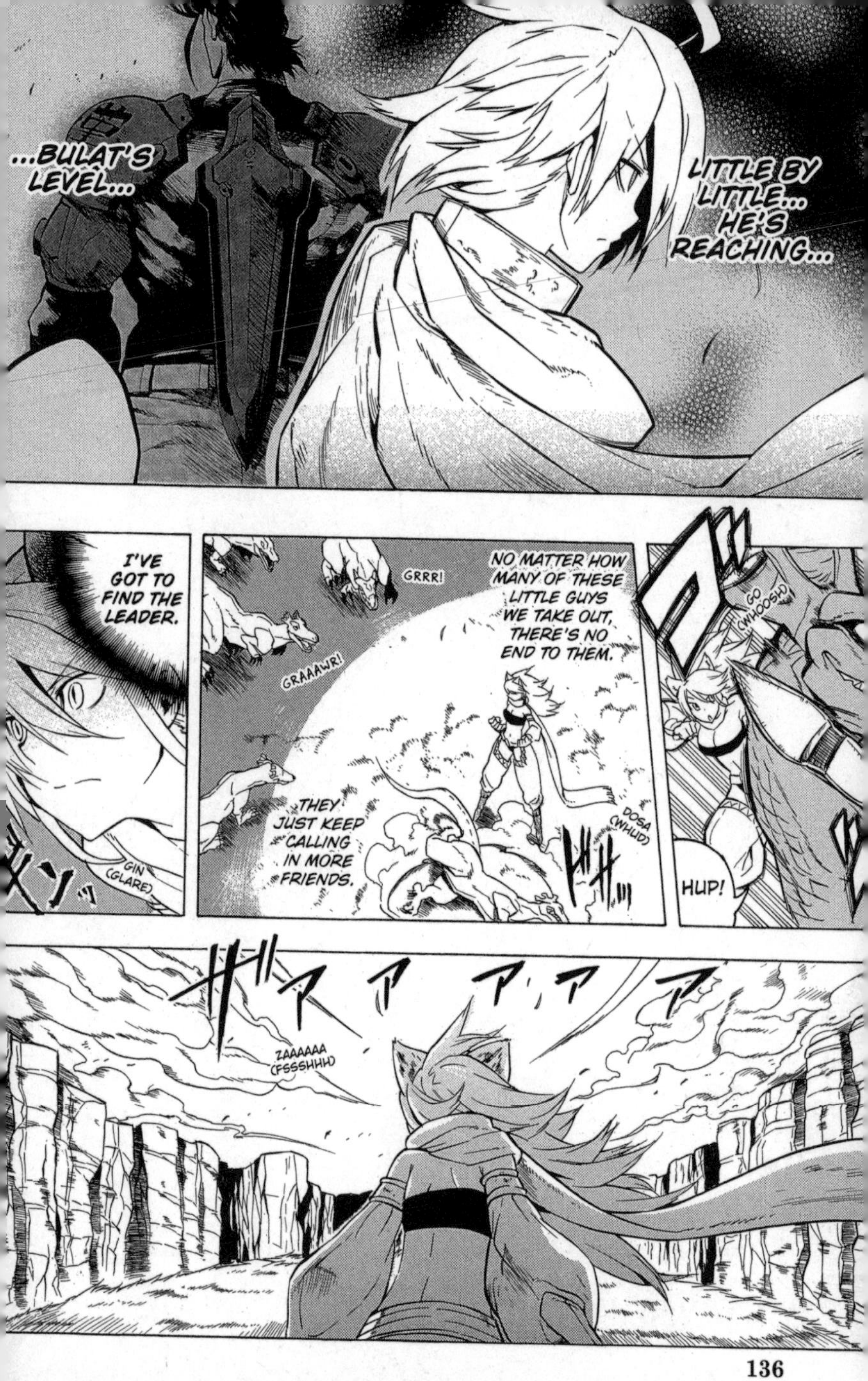
LITTLE BY LITTLE... HE'S REACHING...
...BULAT'S LEVEL...
GO (WHOOSH)
HUP!
NO MATTER HOW MANY OF THESE LITTLE GUYS WE TAKE OUT, THERE'S NO END TO THEM.
GRRR!
GRAAAWR!
THEY JUST KEEP CALLING IN MORE FRIENDS.
DOSA (WHUD)
I'VE GOT TO FIND THE LEADER.
GIN (GLARE)
ZAAAAAA (FSSSHHH)

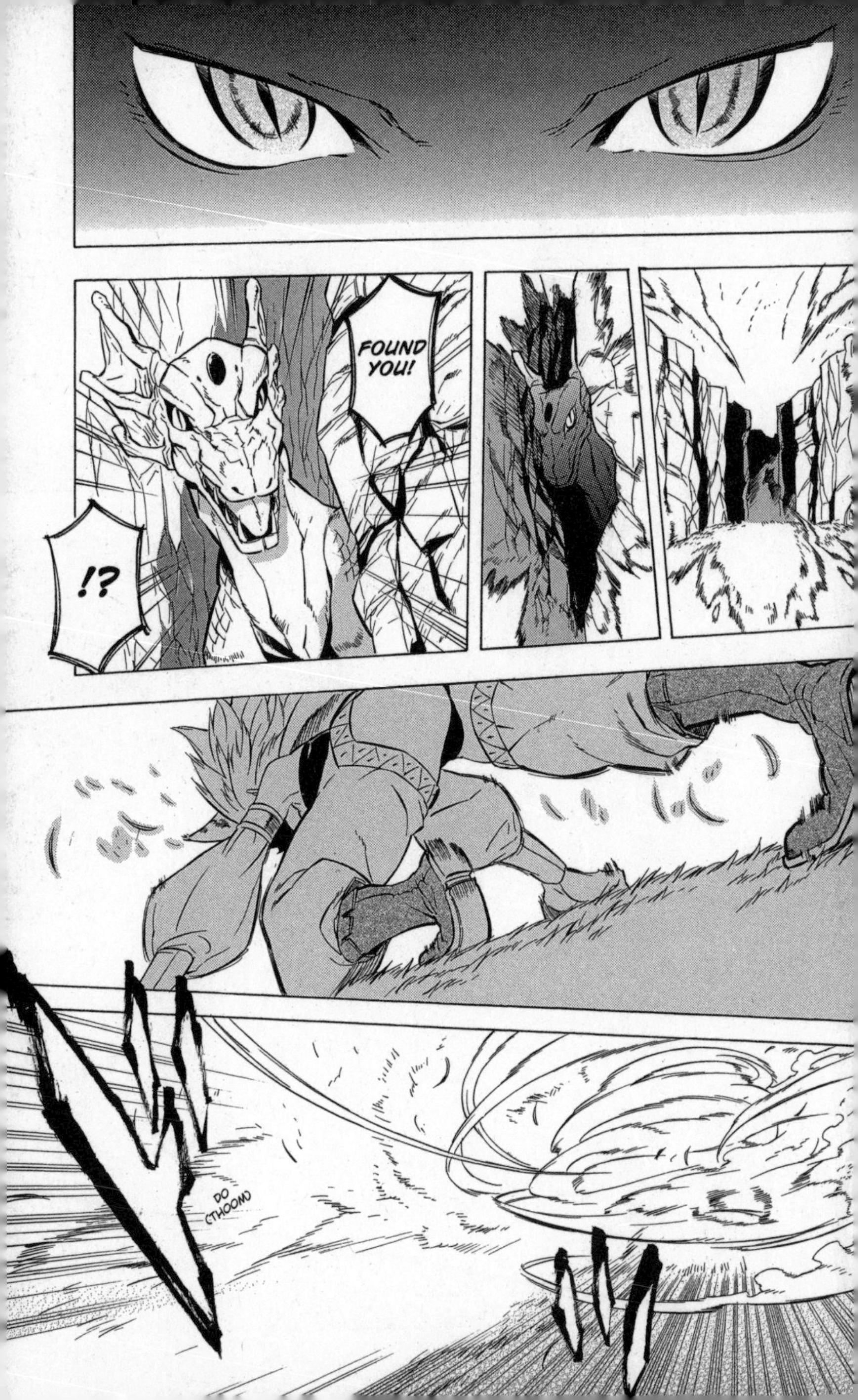
FOUND YOU!
!?
DO
(THOOM)

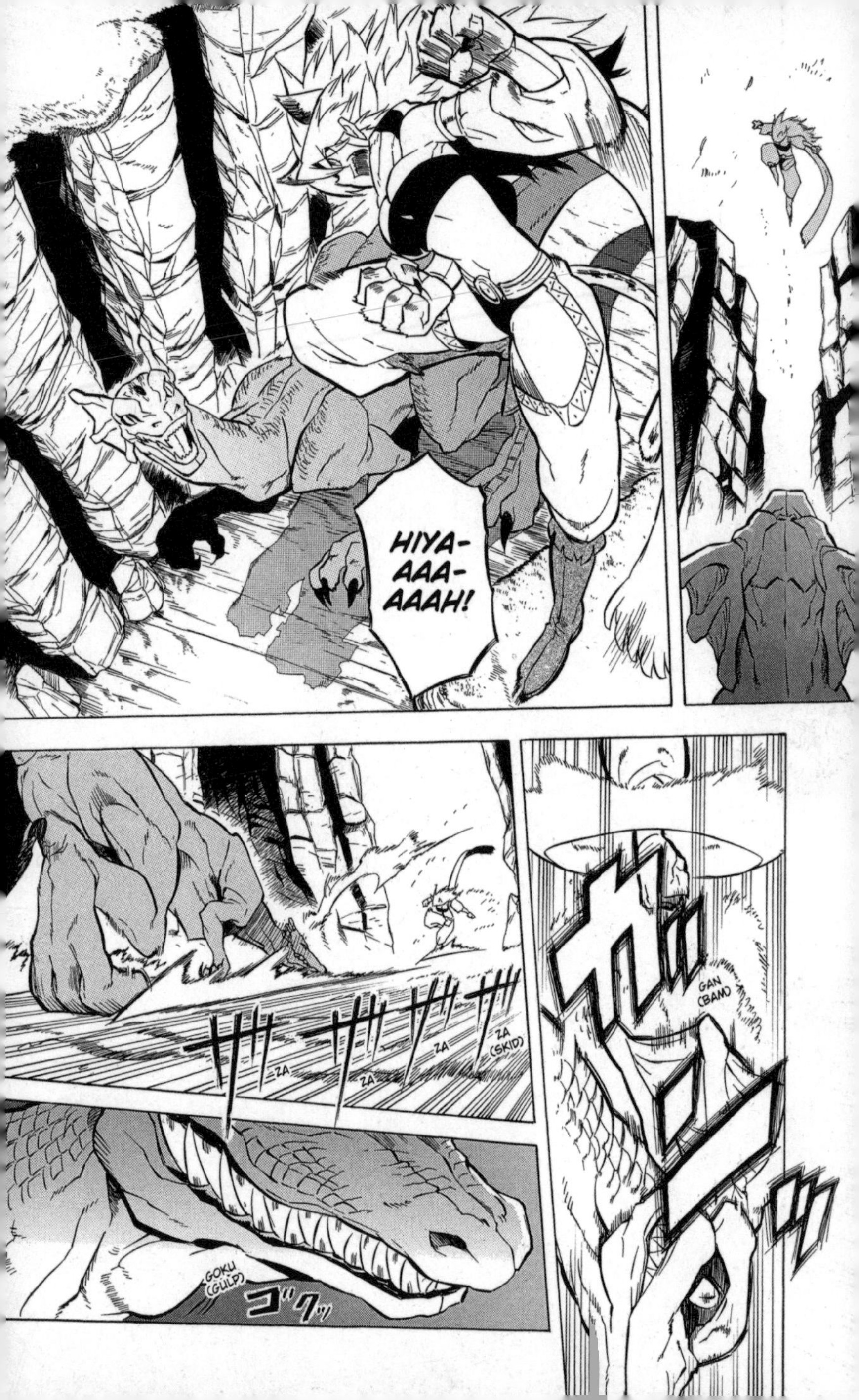
HIYA-
AAA-
AAAH!
GAN
(BAM)
ZA
(SKID)
ZA
ZA
ZA
GOKU
(GULP)
ゴクッ

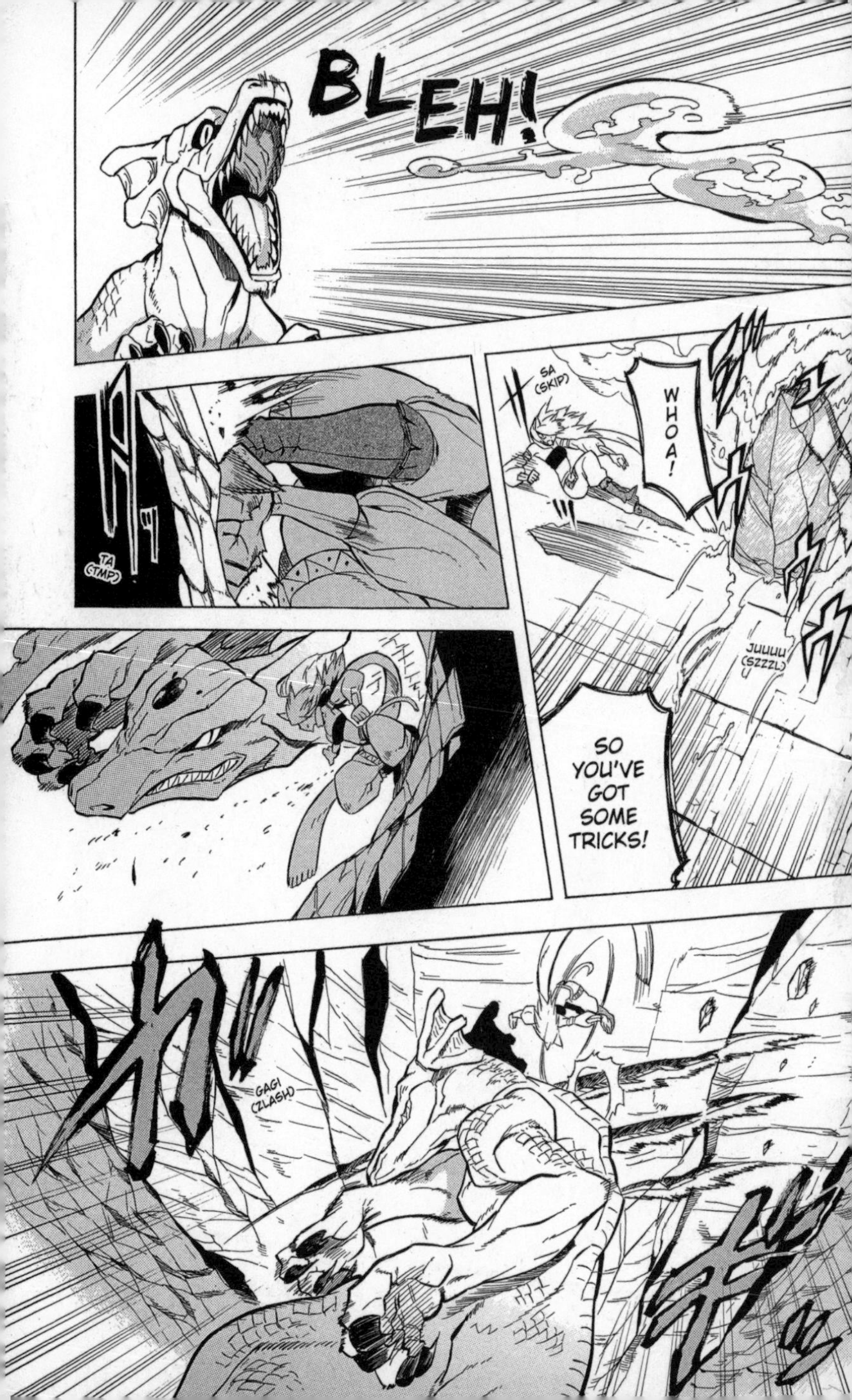
BLEH!
SA (SKIP)
WHOA!
TA (TMP)
JUUUUU (SZZZL)
SO YOU'VE GOT SOME TRICKS!
GAGI (ZLASH)

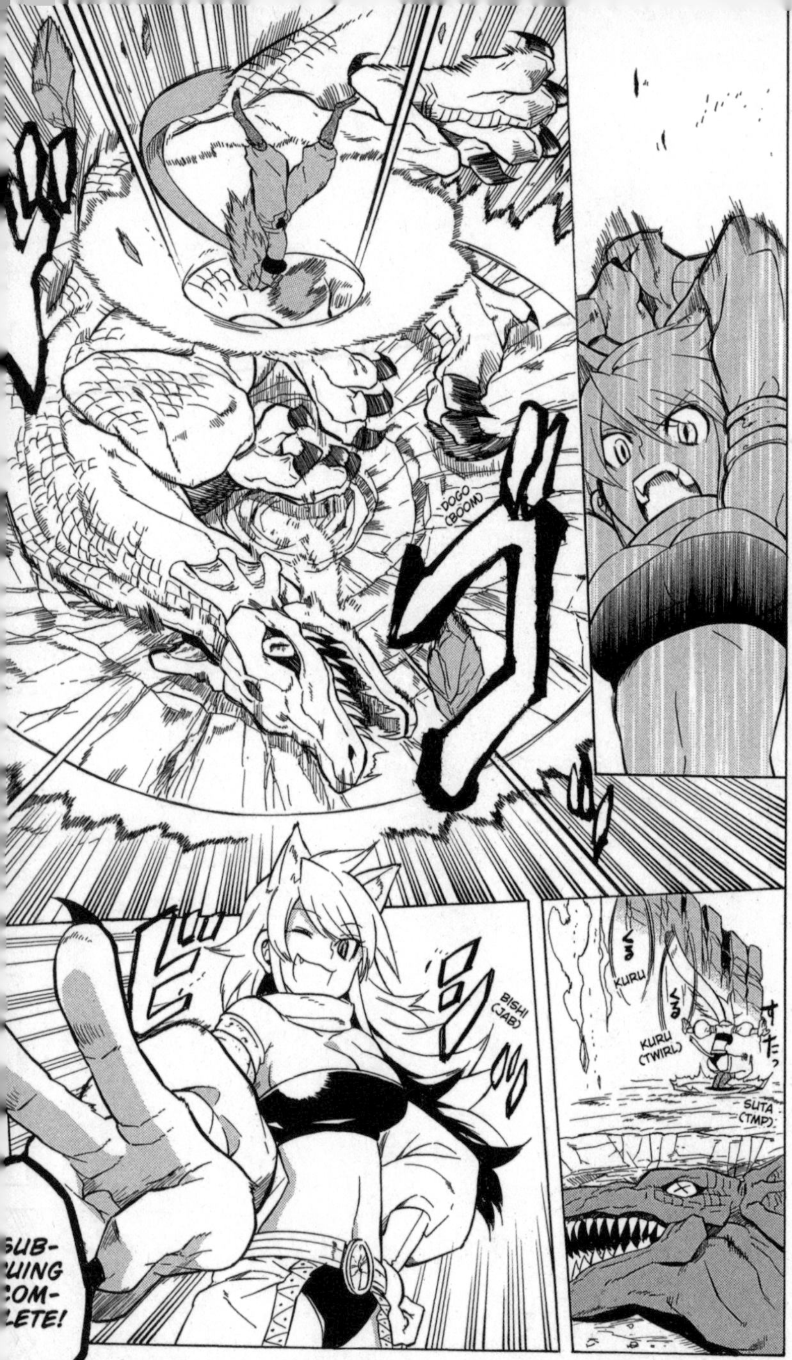

DOGO (BOOM)
BISHI (JAB)
KURU
KURU (TWIRL)
SUTA (TMP)
SUB-
DUING
COM-
PLETE!

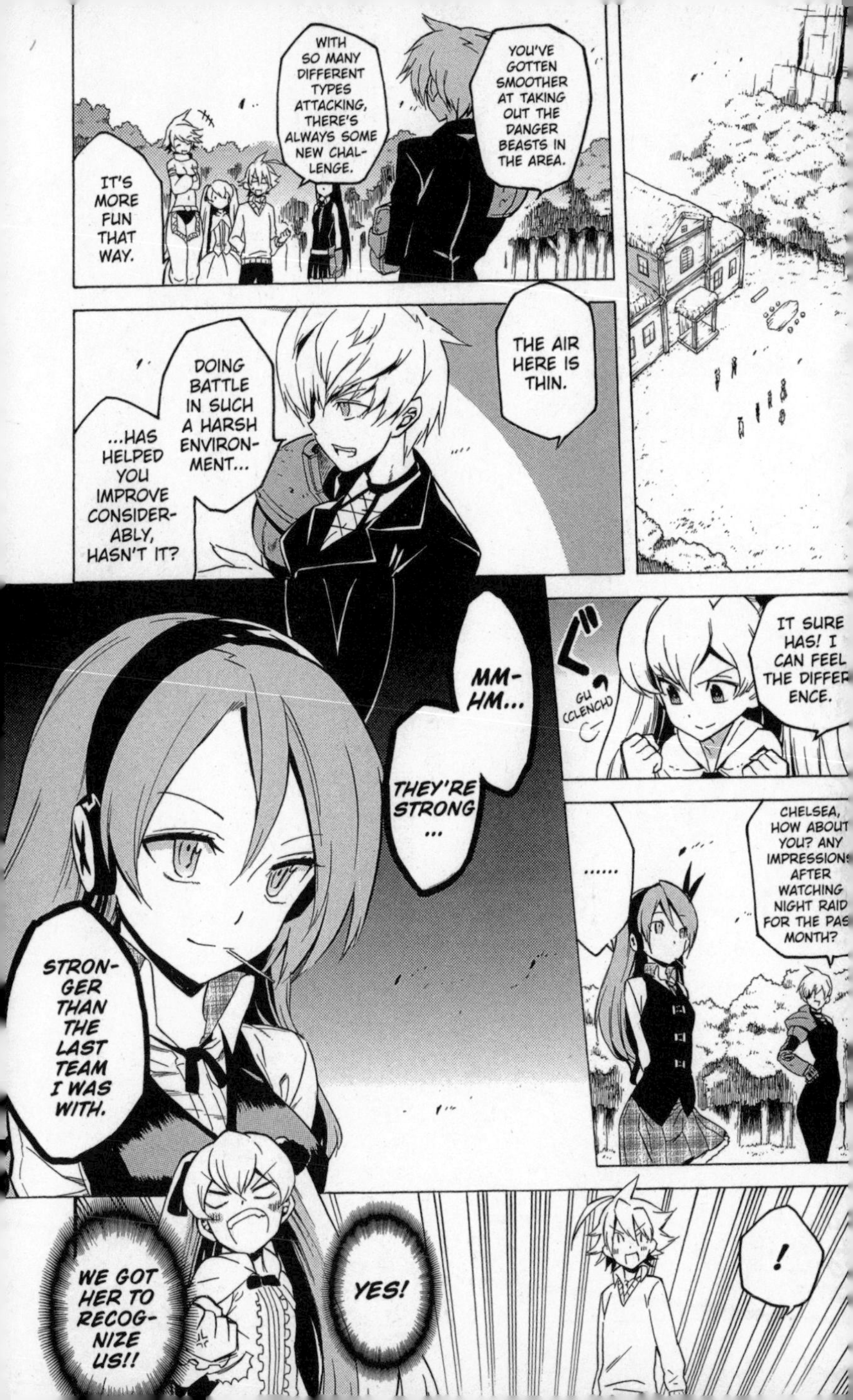
YOU'VE GOTTEN SMOOTHER AT TAKING OUT THE DANGER BEASTS IN THE AREA.
WITH SO MANY DIFFERENT TYPES ATTACKING, THERE'S ALWAYS SOME NEW CHALLENGE.
IT'S MORE FUN THAT WAY.
THE AIR HERE IS THIN.
DOING BATTLE IN SUCH A HARSH ENVIRONMENT...
...HAS HELPED YOU IMPROVE CONSIDERABLY, HASN'T IT?
IT SURE HAS! I CAN FEEL THE DIFFER ENCE.
GU (CLENCH)
CHELSEA, HOW ABOUT YOU? ANY IMPRESSIONS AFTER WATCHING NIGHT RAID FOR THE PAS MONTH?
......
MM-HM...
THEY'RE STRONG...
STRONGER THAN THE LAST TEAM I WAS WITH.
!
YES!
WE GOT HER TO RECOGNIZE US!!

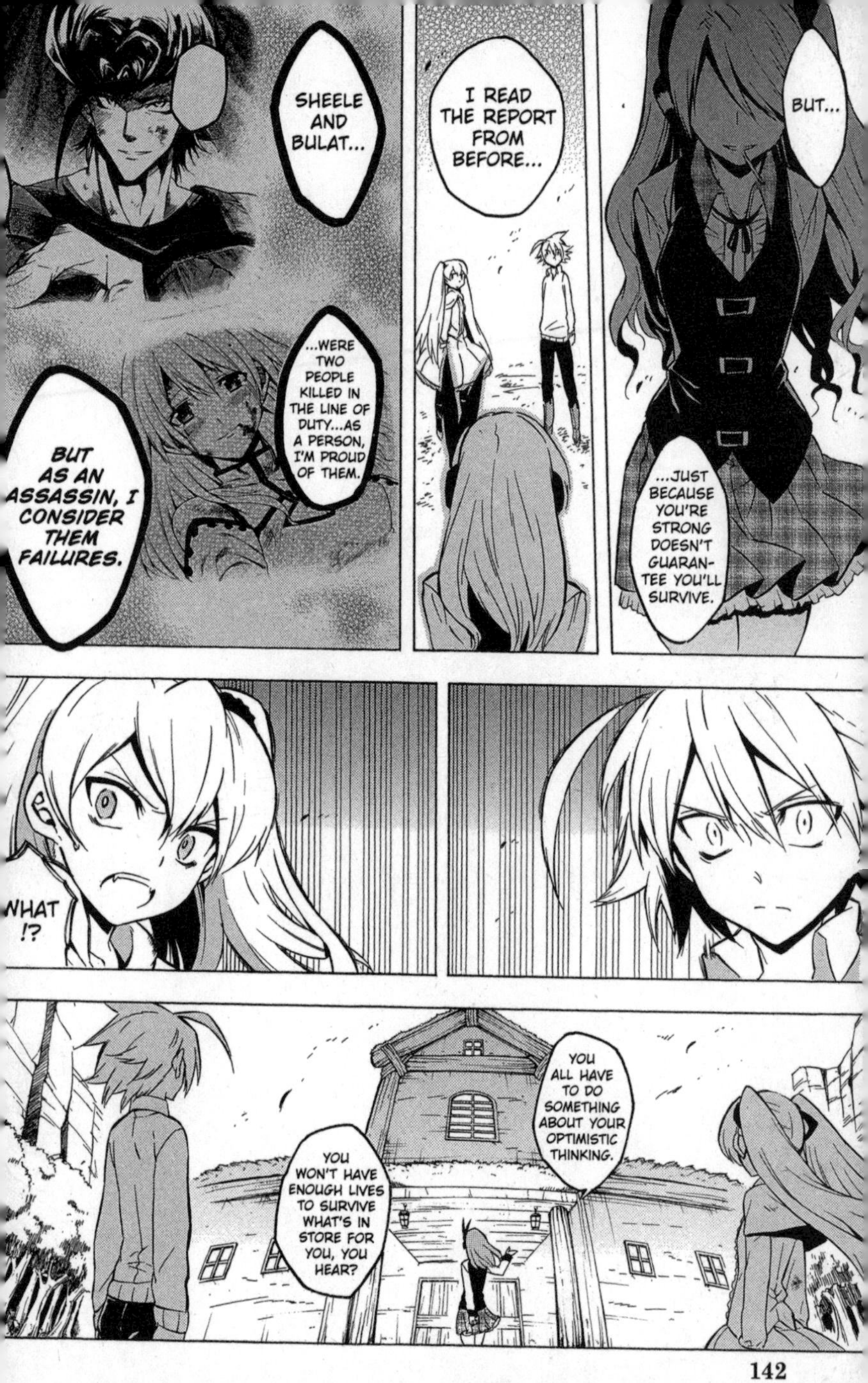
BUT...
...JUST BECAUSE YOU'RE STRONG DOESN'T GUARAN-TEE YOU'LL SURVIVE.
I READ THE REPORT FROM BEFORE...
SHEELE AND BULAT...
...WERE TWO PEOPLE KILLED IN THE LINE OF DUTY...AS A PERSON, I'M PROUD OF THEM.
BUT AS AN ASSASSIN, I CONSIDER THEM FAILURES.
WHAT !?
YOU ALL HAVE TO DO SOMETHING ABOUT YOUR OPTIMISTIC THINKING.
YOU WON'T HAVE ENOUGH LIVES TO SURVIVE WHAT'S IN STORE FOR YOU, YOU HEAR?

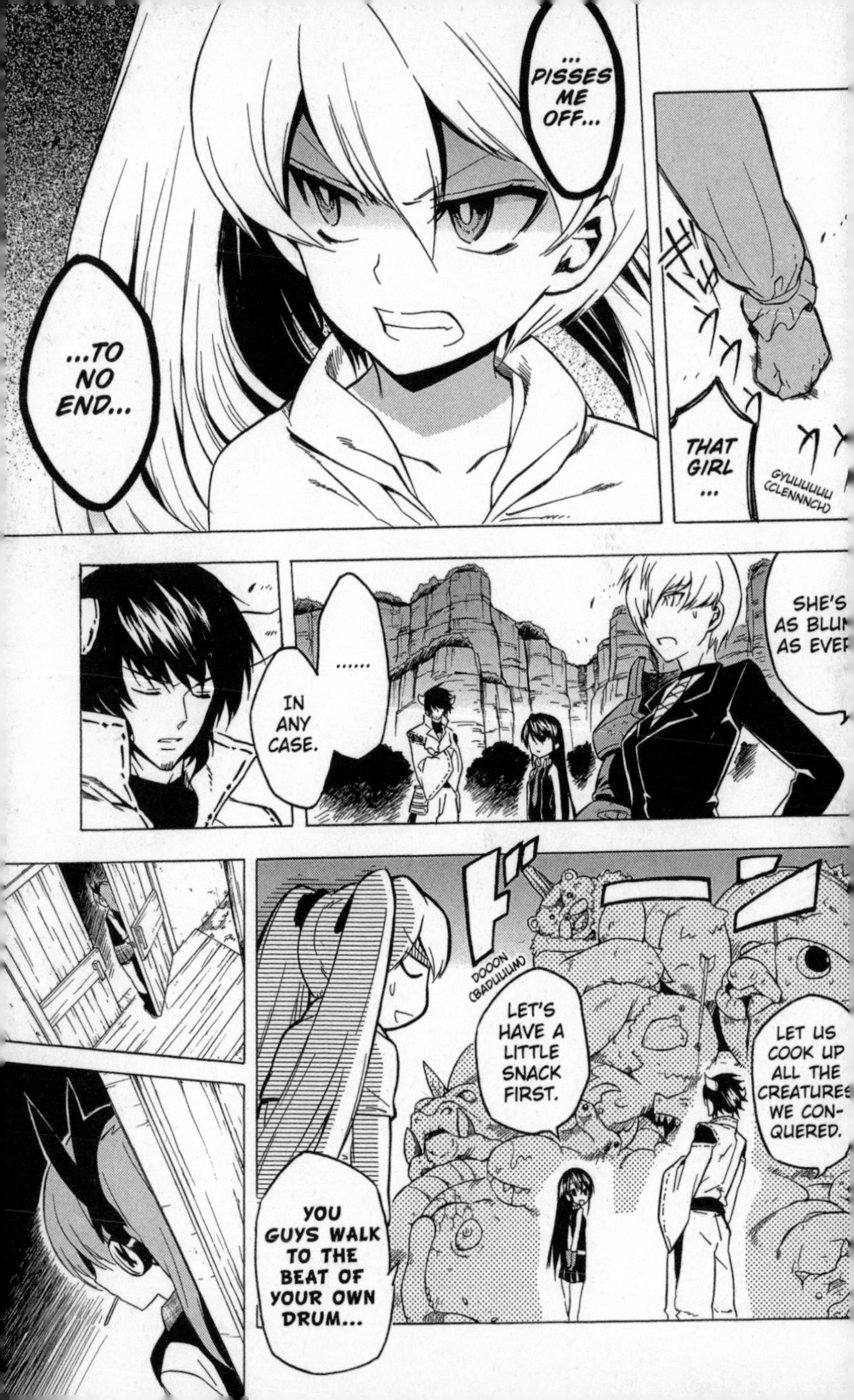
THAT GIRL ...
GYUUUUUUU (CLENNNCH)
... PISSES ME OFF...
...TO NO END...
SHE'S AS BLUN AS EVE
......
IN ANY CASE.
LET US COOK UP ALL THE CREATURES WE CONQUERED.
DOOON (BADUUUM)
LET'S HAVE A LITTLE SNACK FIRST.
YOU GUYS WALK TO THE BEAT OF YOUR OWN DRUM...

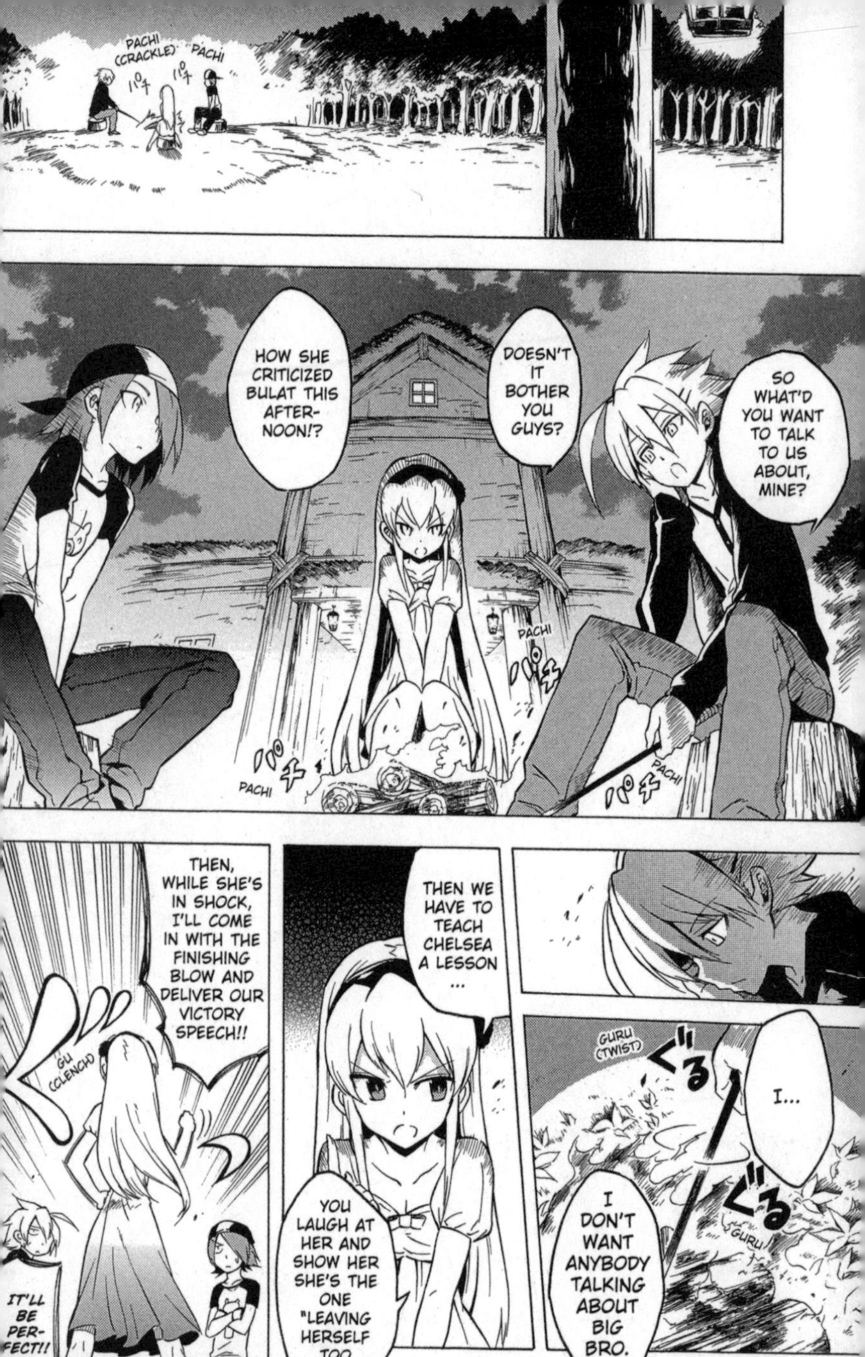
PACHI
(CRACKLE)
PACHI
SO WHAT'D YOU WANT TO TALK TO US ABOUT, MINE?
DOESN'T IT BOTHER YOU GUYS?
HOW SHE CRITICIZED BULAT THIS AFTER-NOON!?
PACHI
PACHI
PACHI
I...
GURU (TWIST)
GURU
I DON'T WANT ANYBODY TALKING ABOUT BIG BRO.
THEN WE HAVE TO TEACH CHELSEA A LESSON ...
YOU LAUGH AT HER AND SHOW HER SHE'S THE ONE "LEAVING HERSELF TOO OPEN."
THEN, WHILE SHE'S IN SHOCK, I'LL COME IN WITH THE FINISHING BLOW AND DELIVER OUR VICTORY SPEECH!!
GU (CLENCH)
IT'LL BE PERFECT!!

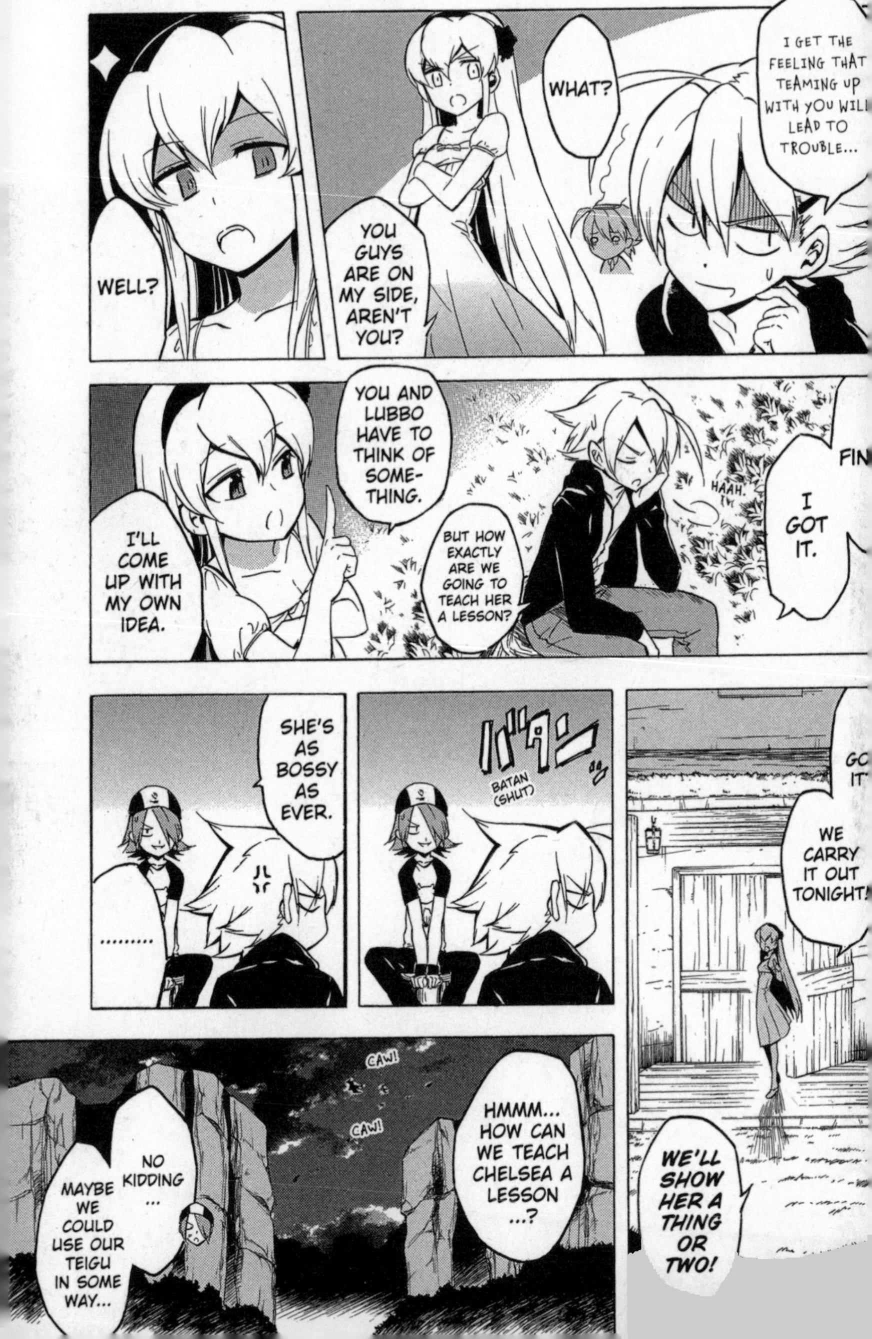
I GET THE FEELING THAT TEAMING UP WITH YOU WILL LEAD TO TROUBLE...
WHAT?
YOU GUYS ARE ON MY SIDE, AREN'T YOU?
WELL?
I GOT IT.
HAAH.
BUT HOW EXACTLY ARE WE GOING TO TEACH HER A LESSON?
YOU AND LUBBO HAVE TO THINK OF SOME-THING.
I'LL COME UP WITH MY OWN IDEA.
WE CARRY IT OUT TONIGHT!
WE'LL SHOW HER A THING OR TWO!
BATAN (SHUT)
SHE'S AS BOSSY AS EVER.
....
CAW!
CAW!
HMMM... HOW CAN WE TEACH CHELSEA A LESSON ...?
NO KIDDING ...
MAYBE WE COULD USE OUR TEIGU IN SOME WAY...

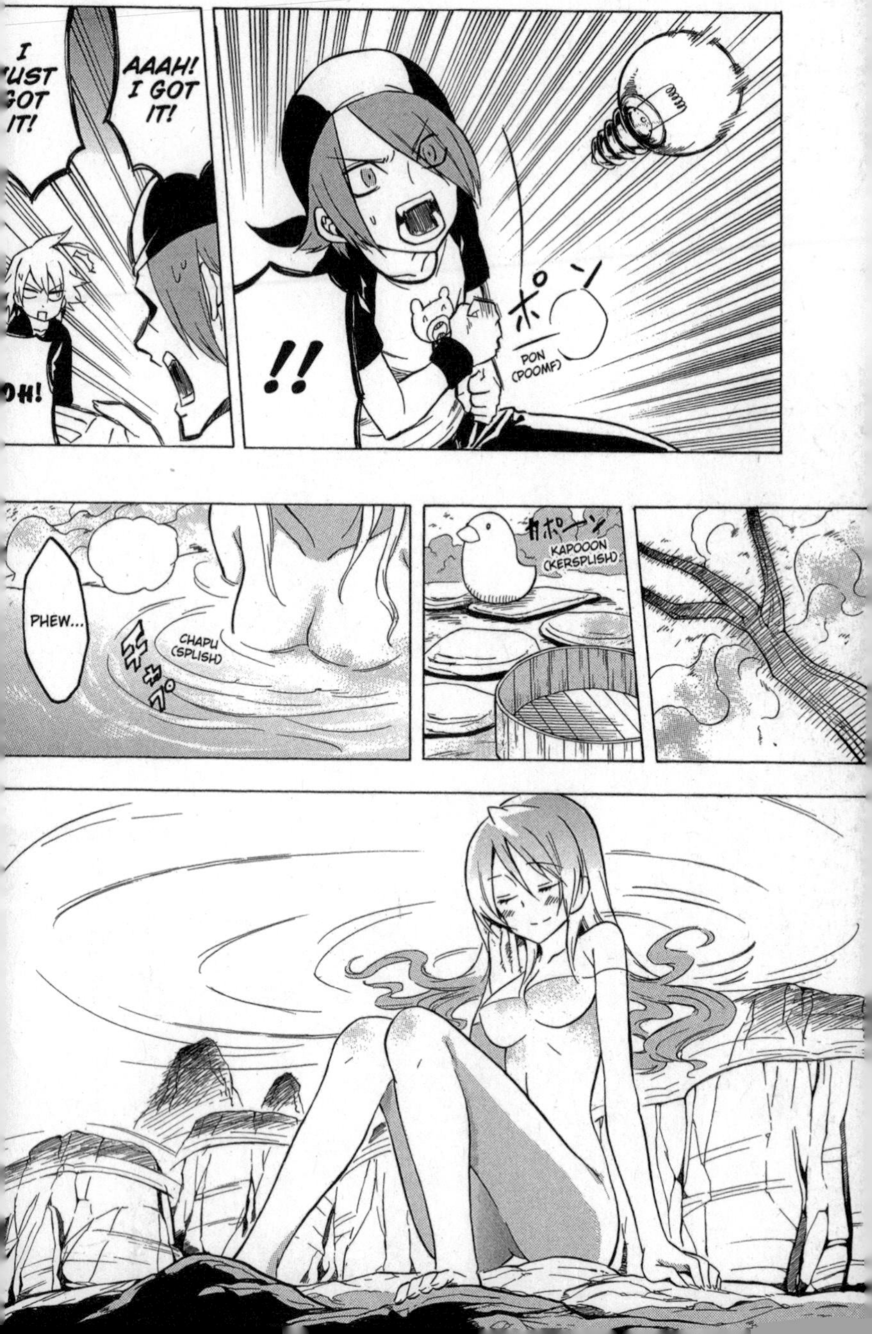

AAAH! I GOT IT!
PON (POOMF)
!!
I JUST GOT IT!
OH!
KAPOOON (KERSPLISH)
CHAPU (SPLISH)
PHEW...

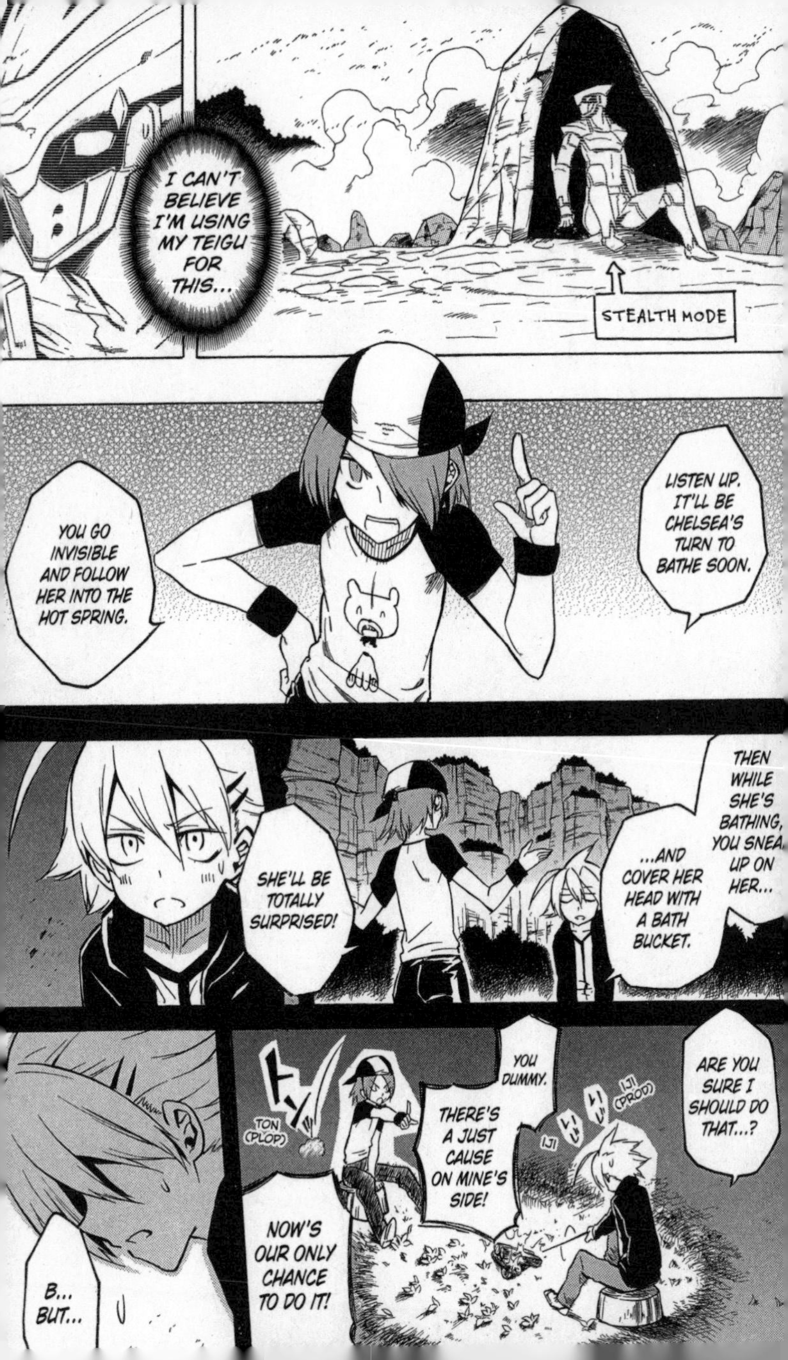
STEALTH MODE
I CAN'T BELIEVE I'M USING MY TEIGU FOR THIS...
LISTEN UP. IT'LL BE CHELSEA'S TURN TO BATHE SOON.
YOU GO INVISIBLE AND FOLLOW HER INTO THE HOT SPRING.
THEN WHILE SHE'S BATHING, YOU SNEA UP ON HER...
...AND COVER HER HEAD WITH A BATH BUCKET.
SHE'LL BE TOTALLY SURPRISED!
ARE YOU SURE I SHOULD DO THAT...?
IJI (PROD)
IJI
YOU DUMMY.
THERE'S A JUST CAUSE ON MINE'S SIDE!
TON (PLOP)
NOW'S OUR ONLY CHANCE TO DO IT!
B... BUT...

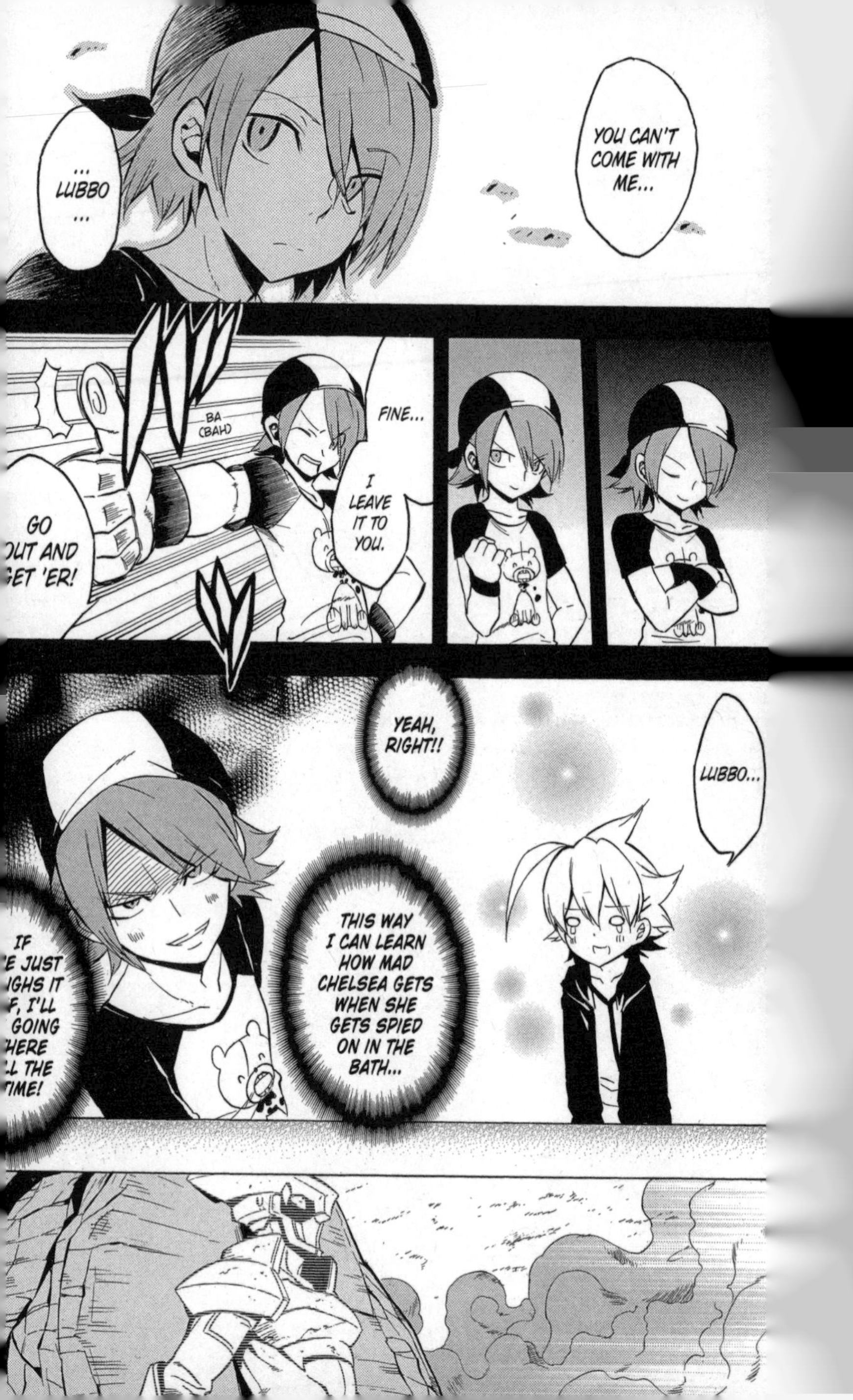
YOU CAN'T COME WITH ME...
... LUBBO ...
FINE... I LEAVE IT TO YOU.
BA (BAH)
GO OUT AND GET 'ER!
LUBBO...
YEAH, RIGHT!!
THIS WAY I CAN LEARN HOW MAD CHELSEA GETS WHEN SHE GETS SPIED ON IN THE BATH...
IF E JUST IGHS IT F, I'LL GOING HERE L THE TIME!

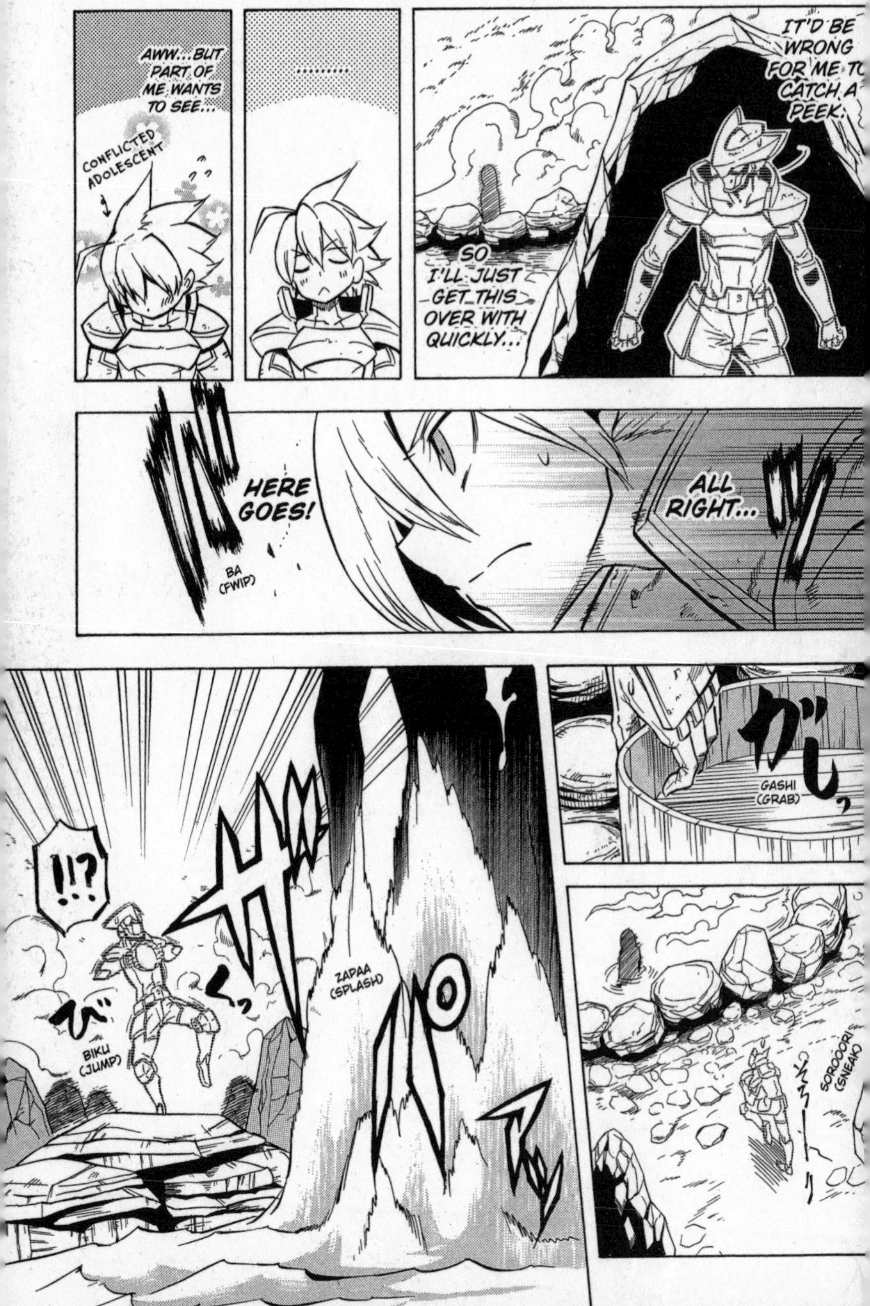

IT'D BE WRONG FOR ME TO CATCH A PEEK.
SO I'LL JUST GET THIS OVER WITH QUICKLY...
....
AWW...BUT PART OF ME WANTS TO SEE...
CONFLICTED ADOLESCENT
ALL RIGHT...
HERE GOES!
BA (FWIP)
GASHI (GRAB)
SOROOORI (SNEAK)
ZAPAA (SPLASH)
!!?
BIKU (JUMP)

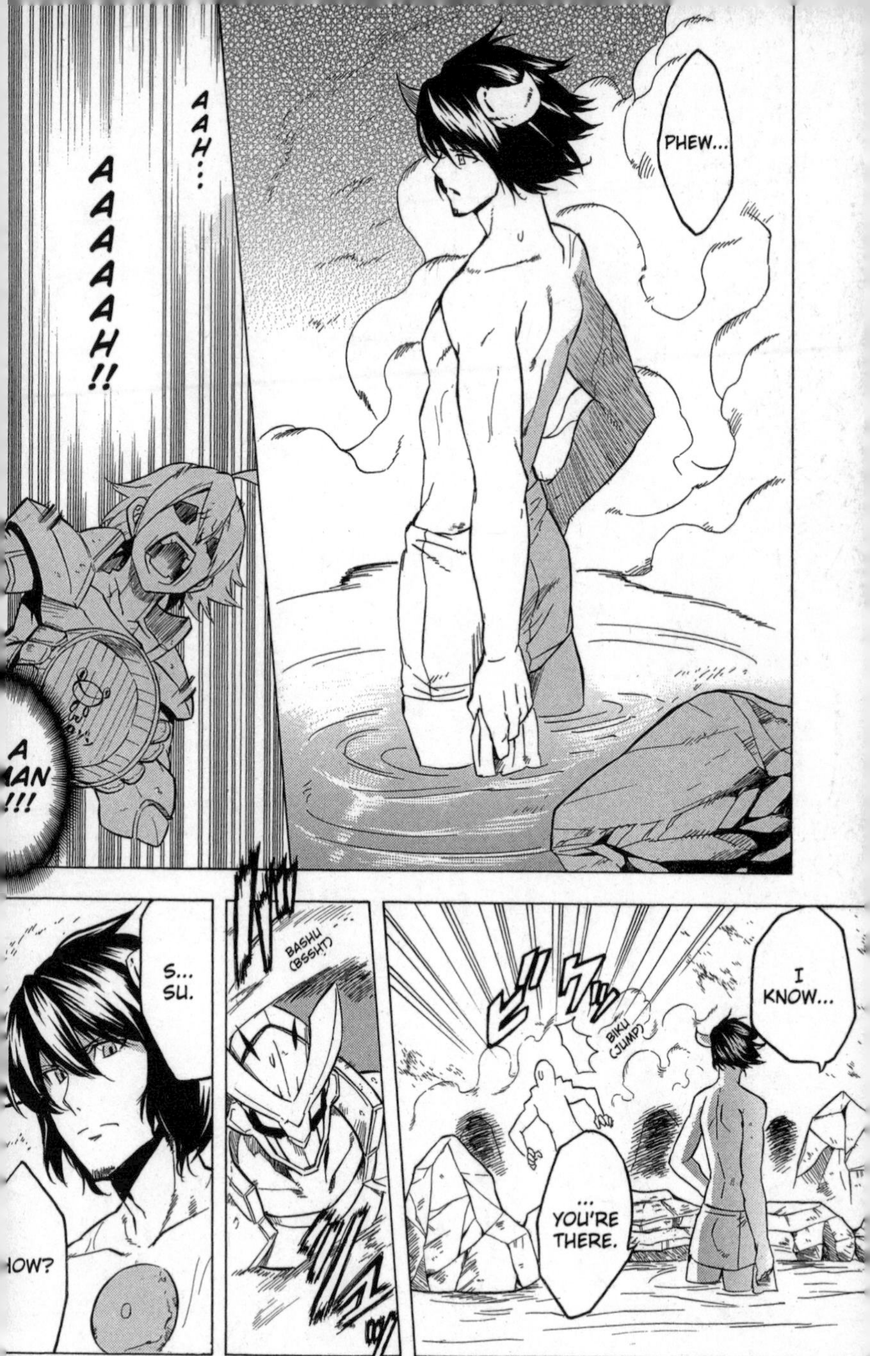
PHEW...
AAH...
AAAAAAH!!
A
MAN
!!!
I
KNOW...
BIKU
(JUMP)
...
YOU'RE
THERE.
BASHU
(BSSHT)
S...
SU.
HOW?

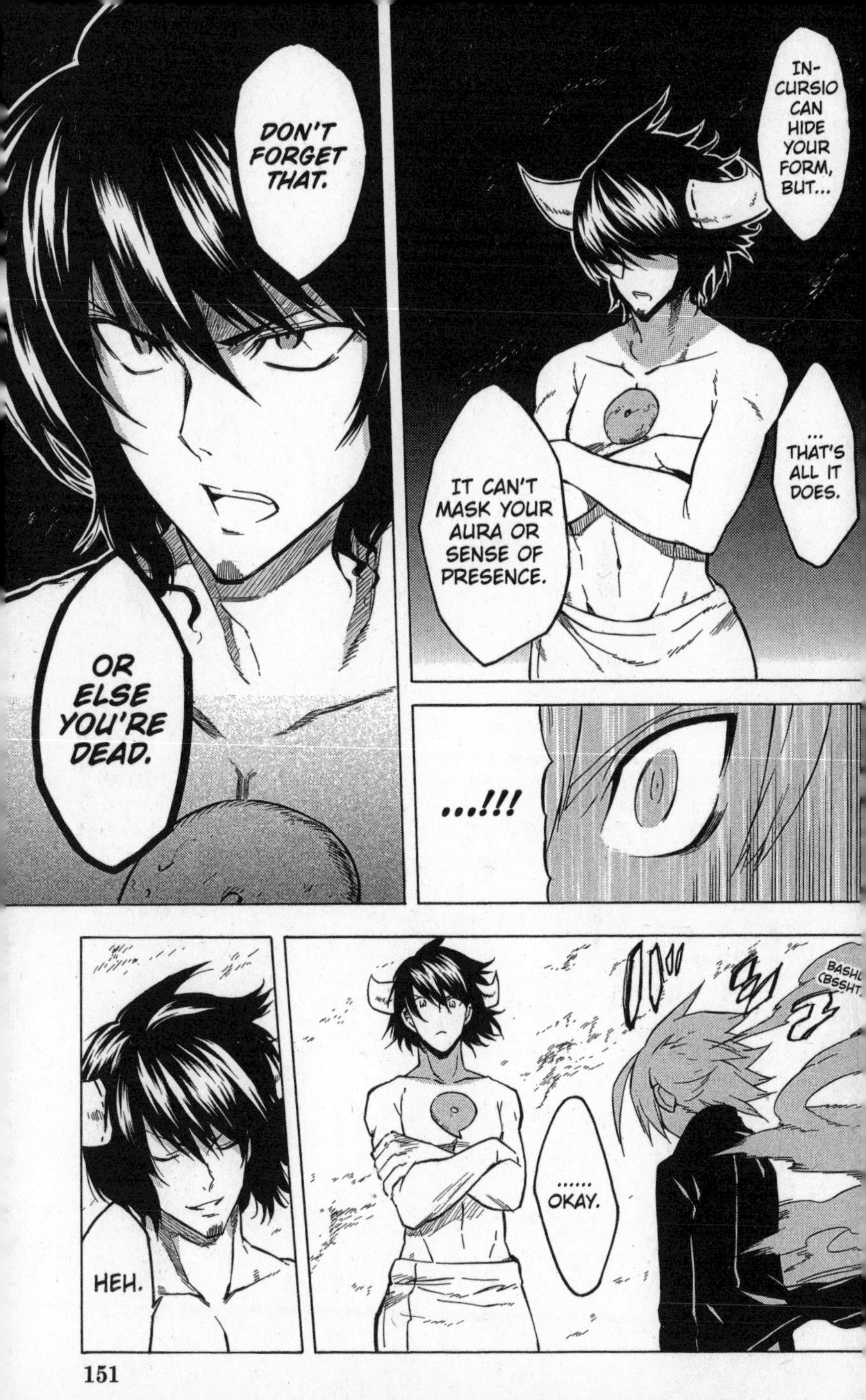

INCURSIO CAN HIDE YOUR FORM, BUT...
...THAT'S ALL IT DOES.
IT CAN'T MASK YOUR AURA OR SENSE OF PRESENCE.
DON'T FORGET THAT.
OR ELSE YOU'RE DEAD.
...!!!
......OKAY.
HEH.

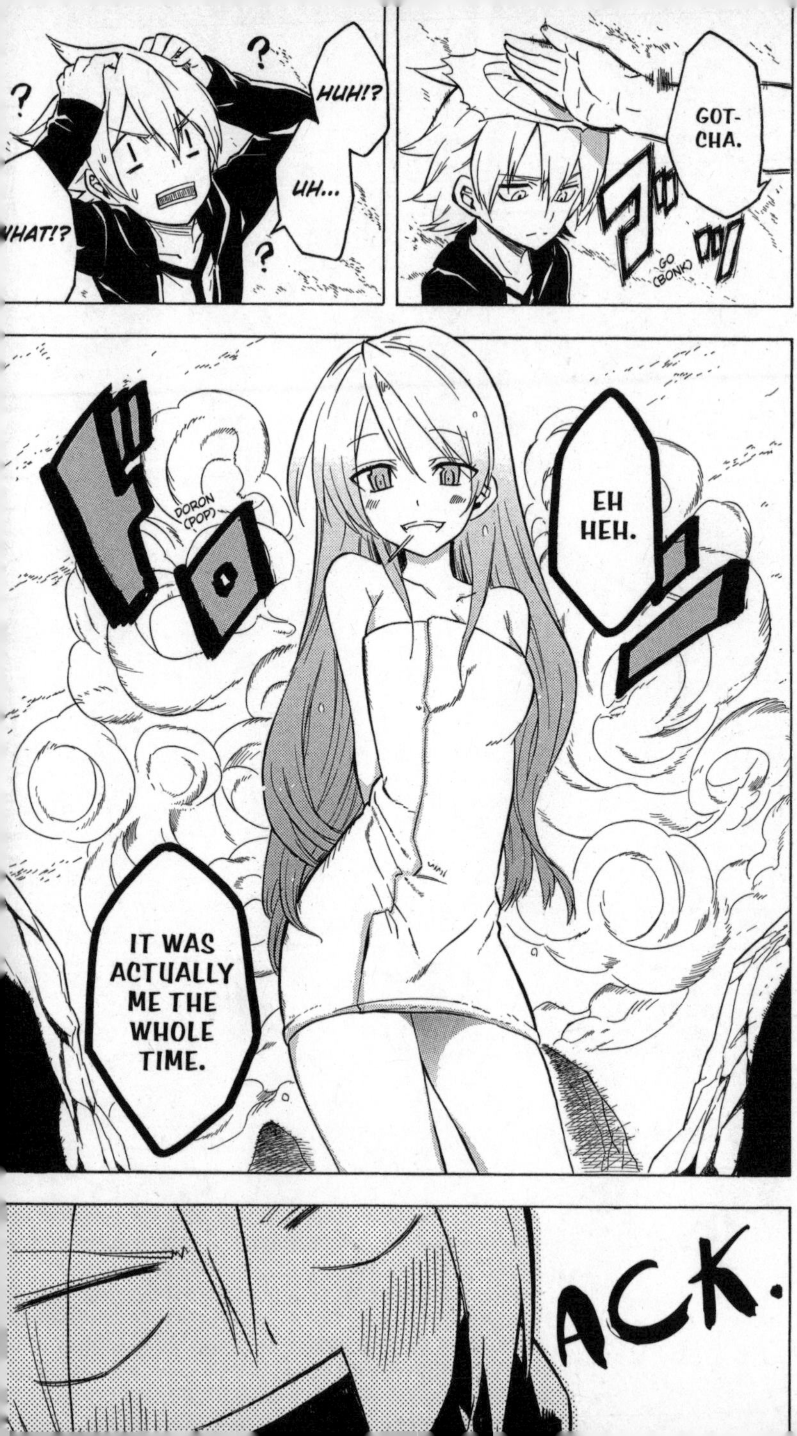
GOT-CHA.
GO (BONK)
HUH!?
UH...
HAT!?
EH HEH.
DORON (POP)
IT WAS ACTUALLY ME THE WHOLE TIME.
ACK.

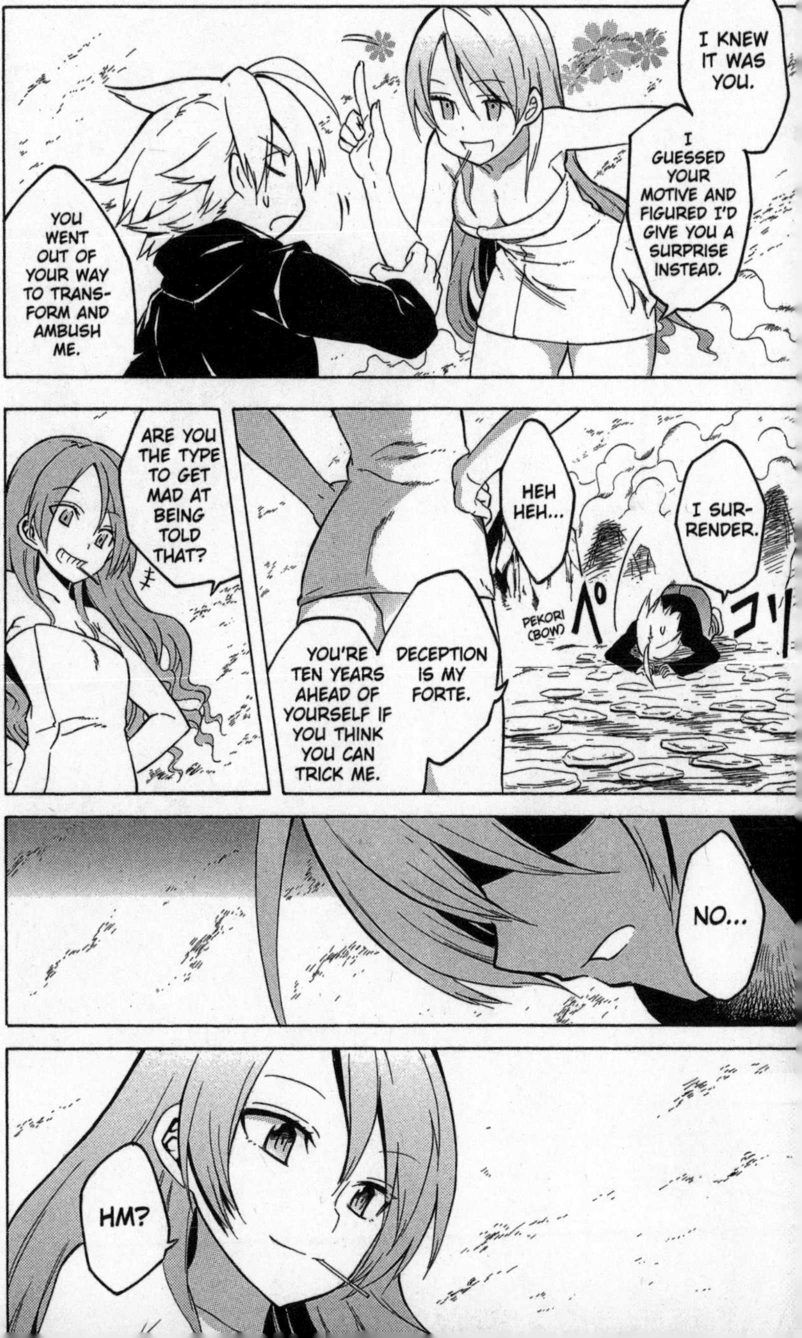
I KNEW IT WAS YOU.
I GUESSED YOUR MOTIVE AND FIGURED I'D GIVE YOU A SURPRISE INSTEAD.
YOU WENT OUT OF YOUR WAY TO TRANS-FORM AND AMBUSH ME.
I SUR-RENDER.
PEKORI (BOW)
HEH HEH...
DECEPTION IS MY FORTE.
YOU'RE TEN YEARS AHEAD OF YOURSELF IF YOU THINK YOU CAN TRICK ME.
ARE YOU THE TYPE TO GET MAD AT BEING TOLD THAT?
NO...
HM?

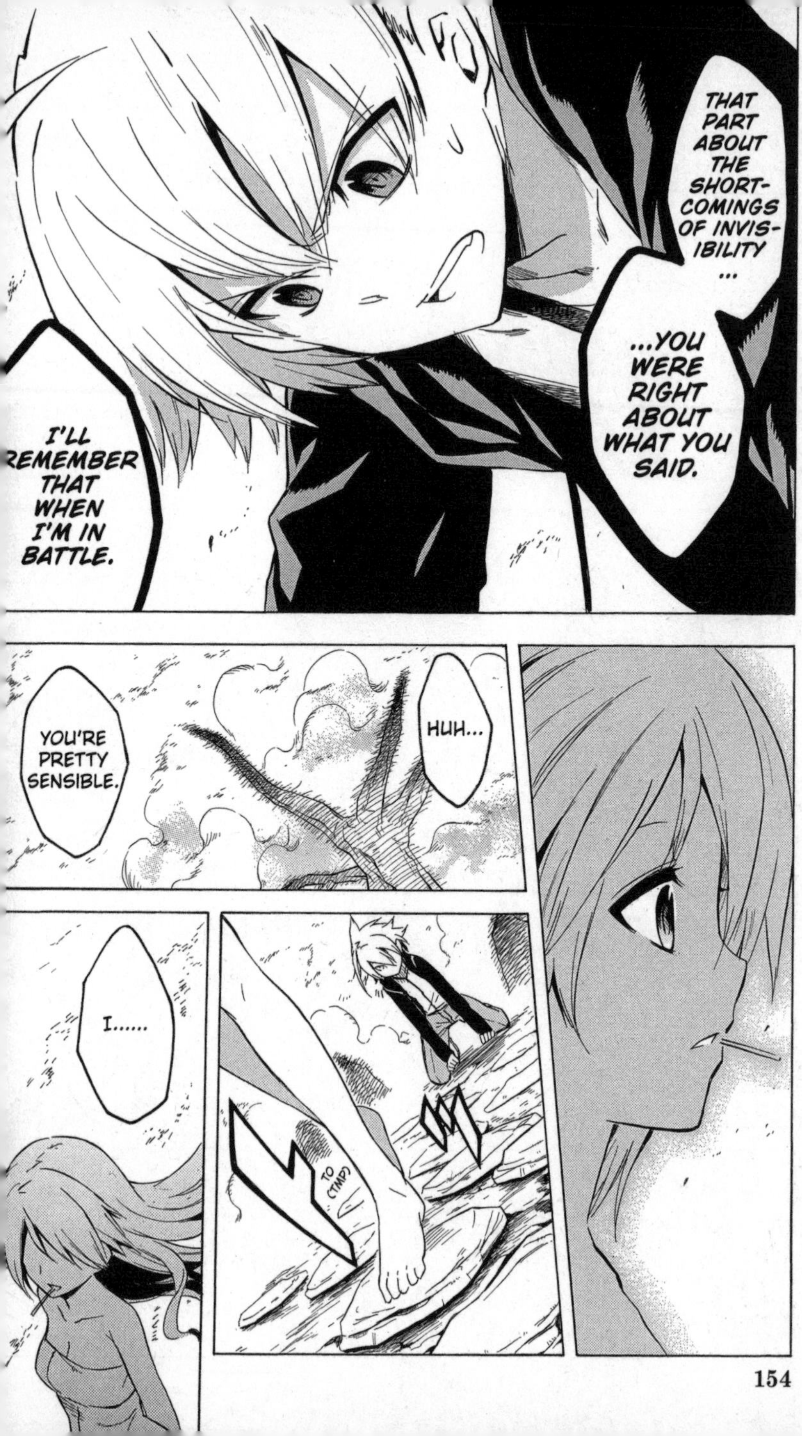
THAT PART ABOUT THE SHORT-COMINGS OF INVISIBILITY...
...YOU WERE RIGHT ABOUT WHAT YOU SAID.
I'LL REMEMBER THAT WHEN I'M IN BATTLE.
HUH...
YOU'RE PRETTY SENSIBLE.
TO (TMP)
I......

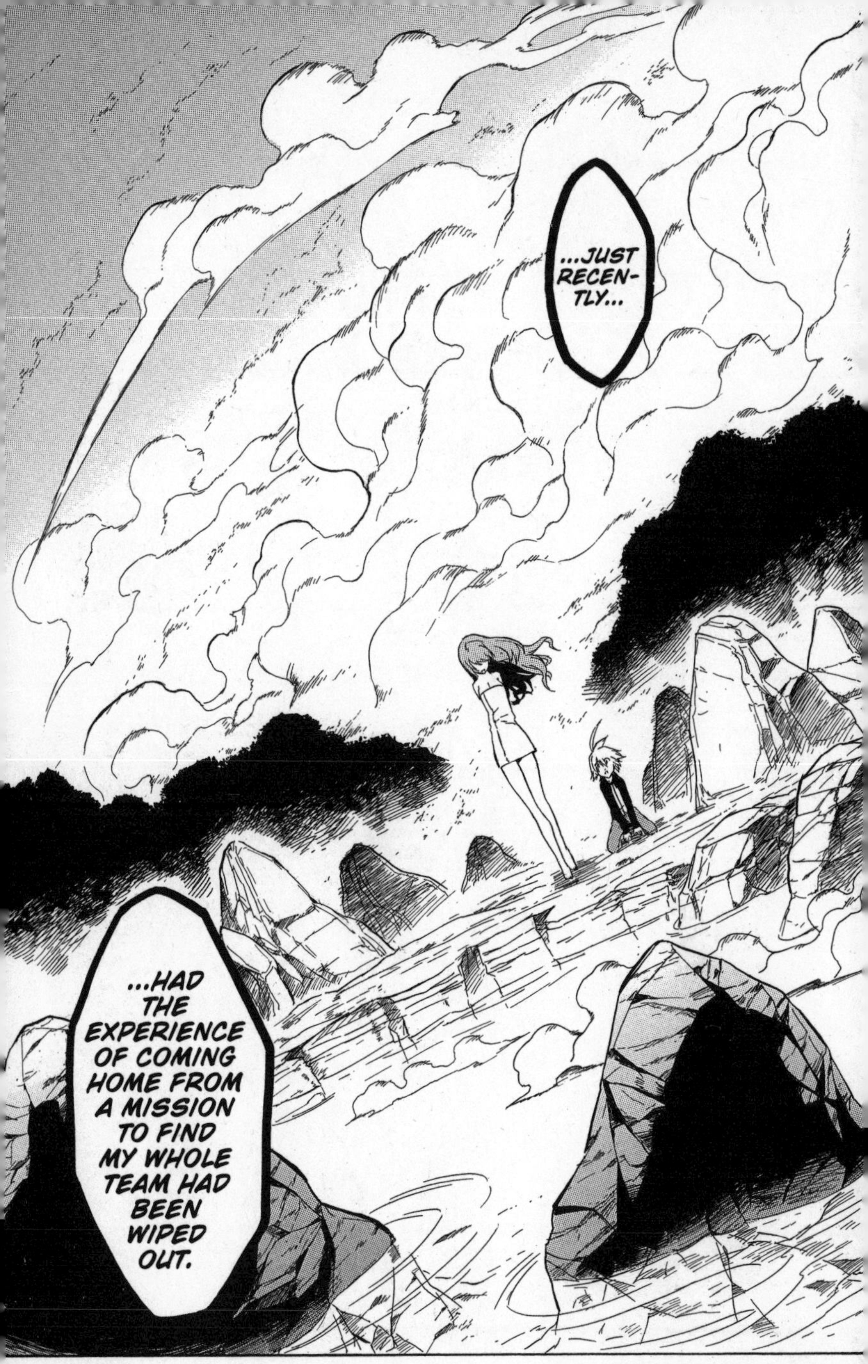
...JUST RECENTLY...
...HAD THE EXPERIENCE OF COMING HOME FROM A MISSION TO FIND MY WHOLE TEAM HAD BEEN WIPED OUT.

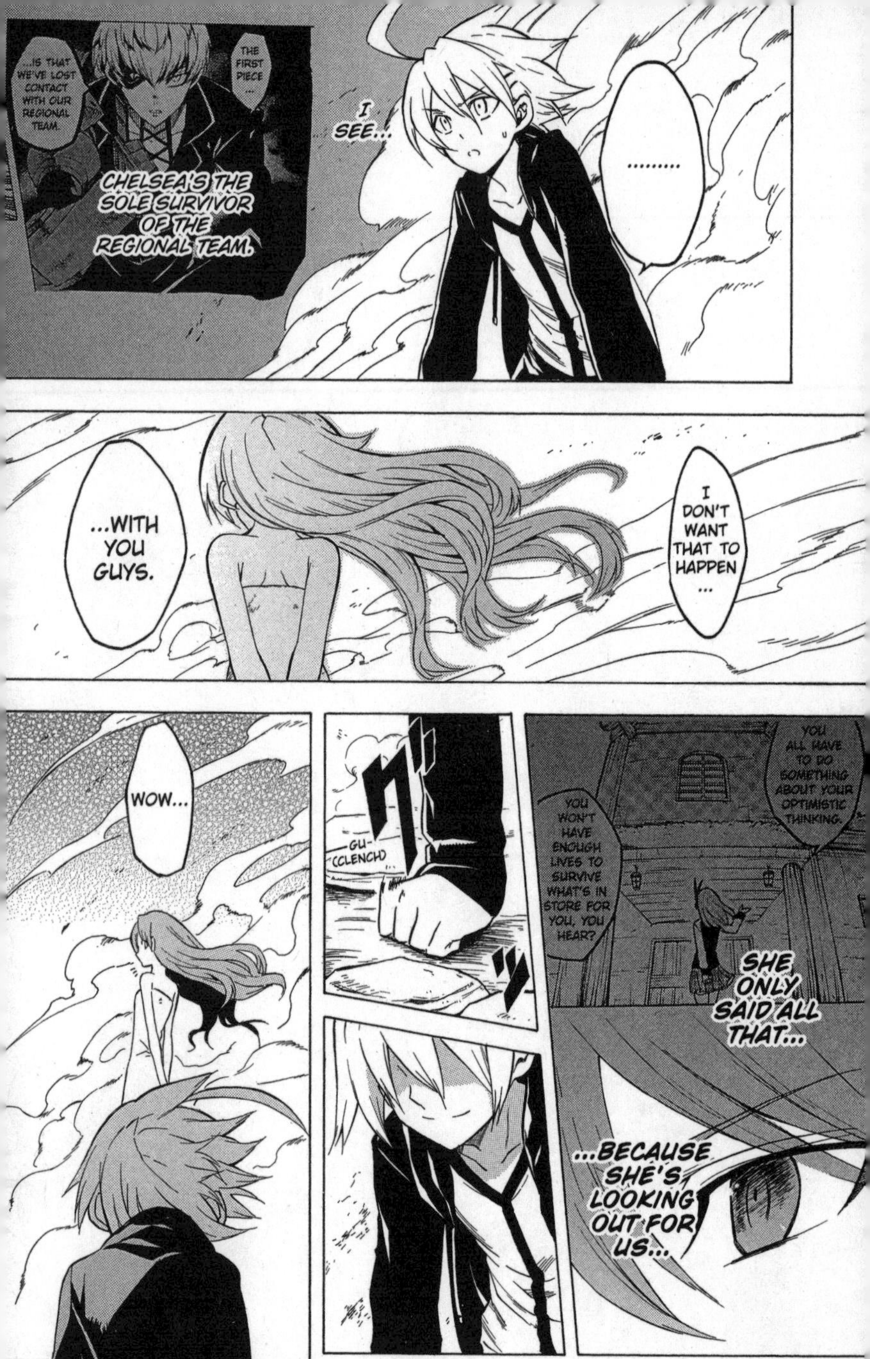
....
I SEE...
THE FIRST PIECE ...
...IS THAT WE'VE LOST CONTACT WITH OUR REGIONAL TEAM.
CHELSEA'S THE SOLE SURVIVOR OF THE REGIONAL TEAM.
I DON'T WANT THAT TO HAPPEN ...
...WITH YOU GUYS.
YOU ALL HAVE TO DO SOMETHING ABOUT YOUR OPTIMISTIC THINKING.
YOU WON'T HAVE ENOUGH LIVES TO SURVIVE WHAT'S IN STORE FOR YOU, YOU HEAR?
GU- (CLENCH)
WOW...
SHE ONLY SAID ALL THAT...
...BECAUSE SHE'S LOOKING OUT FOR US...

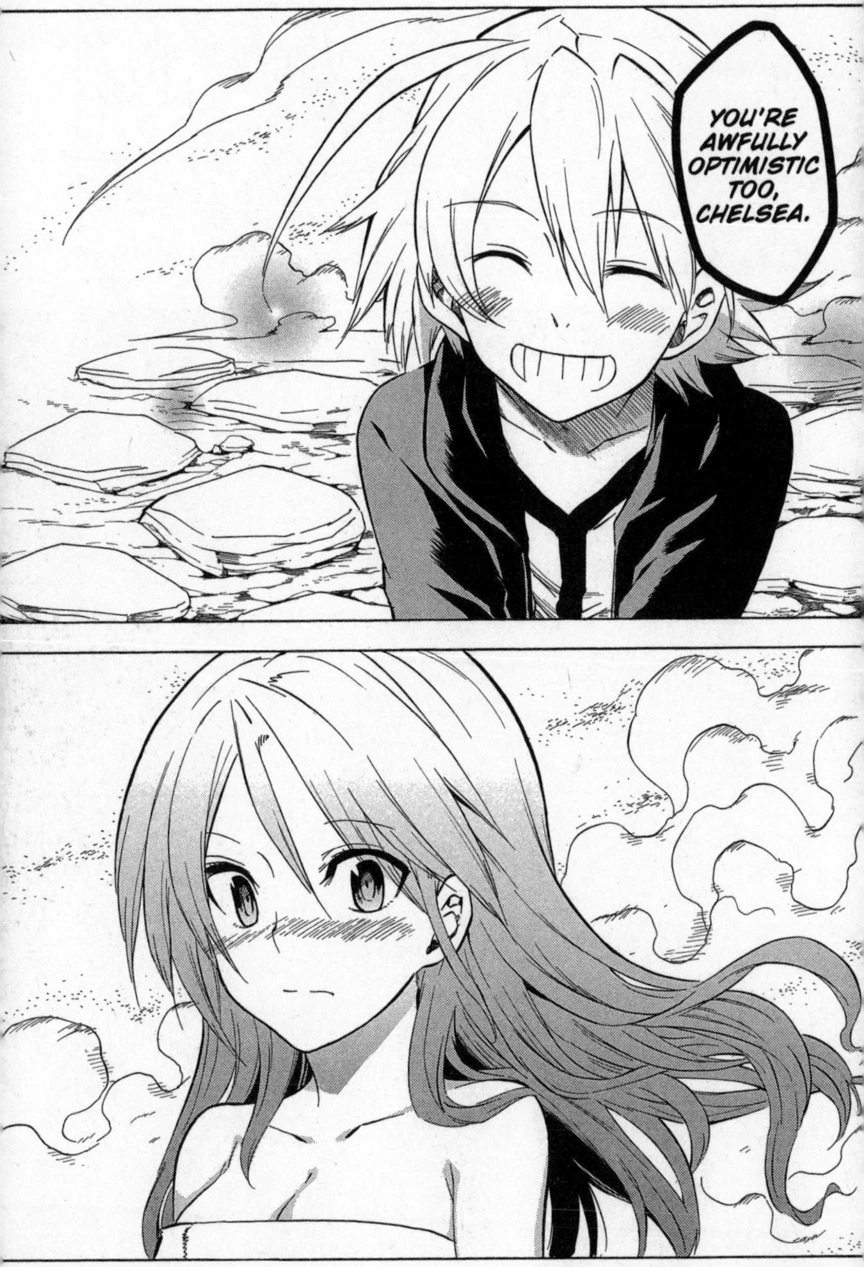
YOU'RE AWFULLY OPTIMISTIC TOO, CHELSEA.

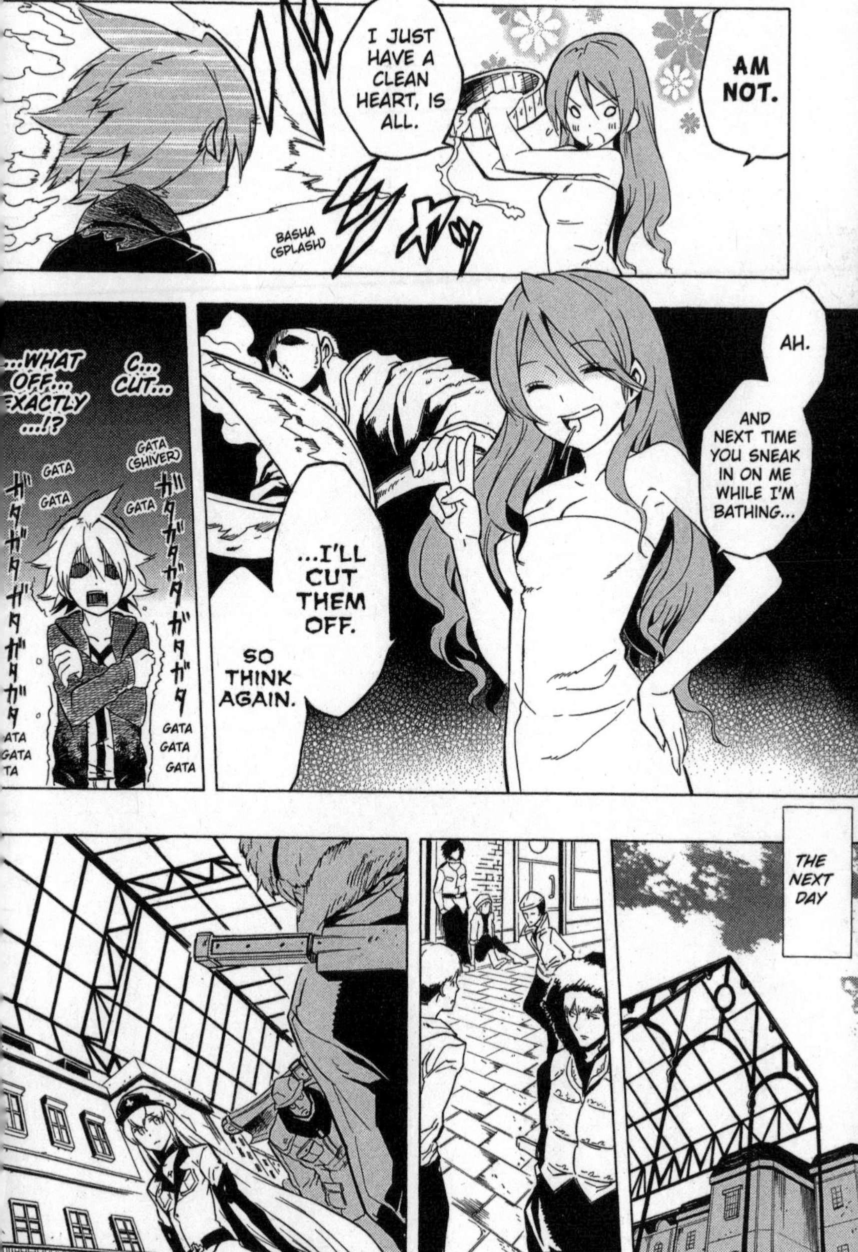
AM NOT.
I JUST HAVE A CLEAN HEART, IS ALL.
BASHA (SPLASH)
AH.
AND NEXT TIME YOU SNEAK IN ON ME WHILE I'M BATHING...
...I'LL CUT THEM OFF.
SO THINK AGAIN.
C... CUT...
...WHAT OFF... EXACTLY ...!?
GATA (SHIVER)
GATA GATA
GATA GATA
GATA GATA GATA
THE NEXT DAY

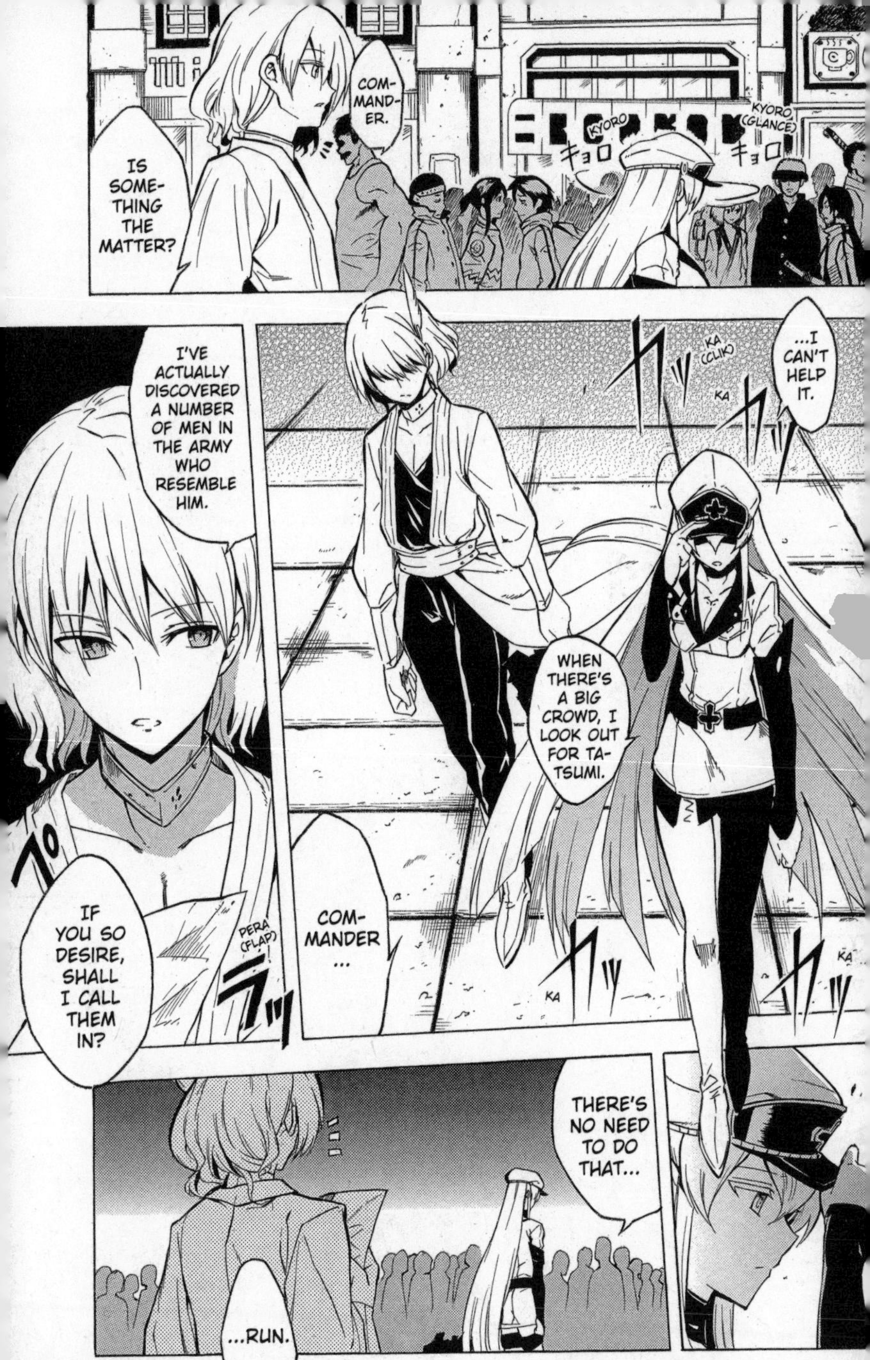
KYORO
KYORO (GLANCE)
COMMANDER.
IS SOMETHING THE MATTER?
...I CAN'T HELP IT.
KA (CLIK)
KA
WHEN THERE'S A BIG CROWD, I LOOK OUT FOR TATSUMI.
KA
KA
COMMANDER...
I'VE ACTUALLY DISCOVERED A NUMBER OF MEN IN THE ARMY WHO RESEMBLE HIM.
PERA (FLAP)
IF YOU SO DESIRE, SHALL I CALL THEM IN?
THERE'S NO NEED TO DO THAT...
...RUN.

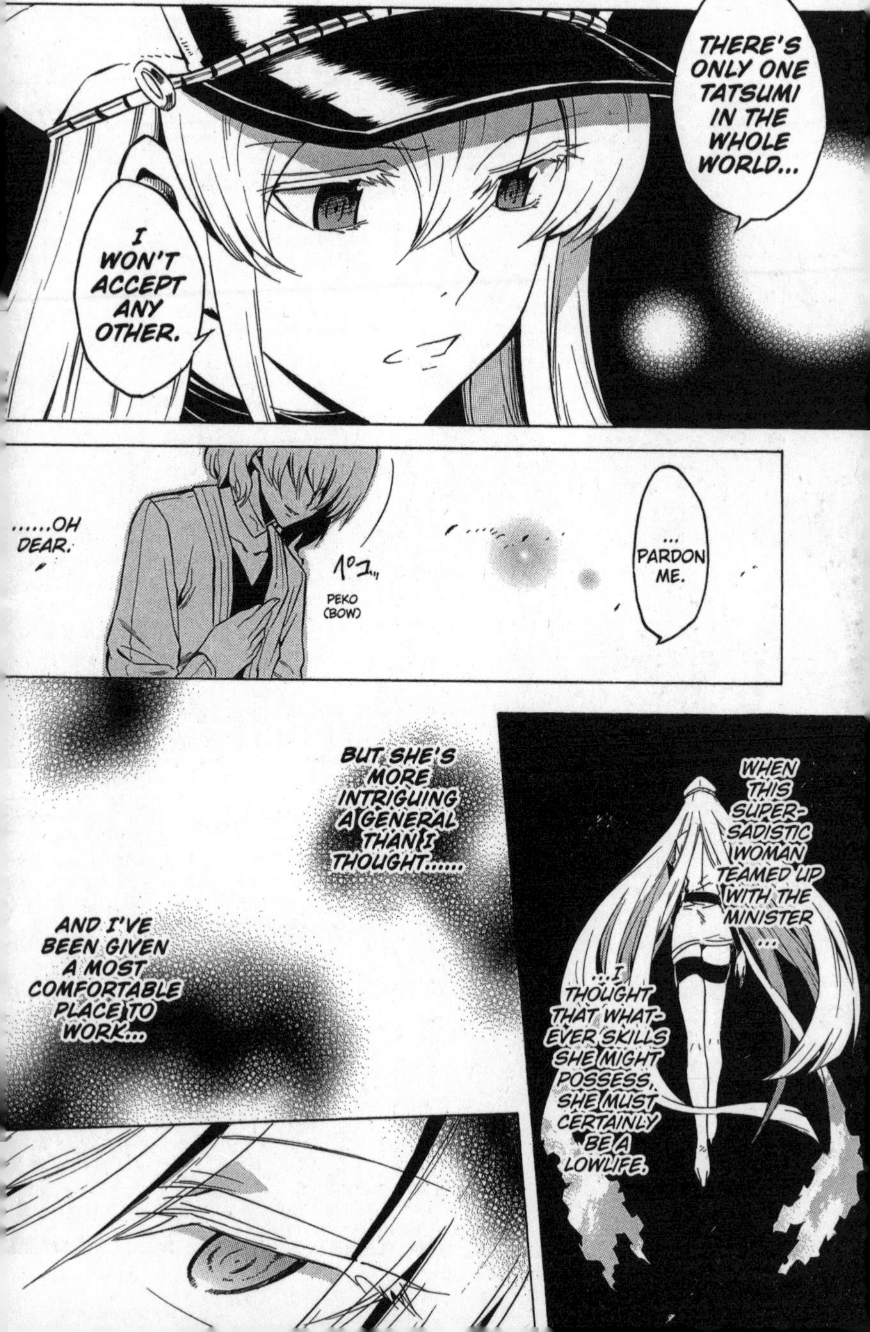
THERE'S ONLY ONE TATSUMI IN THE WHOLE WORLD...
I WON'T ACCEPT ANY OTHER.
...PARDON ME.
PEKO (BOW)
......OH DEAR.
WHEN THIS SUPER-SADISTIC WOMAN TEAMED UP WITH THE MINISTER...
...I THOUGHT THAT WHAT-EVER SKILLS SHE MIGHT POSSESS, SHE MUST CERTAINLY BE A LOWLIFE.
BUT SHE'S MORE INTRIGUING A GENERAL THAN I THOUGHT......
AND I'VE BEEN GIVEN A MOST COMFORTABLE PLACE TO WORK...

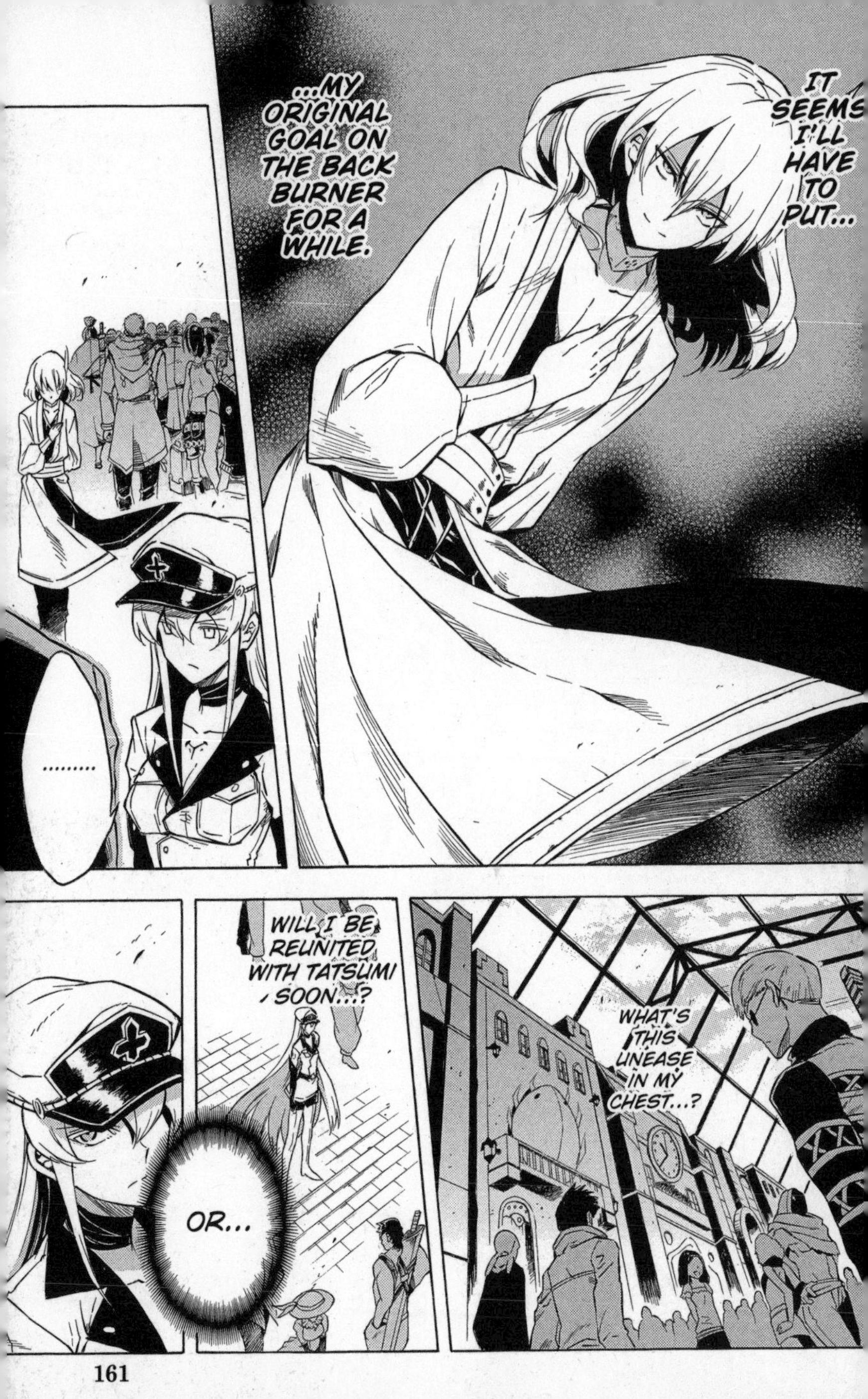
IT SEEMS I'LL HAVE TO PUT...
...MY ORIGINAL GOAL ON THE BACK BURNER FOR A WHILE.
....
WHAT'S THIS UNEASE IN MY CHEST...?
WILL I BE REUNITED WITH TATSUMI SOON...?
OR...

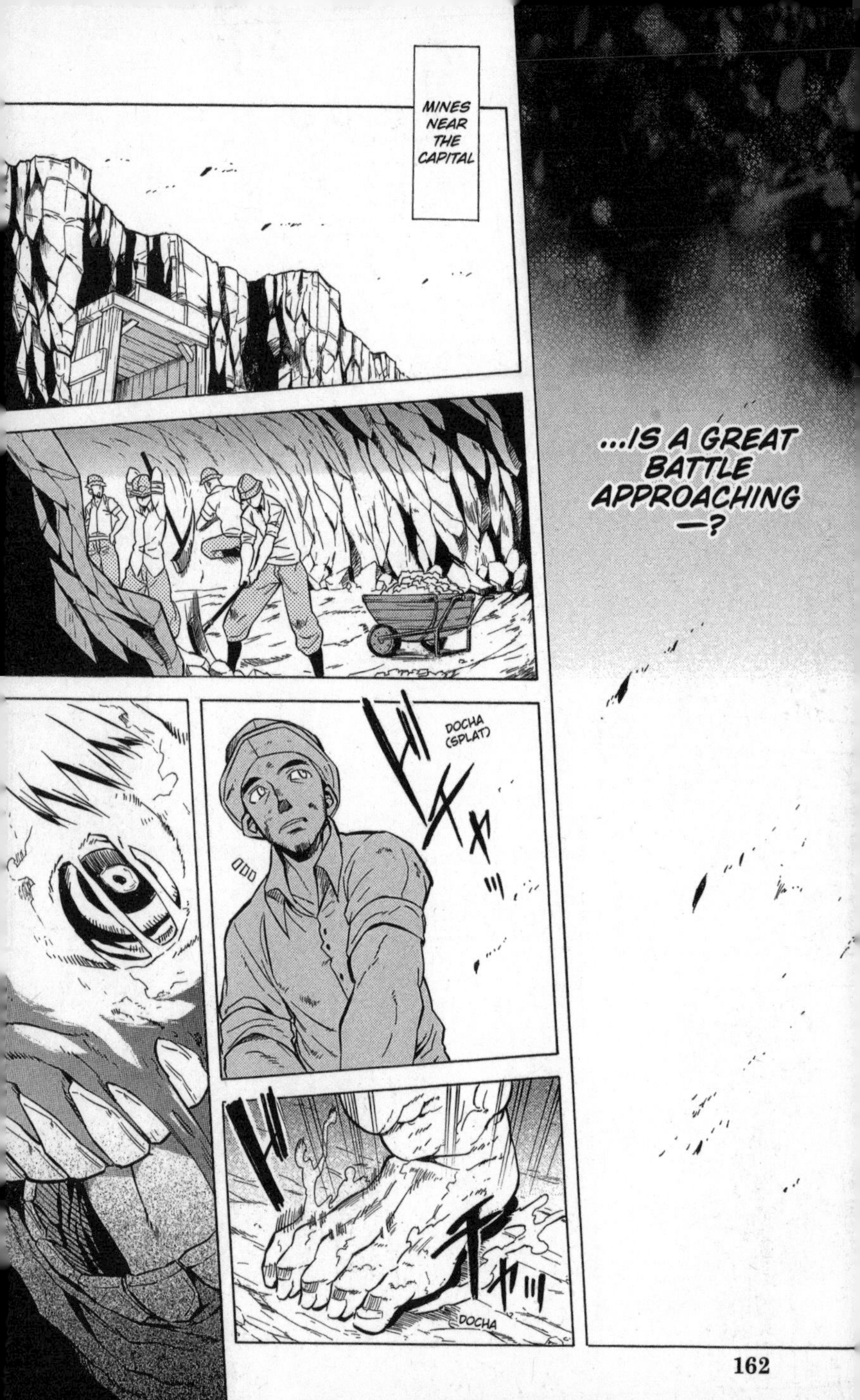
...IS A GREAT BATTLE APPROACHING—?
MINES NEAR THE CAPITAL
DOCHA (SPLAT)
DOCHA

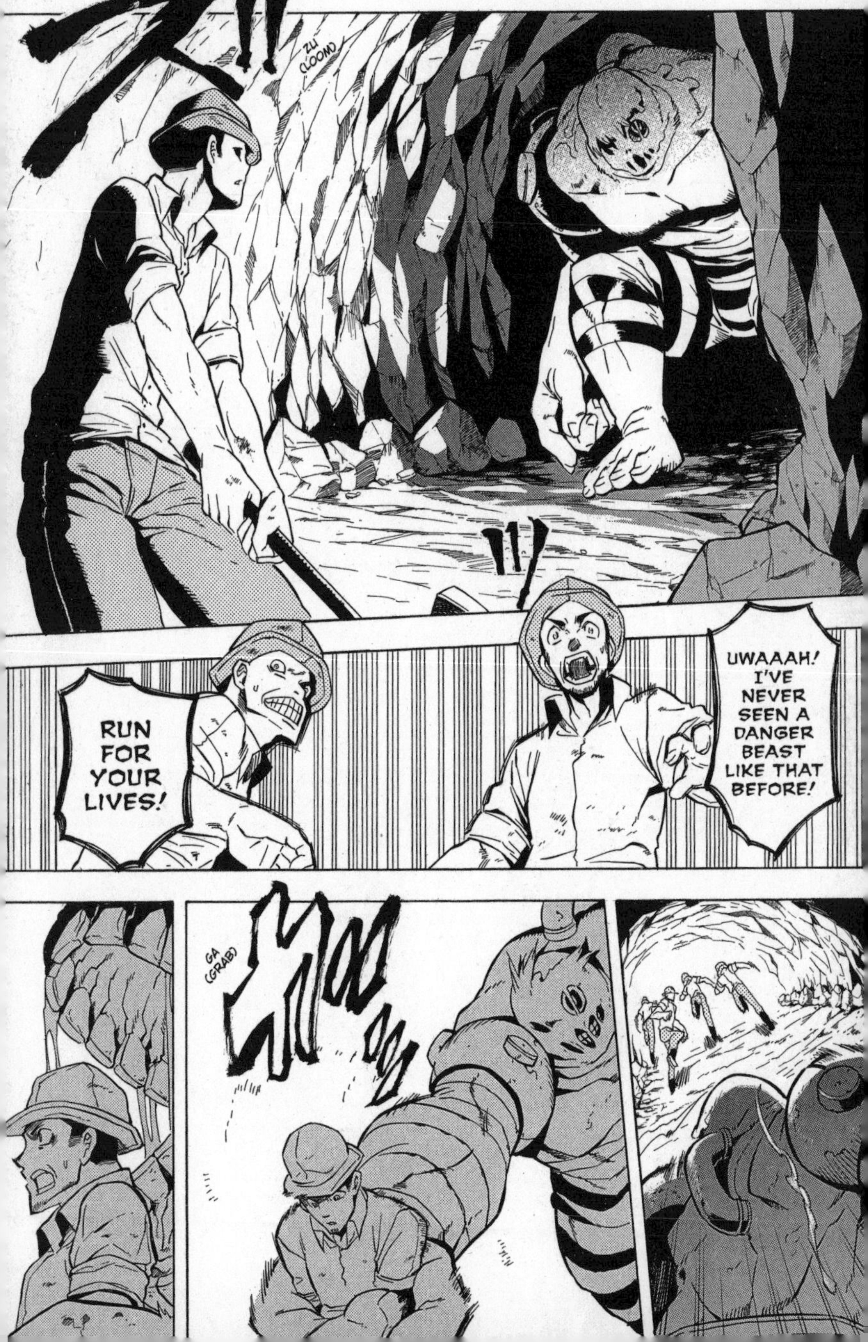
ZU (LOOM)
UWAAAH! I'VE NEVER SEEN A DANGER BEAST LIKE THAT BEFORE!
RUN FOR YOUR LIVES!
GA (GRAB)

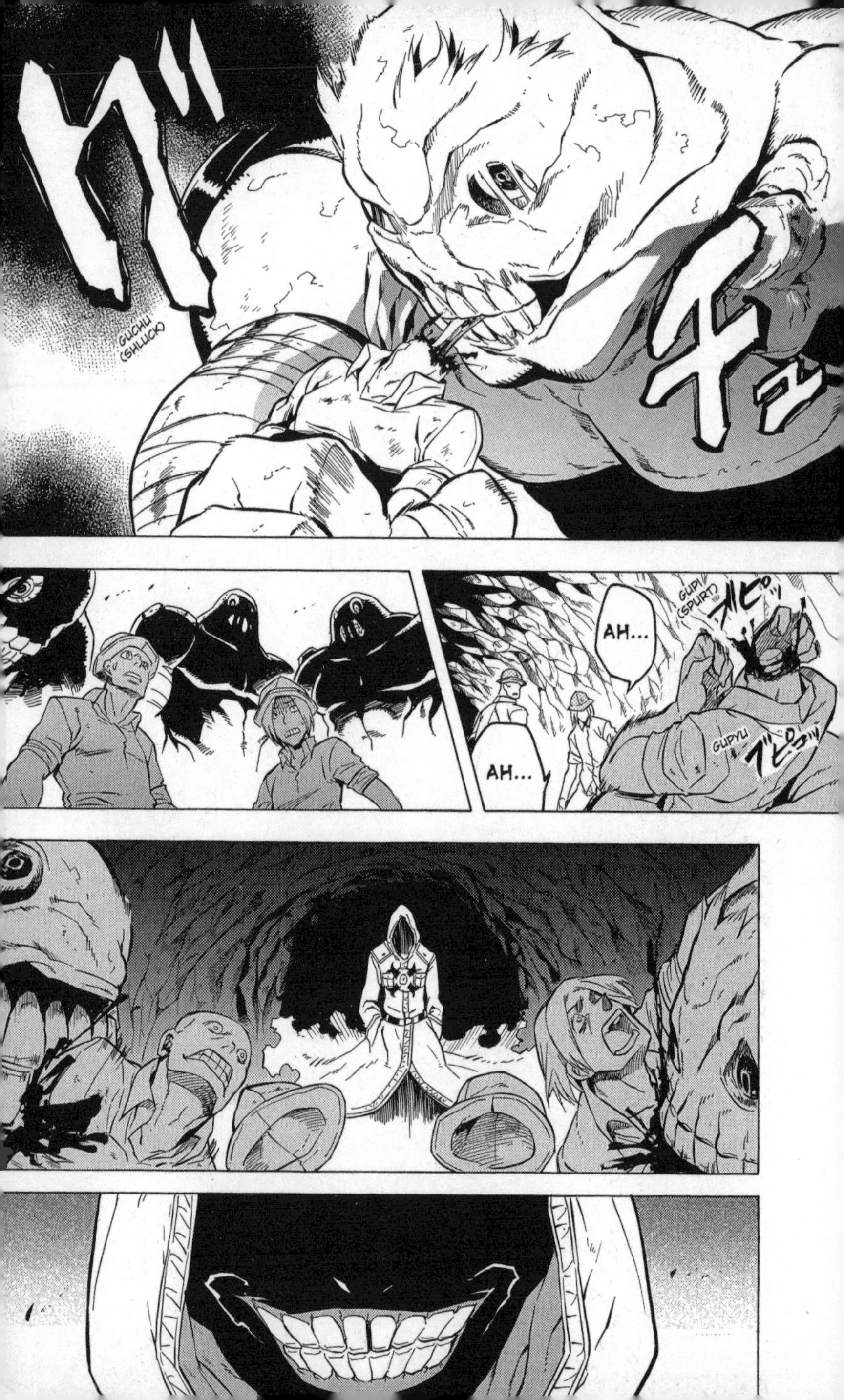
GUCHU (SHLUCK)
GUPI (SPURT)
AH...
AH...
GUPYU
...
...

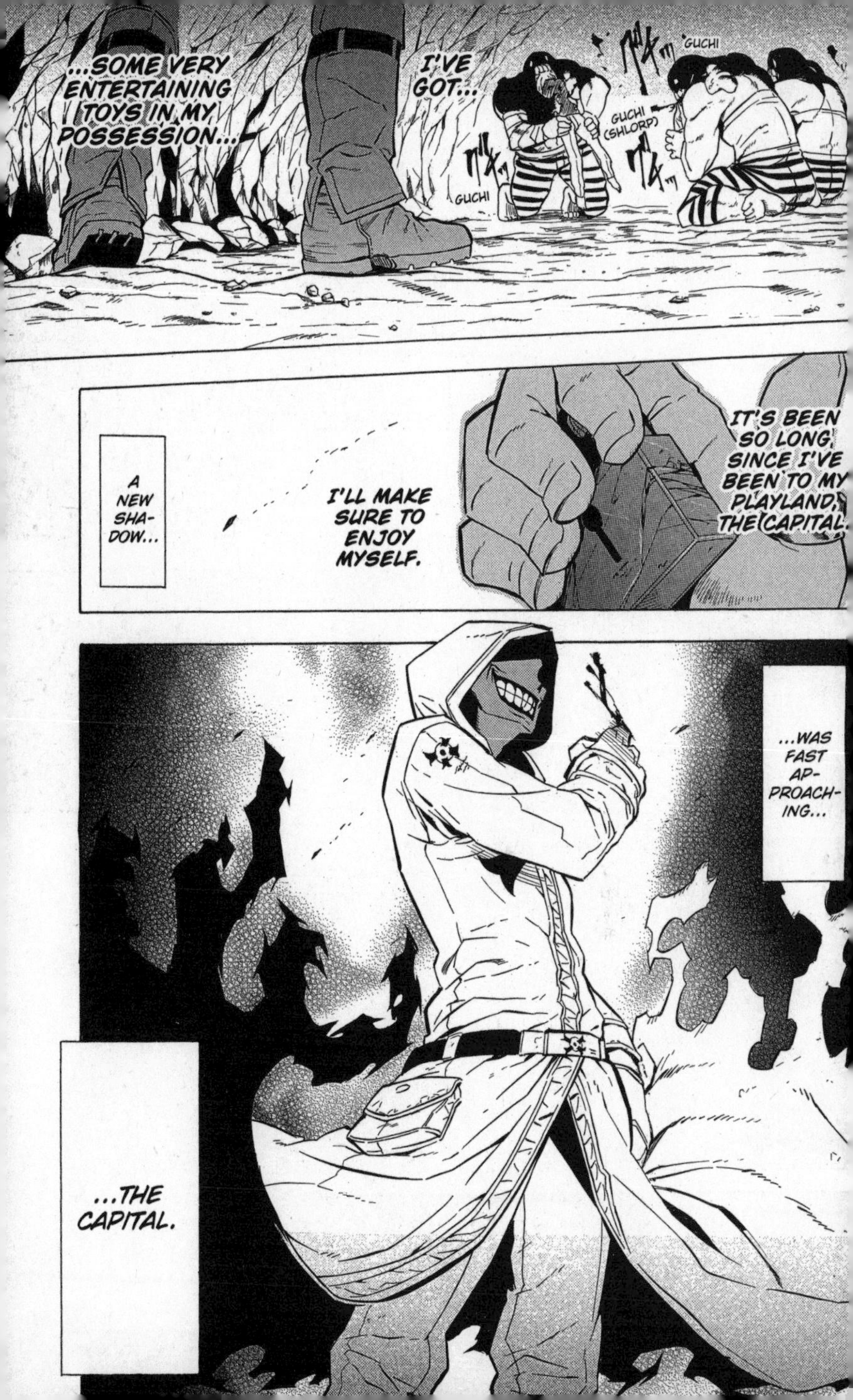
...SOME VERY ENTERTAINING TOYS IN MY POSSESSION...
I'VE GOT...
GUCHI
GUCHI (SHLORP)
GUCHI
A NEW SHA-DOW...
I'LL MAKE SURE TO ENJOY MYSELF.
IT'S BEEN SO LONG SINCE I'VE BEEN TO MY PLAYLAND, THE CAPITAL.
...WAS FAST AP-PROACH-ING...
...THE CAPITAL.

Akame ga KILL!
Rough Sketches 4

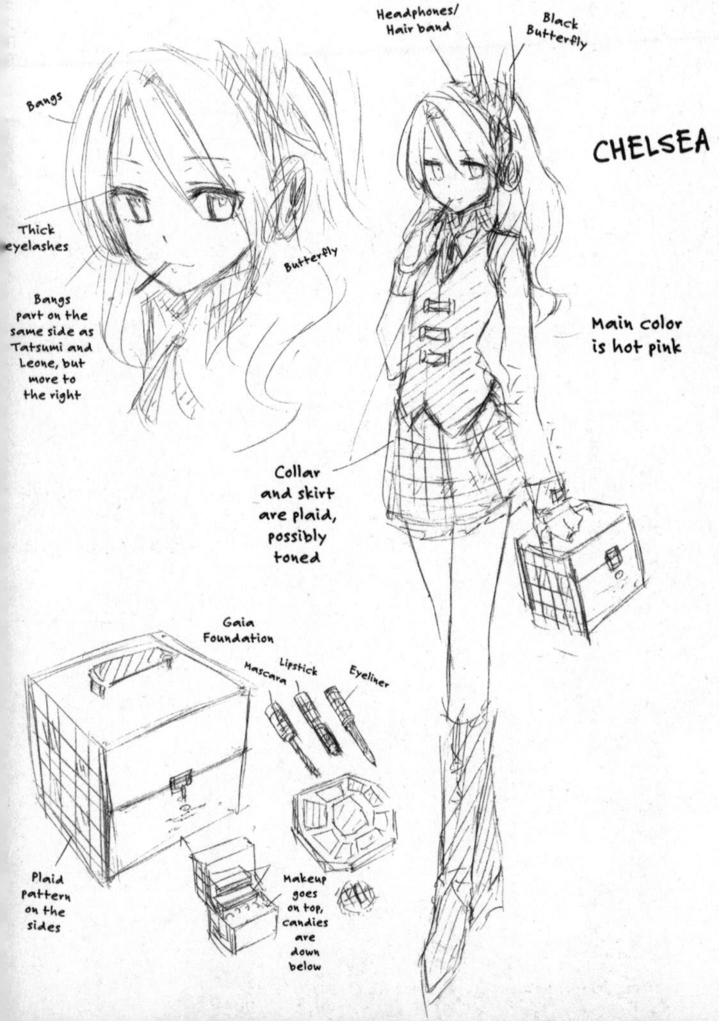
Headphones/
Hair band
Black
Butterfly
Bangs
CHELSEA
Thick
eyelashes
Butterfly
Bangs
part on the
same side as
Tatsumi and
Leone, but
more to
the right
Main color
is hot pink
Collar
and skirt
are plaid,
possibly
toned
Gaia
Foundation
Lipstick
Mascara
Eyeliner
Plaid
pattern
on the
sides
Makeup
goes
on top,
candies
are
down
below

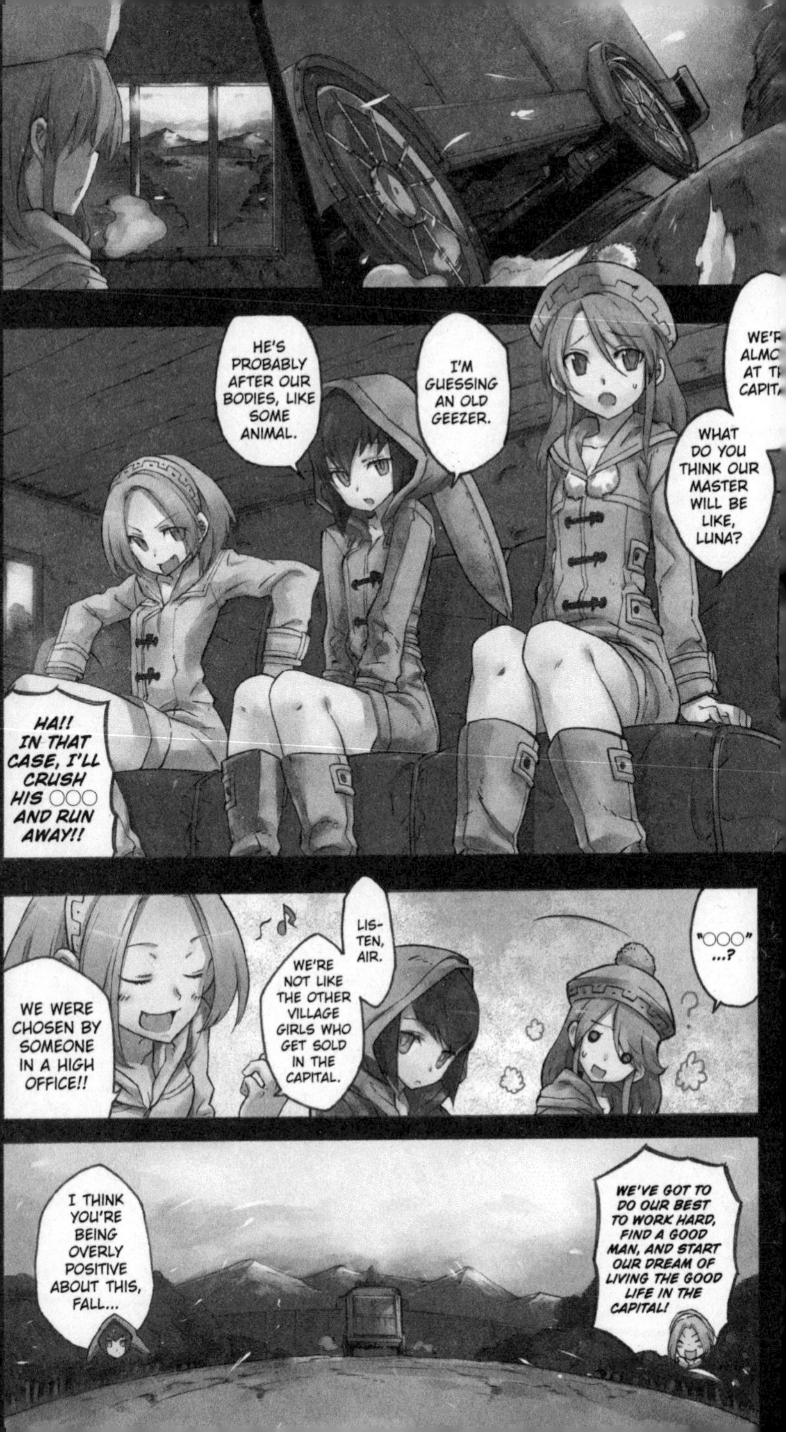
WE'R ALMO AT TH CAPITA
WHAT DO YOU THINK OUR MASTER WILL BE LIKE, LUNA?
I'M GUESSING AN OLD GEEZER.
HE'S PROBABLY AFTER OUR BODIES, LIKE SOME ANIMAL.
HA!! IN THAT CASE, I'LL CRUSH HIS ○○○ AND RUN AWAY!!
"○○○" ...?
LIS-TEN, AIR.
WE'RE NOT LIKE THE OTHER VILLAGE GIRLS WHO GET SOLD IN THE CAPITAL.
WE WERE CHOSEN BY SOMEONE IN A HIGH OFFICE!!
WE'VE GOT TO DO OUR BEST TO WORK HARD, FIND A GOOD MAN, AND START OUR DREAM OF LIVING THE GOOD LIFE IN THE CAPITAL!
I THINK YOU'RE BEING OVERLY POSITIVE ABOUT THIS, FALL...

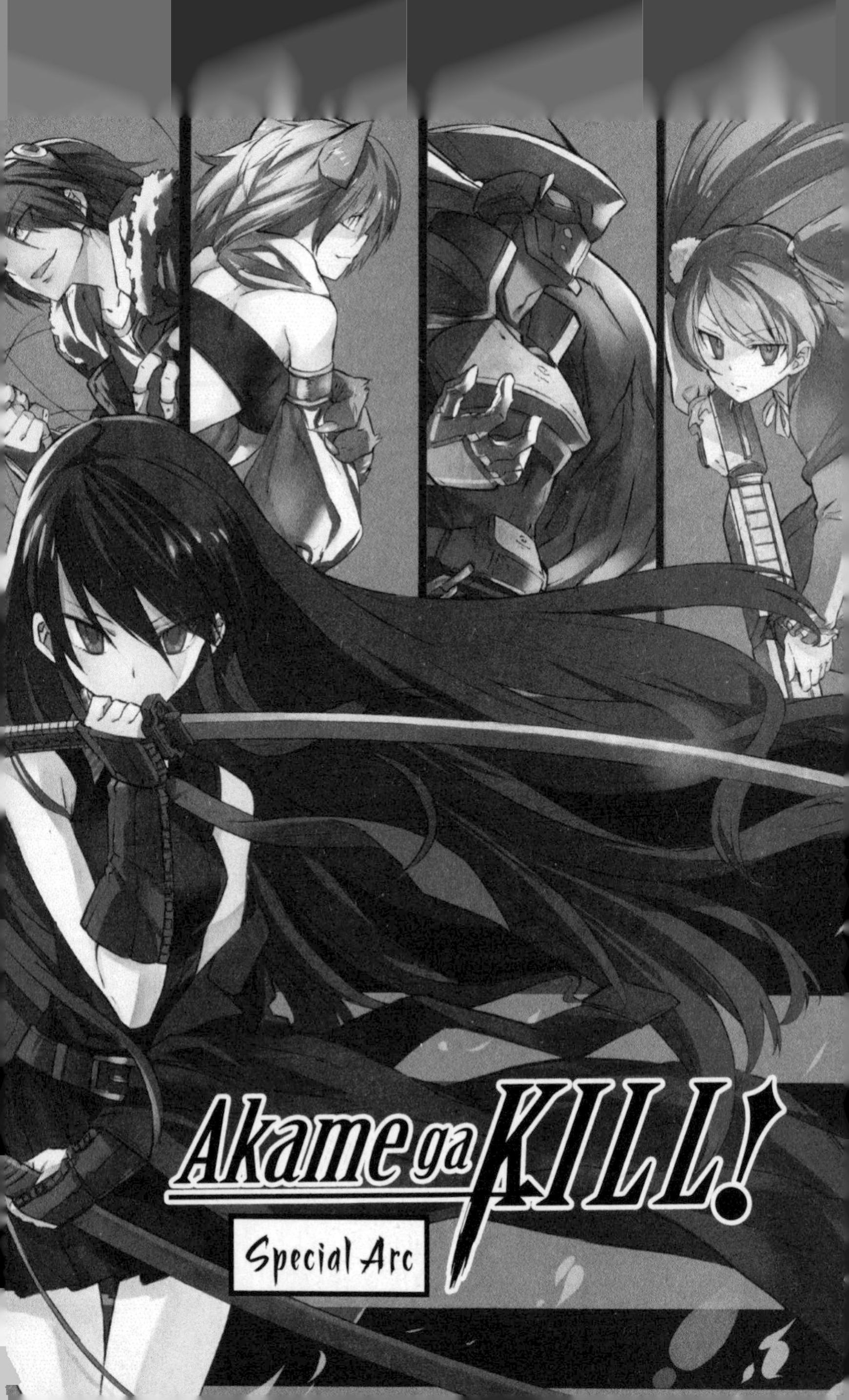
Akame ga KILL!
Special Arc

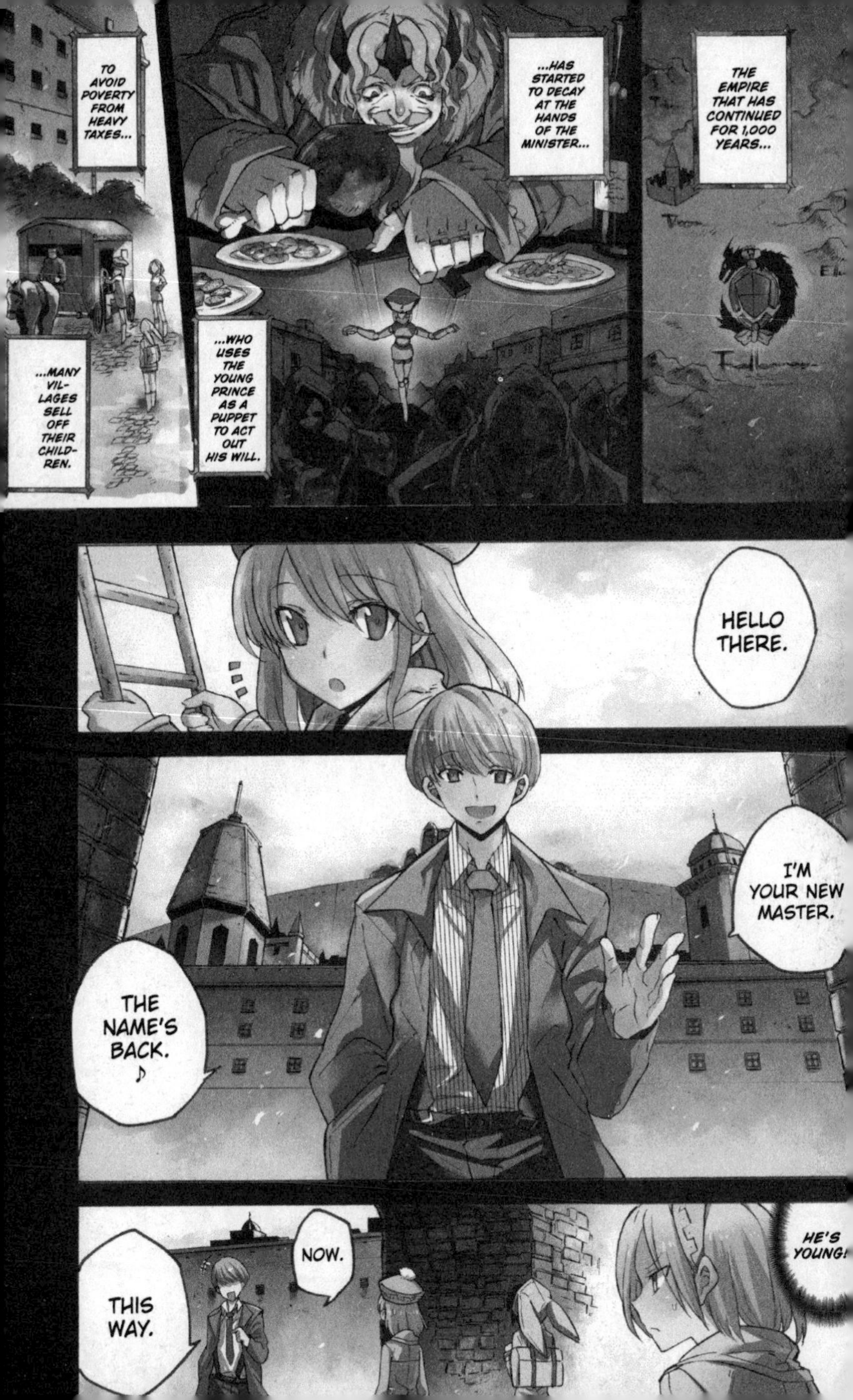
THE EMPIRE THAT HAS CONTINUED FOR 1,000 YEARS...
...HAS STARTED TO DECAY AT THE HANDS OF THE MINISTER...
...WHO USES THE YOUNG PRINCE AS A PUPPET TO ACT OUT HIS WILL.
TO AVOID POVERTY FROM HEAVY TAXES...
...MANY VIL-LAGES SELL OFF THEIR CHILD-REN.
HELLO THERE.
I'M YOUR NEW MASTER.
THE NAME'S BACK. ♪
HE'S YOUNG!
NOW.
THIS WAY.

Akame ga KILL!

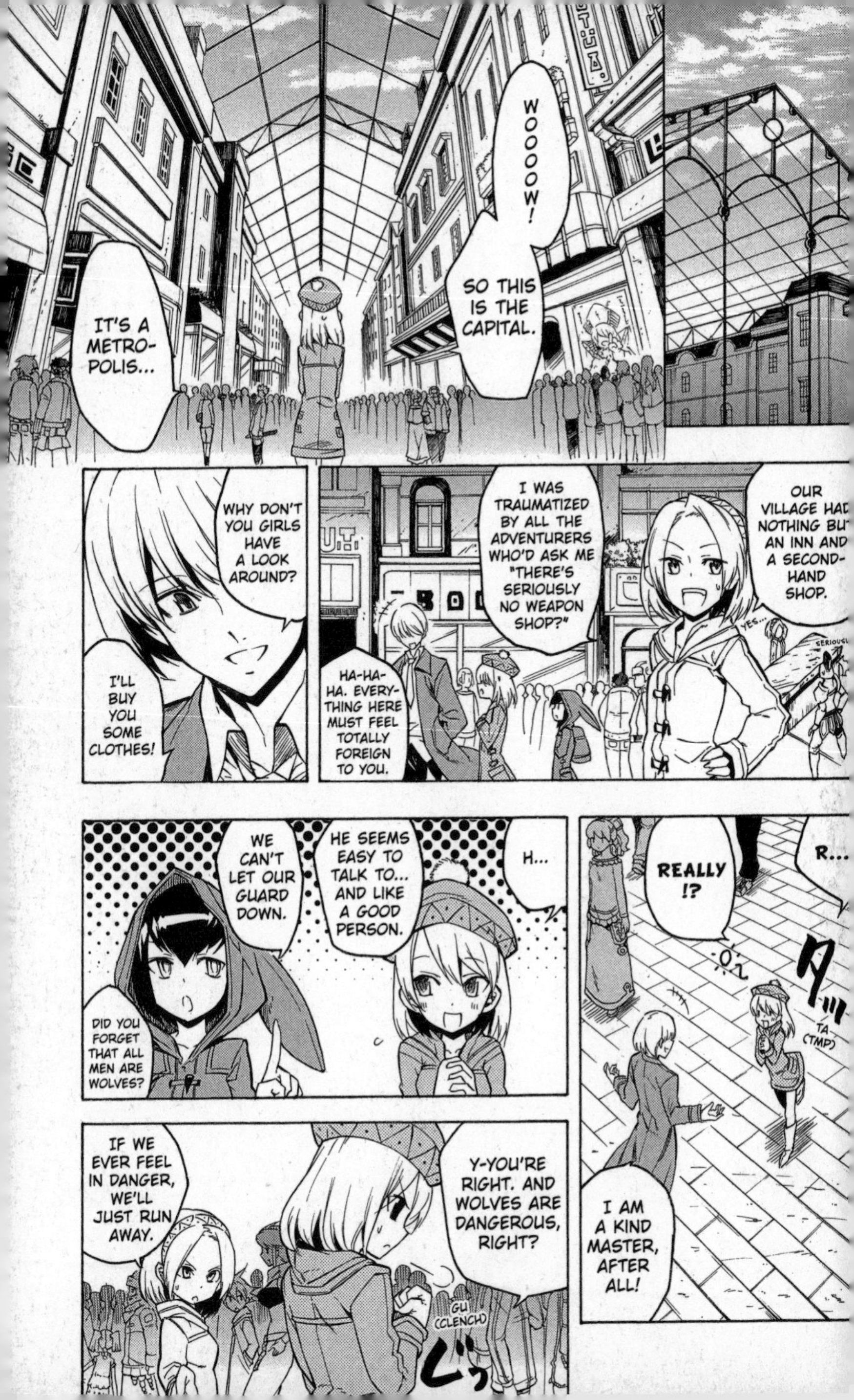
WOOOOOW!
SO THIS IS THE CAPITAL.
IT'S A METROPOLIS...
OUR VILLAGE HAD NOTHING BUT AN INN AND A SECOND-HAND SHOP.
YES...
I WAS TRAUMATIZED BY ALL THE ADVENTURERS WHO'D ASK ME "THERE'S SERIOUSLY NO WEAPON SHOP?"
HA-HA-HA. EVERYTHING HERE MUST FEEL TOTALLY FOREIGN TO YOU.
WHY DON'T YOU GIRLS HAVE A LOOK AROUND?
I'LL BUY YOU SOME CLOTHES!
R...
REALLY!?
TA (TMP)
I AM A KIND MASTER, AFTER ALL!
H...
HE SEEMS EASY TO TALK TO... AND LIKE A GOOD PERSON.
WE CAN'T LET OUR GUARD DOWN.
DID YOU FORGET THAT ALL MEN ARE WOLVES?
Y-YOU'RE RIGHT. AND WOLVES ARE DANGEROUS, RIGHT?
GU (CLENCH)
IF WE EVER FEEL IN DANGER, WE'LL JUST RUN AWAY.

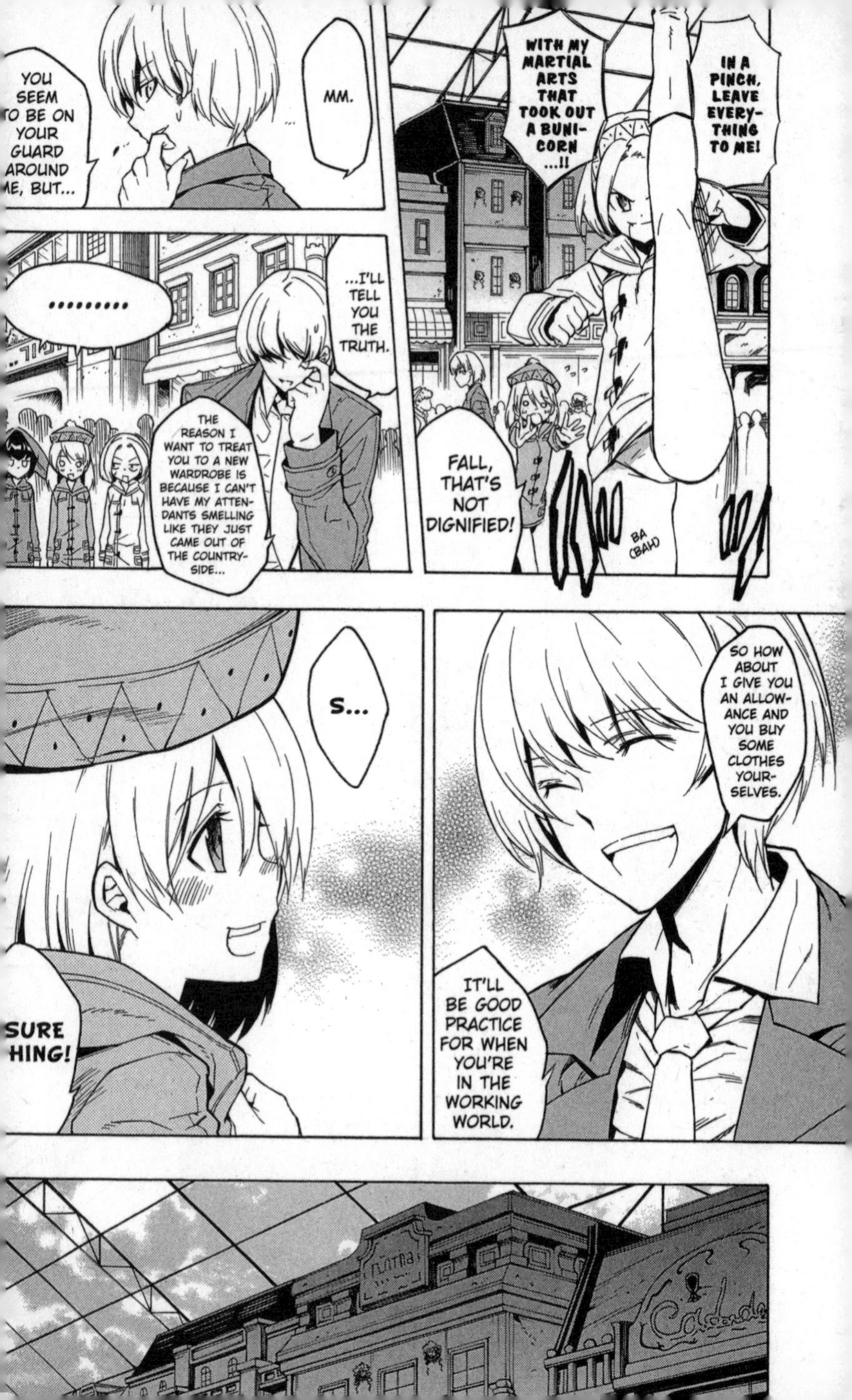
IN A PINCH, LEAVE EVERY-THING TO ME!
WITH MY MARTIAL ARTS THAT TOOK OUT A BUNI-CORN ...!!
MM.
YOU SEEM TO BE ON YOUR GUARD AROUND ME, BUT...
FALL, THAT'S NOT DIGNIFIED!
BA (BAH)
...I'LL TELL YOU THE TRUTH.
....
THE REASON I WANT TO TREAT YOU TO A NEW WARDROBE IS BECAUSE I CAN'T HAVE MY ATTEN-DANTS SMELLING LIKE THEY JUST CAME OUT OF THE COUNTRY-SIDE...
SO HOW ABOUT I GIVE YOU AN ALLOW-ANCE AND YOU BUY SOME CLOTHES YOUR-SELVES.
IT'LL BE GOOD PRACTICE FOR WHEN YOU'RE IN THE WORKING WORLD.
S...
SURE HING!

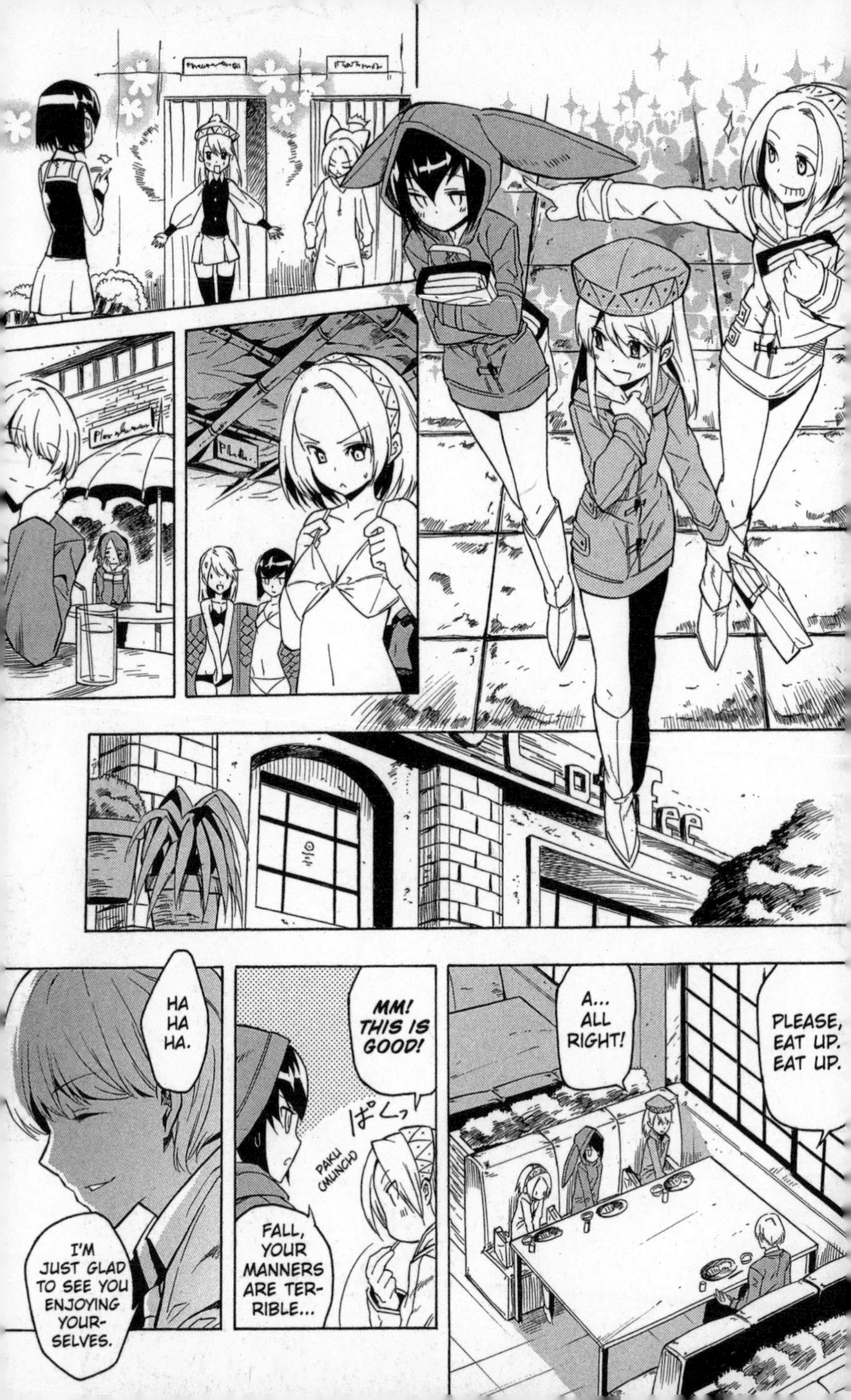
PLEASE, EAT UP. EAT UP.
A... ALL RIGHT!
MM! THIS IS GOOD!
ぱくっ
PAKU (MUNCH)
FALL, YOUR MANNERS ARE TER-RIBLE...
HA HA HA.
I'M JUST GLAD TO SEE YOU ENJOYING YOUR-SELVES.

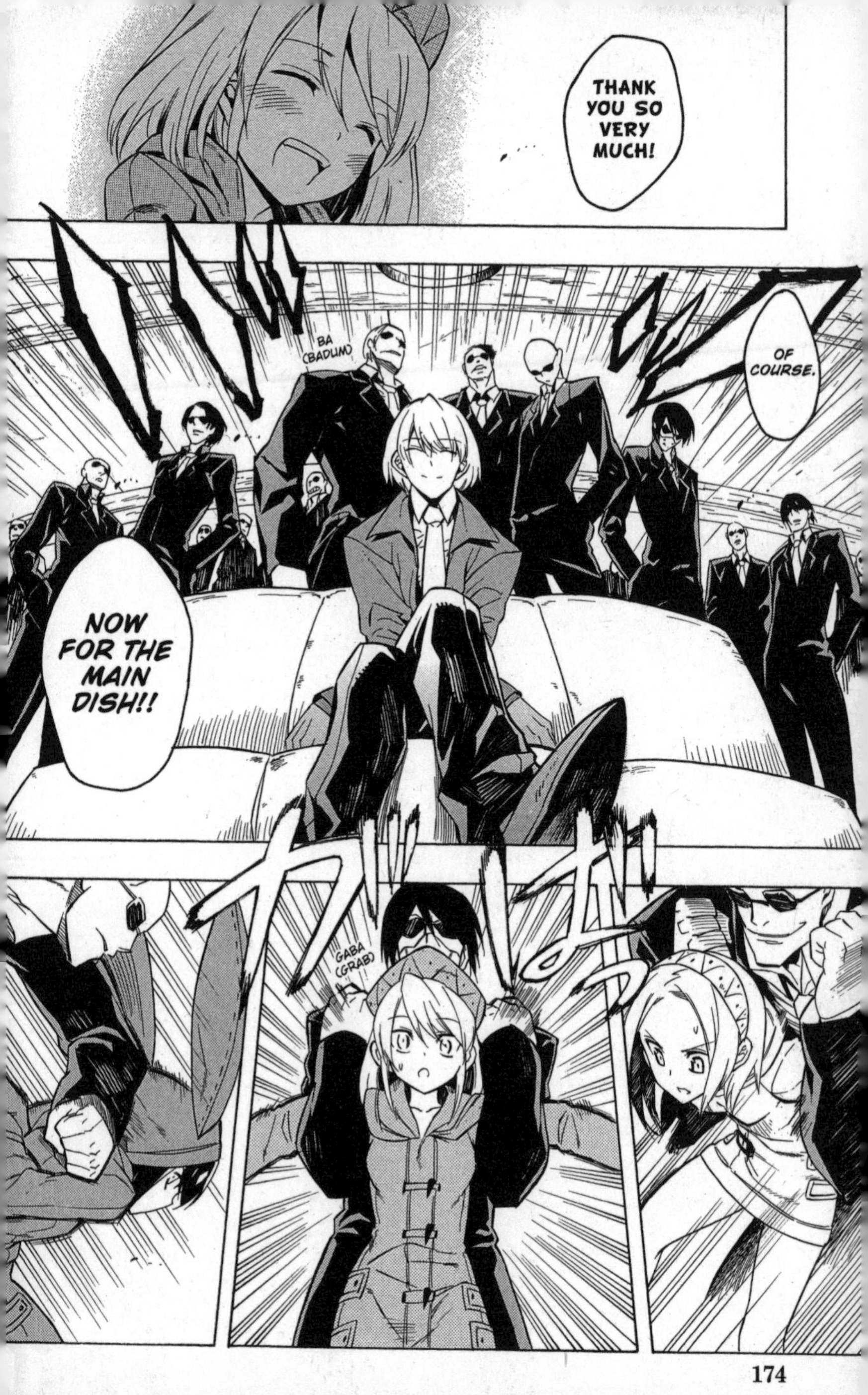
THANK YOU SO VERY MUCH!
OF COURSE.
BA (BADUM)
NOW FOR THE MAIN DISH!!
GABA (GRAB)

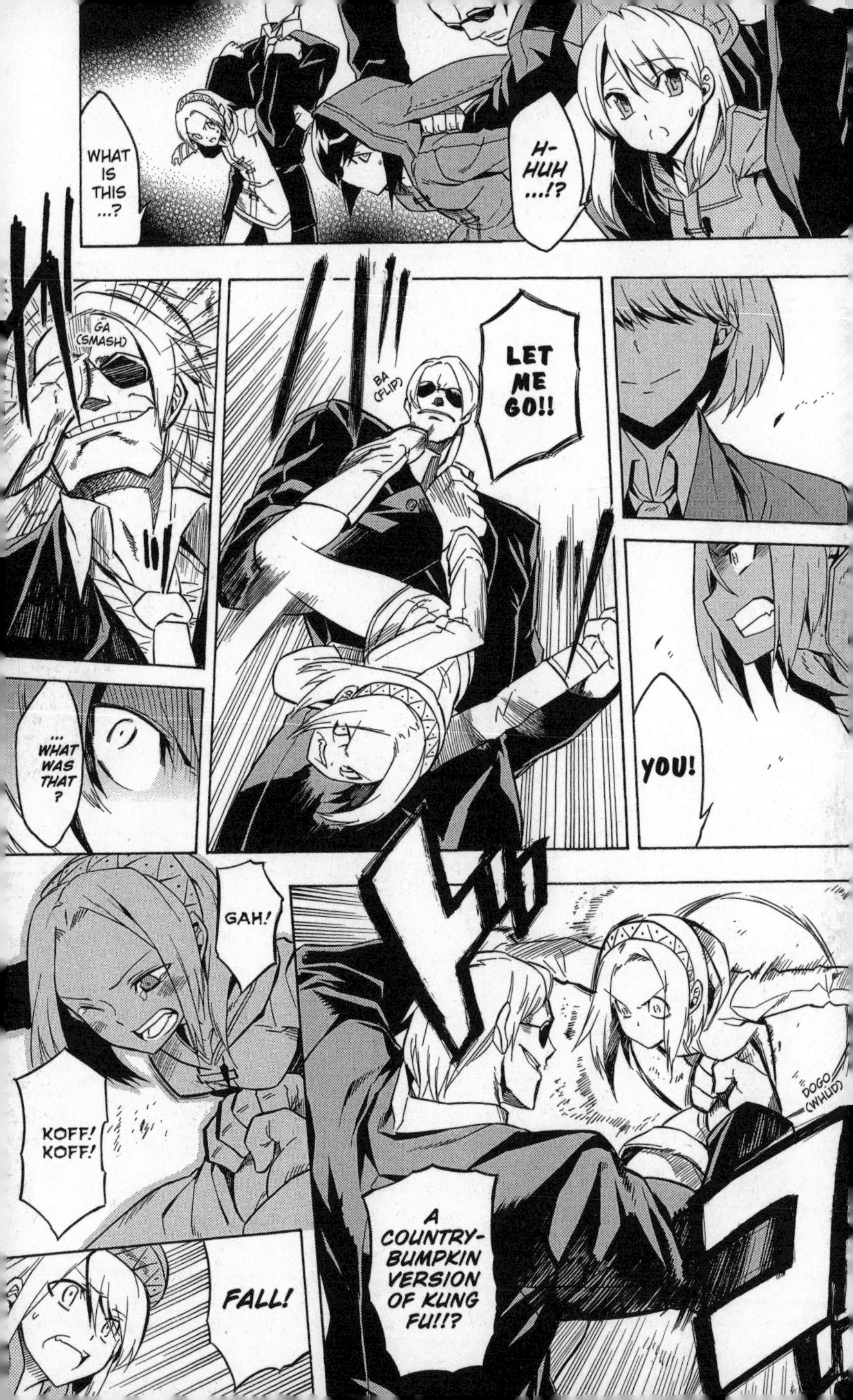
H-HUH ...!?
WHAT IS THIS ...?
YOU!
LET ME GO!!
BA (FLIP)
GA (SMASH)
...WHAT WAS THAT?
DOGO (WHUD)
A COUNTRY-BUMPKIN VERSION OF KUNG FU!!?
GAH!
KOFF! KOFF!
FALL!

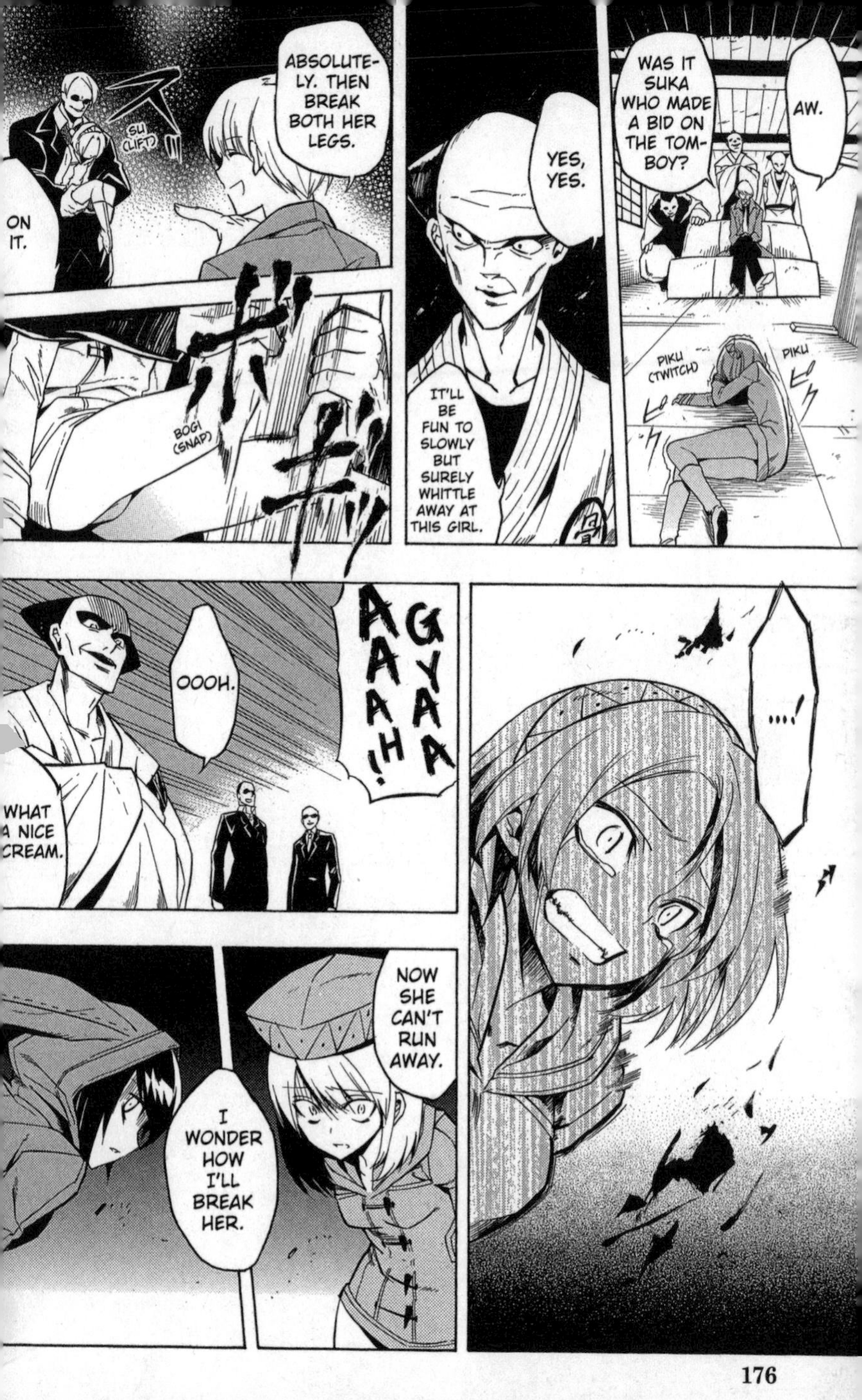
AW.
WAS IT SUKA WHO MADE A BID ON THE TOMBOY?
PIKU (TWITCH)
PIKU
YES, YES.
IT'LL BE FUN TO SLOWLY BUT SURELY WHITTLE AWAY AT THIS GIRL.
ABSOLUTE-LY. THEN BREAK BOTH HER LEGS.
SU (LIFT)
ON IT.
BOGI (SNAP)
...!
GYAAA AAAH!
OOOH.
WHAT A NICE CREAM.
NOW SHE CAN'T RUN AWAY.
I WONDER HOW I'LL BREAK HER.

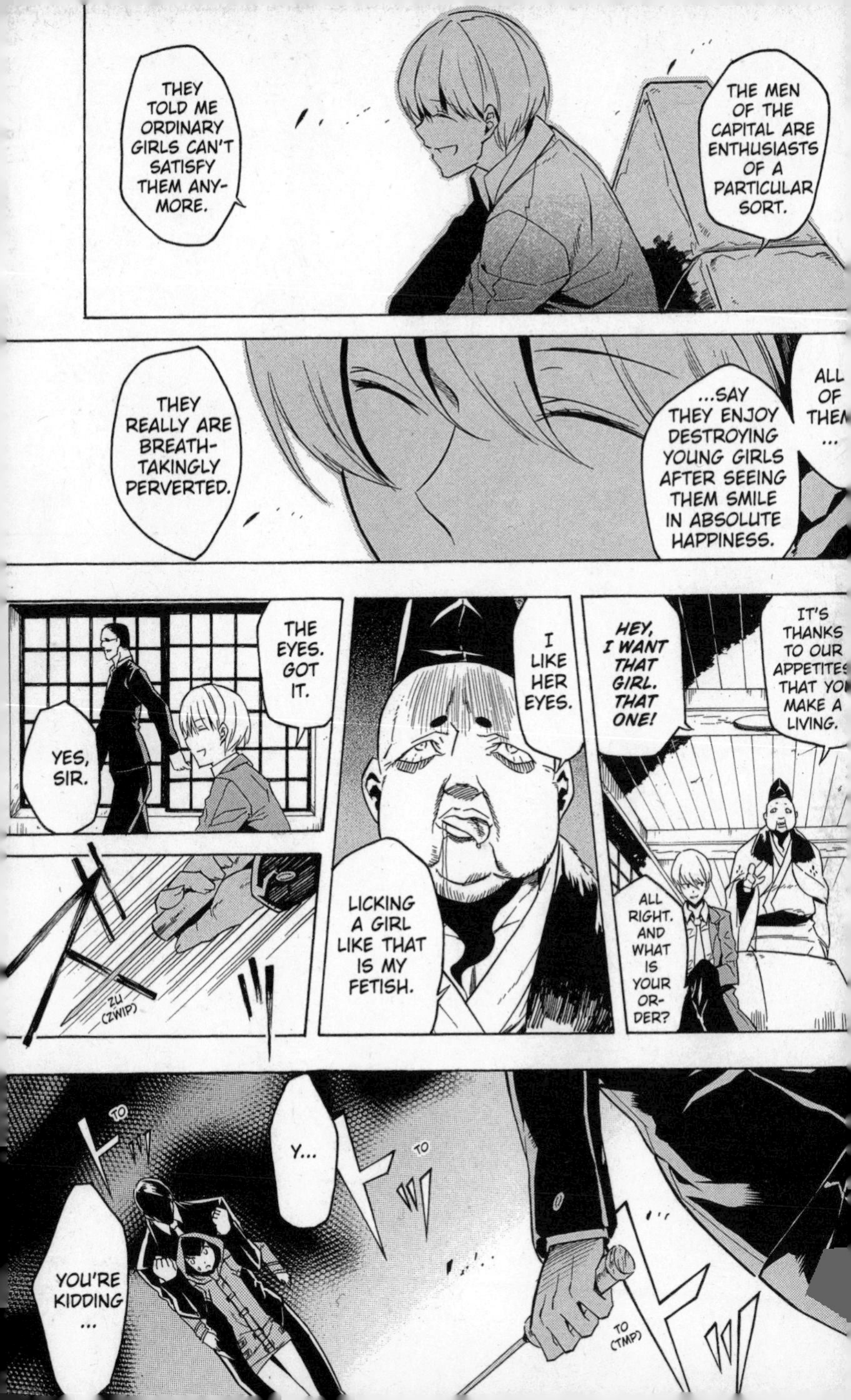
THE MEN OF THE CAPITAL ARE ENTHUSIASTS OF A PARTICULAR SORT.
THEY TOLD ME ORDINARY GIRLS CAN'T SATISFY THEM ANYMORE.
ALL OF THEM ...
...SAY THEY ENJOY DESTROYING YOUNG GIRLS AFTER SEEING THEM SMILE IN ABSOLUTE HAPPINESS.
THEY REALLY ARE BREATHTAKINGLY PERVERTED.
IT'S THANKS TO OUR APPETITES THAT YOU MAKE A LIVING.
HEY, I WANT THAT GIRL. THAT ONE!
ALL RIGHT. AND WHAT IS YOUR ORDER?
I LIKE HER EYES.
LICKING A GIRL LIKE THAT IS MY FETISH.
THE EYES. GOT IT.
YES, SIR.
ZU (ZWIP)
TO (TMP)
TO
Y...
TO
YOU'RE KIDDING ...

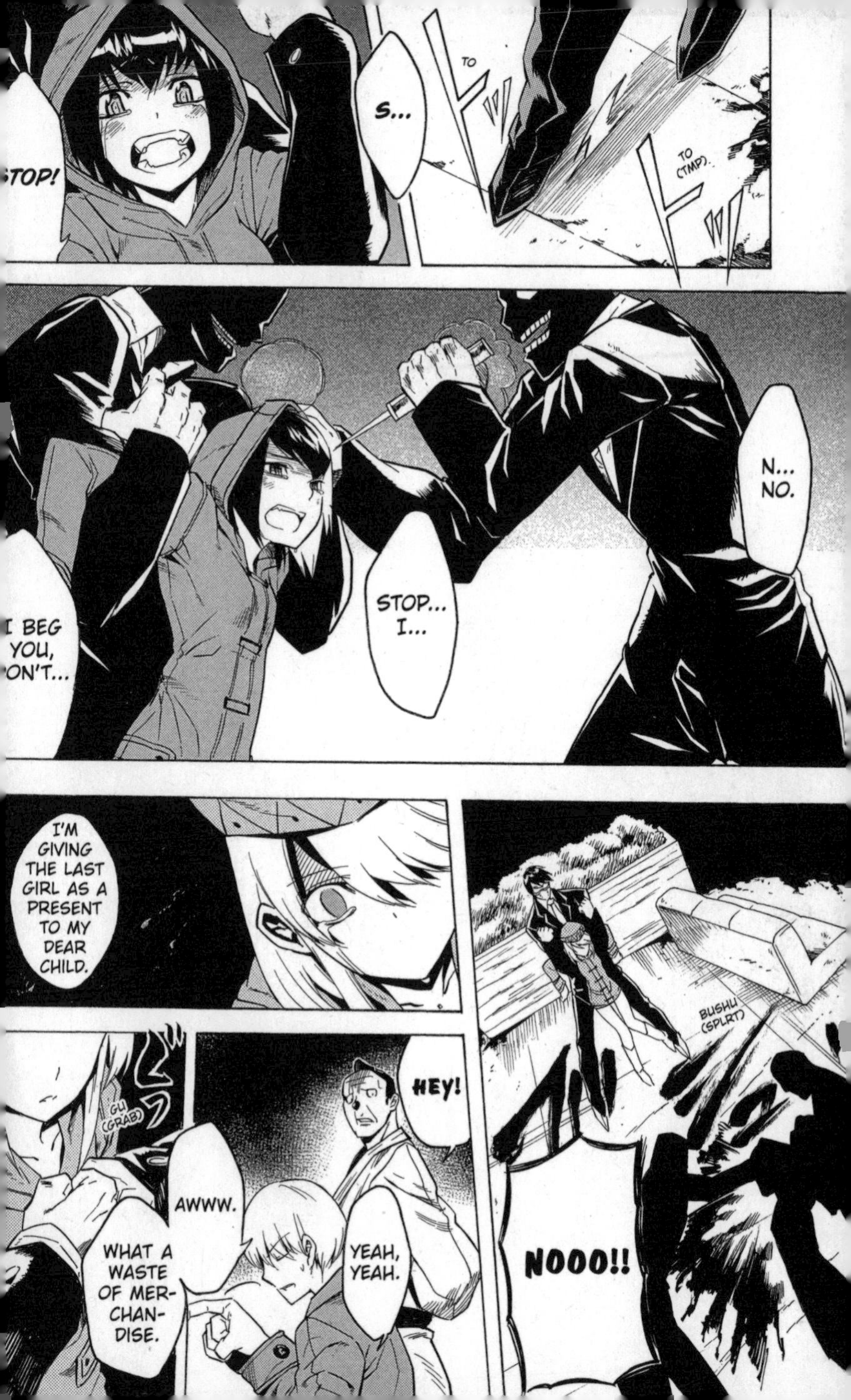
TO
TO (TMP)
S...
STOP!
N... NO.
STOP... I...
I BEG YOU, DON'T...
BUSHU (SPLRT)
NOOO!!
I'M GIVING THE LAST GIRL AS A PRESENT TO MY DEAR CHILD.
HEY!
YEAH, YEAH.
AWWW.
WHAT A WASTE OF MER-CHAN-DISE.
GU (GRAB)

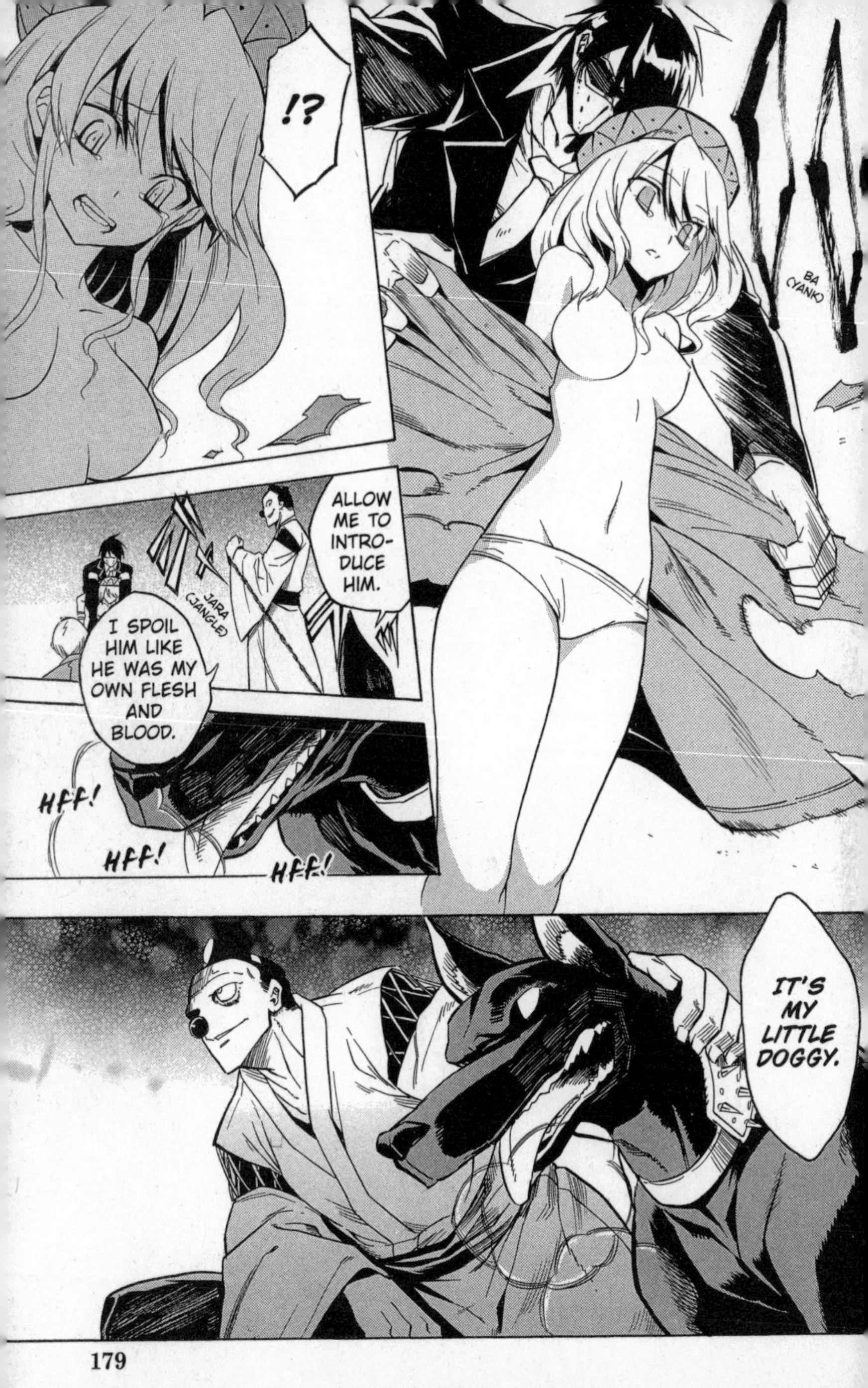
BA (YANK)
!?
ALLOW ME TO INTRODUCE HIM.
JARA (JANGLE)
I SPOIL HIM LIKE HE WAS MY OWN FLESH AND BLOOD.
HFF!
HFF!
HFF!
IT'S MY LITTLE DOGGY.

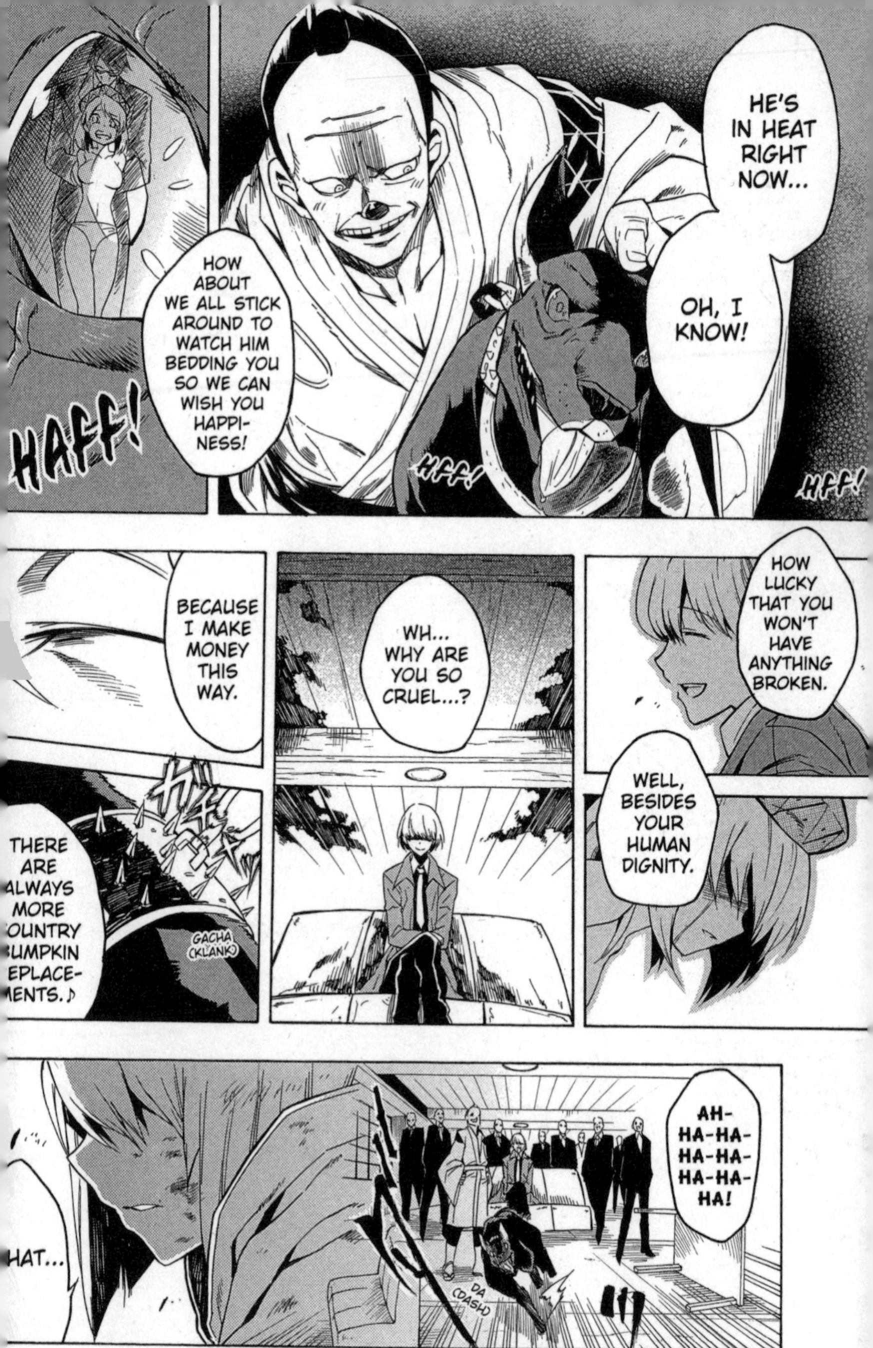
HE'S IN HEAT RIGHT NOW...
OH, I KNOW!
HOW ABOUT WE ALL STICK AROUND TO WATCH HIM BEDDING YOU SO WE CAN WISH YOU HAPPI-NESS!
HFF!
HFF!
HAFF!
HOW LUCKY THAT YOU WON'T HAVE ANYTHING BROKEN.
WH... WHY ARE YOU SO CRUEL...?
BECAUSE I MAKE MONEY THIS WAY.
WELL, BESIDES YOUR HUMAN DIGNITY.
GACHA (KLANK)
THERE ARE ALWAYS MORE OUNTRY UMPKIN EPLACE-MENTS.♪
AH-HA-HA-HA-HA-HA-HA-HA!
DA (DASH)
HAT...

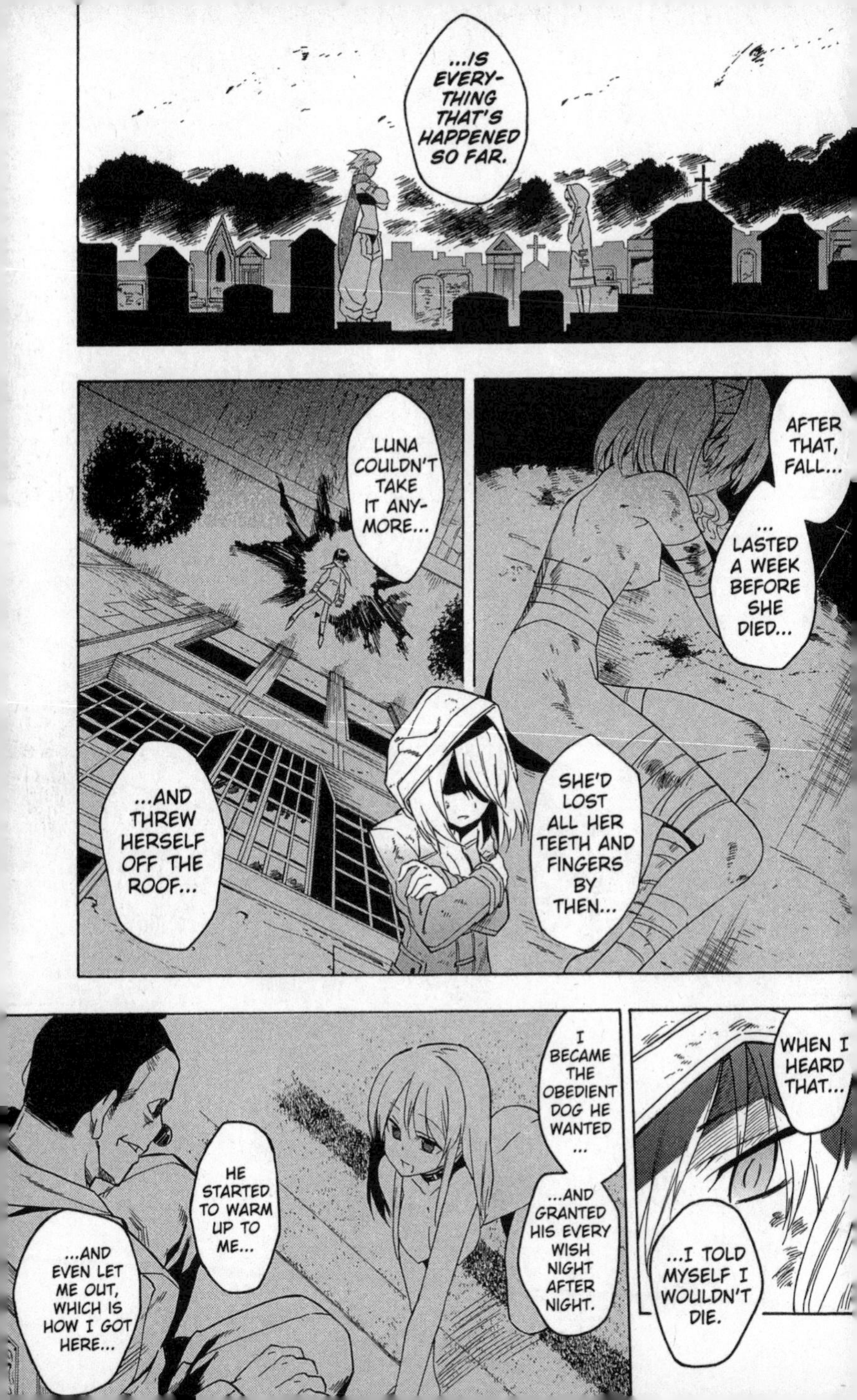
...IS EVERYTHING THAT'S HAPPENED SO FAR.
AFTER THAT, FALL...
...LASTED A WEEK BEFORE SHE DIED...
SHE'D LOST ALL HER TEETH AND FINGERS BY THEN...
LUNA COULDN'T TAKE IT ANYMORE...
...AND THREW HERSELF OFF THE ROOF...
WHEN I HEARD THAT...
...I TOLD MYSELF I WOULDN'T DIE.
I BECAME THE OBEDIENT DOG HE WANTED...
...AND GRANTED HIS EVERY WISH NIGHT AFTER NIGHT.
HE STARTED TO WARM UP TO ME...
...AND EVEN LET ME OUT, WHICH IS HOW I GOT HERE...

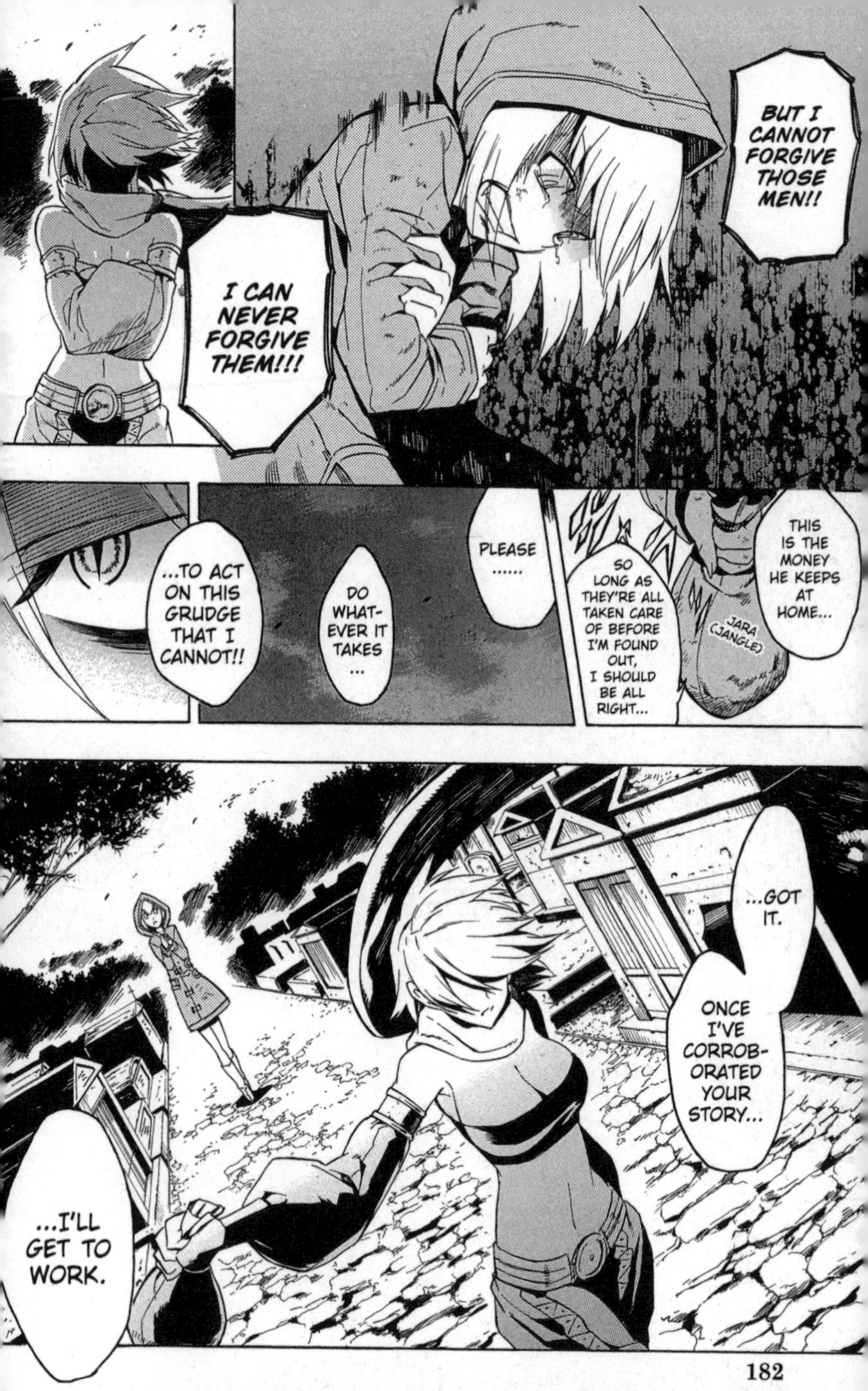
BUT I CANNOT FORGIVE THOSE MEN!!
I CAN NEVER FORGIVE THEM!!!
THIS IS THE MONEY HE KEEPS AT HOME...
JARA (JANGLE)
SO LONG AS THEY'RE ALL TAKEN CARE OF BEFORE I'M FOUND OUT, I SHOULD BE ALL RIGHT...
PLEASE ......
DO WHATEVER IT TAKES ...
...TO ACT ON THIS GRUDGE THAT I CANNOT!!
...GOT IT.
ONCE I'VE CORROBORATED YOUR STORY...
...I'LL GET TO WORK.

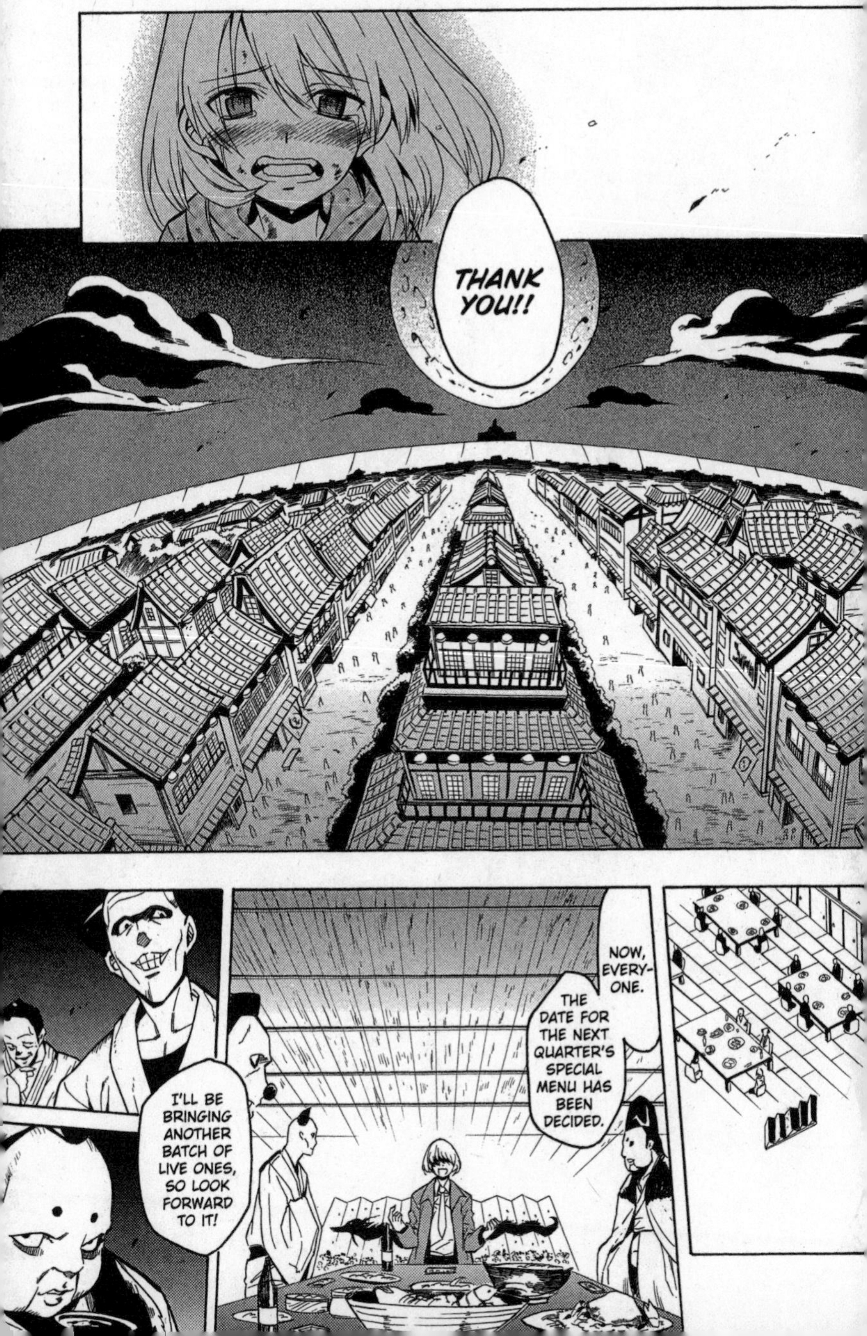
THANK YOU!!
NOW, EVERY-ONE.
THE DATE FOR THE NEXT QUARTER'S SPECIAL MENU HAS BEEN DECIDED.
I'LL BE BRINGING ANOTHER BATCH OF LIVE ONES, SO LOOK FORWARD TO IT!

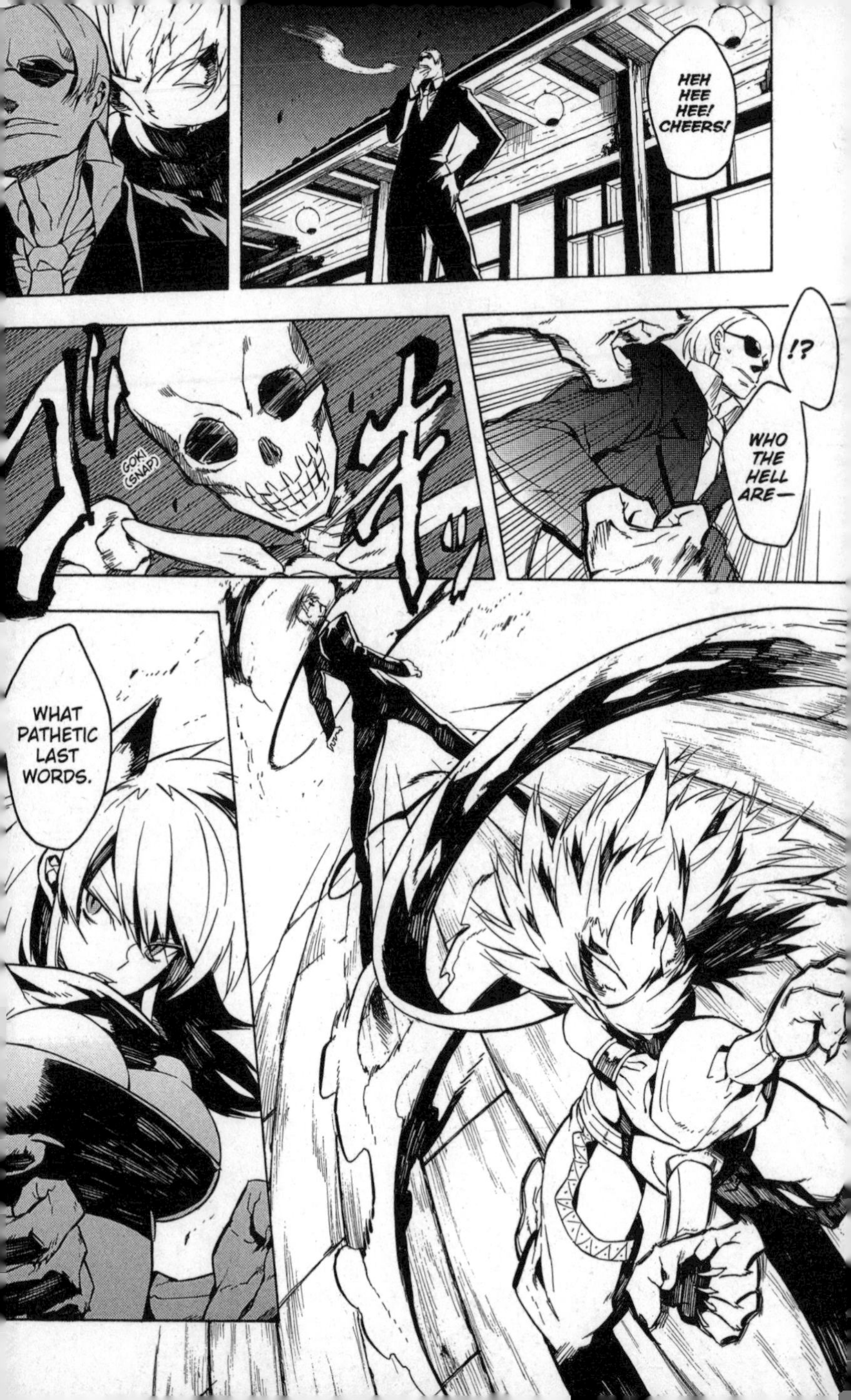
HEH HEE HEE! CHEERS!
!?
WHO THE HELL ARE—
GOKI (SNAP)
WHAT PATHETIC LAST WORDS.

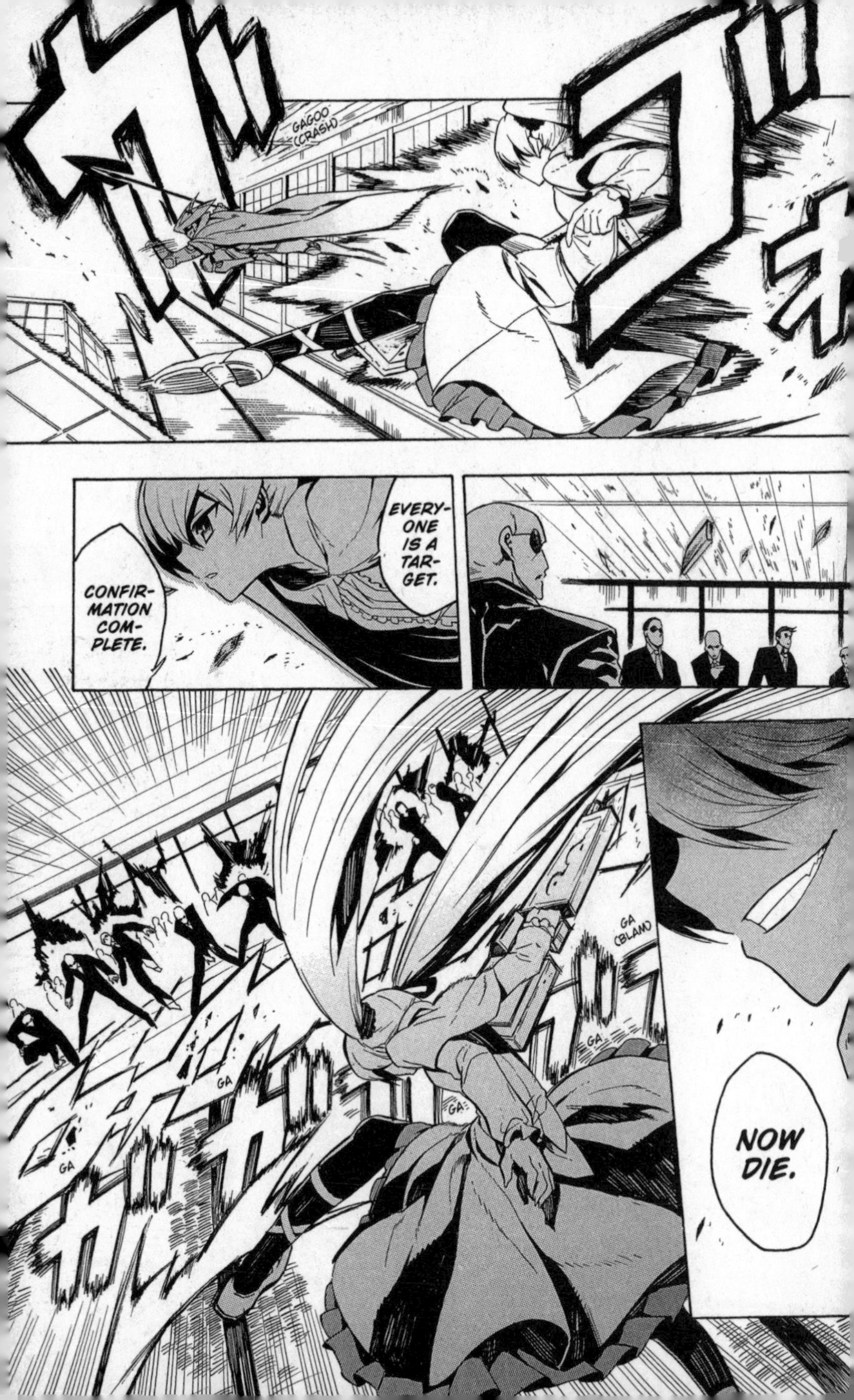
GAGOO (CRASH)
EVERY-ONE IS A TAR-GET.
CONFIR-MATION COM-PLETE.
GA (BLAM)
GA
GA
GA
GA
NOW DIE.

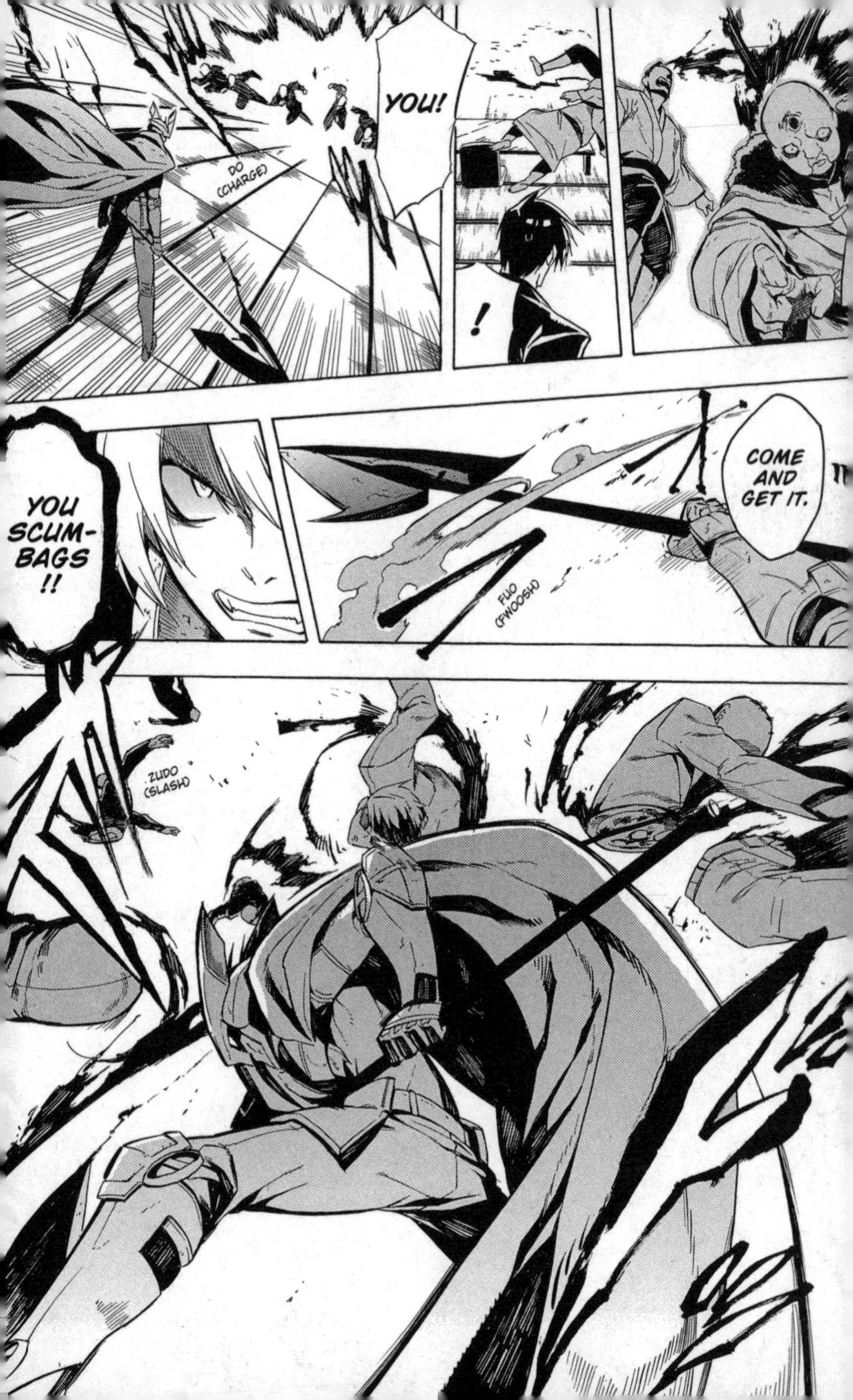
!
YOU!
DO
(CHARGE)
COME AND GET IT.
FUO
(FWOOSH)
YOU SCUM-BAGS !!
ZUDO
(SLASH)

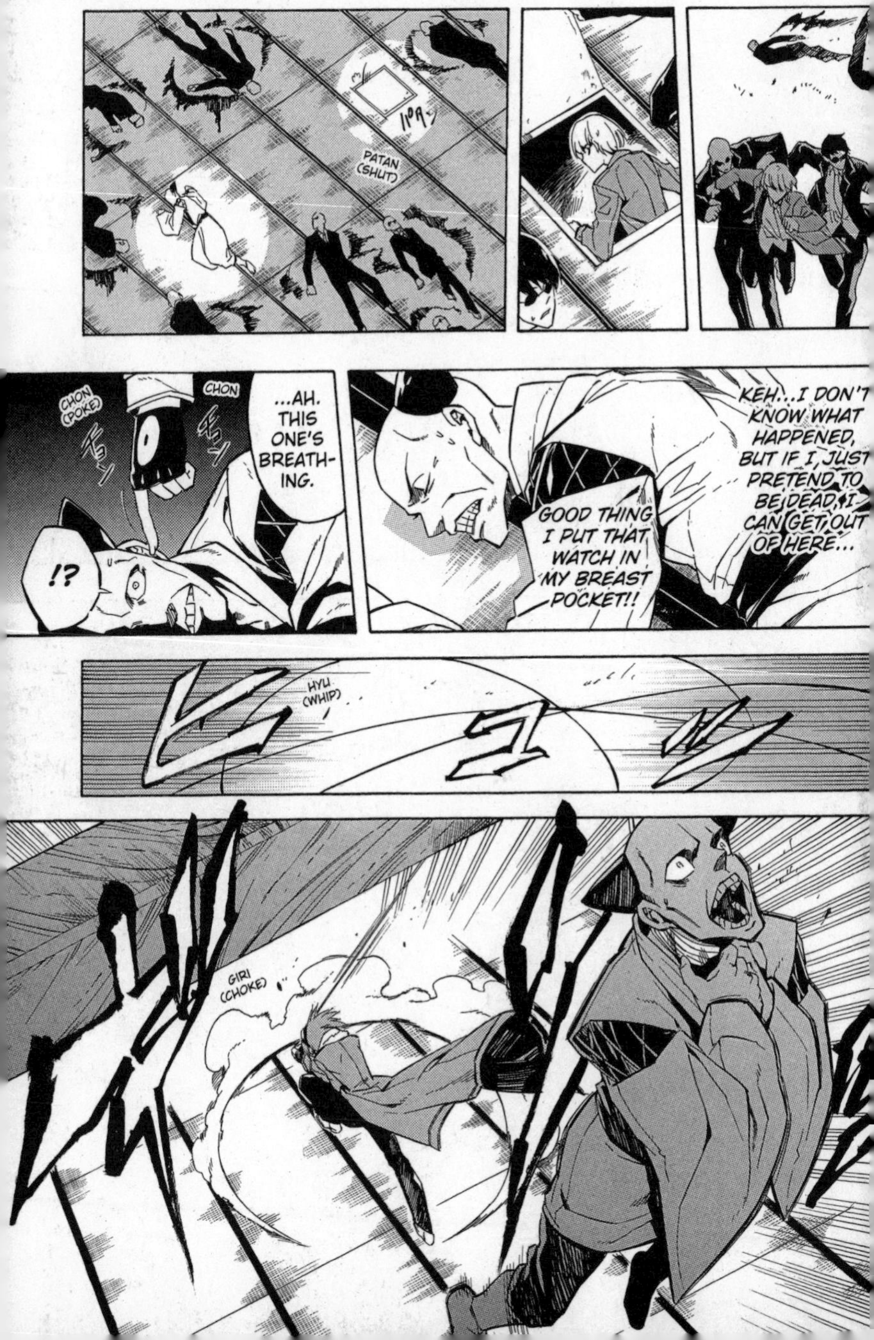
PATAN (SHUT)
KEH...I DON'T KNOW WHAT HAPPENED, BUT IF I JUST PRETEND TO BE DEAD, I CAN GET OUT OF HERE...
GOOD THING I PUT THAT WATCH IN MY BREAST POCKET!!
...AH. THIS ONE'S BREATHING.
CHON
CHON (POKE)
!?
HYU (WHIP)
GIRI (CHOKE)

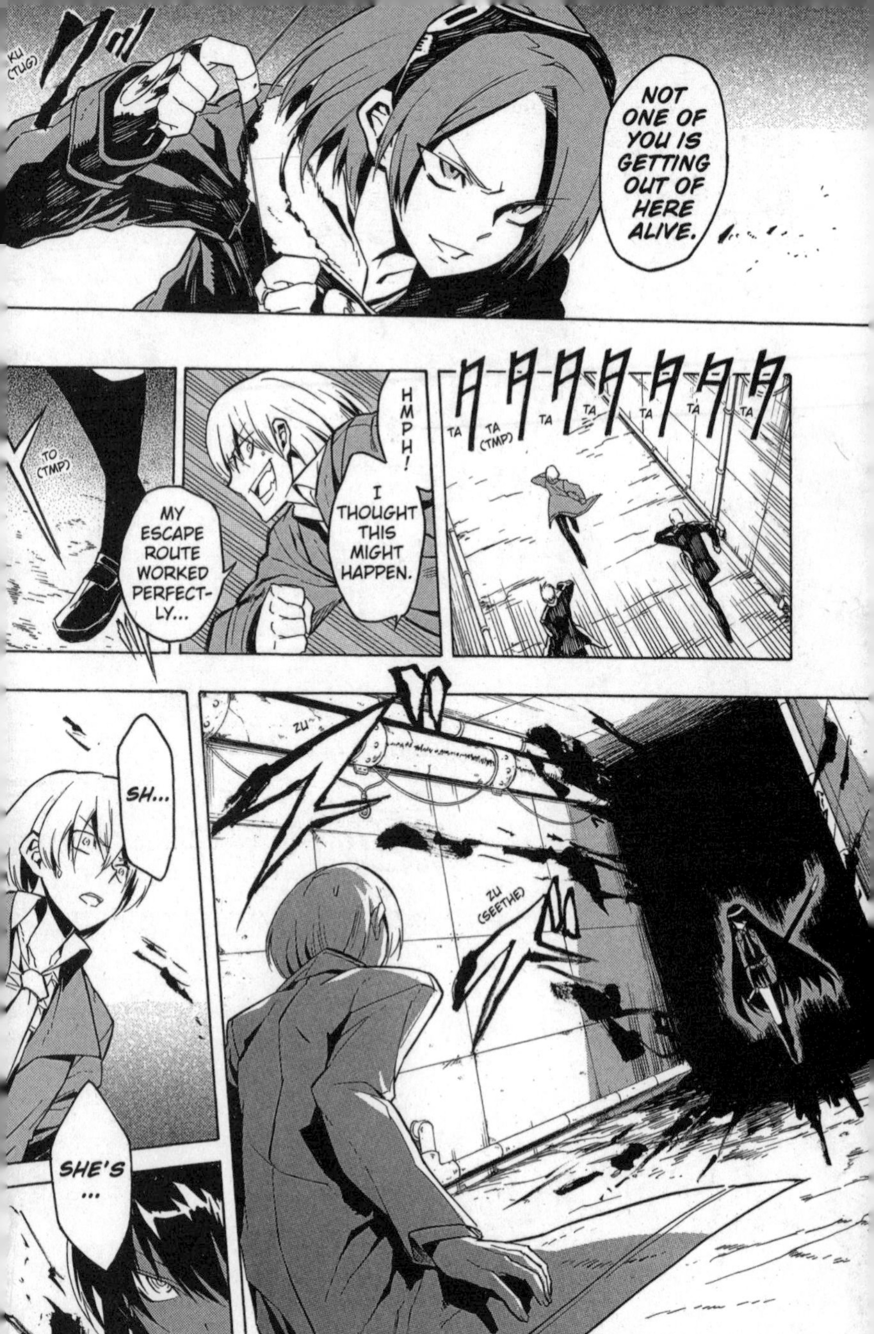
KU (TUG)
NOT ONE OF YOU IS GETTING OUT OF HERE ALIVE.
TA TA TA (TMP) TA TA TA TA TA
HMPH!
I THOUGHT THIS MIGHT HAPPEN.
TO (TMP)
MY ESCAPE ROUTE WORKED PERFECTLY...
ZU
ZU (SEETHE)
SH...
SHE'S...

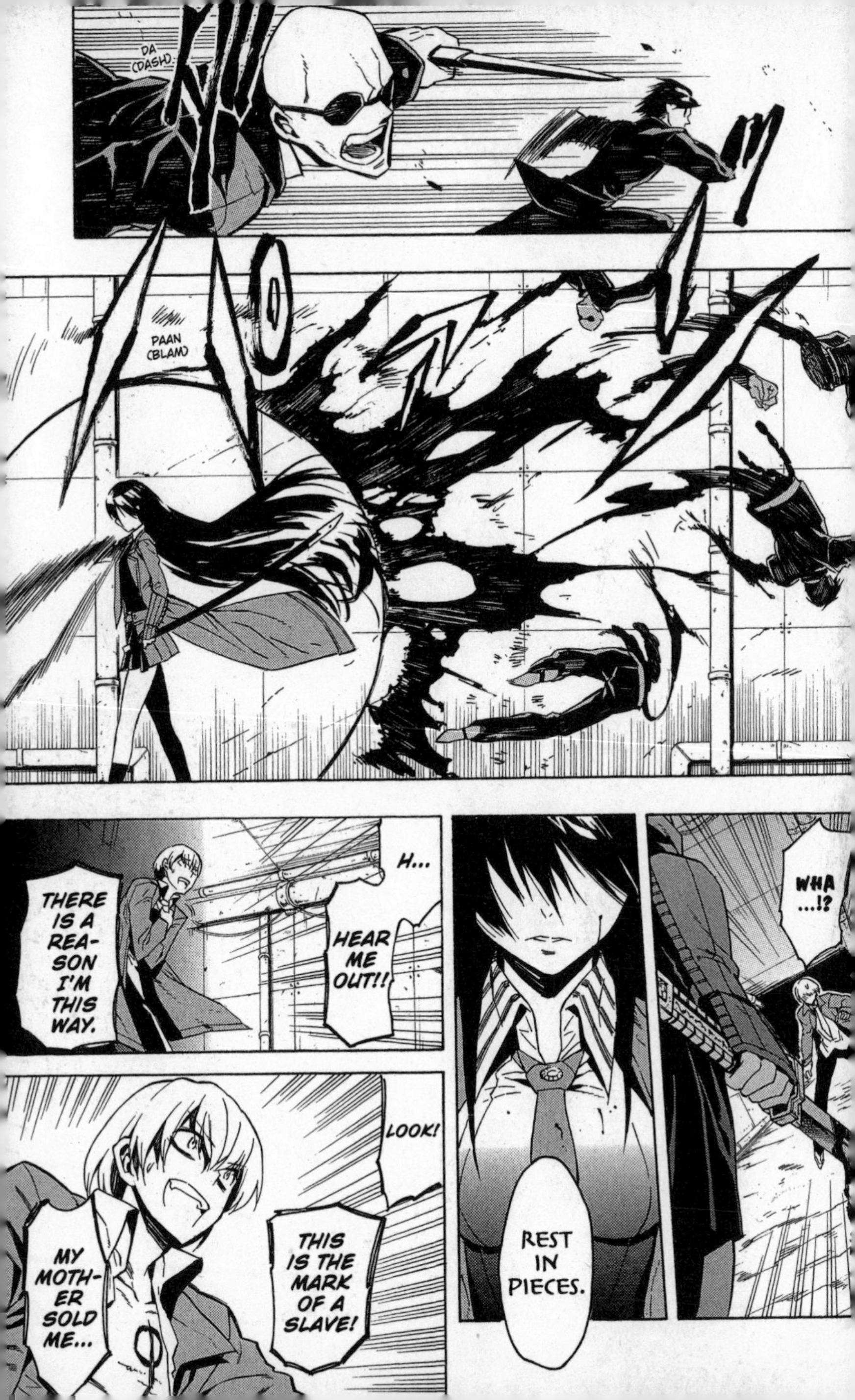
DA (DASH)
PAAN (BLAM)
WHA ...!?
H...
HEAR ME OUT!!
THERE IS A REASON I'M THIS WAY.
LOOK!
THIS IS THE MARK OF A SLAVE!
MY MOTHER SOLD ME...
REST IN PIECES.

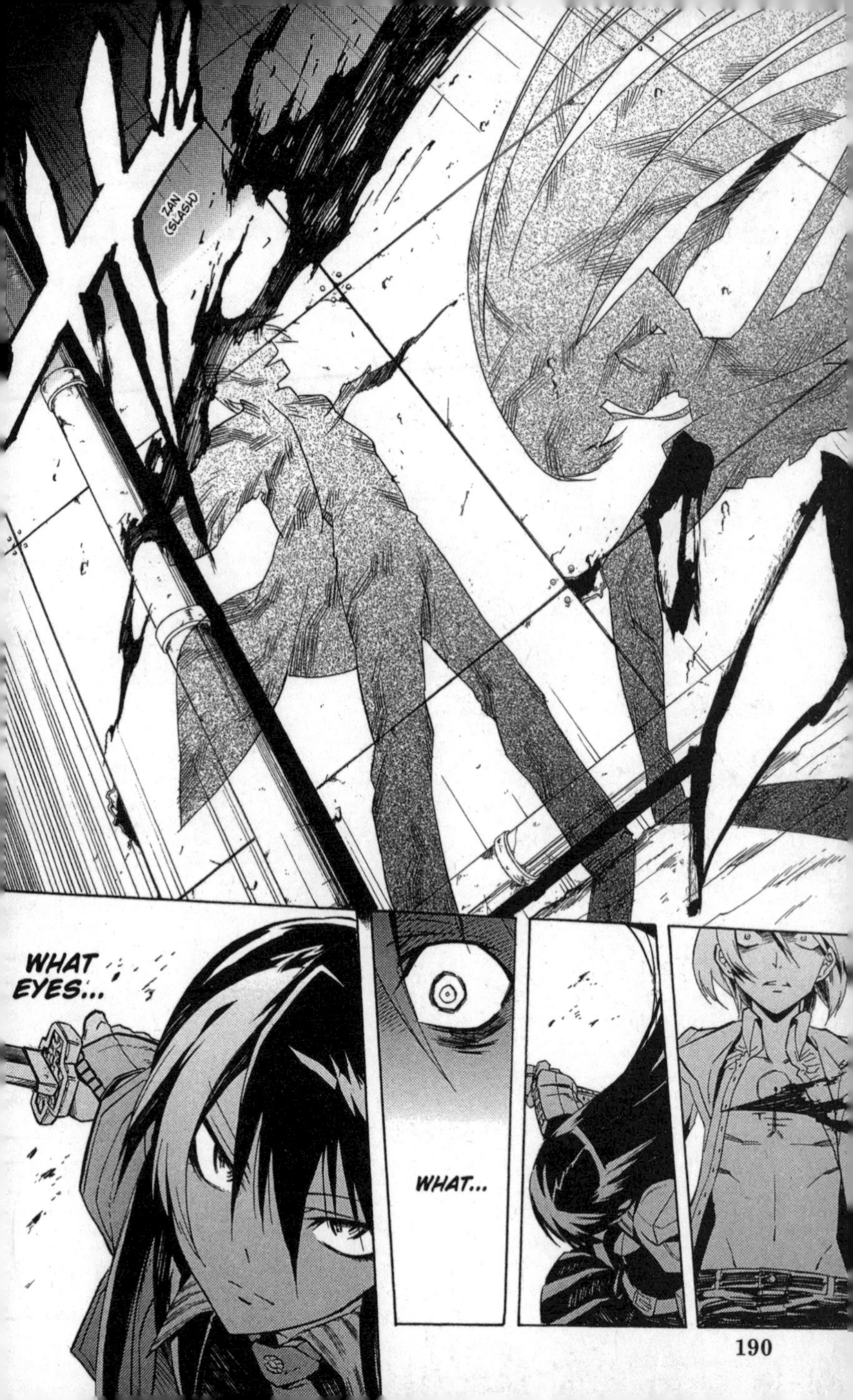
ZAN (SLASH)
WHAT...
WHAT EYES...

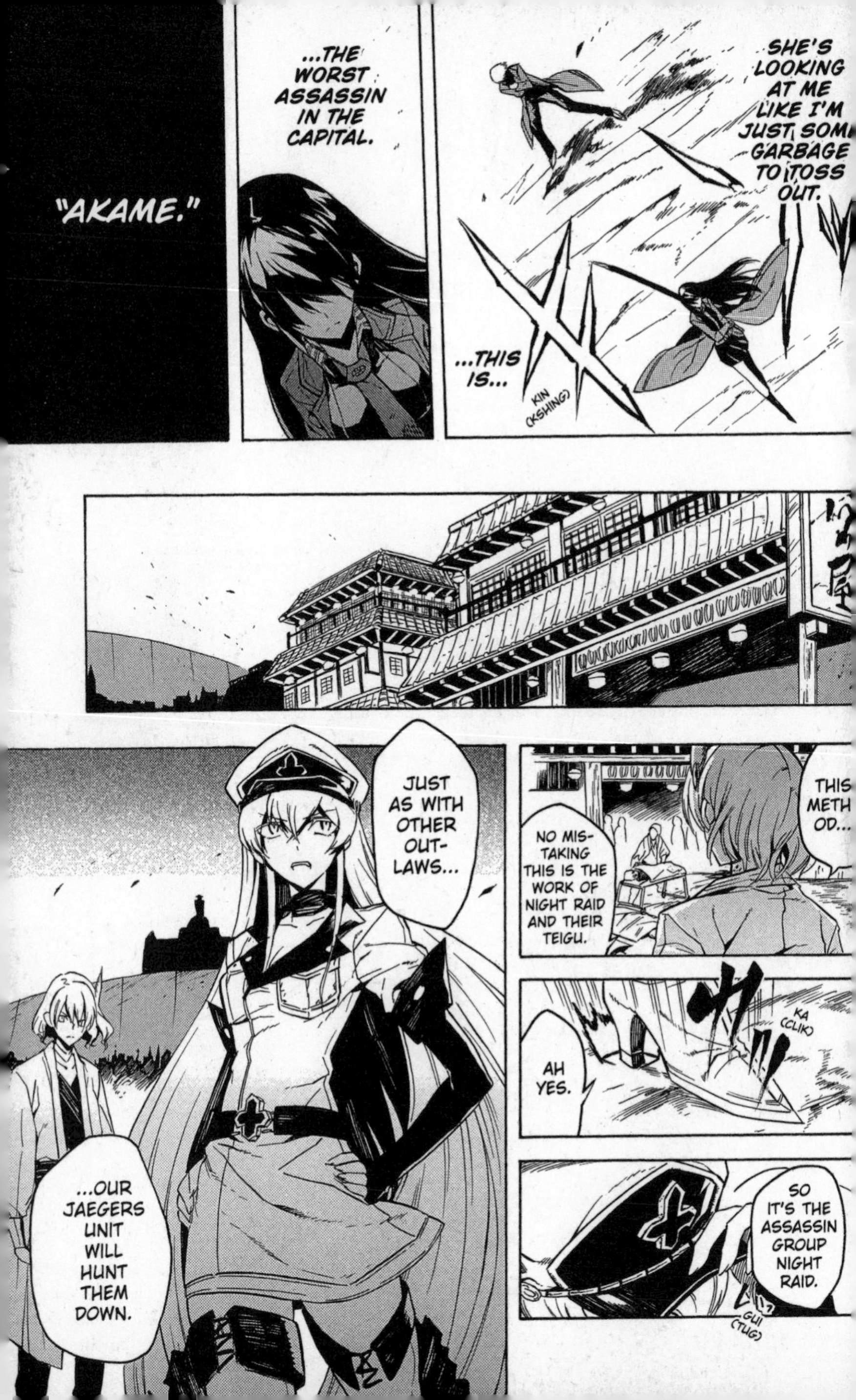
SHE'S LOOKING AT ME LIKE I'M JUST SOM GARBAGE TO TOSS OUT.
...THIS IS...
KIN (KSHING)
...THE WORST ASSASSIN IN THE CAPITAL.
"AKAME."
THIS METHOD...
NO MISTAKING THIS IS THE WORK OF NIGHT RAID AND THEIR TEIGU.
AH YES.
KA (CLIK)
SO IT'S THE ASSASSIN GROUP NIGHT RAID.
GUI (TUG)
JUST AS WITH OTHER OUTLAWS...
...OUR JAEGERS UNIT WILL HUNT THEM DOWN.

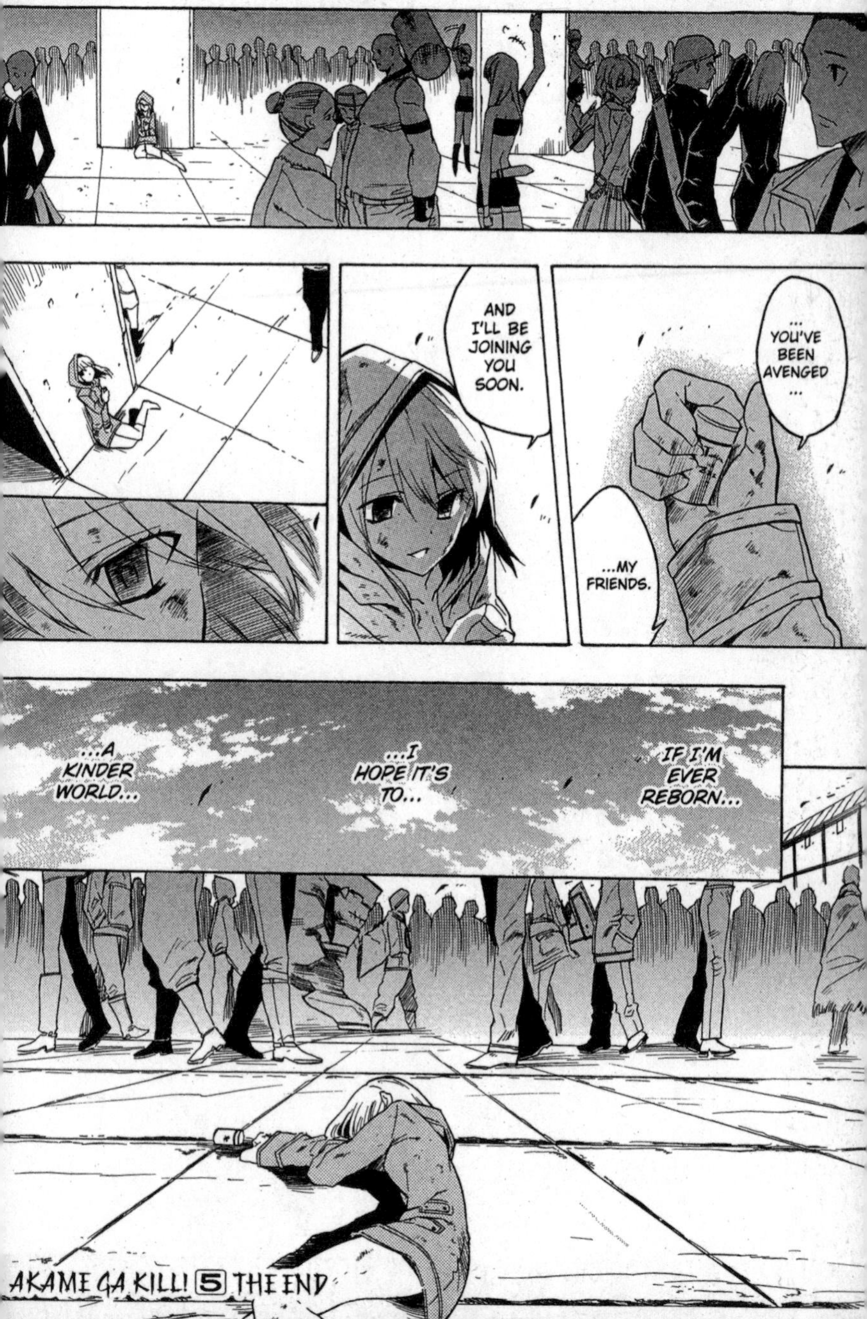
...YOU'VE BEEN AVENGED...
...MY FRIENDS.
AND I'LL BE JOINING YOU SOON.
IF I'M EVER REBORN...
...I HOPE IT'S TO...
...A KINDER WORLD...
AKAME GA KILL! 5 THE END

Akame ga KILL!
Rough Sketches 5

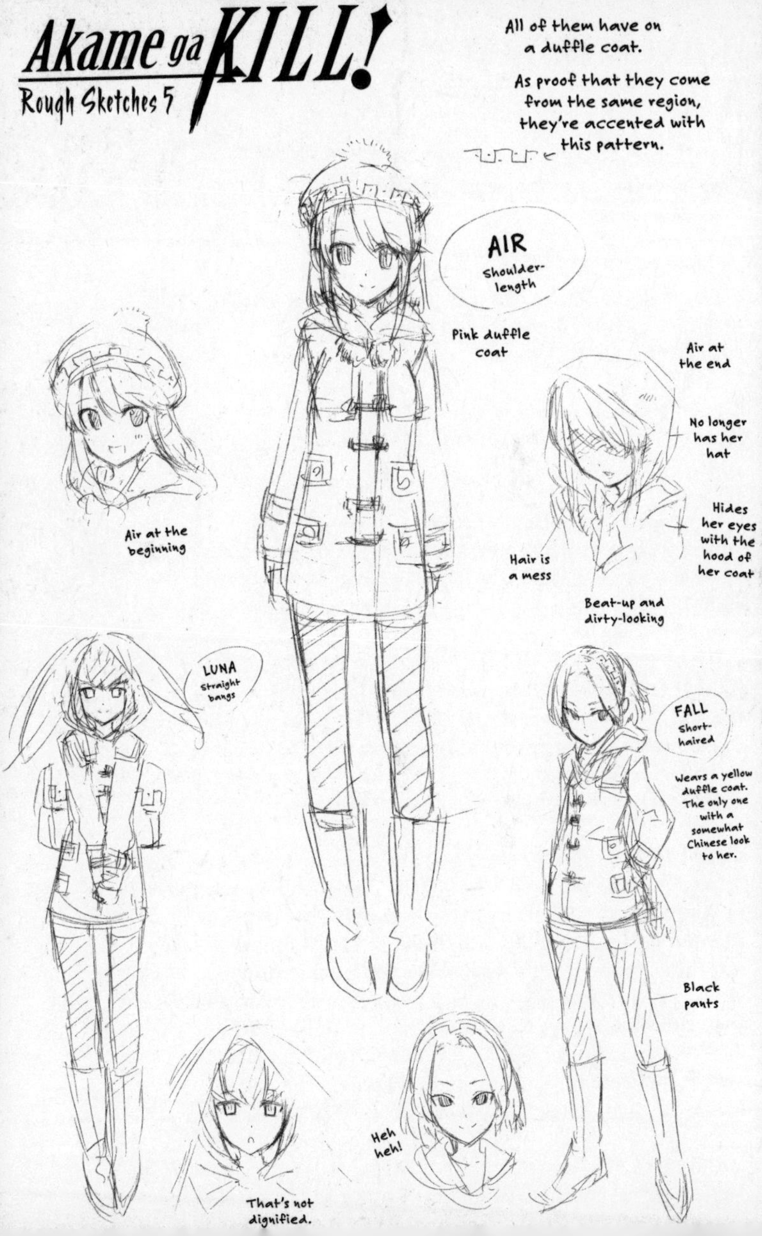

All of them have on a duffle coat.
As proof that they come from the same region, they're accented with this pattern.
AIR
Shoulder-length
Pink duffle coat
Air at the beginning
Air at the end
No longer has her hat
Hides her eyes with the hood of her coat
Hair is a mess
Beat-up and dirty-looking
LUNA
Straight bangs
FALL
Short-haired
Wears a yellow duffle coat. The only one with a somewhat Chinese look to her.
Black pants
Heh heh!
That's not dignified.

TAKAHIRO's POSTSCRIPT

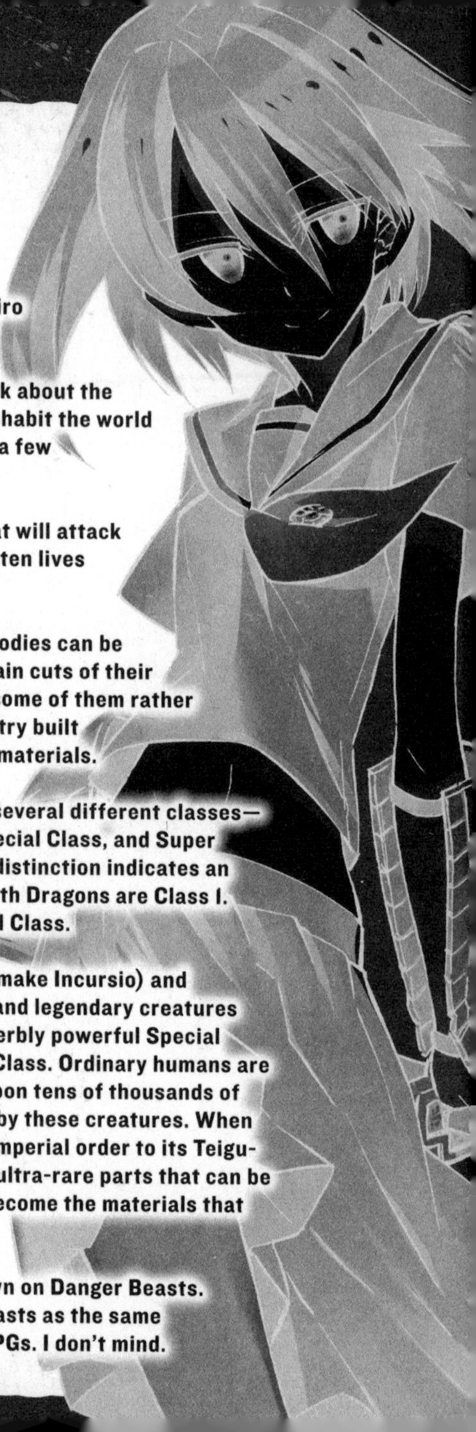

Hello.
This is the artist of this work, Takahiro from Minato Soft.

I'd like to take this opportunity to talk about the concept of the Danger Beasts that inhabit the world of *Akame*. After all, they made quite a few appearances in this volume.

The Empire calls these creatures that will attack any human they encounter and threaten lives "Danger Beasts."

Components of the Danger Beasts' bodies can be sourced for crafting armor, and certain cuts of their meat are particularly tasty, making some of them rather valuable. There is a dangerous industry built around harvesting and selling these materials.

Danger Beasts are categorized into several different classes—Class 4, Class 3, Class 2, Class 1, Special Class, and Super Class—where each ascending class distinction indicates an increase in the Beast's strength. Earth Dragons are Class 1. Evil Birds and Air Mantas are Special Class.

Tyrant (the dragon that was used to make Incursio) and other such Beasts are mythological and legendary creatures ranked as Super Class. Even the superbly powerful Special Class is nothing compared to Super Class. Ordinary humans are no match for them, and thousands upon tens of thousands of victims are estimated to have fallen by these creatures. When they show up, the Empire issues an Imperial order to its Teigu-wielding generals to conquer it. The ultra-rare parts that can be harvested from the Beasts' bodies become the materials that makes up most Teigu.

...And there you have it, a full rundown on Danger Beasts. You can also just think of Danger Beasts as the same types of monsters that show up in RPGs. I don't mind.

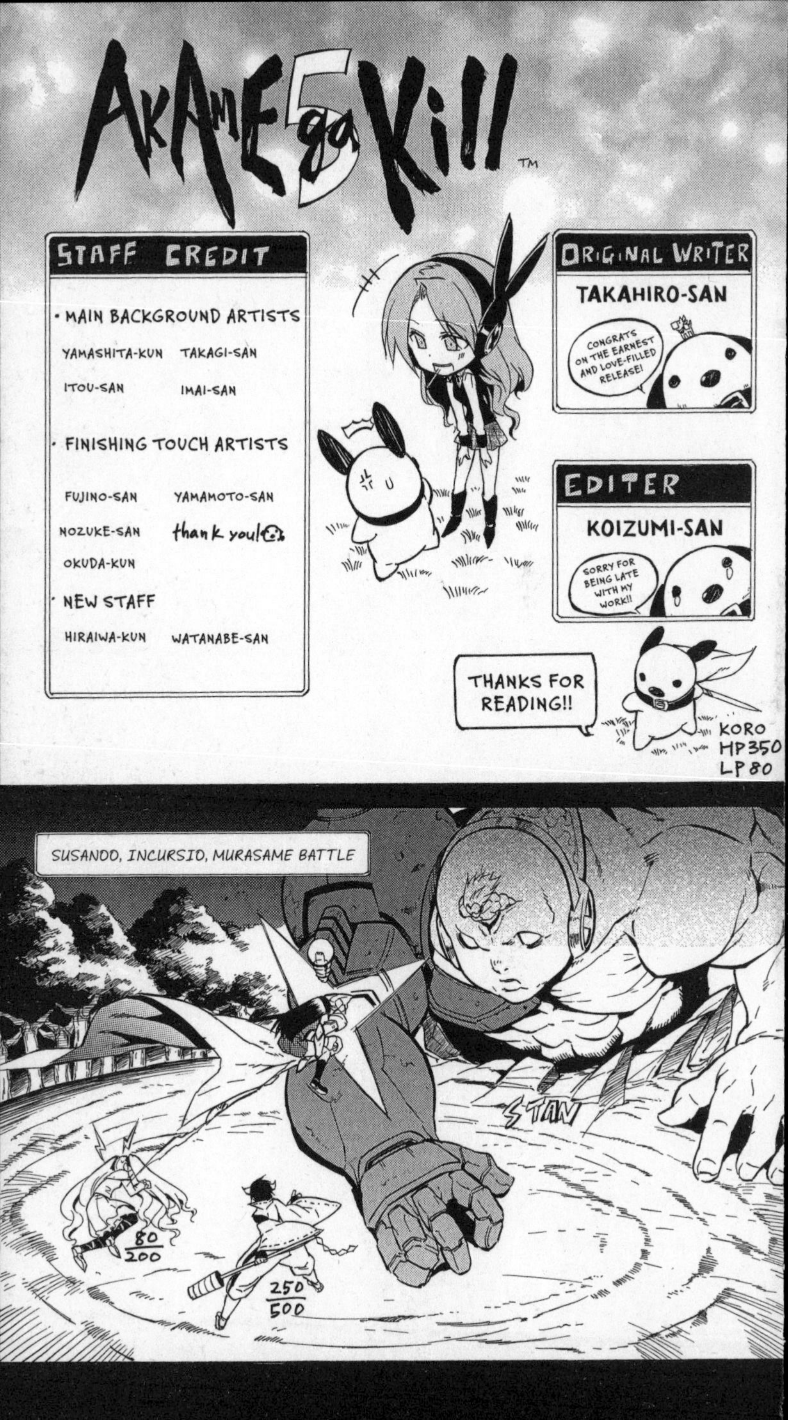
Akame ga Kill 5 ™
STAFF CREDIT
• MAIN BACKGROUND ARTISTS
YAMASHITA-KUN TAKAGI-SAN
ITOU-SAN IMAI-SAN
• FINISHING TOUCH ARTISTS
FUJINO-SAN YAMAMOTO-SAN
NOZUKE-SAN thank you!
OKUDA-KUN
• NEW STAFF
HIRAIWA-KUN WATANABE-SAN
ORIGINAL WRITER
TAKAHIRO-SAN
CONGRATS ON THE EARNEST AND LOVE-FILLED RELEASE!
EDITER
KOIZUMI-SAN
SORRY FOR BEING LATE WITH MY WORK!!
THANKS FOR READING!!
KORO HP350 LP80
SUSANOO, INCURSIO, MURASAME BATTLE
STAN
80/200
250/500

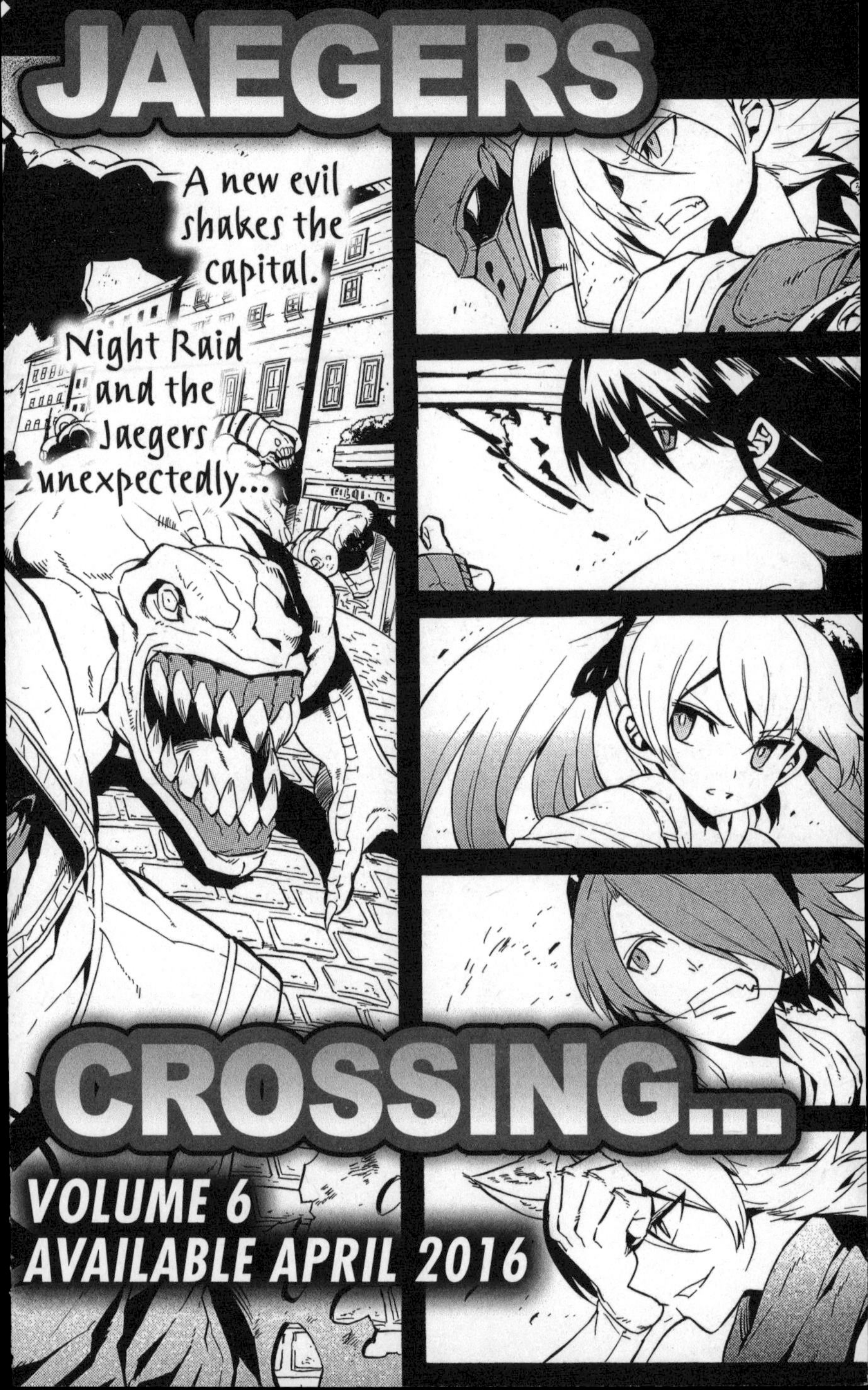
JAEGERS
A new evil shakes the capital.
Night Raid and the Jaegers unexpectedly...
CROSSING...
VOLUME 6
AVAILABLE APRIL 2016

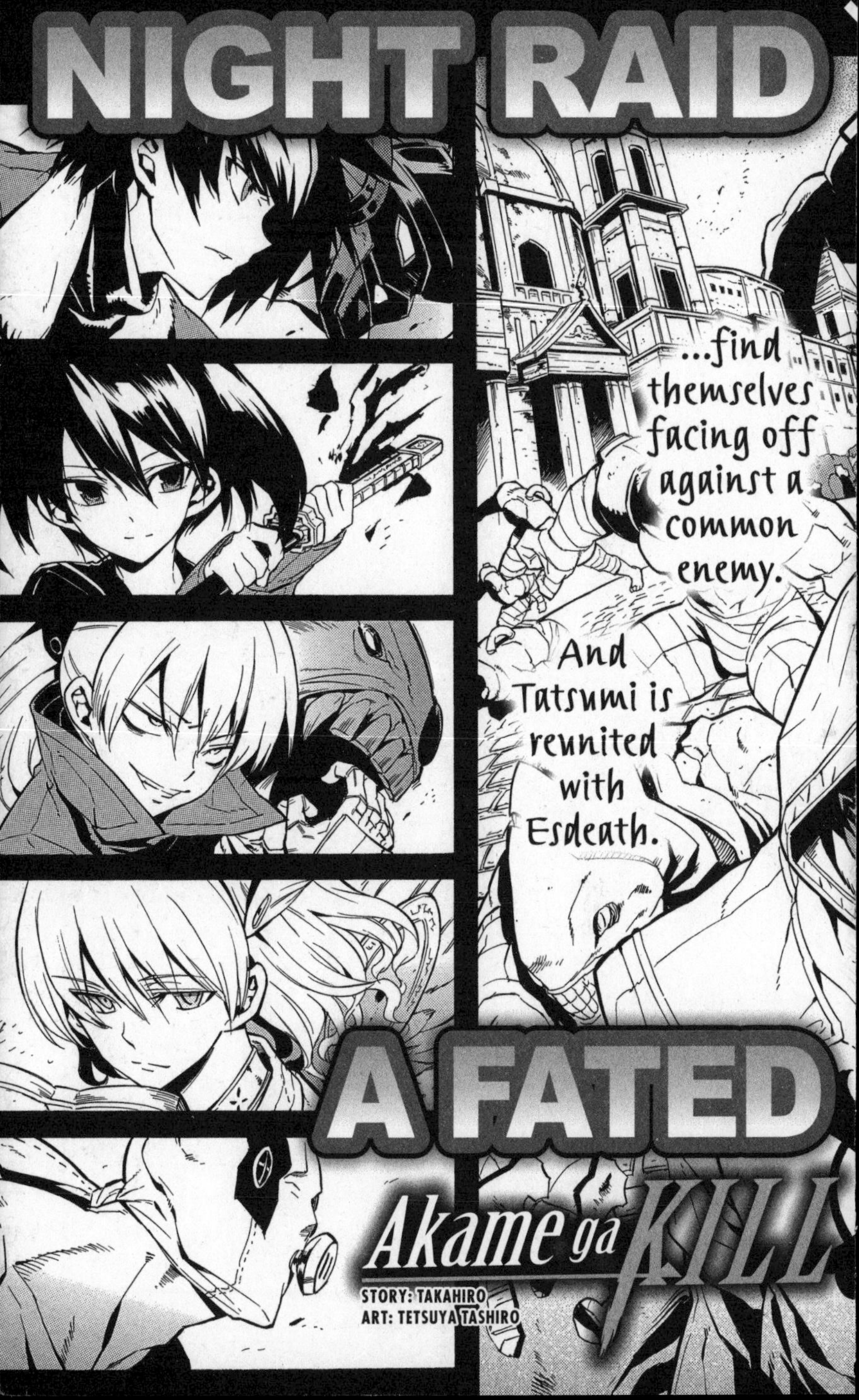

NIGHT RAID
...find themselves facing off against a common enemy.
And Tatsumi is reunited with Esdeath.
A FATED
Akame ga KILL
STORY: TAKAHIRO
ART: TETSUYA TASHIRO

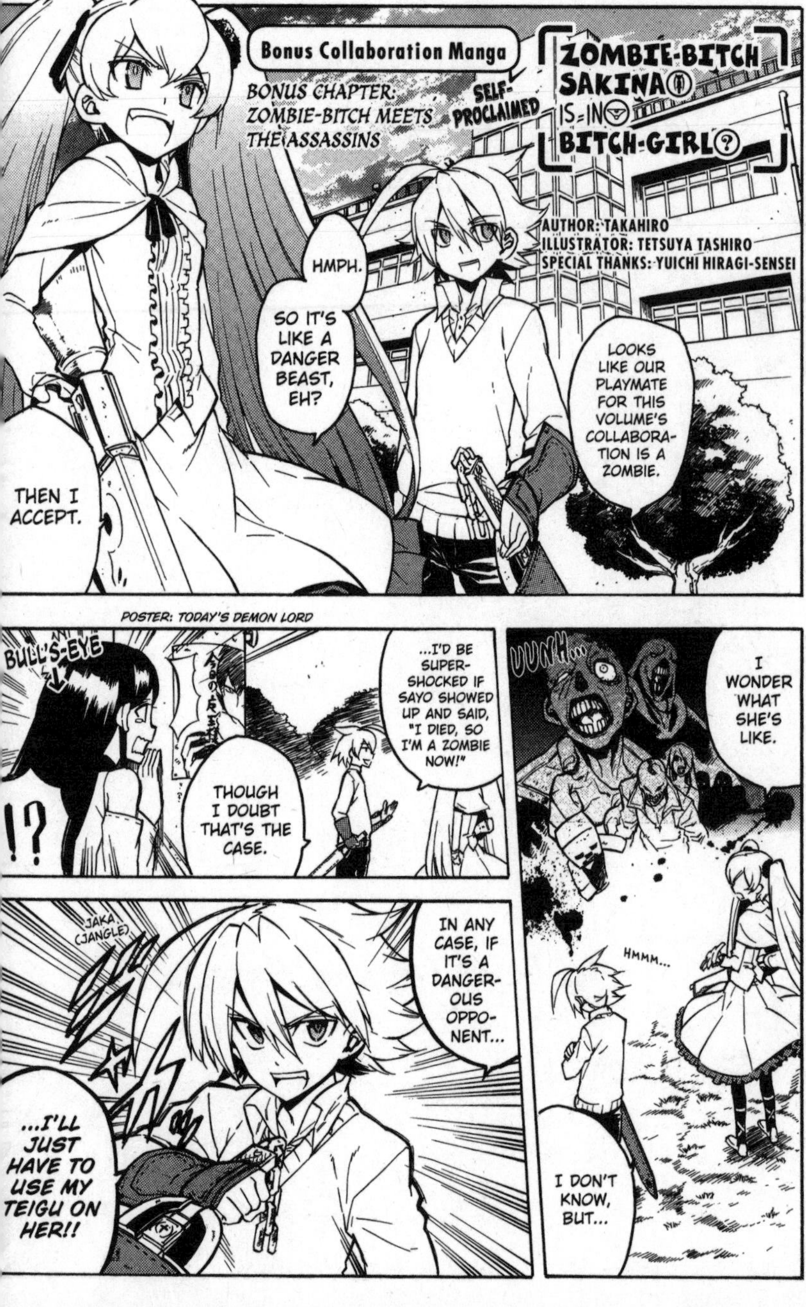
Bonus Collaboration Manga
BONUS CHAPTER: ZOMBIE-BITCH MEETS THE ASSASSINS
SELF-PROCLAIMED
ZOMBIE-BITCH SAKINA IS IN BITCH-GIRL
AUTHOR: TAKAHIRO
ILLUSTRATOR: TETSUYA TASHIRO
SPECIAL THANKS: YUICHI HIRAGI-SENSEI
LOOKS LIKE OUR PLAYMATE FOR THIS VOLUME'S COLLABORATION IS A ZOMBIE.
HMPH.
SO IT'S LIKE A DANGER BEAST, EH?
THEN I ACCEPT.
POSTER: TODAY'S DEMON LORD
I WONDER WHAT SHE'S LIKE.
UUNH...
...I'D BE SUPER-SHOCKED IF SAYO SHOWED UP AND SAID, "I DIED, SO I'M A ZOMBIE NOW!"
THOUGH I DOUBT THAT'S THE CASE.
BULL'S-EYE
!?
HMMM...
I DON'T KNOW, BUT...
IN ANY CASE, IF IT'S A DANGEROUS OPPONENT...
JAKA (JANGLE)
...I'LL JUST HAVE TO USE MY TEIGU ON HER!!

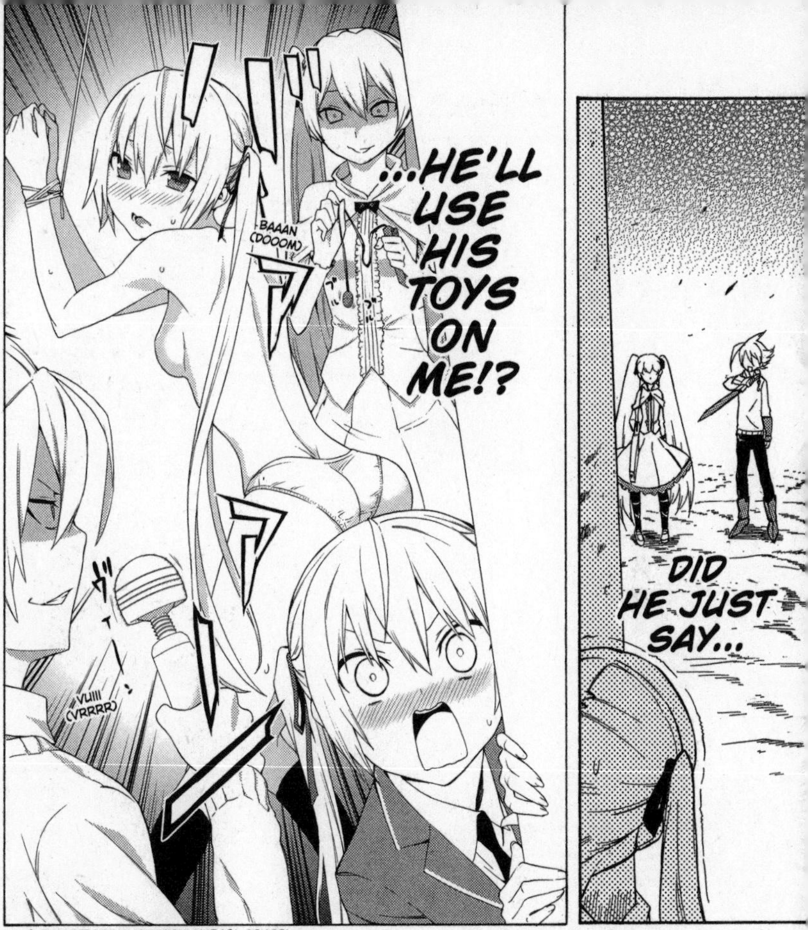
DID HE JUST SAY...
...HE'LL USE HIS TOYS ON ME!?
BAAAN (DOOOM)
VUIII (VRRRR)

⬆ ILLUSTRATION: YUUKICHI HIIRAGI-SENSEI

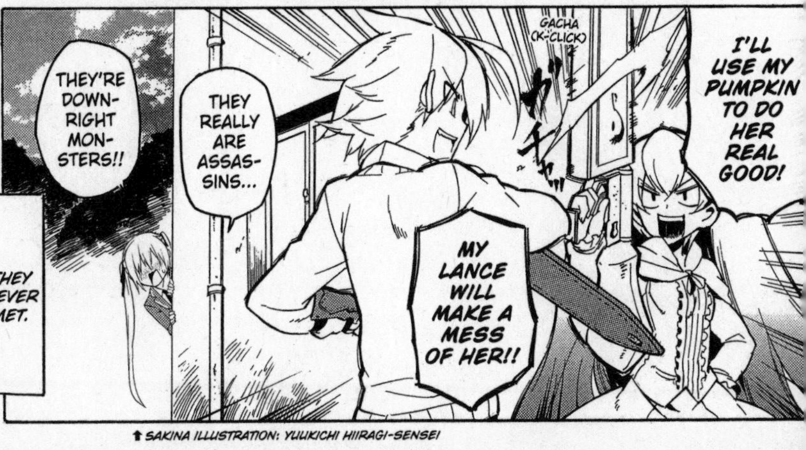
I'LL USE MY PUMPKIN TO DO HER REAL GOOD!
GACHA (K-CLICK)
MY LANCE WILL MAKE A MESS OF HER!!
THEY REALLY ARE ASSAS-SINS...
THEY'RE DOWN-RIGHT MON-STERS!!
THEY NEVER MET.

⬆ SAKINA ILLUSTRATION: YUUKICHI HIIRAGI-SENSEI

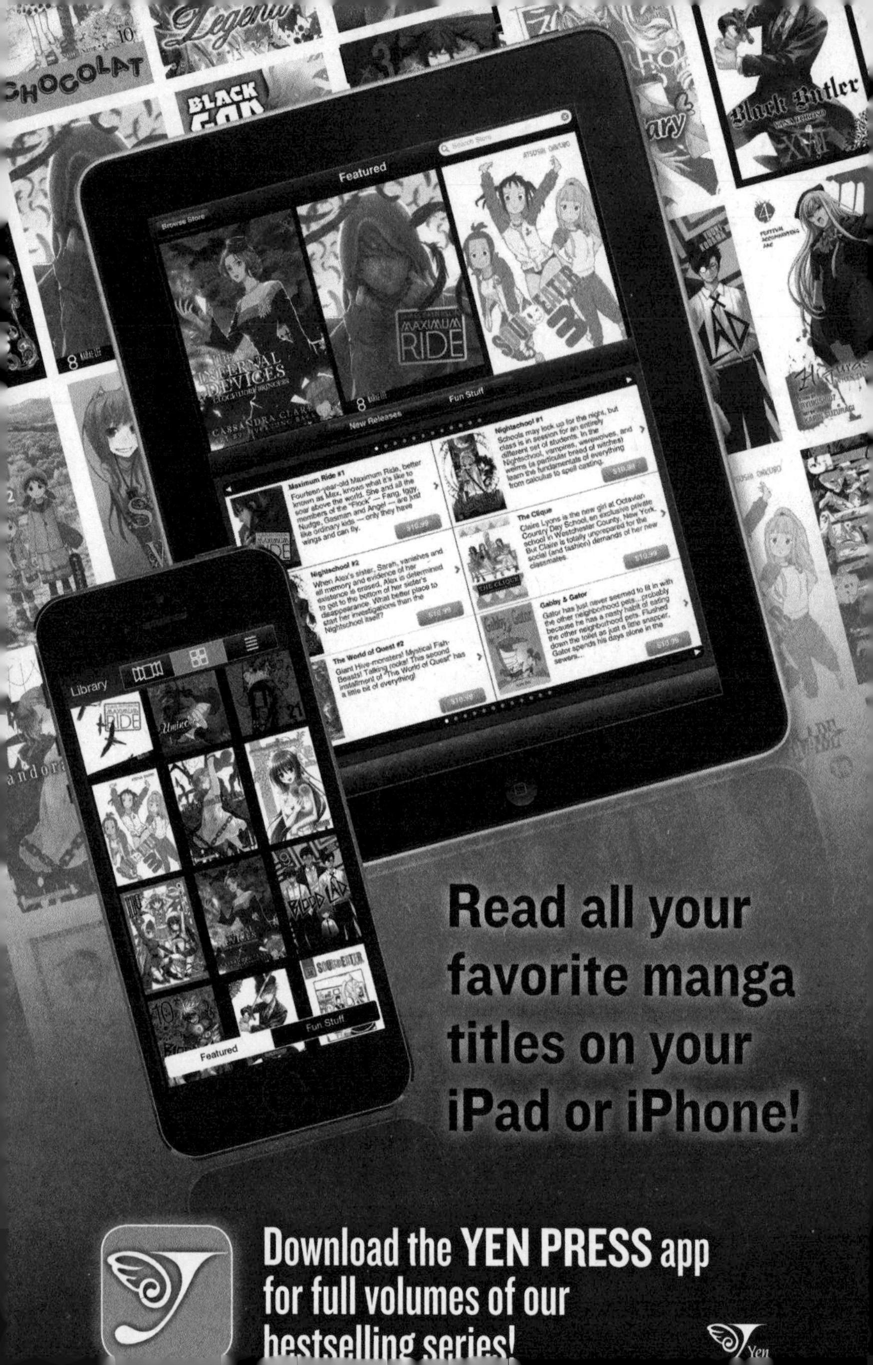
Read all your favorite manga titles on your iPad or iPhone!
Download the YEN PRESS app for full volumes of our bestselling series!
Yen

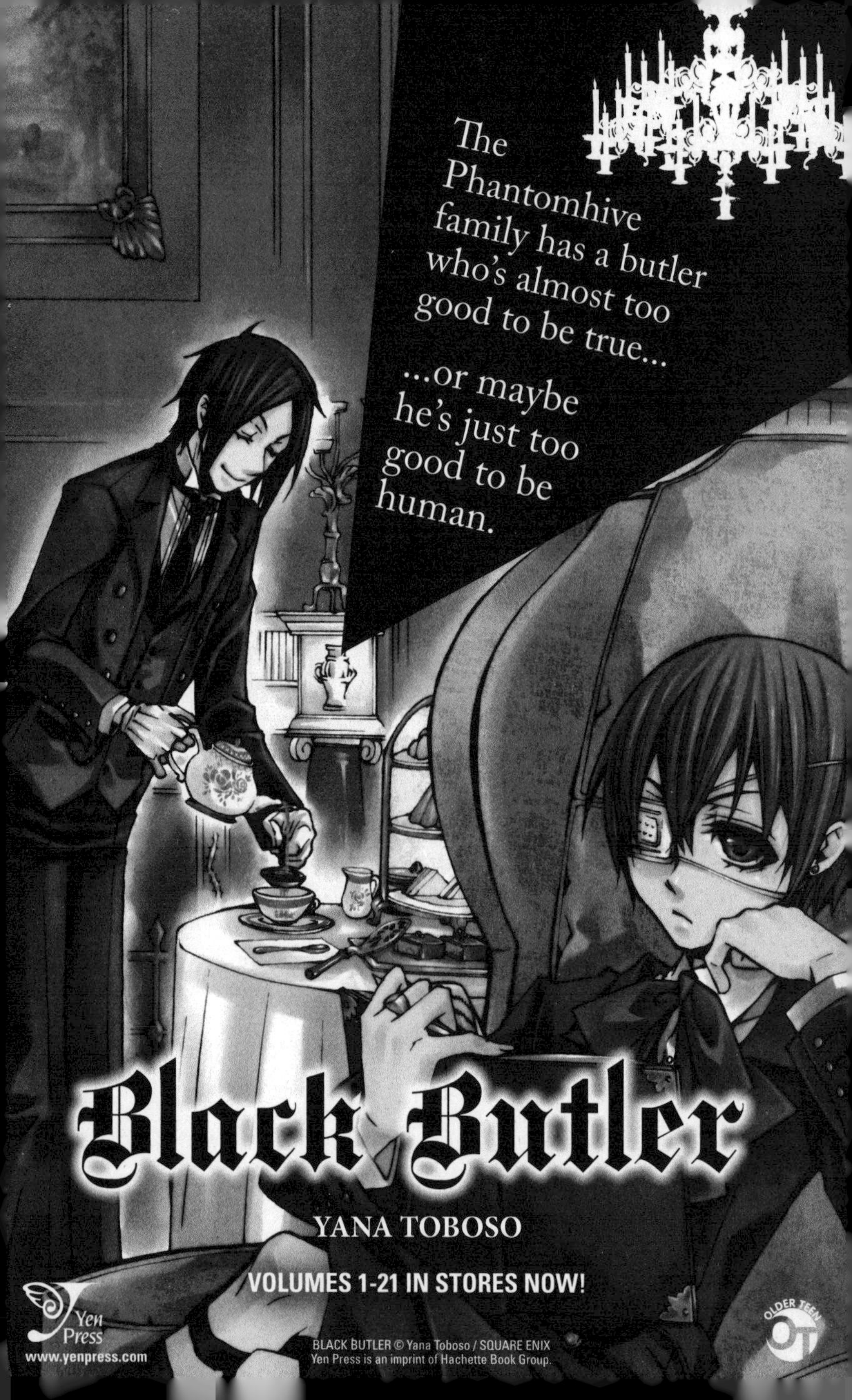

The Phantomhive family has a butler who's almost too good to be true...
...or maybe he's just too good to be human.
Black Butler
YANA TOBOSO
VOLUMES 1-21 IN STORES NOW!
Yen Press
www.yenpress.com
OLDER TEEN
OT
BLACK BUTLER © Yana Toboso / SQUARE ENIX
Yen Press is an imprint of Hachette Book Group.

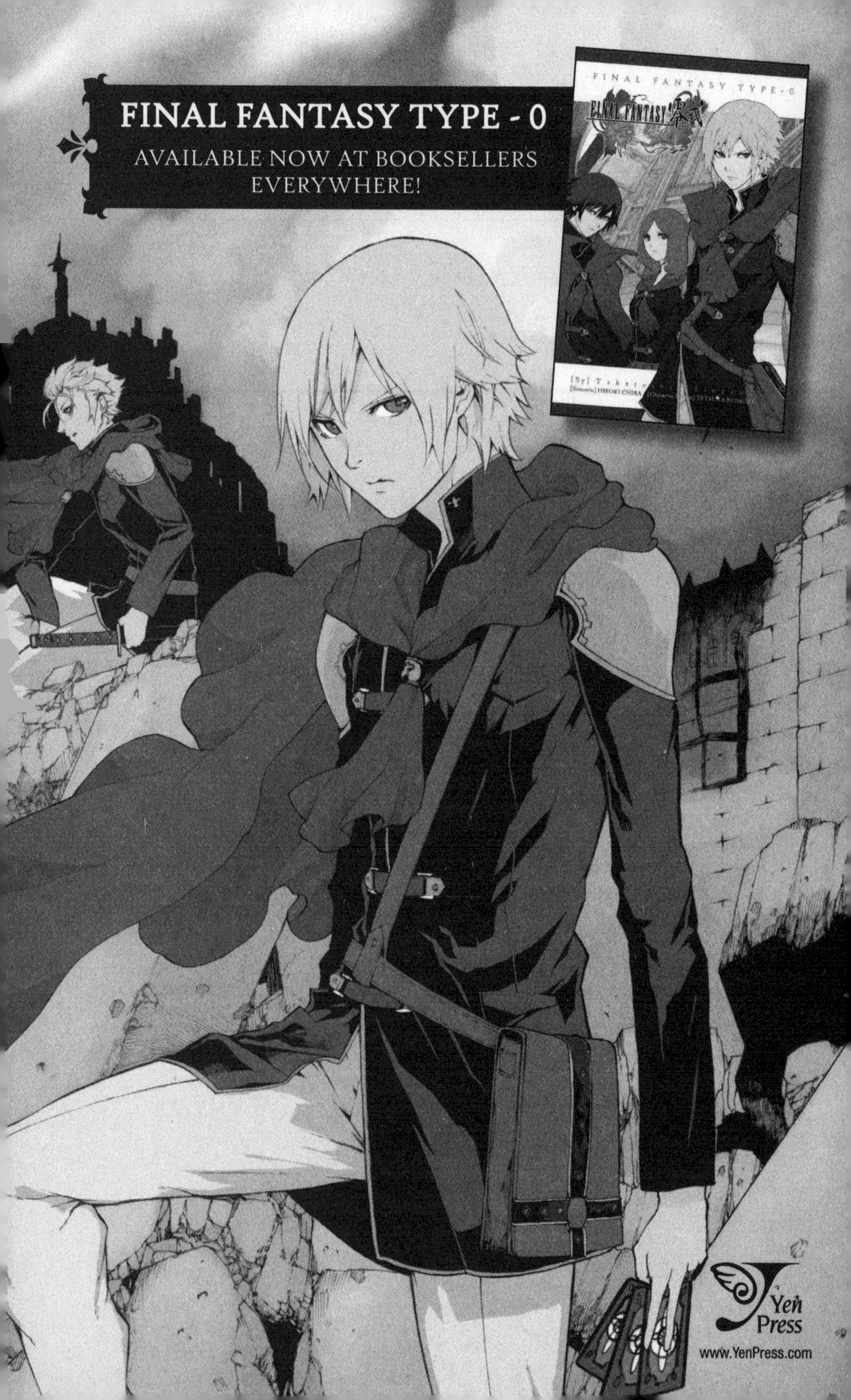
FINAL FANTASY TYPE - 0
AVAILABLE NOW AT BOOKSELLERS
EVERYWHERE!
FINAL FANTASY TYPE-0
Yen Press
www.YenPress.com

FINAL FANTASY 零式 TYPE-0

Art: TAKATOSHI SHIOZAWA
Character Design: TETSUYA NOMURA
Scenario: HIROKI CHIBA

The cadets of Akademeia's Class Zero are legends, with strength and magic unrivaled, and crimson capes symbolizing the great Vermilion Bird of the Dominion. But will their elite training be enough to keep them alive when a war breaks out and the Class Zero cadets find themselves at the front and center of a bloody political battlefield?!

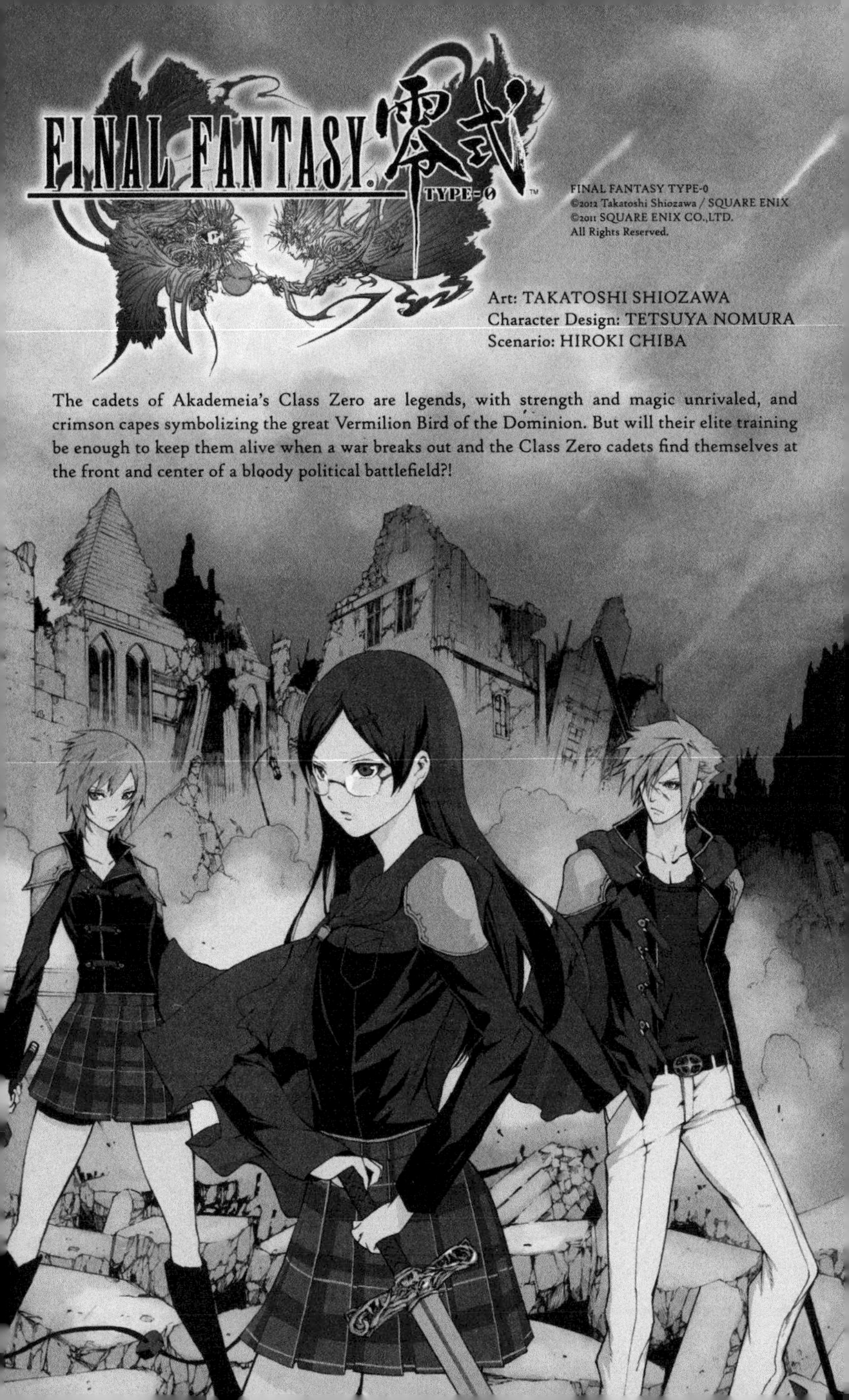

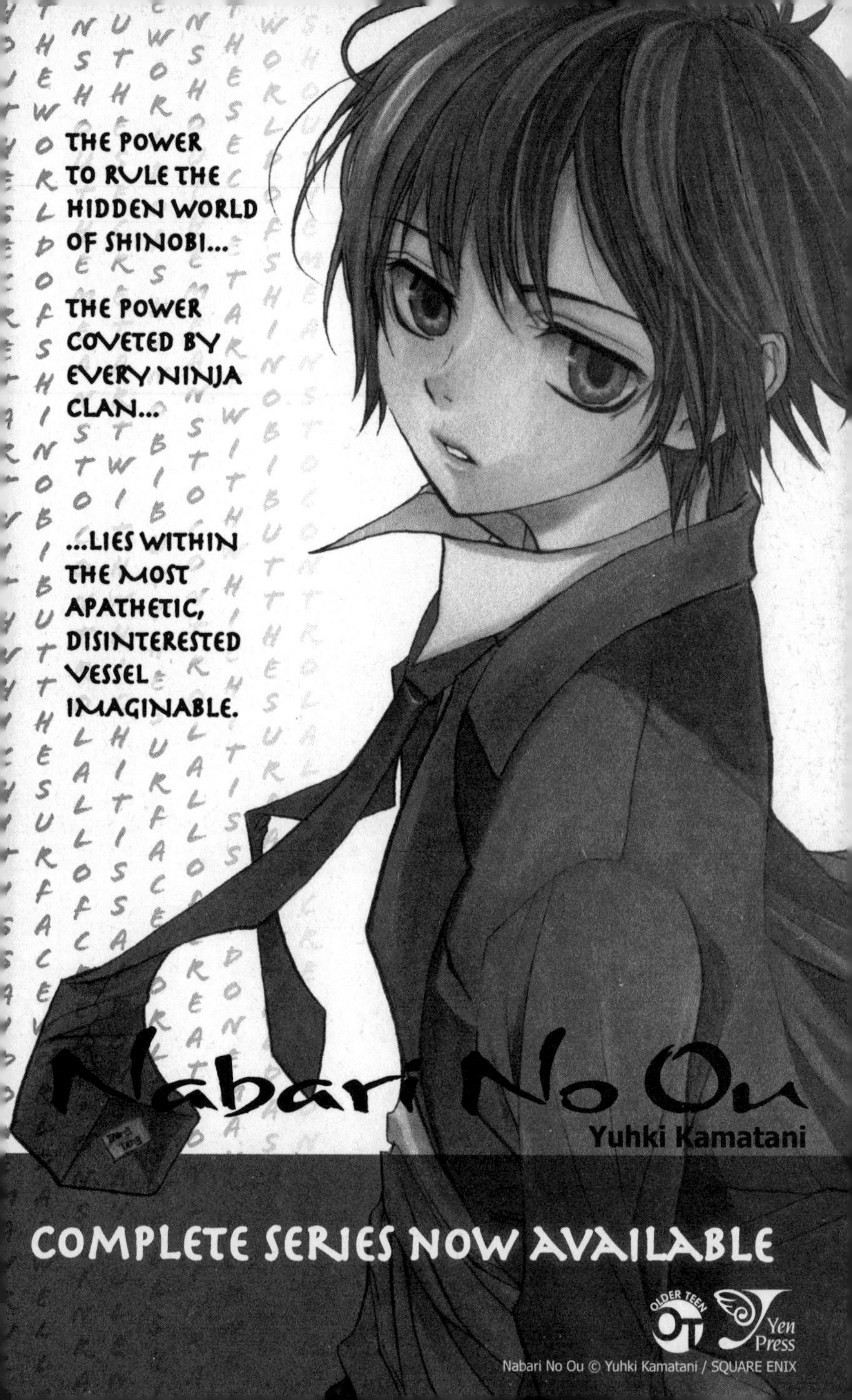
THE POWER TO RULE THE HIDDEN WORLD OF SHINOBI...
THE POWER COVETED BY EVERY NINJA CLAN...
...LIES WITHIN THE MOST APATHETIC, DISINTERESTED VESSEL IMAGINABLE.
Nabari No Ou
Yuhki Kamatani
COMPLETE SERIES NOW AVAILABLE
OLDER TEEN OT
Yen Press
Nabari No Ou © Yuhki Kamatani / SQUARE ENIX

COMPLETE SERIES
NOW AVAILABLE!

DING-
DONG!

DEAD-
DONG!

DON'T BE
LATE FOR
THE "NOT"
CLASS
AT DEATH
WEAPON
MEISTER
ACADEMY!

SOUL EATER NOT!

ATSUSHI OHKUBO

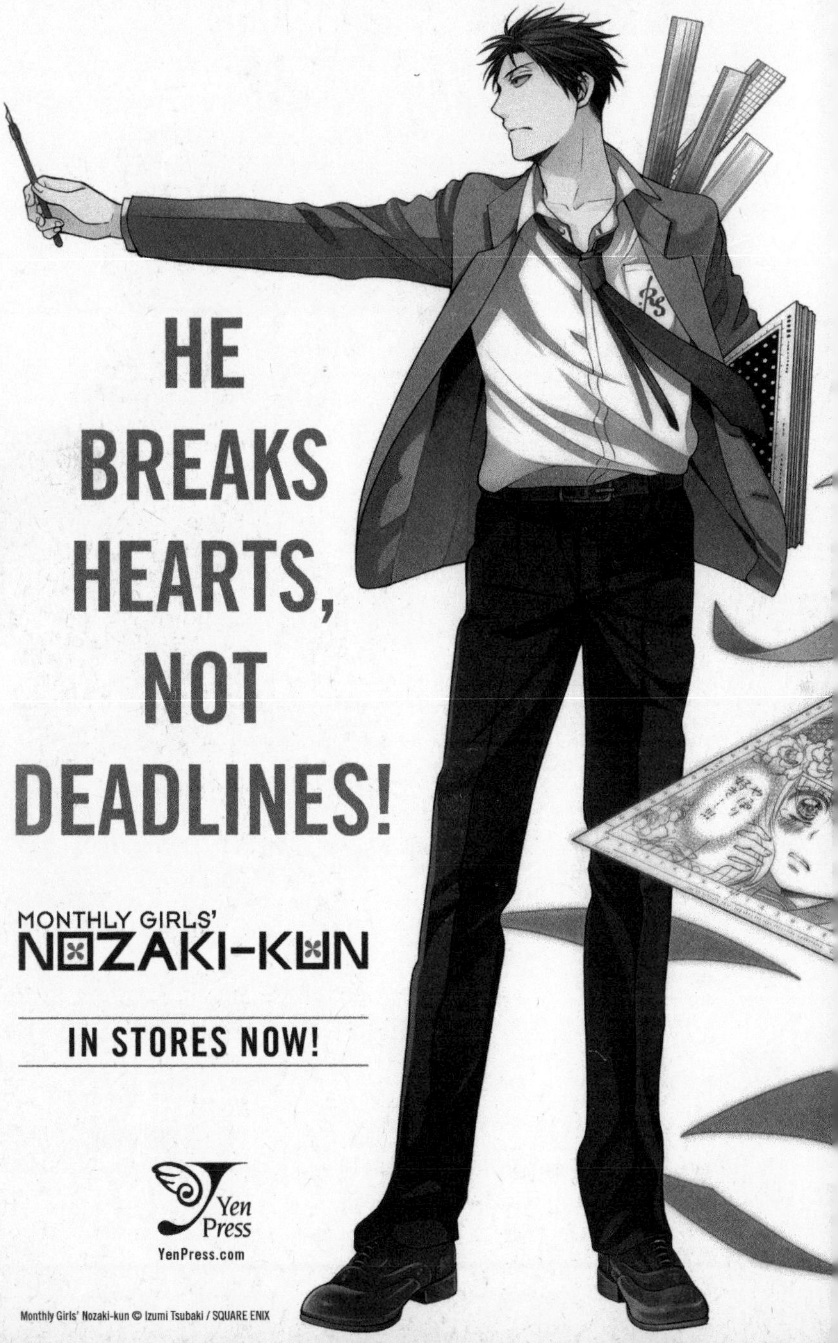
HE BREAKS HEARTS, NOT DEADLINES!
MONTHLY GIRLS'
NOZAKI-KUN
IN STORES NOW!
Yen Press
YenPress.com
Monthly Girls' Nozaki-kun © Izumi Tsubaki / SQUARE ENIX

AKAME GA KILL! 5

TAKAHIRO
TETSUYA TASHIRO

Translation: Christine Dashiell • Lettering: Erin Hickman

AKAME GA KILL! Vol. 5
© 2012 Takahiro, Tetsuya Tashiro / SQUARE ENIX CO., LTD. First published in Japan in 2012 by SQUARE ENIX CO., LTD. English translation rights arranged with SQUARE ENIX CO., LTD. and Hachette Book Group through Tuttle-Mori Agency, Inc., Tokyo.

Translation © 2016 by SQUARE ENIX CO., LTD.

Yen Press
Hachette Book Group
1290 Avenue of the Americas
New York, NY 10104

www.HachetteBookGroup.com
www.YenPress.com

Yen Press is an imprint of Hachette Book Group, Inc. The Yen Press name and logo are trademarks of Hachette Book Group, Inc.

First Yen Press Edition: January 2016

Library of Congress Control Number: 2015952579

ISBN: 978-0-316-34007-6

10 9 8 7 6 5 4 3 2 1

BVG

Printed in the United States of America